POVERTY AND SOCIAL SECURITY

POVERTY AND SOCIAL SECURITY

A. B. Atkinson
Thomas Tooke Professor of Economic Science and Statistics

HARVESTER WHEATSHEAF

New York   London   Toronto   Sydney   Tokyo

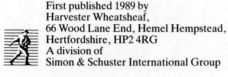

First published 1989 by
Harvester Wheatsheaf,
66 Wood Lane End, Hemel Hempstead,
Hertfordshire, HP2 4RG
A division of
Simon & Schuster International Group

Printed and bound in Great Britain by
BPCC Wheatons Ltd, Exeter

British Library Cataloguing in Publication Data

Atkinson, A. B. (Anthony Barnes), *1944–*
  Poverty and social security.
  1. Great Britain. Poverty relief. Policies of
  government
  I. Title
  362.5′56′0941

  ISBN 0–7450–0024–X
  ISBN 0–7450–0025–8 pbk

1 2 3 4 5   93 92 91 90 89

600362711 7

CC

CONTENTS

PREFACE

This volume contains eighteen essays on poverty and social security written over the past decade. As such, it is complementary to the collection of my papers, *Social Justice and Public Policy*, published by Wheatsheaf Books in 1983. There are of course close connections. The measurement of poverty is related to the measurement of inequality, which is one of the principal topics of the earlier volume. Similarly, the practical issues of the design of income maintenance and taxation discussed here are illuminated by the more theoretical articles in that collection. At the same time, the present collection differs in being particularly concerned with one major objective of policy – the abolition of poverty – and with one set of policy instruments – those income transfer programmes conventionally referred to as 'social security'. It also contains a larger proportion of empirical material, dealing with the effectiveness of present policies and with alternative reforms of the benefit system. These practical policy applications relate largely to the United Kingdom, but reference is made to other OECD countries, and it is hoped that the methods of analysis will be of wider interest.

The empirical work reported in these chapters is the result of three major research programmes in which I have been involved, and I would like to acknowledge the support of the bodies which funded this research and the substantial contribution made by my colleagues on these programmes. The first in chronological order is the Rowntree follow-up project, which I directed jointly with Professor Alan Maynard of the University of York. The research reported in Chapters 4 and 5 was supported by the Joseph Rowntree Memorial Trust and by the Nuffield Foundation. The success of this project would not have been possible without the skill and enthusiasm of Chris Trinder, who worked on it from the outset, and the painstaking and imaginative work on the data by Holly Sutherland, who has continued to work with me and who is co-author of four of the chapters in this volume.

A large number of the chapters draw on the work of the ESRC Programme on Taxation, Incentives and the Distribution of Income, which I direct jointly with Professors Mervyn King and Nicholas Stern, and I should like to thank the Council for its support over the period 1978–89. I am particularly grateful to those who have taken part in the programme.

Not only have they been co-authors for over half of the chapters, but I have learned a great deal from our working together, and it has been a most enjoyable and stimulating experience. A substantial proportion of the chapters have been circulated in the blue discussion series of the ESRC Programme (Chapters 1–3, 8–16 and 18).

The third research programme is the Welfare State Programme, currently jointly directed with John Hills and Julian Le Grand, and financed by Suntory Limited. This programme, with its coverage of other areas of public spending such as health and housing, and its concern to blend quantitative analysis with an interdisciplinary understanding of the welfare state, has again been a valuable source of stimulus.

Of the eighteen essays, seven are published for the first time, and several others are not readily available (one, for example, has only been published in German). It is hoped that the present volume will make them more accessible, as well as helping bring out the connection between different pieces of research. To this latter end, I have made a number of editorial changes, incorporating cross-references and eliminating some minor overlap. The essays were written at a number of dates over the past decade. In some cases there have been subsequent changes in policy. For example, family income supplement – the subject of Chapter 12 – was replaced by Family Credit in April 1988. However, the concern of this chapter with incomplete take-up of benefits remains a live issue, and I have left the chapter largely unchanged. In the Introduction to each of the three Parts, I have referred to developments up to September 1988.

I am grateful to my co-authors for agreeing to our papers being printed in this volume, and to those who have aided its production. At the Suntory-Toyota International Centre for Economics and Related Disciplines at the LSE, Leila Alberici, Jane Dickson, Prue Hutton, Debbie Murrells and Anne Robinson have all been most helpful. Fiona Coulter provided useful research assistance.

A. B. Atkinson
London School of Economics

ACKNOWLEDGEMENTS

The authors and publishers would like to thank the following for permission to reprint the essays in this volume:

Econometric Society (Chapter 2), Basil Blackwell (Chapter 4), Leerstoel P. W. Segers (Chapter 6), Elsevier Science Publishers B.V. (Chapter 9), HMSO (Chapter 10), Policy Studies Institute (Chapters 13 and 14), National Institute of Economic and Social Research (Chapter 15).

NOTE

The tables marked with the TAXMOD logo have been produced using the TAXMOD Tax-Benefit Model described in Chapter 18.

PART I

POVERTY

INTRODUCTION

Concern with poverty in advanced countries may seem misplaced when viewed against the background of mass poverty on a world scale. The parallel has been drawn with rearranging the deckchairs on the *Titanic* as the ship goes down. A closer parallel in my view is with the position of those on boats steaming to the aid of the sinking vessel. One's first obligation is to persuade those on the bridge to proceed as rapidly as possible (and to overcome their present preoccupation with saving fuel), but those on the rescuing ships should also be concerned that their steerage passengers do not get frostbite on the way. The relief of famine and the redistribution of world income has priority, but hardship in advanced countries may legitimately come second on the list of our concerns.

The focus of the chapters in Part I is with such hardship in advanced countries. Poverty, which is discussed both theoretically and empirically, has therefore to be seen in terms of deprivation rather than destitution; what is at stake is ability to function rather than physical survival. The definition of such a poverty line does, of course, raise major issues, including the relation between the poverty line and the general level of living in a particular society. This is one of the topics considered in Chapter 1, which reviews a wide variety of conceptual problems in the analysis of poverty, making reference to studies of poverty in the United States, Britain and other OECD countries. Are we concerned about standards of living or – as is usually measured – levels of income? How is the poverty standard defined, and how can we compare poverty at different dates? What should be the unit of analysis – the individual, the family or the household? And how should we treat families of differing composition? What should be the period of assessment and what account should be taken of the duration of poverty?

One general theme running through this, and other chapters, is that there is a diversity of judgements about how poverty should be measured and that we need to recognize this diversity explicitly in the procedures adopted. This is illustrated by Chapter 2, which was presented as the Walras–Bowley Lecture at the 1985 World Congress of the Econometric Society. This examines in depth three issues. The first is the choice of poverty line. The fact that there is likely to be disagreement about the choice means that we may only be able to make comparisons, and not to measure differences, and that the comparisons may lead only to a partial rather than a complete ordering. The emphasis is however on what *can* be said, rather than on the difficulties, and the chapter sets out conditions under which definite conclusions may be reached despite the existence of disagreement, illustrating their application by reference to data for the United States.

The choice of *measures* of poverty has been the subject of an extensive literature following the article by Sen (1976a). He, like Watts (1968), criticized the widespread reliance on the 'head count' measure of poverty, and suggested alternative indicators. This opens the possibility of further disagreement, with, for example, poverty having increased according to one indicator but decreased according to another. In Chapter 2, a different approach is suggested, considering a class of poverty measures which satisfy certain general properties and seeking conditions under which all members of the class give the same ranking. The approach is similar to that adopted to the measurement of inequality in Atkinson (1970) and the conditions are analogous to Lorenz curves not intersecting. The key concept turns out to be the 'poverty deficit curve', $\Phi(Z)$, which measures the total deficit from Z of all incomes which fall below Z. In other words, it is the poverty gap, but taken for different values of the poverty line Z. What we require in order to reach an unambiguous conclusion – for instance when comparing the situation before and after a policy change – is that the poverty deficit be less for all values of Z up to the highest poverty line believed relevant. This is a criterion which is easily applied in practice.

The next two chapters are concerned with the measurement of poverty in Britain (Chapter 3) and York (Chapter 4). In this, and other work, I have been especially concerned with the *comparison* of the findings of different studies. The particular focus here is with the comparison of different studies at different dates and with the trends in poverty over time. Chapter 3 compares the evidence about poverty in Britain in the 1930s, drawing on local studies of the cities of Southampton, York and Bristol, with that available from national surveys in the 1980s. Chapter 4 is a re-analysis of the information collected by Seebohm Rowntree in his survey of York in 1950, a survey which is particularly significant in providing a link between his work, which spanned the first half of the twentieth century, and later national studies.

This review of the historical experience of one country over a 50-year period serves to illustrate a number of the conceptual points made in Chapters 1 and 2. In Chapter 4, we show for example the considerable difference between Rowntree's own assessment of the extent of poverty in 1950 and that which would have been obtained had he applied the national assistance scale as in subsequent studies such as that of Abel-Smith and Townsend. These poverty criteria differ in a number of respects, but among the most important was the fact that Rowntree adopted a *household* basis whereas national assistance was based on the *family* unit. This change in the method of calculation has recently been reversed in Britain (see below). Chapter 3 considers the comparison of poverty lines at different dates and shows how the *structure* of the poverty line has changed between the 1930s and the 1980s, with those over pension age being favoured relative to those under pension age, and the scales for men and women being brought into line. Any comparison of the poverty standard in the 1930s with that in the 1980s depends therefore on the composition of the family considered.

The analysis of Chapters 3 and 4 also brings out the need to consider the sources of the data and their comparability. In this, the existence of full documentation is of prime importance. Standards here vary considerably, and, although the report by Rowntree and Lavers (1951) was perhaps extreme in the paucity of information provided, the difficulties (described in Chapter 4) that we had in reconstructing their procedures serve to demonstrate the crucial role of documentation. The reader was not even told, for example, the size of the sample on which the results were based – in contrast to the much fuller account given of the 1936 and 1899 surveys in Rowntree (1901, 1941). Without access to the original working papers of Seebohm Rowntree, it was very difficult to assess the validity of the 1950 findings – findings which were very influential in postwar Britain.

The problems of documentation are perhaps not widely appreciated because few economists attempt the kind of comparative study described in Chapters 3 and 4. There has however been a welcome interest in recent years in *cross-country* comparisons, most notably in the Luxembourg Income Study, which has brought together and put on a comparable basis micro-data sets for a set of industrialized countries, including Australia, Canada, Finland, France, Israel, Italy, Netherlands, Norway, Sweden, Switzerland, United Kingdom, United States and West Germany. For the first results of cross-country analyses, see Smeeding *et al.* (1989).

The British data included in the Luxembourg Income Study are those collected in the *Family Expenditure Survey*, and these are the basis for the official Department of Health and Social Security (DHSS) estimates of the number of low-income families referred to in Chapters 1 and 3. (The most recent are those for 1985 published in Department of Health and Social Security (1988b).) As is discussed in Chapter 3, the DHSS estimates have definite advantages over the earlier studies by Rowntree and others, including the fact that they relate to a national sample, rather than a single city such as York. At the same time, the official estimates in Britain contained only very limited information – in contrast to the 247 pages published in the United States.

It is therefore very welcome that the DHSS has carried out a review of the low-income calculations, the results of which have been published in

Department of Health and Social Security (1988a). As a result, there have been major changes in methodology. The use of supplementary benefit (now Income Support) as a yardstick has been dropped and replaced by fractions of average income. The figures published for 1981, 1983 and 1985 (Department of Health and Social Security, 1988a) show the percentages below 50, 60, 70, 80, 90 and 100 per cent of average income (applying an equivalence scale). This may be seen as adopting a thoroughly relative approach along the lines suggested by Fuchs (1965) (see Chapter 1). This provides much fuller information, although the review stopped short of publishing the poverty deficit curve advocated in Chapter 2. There were however other changes in methodology, most significantly the adoption of a household rather than a family unit basis, reversing the shift described in Chapter 3. On this, and other aspects of the new figures, see the report of the House of Commons Social Services Committee (1988).

The measures of poverty that have been considered so far have been largely based on income. In Chapter 5, we consider other indicators of deprivation, taking a wider perspective of the problem. This chapter is again based on the 1950 Rowntree survey of York, but in this case includes evidence from our 1975–78 follow-up of the children of the families interviewed in 1950. The main focus is indeed on the extent of intergenerational continuities in deprivation. In our book on the follow-up study (Atkinson, Maynard and Trinder, 1983), we show for example that the children of families with low incomes in 1950 have nearly twice the chance of having low incomes themselves as those whose parents did not have low incomes. Chapter 5 considers deprivation more broadly in terms of housing, family status and job instability.

In the comparison of the 1930s and 1980s in Chapter 3, the role of unemployment features significantly, and this is taken further in Chapter 6, which was delivered as the first P. W. Segers Lecture in Antwerp. This makes use of the DHSS low-income estimates. It then goes on to examine some of the mechanisms underlying the rise in the incidence of low incomes and the prospects for the future. This provides a natural bridge to Parts II and III dealing with social security and its reform.

1 · HOW SHOULD WE MEASURE POVERTY? SOME CONCEPTUAL ISSUES

INTRODUCTION

The aim of this chapter is to review some of the conceptual issues in the measurement of poverty, trying to identify the dimensions in which legitimate differences of judgement may arise, and to suggest ways in which progress may be made. It should be stressed at the outset that the coverage is selective, reflecting my own particular interests, and that there are important topics not covered here.

The discussion is largely theoretical, but I would like to start by quoting briefly from the official evidence about poverty in Britain. In doing this, I am not making any attempt to assess the validity of the statistics, and the conclusions drawn are meant only to illustrate the methodological discussion. Any substantive conclusions would require a more thorough investigation of the empirical evidence. The introduction of the figures should be seen as a restraint on the tendency of the chapter to concern itself with theoretical refinements and as an earnest of my intention to be of assistance to those who have to translate concepts into numbers.

The official evidence takes the form of estimates made by the Department of Health and Social Security of the number of people and families in Great Britain with incomes below the supplementary benefit (SB) level, a level which sets the ceiling for entitlement to means-tested assistance but which is frequently taken as a poverty standard. The estimates are obtained from the *Family Expenditure Survey* which is a nationally representative sample of households carried out on a continuous basis. Table 1.1 shows that in 1981, 2.8 million people were living in families which were below the SB level, that is, 5.3 per cent of the total population. Official figures of this type (but not precisely the same form) have been produced since 1972, and those for 1976 (a year when considerable detail

Revised version of a lecture at the Berlin Symposium on Statistics for the Measurement of Poverty organized on behalf of the European Community by the Sonderforschungsbereich 3 of the University of Frankfurt and the Deutsches Institut für Wirtschaftsforschung, Berlin. [Section 5 of the paper presented in Berlin has been omitted to avoid overlap with Chapter 2.] I am grateful to the participants, particularly the discussant Tim Smeeding, and to Frank Cowell, Ruth Hancock, Julian Le Grand and Jill Smith for their helpful comments.

Table 1.1 Official estimates of families below supplementary benefit level in Great Britain

| | Numbers (thousands) with incomes | | | | | | Those in receipt of SB plus those | | | | | |
| | Below 90% of SB level | | Below SB level | | In receipt of SB | | Below 110% of SB level | | Below 120% of SB level | | Below 140% of SB level | |
	F	P	F	P	F	P	F	P	F	P	F	P
1981												
Over pension age	—	—	880	1,120	1,670	1,960	3,160	3,980	3,770	4,820	4,530	5,890
Under pension age	—	—	880	1,690	1,350	2,880	2,550	5,340	2,890	6,310	3,830	9,100
of which, single persons												
without children	—	—	560	560	640	640	1,370	1,370	1,470	1,470	1,730	1,730
couples without children	—	—	60	120	100	200	180	360	230	470	370	730
families with children	—	—	260	1,020	620	2,030	1,010	3,610	1,190	4,370	1,750	6,640
Total	—	—	1,760	2,810	3,010	4,840	5,700	9,310	6,650	11,120	8,350	15,000
1976												
Over pension age	290	340	700	870	1,660	1,950	2,930	3,630	3,720	4,710	4,590	6,000
Under pension age	460	820	650	1,410	960	2,130	1,860	4,360	2,280	5,680	3,270	8,850
of which, single persons												
without children	280	280	360	360	410	410	840	840	940	940	1,160	1,160
couples without children	50	100	70	130	80	160	180	350	240	470	400	780
families with children	130	440	230	920	460	1,560	840	3,170	1,100	4,260	1,720	6,910
Total	740	1,170	1,350	2,280	2,610	4,090	4,780	8,000	5,990	10,400	7,860	14,860

Sources:
1981: Department of Health and Social Security, *Tables on Families with Low Incomes – 1981*, unpublished.
1976: *Social Trends 1979*, Table 6.26; and *Social Security Statistics 1977*, Table 47.07.

Notes:
1. F = Families; P = Persons.
2. The total number of families in 1981 was 27 million and the total number of persons 53.4 million. The total number of families in 1976 was 25.1 million and the total number of persons 53.0 million.
3. The estimates for the two years are not fully comparable for several reasons, including the fact that in 1976 incomes reported in the survey were adjusted to an end-of-year basis, and the introduction of automatic heating additions in 1981.
4. Because of rounding, the sum of component parts may not add to the total.

was published) are shown in the lower part of Table 1.1. At that date, 2.3 million people were in families below the SB level, 4.3 per cent of the total population. As noted in the table, the estimates are not fully comparable, but this is not the only aspect which needs to be given careful consideration before one can draw conclusions about the trend in the extent of poverty over time.

The findings in Table 1.1 are based on comparing the total income of a family, denoted below by Y, with a prescribed poverty standard, referred to as Z. This approach to the recording of the extent of poverty raises several crucial questions:

1. What is the concept of income, and why are we concerned with income rather than standards of living?
2. How is the poverty standard, Z, defined? What happens if people hold different views about its definition? What meaning can be attached to poverty at different dates, such as 1976 and 1981?
3. How should we treat families of differing composition? Should the family be the unit of analysis, rather than the household? Should the individual be our main concern?
4. What should be the period of assessment? What account should be taken of wealth? How does the duration of poverty enter our considerations?
5. The figures show the 'head-count' of poverty; the US figures show also the poverty deficit. How should we measure the exent of poverty? Should we follow those authors who have proposed measures of poverty akin to those of inequality?

Questions 1–4 form the subject of sections 1–4 of this chapter; Question 5 is examined in Chapter 2. In each case, a variety of answers may be given; and one of the main points of the chapter is to bring out the different enterprises on which people may be embarked when they set out to 'measure poverty'.

1 CONCEPT OF RESOURCES

The estimates in Table 1.1 treat a family as being below the SB level if its cash income in a particular period is below the specified scale. The first point to be made about such a concept is that poverty is based on objective circumstances of the family and not on the family's own assessment. The measurement of poverty is concerned, on this approach, with the level of resources and not with the subjective evaluation of its position by the family in question. For those approaching the subject from a welfare-economic perspective, our concern is with Y, the level of resources, not with the family's personal sense of well-being $U(Y)$. In the terminology of

Sen (1977), it is a 'non-welfarist' approach. It is neither necessary nor sufficient that its members feel themselves to be deprived. This is not, of course, to deny that the feelings of deprivation, exclusion or frustration associated with low levels of resources may be a powerful reason for our concern in the first place.

In this chapter the focus will be on the objective indicators which have been the traditional basis for the investigation of poverty. The fact that they are typically all that we observe is one major reason for this being so, but it may also be argued that even if information on the family's own assessment were available, then it would not modify our judgement based on hard cash. Against this may be levelled the objection that such a position is essentially paternalistic; that it represents society imposing its own valuation – a further indignity for the poor.

There is a second sense in which the description 'subjective' may be used. This is where the indicator, Y, is observed income, but the poverty standard, Z, is based on the subjective judgements of the population as a whole. A subjective approach in this sense is not ruled out in what follows. The use of subjective considerations in the establishment of poverty standards has been explored particularly in the work of van Praag and colleagues (for example, Goedhart et al., 1977; van Praag et al., 1980, 1982a, 1982b). A recent study in Britain is that of Mack and Lansley (1985).

The indicator of poverty may take a variety of forms, and three broad approaches may be distinguished:

1. Consumption of specific goods.
2. Total expenditure.
3. Total income.

The first of these may be seen as parallel to the concept of 'specific egalitarianism' introduced by Tobin (1970); and he himself refers to 'biological or social necessities which are scarce in aggregate supply, so scarce that if they are unequally distributed, some citizens must be consuming below a tolerable minimum' (1970, p. 266). People are concerned if there are families with too little to eat, with inadequate housing, or who are ill-clothed. Society may set specific consumption targets, which I denote by X^* (this denoting a vector of commodity targets). In the context of developing countries, such considerations have been discussed in recent years under the heading of 'basic needs' (see, for example, Chichilnisky, 1982; Srinivasan, 1977).

The specific poverty approach leads to concern with the number of people with inadequate diets, the number with sub-standard housing, etc. We would have a multidimensional approach to the measurement of poverty, with the extent of overlap between the groups – the extent of 'multiple deprivation' – being of particular interest (see Chapter 5).

The alternative to such a multidimensional approach is to seek to reduce the analysis to a single indicator. From the list of minimum requirements, X^*, we could calculate the cost of purchasing them, $P.X^*$, and set $E^* = P.X^*$ as the minimum level of spending. This is in essence the approach which was followed by Rowntree (1901) and many subsequent studies. The problems with such an approach are considered in section 2; for the present, the principal point is that there is an important choice between *expenditure*, as used above, and *income* as the indicator of poverty.

Views differ as to whether we are concerned with low income or low spending, yet this fundamental distinction is rarely made explicitly. It is interesting in this respect to note the evolution of postwar studies of poverty in Britain. Abel-Smith and Townsend (1965), who pioneered the use of the *Family Expenditure Survey* for the measurement of poverty, were concerned with 'low levels of living'. For the first period studied (1953–54), there was no adequate income information, and the assessment was based on total expenditure; for the second period (1960) the expenditure totals could not readily be obtained, and they used 'normal' income, a concept which they preferred to actual last period income as being 'closer to what we intended to mean by level of living' (1965, p. 22). Abel-Smith and Townsend were careful to draw attention to the implications of these choices, and to note the difference between income and expenditure (see also Townsend, 1970); however, subsequent investigators, myself (1969) included, adopted the income definition without typically recognizing the shift in emphasis.

There are several reasons why an analysis based on income may lead to different conclusions from one based on expenditure. A family may have an income below Z but be able to attain a level of expenditure above the poverty line by running down savings or by borrowing. Budget studies commonly report significant dissaving by low-income groups. It could arise where they receive benefits in kind (such as free housing), or where they share consumption with others (as where an elderly person lives with children). In these cases, it could be argued that income has not been correctly measured, although it should be noted that in the case of shared consumption this would require a full accounting for the spillover effects. Conversely, receipt of an income above Z does not imply that a minimum target level of consumption can be achieved. As noted by Srinivasan, 'the failure of the poor to get their basic needs presumably reflects not only the unequal initial distribution of real purchasing power, but also market imperfections and failures' (1977, pp. 18–19). Access to housing, for example, may be subject to rationing.

Income and expenditure may also give different answers because of the choices made by the families. The actual level of spending may reflect tastes as much as consumption possibilities, a problem which has been well recognized: 'to *choose* not to go on holiday or eat meat is one thing: it may interest sociologists, but it is of no interest to those concerned with poverty. To have little or no *opportunity* to take a holiday or buy meat is entirely different' (Piachaud, 1981b, p. 421).

In considering these approaches to the indicator of poverty, we can discern two rather different conceptions. The first is concerned with the *standard of living*, and it leads in the direction of studying total expenditure (or the consumption of specific commodities). This approach is perhaps the natural one for those who see concern for poverty as stemming from individual caring or compassion for others (or utility interdependence). The second conception is that of poverty as concerned with the *right to a minimum level of resources*. On this basis, families are entitled, as citizens, to a minimum income, the disposal of which is a matter for them. This approach may be more appealing to those who see concern for poverty as based on a notion as to what constitutes a good society. The rights approach does indeed bring us close to the theory of justice, but should be kept distinct. Thus, the right to a minimum level of income may be seen as a prerequisite for participation in a particular society, with this having priority over other distributive principles.

That the standard of living and minimum rights conceptions of poverty may lead to different approaches is illustrated by the setting of the poverty line for men and women. On a standard of living approach, it may be defensible to set differing minima, reflecting, for example, differing nutritional requirements (as was the case with the United States official poverty line); but on a rights approach such differentiation would be hard to justify, and equal treatment may follow as a corollary.

The notion of 'rights' has been less fully discussed than that of standards of living (although it has obviously concerned lawyers in this field; see, for example, Reich, 1964; Michelman, 1973; Vernier, 1981), and it raises a number of questions. In particular, one cannot necessarily treat all sources of income as equivalent. The receipt of income is typically conditional. In the case of earnings, we may not regard it as objectionable that earnings be conditional on working but we might feel differently about a system of slavery. The receipt by an elderly person of a transfer from a child may be conditional on going to live with that child, and this may not be regarded as acceptable, as evidenced by the often expressed goal of ensuring that old people should be able to live on their own and not be forced to change their housing arrangements for financial reasons. This may lead us to apply a 'discount' to income which is contingent on moving. The same argument could, more controversially, be applied to means-tested state benefits. The incomplete take-up of such benefits, even when the person is informed of entitlement, is an indication of the *discount* effectively applied on account of the stigma attached and the uncertainty surrounding its payment.

To sum up, it has been suggested that we need to distinguish between a 'standard of living' approach, which may be represented by consumption of specific commodities, such as food or housing, or by total expenditure, and a 'minimum rights' approach, concerned with income, where we may want to distinguish between different sources of income.

2 DEFINITION OF THE POVERTY LINE

The problems which arise in the determination of the poverty line have been extensively discussed in the literature and it is now generally recognized that there is scope for a wide variety of opinion. This is most obvious in the case of the rights approach, where the determination of the minimum level of income, Z, is explicitly a social judgement, but it applies also to the standard of living approach. Suppose that we adopt a target set of consumptions, X^*, and that we are willing to aggregate them into a single indicator based on total expenditure. Then, as noted above, it is natural to define E^* as $P.X^*$, or more generally as:

$$E^* = (1 + h) P.X^*$$

where h is a provision for inefficient expenditure or waste, or a recognition that a family will not necessarily allocate its expenditure to the target goods, or a provision for items not included in the list X^*. One thinks for example of the provision for 10 per cent of wastage of all foods, and hence of nutrients, in the analysis of the adequacy of diets in the *National Food Survey* (for example, Ministry of Agriculture, Fisheries and Food, 1984). One can interpret in these terms the poverty standard developed by Orshansky (1965) for the United States, where the $P.X^*$ was based on the value of food requirements and h makes provision for necessary spending on other goods ($(1 + h)$ is equal to the reciprocal of the estimated share of food in total spending). It is evident that both X^* and h are areas where opinion may differ as to the appropriate level. This is true even for food, and for other items the derivation of reasonable standards is difficult: 'many people have been uneasily aware of the problems of defining necessities like housing, clothing, or fuel and light. . . . A family could go to bed early and spend nothing on electricity' (Townsend, 1973, p. 39).

It is not my intention to rehearse these arguments here; rather, I would like to examine the consequences for the measurement of poverty of the fact that such differences of opinion exist. In doing so, I am following the lead of Sen (1979), who noted that 'one may be forced to use more than one criterion because of non-uniformity of accepted standards, and look at the *partial* ordering generated by the criteria taken together' (p. 286), an approach which has also been explored by Foster and Shorrocks (1984).

Suppose that we have a range of possible poverty lines, so that $Z^- \leqslant Z \leqslant Z^+$, where this range is denoted by Z^*. (I refer to income, but the argument applies equally to expenditure.) What can we say? As discussed further in Chapter 2, a very natural way to proceed is to say that we can make unambiguous comparisons if the number in poverty is lower for all Z in the range, or higher for all Z in the range, but that we cannot rank two situations if the number in poverty is higher for some Z and lower for other Z in the range Z^*. In other words, for there to be definitely less poverty with one distribution of income than with another, we require that the cumulative distribution of Y be everywhere below that of the other in the range of possible poverty lines.

The application of this simple idea is illustrated in Figure 1.1, where the extent of poverty in Britain in 1981 is compared with that in 1976 on the basis that the poverty line is the supplementary benefit (SB) standard in both cases, an assumption which is discussed below. The number of people in poverty is expressed as a percentage of the total population. The figure assumes that those families receiving SB are exactly at the SB level. In Figure 1.1 the cumulative distributions do not intersect in the range from 100–140 per cent of the SB scale. If we could agree that the poverty line lies in this range, then we would reach a definite conclusion: according to these figures, poverty had increased between 1976 and 1981. In Figure 1.2, the analysis is restricted to families where the head is above the minimum pension age, and this shows a situation where the cumulative distributions intersect and no unambiguous conclusion can be reached. Taking the

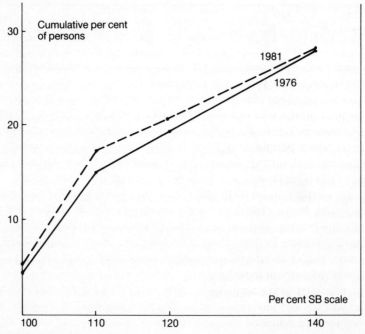

Figure 1.1 Cumulative percentage below poverty line in Britain, 1976 and 1981

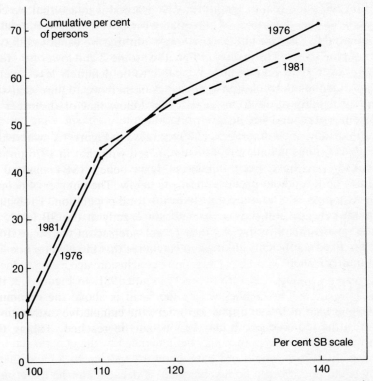

Figure 1.2 As Figure 1.1 but restricted to families where head is above pension age

figures at face value, it appears that 'serious' poverty has worsened and the number with less severe poverty has declined.

Any conclusion about changes in the extent of poverty over time must of course depend on the way in which the poverty standard itself is adjusted. On the minimum rights approach, this is again explicitly a matter for judgement. Some people may hold that the level of income should be maintained in real terms; that is they would like to see an 'absolute' standard. Others may opt for a 'relative' standard which adjusts the poverty line as the general level of income rises. A well-known example is the proposal by Fuchs (1965) that the poverty line should be one half the median family income. If there are such differences of opinion, all that one can realistically hope to do is to narrow down the range of disagreement: for example, that Z should be increased at least in line with prices and by up to a specified amount in real terms.

The standard of living approach may at first sight offer the prospect of more definite advice: the components X^* and h provide a fixed basis, and E^* should then be adjusted in line with prices. We may not find it easy to agree on X^* and h, but we can agree that a comparison over time should be based on the same real expenditure. This leads us again to an 'absolute' approach to the definition of poverty, where the poverty standard is uninfluenced by changes in the general level of incomes in the society. It is not however so straightforward. First, the parameter h may not remain constant over time and it may be influenced by the general level of incomes. On the interpretation as efficiency of spending, it may be affected by the availability of different goods: what foods are on sale depends on the incomes of others. On the interpretation in terms of spending patterns, the ratio of, say, food in total expenditure may change over time, and with it the poverty line implied by a particular X^*.

Secondly, we have been talking in terms of 'goods', whereas the literature on household production has rightly pointed to the need to see goods as inputs into household activities, with the level of such activities being our concern, not the purchase of goods as such. On this basis, we have to rewrite the objective as a target level of activities, say A^*, so that if there are fixed coefficients linking goods requirements to activities, with an input-matrix I, then

$$E^* = (1 + h) P I A^*$$

The significance of this approach is that even when we take a fixed set of activities, the required goods may be changing because of changes in the input-matrix I, and this in turn may be influenced by the general standards of living. In 1976 it would not have been a handicap to a child that his family could not afford a home computer; a decade later he might find it more difficult to follow lessons than his classmates with their Amstrad machines.

The approach just described has some similarity with that of Sen (1983), but he goes on to suggest that an activity model serves to close the gap between relative and absolute definitions of poverty: 'if we view the problem of conceptualising poverty in this light, then there is no conflict between the irreducible absolutist element in the notion of poverty [and] thoroughgoing relativity' (1983, p. 161). This seems misleading, since there is a clear difference, at least in principle, between those who would hold constant the level of activities, and those who would be influenced in the specification of activities by the prevailing customs and expectations of the society. This is, for example, the central concern of Townsend's develop-ment of alternative measures of poverty based on the capacity of families to participate in the 'community's style of living' (1979, p. 249).

With the standard of living approach, as with the rights approach, there is room for disagreement about the adjustment of the poverty line over time. Again, the obvious approach is to recognize this explicitly and to construct a 'confidence interval' about the estimated poverty percentage, based on alternative assumptions about the adjustment of the poverty standard over time: for example that (i) the poverty line had risen in line with the retail prices index, or (ii) that the poverty line had risen in line with average gross earnings.

The procedures proposed in this section introduce sources of ambiguity into the measurement of poverty; and economists have been criticized for seeking to blur the issue. It would patently be preferable to specify a single poverty standard and hence obtain a clearcut measure of the extent of poverty. This would however represent an 'all or nothing' approach, since those who disagree with the standard are likely to reject the findings out of hand. The intermediate path suggested in this section leads to less definite answers but, one hopes, commands a wider degree of support.

3   DIFFERENCES IN NEEDS AND THE UNIT OF ANALYSIS

Definition of the poverty standard depends not just on its level but also on the treatment of families of different sizes and with differing needs. Here attention is focused on the provision for families with different number of members; similar considerations apply to special provisions for the aged, the handicapped, etc.

The SB scale, like poverty scales in other countries, embodies differential rates, with couples receiving some 160 per cent of the amount for a single person, and children around either a third or a half depending on age. These differentials have a long history, but they have undoubtedly been influenced by the research on 'equivalence scales'. This has generated a vast literature (for a review, see Deaton and Muellbauer, 1980), which cannot be surveyed in full here. It is, however, important to consider its relation to different approaches to the measurement of poverty and the implications for the choice of unit of analysis.

For purposes of exposition, let us take the three sub-groups of families with head below pension age shown in Table 1.1: single persons without children, couples without children, and families with children (subsuming single-parent families with two-parent families). Their respective poverty lines are denoted by Z, mZ and cZ. The SB scale sets $m = 1.6$ and $c = (1.93+)$. The problem is to obtain values for m and c; and the extensive literature has shown that this too is a matter where judgement plays a significant role.

It is tempting to assume that in this area at least one can obtain a firm base from observation of consumer behaviour. One of the early methods – that proposed by Rothbarth (1943) – provides an illustration. By taking a commodity consumed by adults as an indicator of the level of living, one can measure the income required with different family types by taking the levels of income at which expenditure per person on, say, clothing is the same. The difficulty is that one is assuming that preferences for that commodity are independent of family composition; and this is an essentially arbitrary assumption. With other methods based on observed consumption patterns, identifying restrictions are similarly required.

Perhaps more importantly, the ethical status of such scales is far from transparent. Consumption patterns estimated conditionally on family composition cannot be used to draw conclusions about welfare levels with different compositions (Pollak and Wales, 1979). If the analysis is extended to include choice over household composition (Gronau, 1983, discusses fertility decisions, but also important are marriage and children leaving home), then there would remain the issue as to how far social judgements should be based on the private valuations implicit in such decisions. Society may, for example, want to modify the parental evaluation to take account of the interests of the children.

Nor does the adoption of other approaches solve the problem. If instead one seeks to consider the specification of A^* and the matrix I, and how they vary with family size, then one is back again with matters of judgement. The same is true with the rights approach to the measurement of poverty. It is not therefore surprising that a wide range of equivalence scales have been proposed in practice. Lazear and Michael (1980), for example, compare the Bureau of Labor Statistics and Orshansky estimates of m, which are 1.67 and 1.26 respectively, with their own, which is 1.06. For a couple with one child, the estimates are 2.28, 1.51 and 1.28. Similarly, van Praag, Spit and van de Stadt (1982) draw attention to the very different relationship between the poverty line and family size which they find applying the Leyden approach rather than the Orshansky method to data for the Netherlands. In view of this, it seems preferable to take explicit account once again of the scope for differences of opinion, and to settle for the more modest goal of making a partial ordering. This is the approach explored in Atkinson (1988), making use of the results in Atkinson and Bourguignon (1987).

Central to the discussion of equivalance scales has been the assumption – often implicit – that the standard of living is common to all members of the family. Studies such as that by Nicholson (1949) of the variations in working-class expenditure, one of the pioneering applications of the Rothbarth method, did not examine the possibility of differences between husbands and wives in their levels of living. He refers to separate figures for expenditure by the husband and wife on clothing, but uses the combined total. In the study of poverty, the *intra-family* distribution is clearly a crucial question, since it is quite possible that one member of the family has a lower level of living than the others. The distribution within the family is a subject about which we know very little, but there are fragmentary statistics to bear out the anecdotal evidence that there is significant inequality. Pahl (1983) quotes the finding that a sizeable proportion of women who have left their husbands report being 'better off' on supplementary benefit than living with their husbands, the figures ranging from 18 to 33 per cent. This has to be interpreted carefully, not least because the personal circumstances may colour recollection. Those wives leaving their husbands are more likely to be drawn from those where family resources were unequally distributed and, if financial stress is a factor leading to marital breakdown, from those families which were in any case below the SB level. And the wives may be seeking to justify their decision. Nevertheless, this kind of evidence suggests that there are indeed grounds for concern.

What are the implications of within-family inequality? On a standard of living approach, it means that it is no longer legitimate to look at the aggregate unit; we have to consider the position of individuals. If women have an inadequate diet even though the food consumption of the family as a whole is above the minimum, then this is a matter for concern. Food is taken in this example since it is clearly a private good, whereas other items of consumption may in effect be 'public' for the family, such as housing. In these latter cases, the spillover may be such that all members enjoy broadly equal levels of living. This may be the grounds for focusing on individual items – the specific poverty approach.

If we take total expenditure, then we have to recognize that the extent of individual poverty beneath the surface of the family depends on the unobserved distribution within the family. This again may lead us to attach a confidence interval to the estimated extent of poverty. At first sight, it might appear that the equal division assumption implicit in taking the family unit would give a lower bound. However, the fact that the head-count measure of poverty does not satisfy the general transfer axiom (see Chapter 2) means that this is not necessarily true, although it is the case for certain other poverty measures used such as the poverty gap.

The minimum rights approach to poverty must also be essentially individualistic, but this again raises questions about the nature of the rights and their converse – the obligation to support. A wife may have a right to an equal share in the joint income of a couple. Under the supplementary benefit law, a man is liable to maintain his wife and a woman is liable to maintain her husband. These issues extend beyond the family to the household and the wider circle of relatives. One of the advances of the postwar assistance legislation in Britain was the abolition of the hated 'household means test', which enforced the liability of adult children living at home for their parents, and vice versa. (There are signs that the government would like to reverse this by extending the liability of parents for their children, e.g. through changes to the benefits for young persons and in student support.)

The adoption of a family unit implies on the rights approach that inter-spousal obligations exist and are fulfilled; to apply the same reasoning and take a household basis for assessing poverty would imply that obligations of support existed between members of the household and that they were carried out. If we are concerned lest they not be fulfilled, then we face the same difficulty as with the standard of living approach, namely lack of information. We do, however, have rather more on which to proceed, since the cashflows into the family are largely identified by recipient. If we look at a family budget, then it is the wife who receives her earnings and, typically, the child benefit.

4 TIME PERIOD AND THE DURATION OF POVERTY

The estimates of poverty in Britain in Table 1.1 are based on the family's income in the 'normal employment situation' of the family head. This official definition means that, where the head has been off work due to sickness or unemployment for less than 13 weeks at the time of interview, the family's normal income when the head is in work is taken in determining income. The purpose of this adjustment is to obtain a measure of 'normal' poverty status, although in the case of those experiencing recurrent unemployment it could be argued that some average of the incomes in and out of work would be more appropriate. The use of normal income in such cases, rather than current income, can make a noticeable difference, as has been shown by Beckerman and Clark (1982): for 1974–76, they estimate 5 per cent to be below the poverty line on a normal basis and 6.8 per cent on a current basis (1982, Table 3.3).

The choice of time-period is open to debate. Should we take current income or normal income? Should we move to a longer assessment period, such as the annual income basis used in the United States? As we have seen earlier, the standard of living approach to the measurement of poverty has led investigators to prefer normal to current income as being more closely related to the sustainable level of consumption. Thus, even if we are concerned about consumption in this period, we may want to ignore short-term fluctuations in income which can be smoothed out by dissaving or borrowing. Indeed, in a perfect capital market, where people can borrow or lend at a fixed rate of interest, we may want to take simply the present discounted value of income. In this way, we would be able to combine the flow of resources with the stock of assets. As was proposed by Weisbrod and Hansen (1968), income and net worth need both to be taken into account, the solution proposed by these authors being to convert net worth into an annuity.

There are however substantial problems with this approach. Even in a perfect capital market, the annuitized value of a stock of wealth depends on a person's life-expectancy (and on obligations to heirs). Once we leave the perfect capital market assumption, the outcome depends on the rate of interest at which the person can borrow or lend, and on the credit limits faced. For each individual there is a large number of unobservable, or difficult to observe, parameters, necessary to determine the sustainable level of consumption. All of this may suggest that it would be better to take consumption expenditure itself as a measure of status. After all, the person takes the capital market opportunities into account when deciding how much to consume, so why not take these decisions as embodying the unobserved capital market parameters? This is indeed an argument for the use of *consumption*; unfortunately, this is not the same as the observed *consumption expenditure*. The difference is most obvious in the case of durables, where the services continue for years after purchase, but, as argued by Kay, Keen and Morris (1984), much expenditure has that form, if to a lesser degree. The distribution of outlays will exhibit a higher proportion of people with low values than the underlying distribution of actual consumption: 'observed expenditures are liable to give a seriously distorted picture of the true incidence of poverty' (Kay *et al.*, 1984, p. 170).

Turning to a rights approach, the issues are different. The interpretation of rights to an income must surely be conditional on assets. There must be some combination of income and net worth, but here the judgement is a social one. At what rate should a person be expected to use up his capital? The practice which used to be used in the operation of SB seems relevant here: an assumed rate of amortization of capital. In other words, we arrive at a procedure like that advocated by Hansen and Weisbrod, but with the annuity rate reflecting social judgements.

Lurking behind the discussion of the time-period is concern about the duration of poverty. Here one senses that there are quite different views. For some people, interdependence between consumption at different dates is seen to be such as to impose a greater cost of poverty on those who had previously enjoyed a high level of living. On this basis, a highly mobile poor population would be worse than a static one of the same size. This 'distressed gentlefolk' view is clearly based on the standard of living approach and is equally clearly based on consideration of individual welfare, rather than the social judgements which have been our main concern here.

In general, most people seem to agree that a situation of mobility is better than one where there is persistent poverty. The Institute of Social Research Newsletter item about the study by Duncan (1984) using the Michigan Panel Study of Income Dynamics described its findings of mobility as 'more hopeful' than the view that poverty persisted. Nevertheless, the reasons for this judgement do not seem to have been very fully articulated. Here, we identify two main arguments. The first follows on from the distinction between consumption and expenditure. If we observe only the latter, as an imperfect indicator of the former, then the longer that we observe a low level of expenditure presumably the greater the probability that the person is indeed poor. That is, our evaluation of the *current* status of a person depends on past as well as present observations of expenditure.

The second interpretation is that our social concern is both about the existence of poverty *and* about its duration. The judgement may be made that its consequences become more serious, as time passes, independently of the actual level of living or income. In this case, unlike the first, there is the problem of aggregation. How should the two dimensions – poverty and duration – be traded one against the other in social judgements? Some people may have a lexicographic ordering, giving priority to poverty, and only taking account of duration when there is an equal rank on poverty. Others might allow a trade-off, being willing to exchange some increase in the amount of poverty for a reduction in the average duration.

One of the few authors to address this explicitly is Nicholson (1979), who argues that there is some level of income deficiency which is serious even for short periods and a lesser extent of deprivation which becomes serious if it lasts long enough. The two are combined in the form of the product of the lack of resources and the duration, with it being said that 'poverty is serious when the product exceeds a certain tolerance limit' (Nicholson, 1979, p. 61). If we could agree with Nicholson that the product was the appropriate functional form, then we would have a simple bivariate measure of poverty. If we could agree not on the precise form, but on certain properties, such as a positive weight to the interdependence between duration and poverty, then we could apply the dominance results for the bivariate case derived by Atkinson and Bourguignon (1982).

In this discussion, it has been assumed that information on duration is available. Panel studies, such as the Michigan data, may increasingly provide such information, but in many situations the duration is likely to be unobserved. If therefore the 'true' status depends on both current income and duration, then we have the problem that we are observing an imperfect indicator of poverty status. In just the same way, observed expenditure is an imperfect indicator of actual living standards. One of the conclusions to be drawn from this section is that it may be better to recognize this explicitly and to carry out the analysis in terms of the *probability* that a family is in poverty.

CONCLUDING REFLECTIONS: NEW TECHNOLOGIES AND OLD INSIGHTS

Two themes have been stressed throughout this chapter. The first is that of differences in judgements and the need to face directly the existence of such differences in values. People will disagree about the right level for the poverty line, about the adjustments to be made over time, about the appropriate equivalence scales, about the choice of poverty index, and about the trade-off between poverty and inequality.

I have made a variety of suggestions as to how such differences can be taken into account, steering an intermediate path between providing clearcut answers to questions many people do not want answered and providing no answers at all. However, a concluding reflection concerns the form in which information is made available, and the scope offered by new microcomputing technology. In the days when the production of a statistical table was the product of many hours with a desk-calculator, or more recently of a long wait in the batch queue of a central computing centre, it was understandable that the end-product was a limited selection of tables. Today, when whole surveys can be held on local microcomputers, it seems reasonable to question the form of the output. Should we not provide results in a form that allows the user to specify the aspects of interest? Should the user not be allowed to choose the poverty line and the equivalence scale? Should the user not be allowed to determine the groups of the population for which the results should be produced? Of course, there would have to be safeguards that the data were not misused, so that the program did not produce poverty percentages for families with six children in Barnstaple, but this should not defeat the ingenuity of the programmers, particularly of those with experience in answering Parliamentary Questions.

The second theme has been the role of unobservable variables, such as the distribution of income within the family, or the level of consumption as opposed to consumer expenditure. Here again, we may be able to make progress by making more limited demands. It may be better, for example, to present the findings in terms of the *probability* that a family is in poverty, making explicit the limitations to our knowledge. It may be that we can learn from the econometric work on unobservables; for example, it may be that we should make use of multiple indicators.

But we need also to give thought to the *kind* of information which is collected. The study of poverty today has become increasingly that of secondary analysis of surveys carried out for other purposes; and the information is statistical. One of the contributions of early investigators was that they were actively involved in fieldwork and that a great deal of qualitative and background material entered into their assessment. In particular, they knew a great deal about the localities they studied. When Rowntree reported the percentage in poverty in York and Bowley that in Reading, their results were given credence in part because of the local and background knowledge they brought to bear. Moreover, it was one of the insights of such investigators that the individual family or household should not be seen as an independent observation unrelated to their neighbours or work-mates. The extent and causes of poverty would be documented not just in terms of individual units but also in terms of the experience of localities and communities. The needs of immigrants and those on the margins of society, such as the homeless, excluded by the rigid requirements of survey design or questionnaire coding, would be less easily overlooked, and the investigators would be more likely to respond quickly to changing social problems.

2 · ON THE MEASUREMENT OF POVERTY

INTRODUCTION

The subject I have chosen for this Walras–Bowley chapter is undoubtedly more appropriate for Bowley than for Walras. Sir Arthur Bowley was a pioneer in the measurement of poverty in Britain, notably in bringing statistical rigour to bear on this important but emotive topic. Seventy years ago he produced, with Burnett-Hurst, a book, *Livelihood and Poverty* (1915), which studied the incidence of poverty in five English towns. Ten years later, with Hogg, he produced a sequel called *Has Poverty Diminished?* (1925), examining the changes which had taken place in the intervening period.

The changing extent of poverty is a subject of importance today. Many people are concerned that recession, and Conservative government policy, have led to an increase in poverty; and the official statistics provide grounds for this fear. In Britain, government figures (Department of Health and Social Security, 1983) show that the proportion of families with incomes below the supplementary benefit level increased by around a quarter between 1979 and 1981, the most recent year available. In the United States, the official estimates (US Bureau of the Census, 1985) show 14.4 per cent of the population to be in poverty in 1984, compared with 11.2 per cent in 1974. On the other hand, there are those, especially defenders of the government record, who are sceptical about the claim that poverty has increased. The sceptics point to the unsatisfactory nature of the measures used and the need for reconsideration of basic concepts.

For this reason, I was tempted to echo Bowley and title this chapter *Has Poverty Increased?* However, I have not done so, since the content is methodological rather than substantive. It does not seek to provide a definitive answer to the question as to whether poverty has increased; rather it explores some of the problems which arise in trying to provide

A revised version of the Walras–Bowley Lecture delivered at the Fifth World Congress of the Econometric Society, August 1985, at MIT. I am most grateful to the Editor, the referees, F. A. Cowell, J. Creedy and J. Gordon for their helpful comments and suggestions.
Reprinted from *Econometrica*, Vol. 55, 4 July 1987.

such an answer. There are many more such problems than can be considered in the space available, and I concentrate on three. (In Chapter 1, I have discussed some of the other issues which arise, including the dynamic aspects of poverty and the choice of unit of analysis – individual, family, or household).

First, there is the choice of poverty line – clearly an essential ingredient. It has been recognized since the early days that there is room for differences of view as to the drawing of the line. Those sceptical as to the conclusion that poverty has increased may therefore argue that the choice of a different standard could lead to a reversal of the conclusion.

Secondly, there is the choice of poverty measure. I have simply referred to the proportion of the population in poverty, commonly known as the head-count, but there has been an extensive recent literature on alternative poverty measures. Could different views about the choice of poverty measure lead us to reach different conclusions about what has happened?

Thirdly, sceptics have been heard to complain that those concerned about poverty are really confusing poverty and inequality. Are the numbers quoted for the UK and the US just an alternative measure of income inequality? Here, the sceptics are touching on a raw nerve, since in my view the literature on the measurement of poverty has done little to illuminate the relationship between the two concepts.

Before considering these questions, I should draw attention to one theme that recurs throughout the chapter: that there is likely to be a diversity of judgements affecting all aspects of measuring poverty and that we should recognize this explicitly in the procedures we adopt. This will lead to less all-embracing answers. We may only be able to make comparisons and not to measure differences; and our comparisons may lead only to a partial rather than a complete ordering. But such partial answers are better than no answers. In this, and other aspects, I should acknowledge the influence of the work of Amartya Sen. In particular, he has stressed 'the danger of falling prey to a kind of nihilism [which] takes the form of noting, quite legitimately, a difficulty of some sort, and then constructing from it a picture of total disaster' (1973, p. 78). So that while I shall be taking seriously the objections raised by the sceptics, my emphasis will be on what we *can* say.

1   LEVEL OF THE POVERTY LINE

Beginning with the first question, it is evident that the choice of the poverty line, denoted here by Z, is a matter about which views may differ. Of this, early investigators such as Bowley were well aware. He referred to his poverty line as 'arbitrary, but intelligible' (1925, p. 14), recognizing that others might disagree, as illustrated by the famous occasion in 1920 when he was being cross-examined by Ernest Bevin, the well-known union leader (later Foreign Secretary) during the inquiry into dockworkers' pay. Bowley had given evidence for the employers as to what constituted a minimum basket of goods. Bevin in turn had gone out and bought the recommended diet and came into court with a plate bearing a few scraps of bacon, fish and bread. In a devastating piece of cross-examination, he asked Bowley whether he thought that this was sufficient breakfast for a man who had to carry heavy bags of grain all day.[1]

In terms of the measurement of poverty there is a straightforward procedure, which has been used implicitly for a long time. If we suppose that the poverty line may vary over a certain range $[Z^-, Z^+]$, denoted by Z^*, then we can examine whether or not we obtain the same ranking for all Z in the range Z^*. For the head-count measure, this means comparing over the range Z^* the cumulative distribution, denoted by $F(Y)$, where Y may refer to income or standard of living (for simplicity, I refer to income).

To make this more precise, let us assume that the population is fixed in size, and that $F(Y_1) = 0$ and $F(Y_2) = 1$ for some finite Y_1 and Y_2; for ease of exposition, I take $Y_1 = 0$ and $Y_2 = A$. The corresponding density function is denoted by $f(Y)$. We are interested in comparing two distributions, F and F^1, denoting the difference by $\Delta F \equiv F - F^1$. The difference in the corresponding densities is denoted by Δf. Then we require a *restricted* form of first-degree stochastic dominance condition:

CONDITION I: *For there to be for all $Z \in Z^*$ a reduction, or no increase, in poverty, as measured by the headcount, on moving from the distribution F^1 to F:*

$$\Delta F(Z) \leqslant 0 \quad \text{for all} \quad Z \in [Z^-, Z^+].$$ (I)

The application of this simple condition is illustrated in Figure 2.1, which shows the curves for the US in 1974, 1979 and 1982,[2] taking the range from 50 per cent (75 per cent for 1974) of the official poverty standard to 150 per cent. In the case of the comparison of 1982 with either of the years in the 1970s, the curves do not intersect. This means that we may not be able to say that poverty has gone up by x per cent, since the shift is not uniform, but we can agree about the direction of the change: poverty increased between 1979 and 1982. On the other hand, it is possible that we cannot reach agreement, as when comparing 1974 and 1979, where the curves intersect. We cannot rank 1974 and 1979 if the range of permissible poverty lines extends both above and below the official poverty line (which is the point of intersection in this case).

The same can be done for other poverty measures, such as the poverty deficit, normalized by the poverty line. This is the measure D in Table 2.1, which shows a variety of different poverty measures. Again, let us suppose that there is a range Z^* over which Z may vary. What we then require for

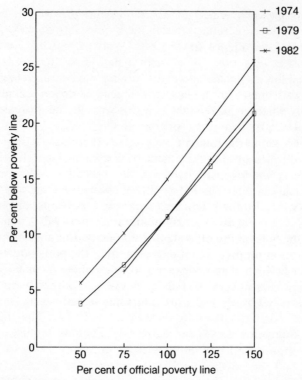

Figure 2.1 Cumulative percentage below different poverty levels in US, 1974, 1979 and 1982

Sources: 1974 from US Department of Health, Education, and Welfare (1976), Table 17; 1979 from US Bureau of the Census (1981), Table 7; 1982 from US Bureau of the Census (1984), Table 7. The 1974 figures are before the introduction of the revised methodology.

agreement that poverty has decreased, or is not higher, is that D be everywhere no higher for all Z in the range Z^*. As noted by Foster and Shorrocks (1984), this is equivalent to a second-degree stochastic dominance condition, although it is important to specify the range over which it must hold. It is a *restricted* second-degree dominance condition:[3]

CONDITION II: *For there to be for all $Z \in Z^*$ a reduction, or no increase, in poverty, as measured by the poverty deficit, on moving from the distribution F^1 to F:*

$$\Delta\Phi(Z) \equiv \int_0^Z \Delta F(Y)\, dY \leqslant 0 \quad \textit{for all} \quad Z \in [Z^-, Z^+]. \tag{II}$$

This result follows from the fact that, integrating by parts,

$$\Delta\Phi(Z) = \int_0^Z [Z - Y]\Delta f(Y)\, dY. \tag{1}$$

The application of this second-degree condition may be illustrated by the US data for 1974 and 1979. In Figure 2.1, the cumulative frequency is lower in 1974 at income levels below the poverty line, at least in the range shown, which suggests that 'serious' poverty is more severe in 1979 and that this would be reflected in the poverty deficit. This is in fact the case. Whereas the head-count measured at the official poverty line is identical in the two years, the poverty deficit per head of the US population, normalized by the poverty line, increased between 1974 and 1979 (derived from US Bureau of the Census, 1981, Table 6). If we take F^1 as the distribution in 1979 and F as that in 1974, then $\Delta\Phi(Z)$ is negative at the official poverty line. As we take values of Z above the official poverty line, then the value of $\Delta\Phi(Z)$ is rising, since ΔF is positive, but there will be a range of Z above and below the official line such that we can reach the definite conclusion for the poverty deficit that poverty increased between 1974 and 1979. A change in the poverty measure has therefore widened the range of possible comparisons.

Before going on to the choice of poverty measure, it should be noted that in Condition I and II families have been assumed to be identical in their needs and the poverty line has been taken as the same for all. In practice, the poverty line is different for families of different size and differing in other respects. There is therefore scope for disagreement not just about the *level* of the poverty line but also about its *structure*. The sceptic may point to the widely varying equivalence scales which are employed and to the possibility that these may give conflicting results.

Table 2.1 Examples of poverty measures

Head-count: $H = \int_0^Z f(Y)\, dY.$

Normalized deficit: $D = \int_0^Z [1 - Y/Z]f(Y)\, dY.$

Watts measure: $W = -\int_0^Z \log_e (Y/Z)f(Y)\, dY.$

Clark *et al.* (second measure): $1/c[1 - (1 - P^*)^c] = 1/c\int_0^Z (1 - (Y/Z)^c)f(Y)\, dY$, where $c \le 1$.

Foster *et al.*: $P_a = \int_0^Z (1 - Y/Z)^a f(Y)\, dY$, where $a \ge 0$.

Moreover, differing weights are used in combining the poverty indices for different groups to arrive at an aggregate measure. Sometimes the total number of *families* is counted; in other cases it is the total number of *people* in poverty. However, all is not lost, since again we may seek a partial ordering. Suppose that we can agree on a ranking of the 'needs' of different types of family such that the poverty line is at least no lower as we move up the ranking: couples should get no less than single persons, couples with one child no less than couples without children, and so on. Suppose that the same applies to the weights in the aggregate poverty index. Families then differ in two dimensions – income and 'needs' – and we can use the results for bivariate stochastic dominance, applied to income inequality measurement in Atkinson and Bourguignon (1987). In the case of the poverty deficit, this leads to conditions for dominance which are quite demanding but which are easy to check. In effect, they involve cumulating not just over incomes but also in the second direction of differences in 'needs' (Atkinson, 1988). And where there is only incomplete agreement on the ranking of 'needs', the conditions may be applied for the alternative rankings.

2 DIFFERENT MEASURES OF POVERTY

The head-count measure, H, used at the outset has been under severe attack. Some twenty years ago, Watts noted that it had 'little but its simplicity to recommend it' (1968, p. 326). In his influential work, Sen has remarked that the degree of support commanded by this measure is 'quite astonishing' (1979, p. 295) and criticized Bowley for his identification of the measurement of poverty with the use of H. Watts, Sen, and a variety of subsequent authors, have therefore proposed alternatives (see Foster, 1984, for a valuable survey), opening the door for the sceptic to claim that these can lead to conflicting conclusions.

In order to explore the properties of different measures, let us consider the class of additively separable poverty measures, P, such that there is a monotonic transformation, $G(P)$, which can be written in the form of the integral of a function $p(Y, Z)$ over the full range of the distribution of incomes, with $p(Y, Z) = 0$ for $Y \geq Z$, but where we express poverty negatively, in that the function G is decreasing in the poverty index, P:

$$G(P) = \int_0^A p(Y, Z) f(Y) \, dY \tag{2}$$

where

$$p(Y, Z) = 0 \quad \text{for} \quad Y \geq Z \quad \text{and } G \text{ is a decreasing function.}$$

We assume that p is non-decreasing in Y, which implies that $p(Y, Z)$ is non-positive. Writing the objective in this way puts it in a form similar to a social welfare function – an aspect developed in the final section of the chapter – and means that an *increase* in G is preferred. Of course, the assumption that the index may be written in this way is restrictive; it excludes for example the index proposed by Sen (1976a). It does, however, encompass a variety of measures, including all of those shown in Table 2.1, as is illustrated in Figure 2.2, where the form of $p(Y, Z)$ is sketched as a function of Y for these different measures.

The objection of Watts to the head-count is that 'poverty is not really a discrete condition. One does not immediately acquire or shed the afflictions we associate with the notion of poverty by crossing any particular income line' (1968, p. 325). In terms of the representation (2), for the head-count the function p is discontinuous at $Y = Z$, taking the value -1 for $Y < Z$, and 0 for $Y \geq Z$. This is illustrated in Figure 2.2 by the heavy line. Here, there is room for difference of opinion. On the one hand, there are those who agree with Watts that there is a continuous gradation as one crosses the poverty line. On the other hand, there are people who see poverty as an either/or condition. A minimum income may be seen as a basic right, in which case the head-count may be quite acceptable as a measure of the number deprived of that right. The same position may be taken if the income level Z is interpreted as that necessary for survival,

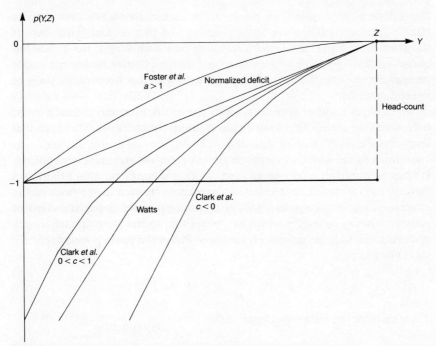

Figure 2.2 Form of the function $p(Y, Z)$ for different poverty measures

although if the probability of survival varies continuously with income we may be back with the position of Watts.

For those who reject the head-count, and require that the function $p(Y, Z)$ be continuous, there are several possible ways in which one could arrive at a replacement for the head-count. One can simply propose measures which look better. Watts himself suggested two, and these are shown in Figure 2.2. First, there is the normalized poverty deficit which replaces the discontinuous p function by a continuous function. The second proposal is more sophisticated, and is designed to allow for the fact that 'poverty becomes more severe at an increasing rate' (1968, p. 326), taking the p function log (Y/Z), where $Y < Z$. This in turn may be seen as a sub-case of the second class of measures suggested in Clark et al. (1981), governed by the parameter c, varying between 1 and $-\infty$, with the Watts case being obtained as c tends to zero. There are other possibilities, such as the class of measures proposed by Foster et al. (1984) and shown in Figure 2.2, based on a power of the (normalized) poverty gap.

Sen, on the other hand, took an axiomatic approach and this has been followed in a number of subsequent articles. In the construction of his index, the key axiom is one which rejects the equal weighting of poverty gaps implied by the poverty deficit (the linearity of the p function), on the grounds that this is insensitive to the distribution of income amongst the poor, and proposes that the poverty gap be weighted by the person's rank in the ordering of the poor. Sen refers to the classic use by Borda of such an equidistance cardinalization of an ordering and to a subjective concern of the poor for their relative position. In my own judgement, the arguments about relative position and ranking are more persuasive for inequality measurement (as in Sen, 1974) than for poverty measurement – a point to which I return.

There is yet another approach which has not been much followed in the literature (the closest that I have seen is Gourieroux, 1980). This approach considers a class of poverty measures satisfying certain properties and seeks conditions under which all members of that class will give the same ranking. It tries to establish common ground, so that we may be able to say that poverty has increased, or decreased, for all poverty measures in a class.

To this end, let us consider the difference in poverty as measured by the class of poverty measures which can be written in the form (2), where p is now assumed to be a continuous function. Poverty is lower, or no higher, if $\Delta G \geqslant 0$, where

$$\Delta G = \int_0^A p(Y, Z) \, \Delta f(Y) \, dY = \int_0^Z p(Y, Z) \, \Delta f(Y) \, dY. \tag{3}$$

Then we have the following condition.

CONDITION IA: *A necessary and sufficient condition for there to be for all*

$Z \in Z^*$ *a reduction, or no increase, in poverty for all measures in the class* *(2), where p is continuous and non-decreasing in Y, on moving from the distribution F^1 to F is that:*

$$\Delta F(Z) \leq 0 \quad \text{for all} \quad Z \in [0, Z^+].$$ (IA)

The sufficiency of this condition may be seen by integrating ΔG by parts (and using the fact that $p(Z, Z) = 0$):[4]

$$\Delta G = - \int_0^Z p_Y \, \Delta F(Y) \, dY.$$ (4)

The non-negativity of ΔG then follows from $p_Y \geq 0$. The necessity may be seen by considering an interval $[Y_0, Y_0 + \varepsilon]$ where $\Delta F(Z) > 0$, and constructing a function p taking the value $-\varepsilon$ for $Y \leq Y_0$, $-(\varepsilon - (Y - Y_0))$ for Y in the interval, and 0 for $Y \geq Y_0 + \varepsilon$. It may be noted that Condition IA is stronger than Condition I and that even though the range of permissible poverty lines is $[Z^-, Z^+]$, rather than $[0, Z^+]$, the condition cannot be weakened where $Z^- > 0$. In the limiting case where we are agreed on the poverty line ($Z^- = Z^+$), we still require $\Delta F(Z) \leq 0$ for all income levels below Z^+.

Suppose that we now make the further assumption that the function $p(Y, Z)$ is (weakly) concave in Y, i.e. where p is differentiable, $p_{YY} \leq 0$. This further assumption is restrictive, as discussed below, but it allows us to make use of a result suggested by a theorem of Fishburn (1977) in the portfolio literature. In that literature, 'poverty' corresponds to below-target returns. The head-count corresponds to the safety-first principle of Roy (1952), the poverty deficit to the Domar Musgrave (1944) measure of risk, and the Foster *et al.* measures to the $\alpha - t$ model of risk analysed by Fishburn. The result is given in Condition IIA.

CONDITION IIA: *A necessary and sufficient condition for there to be for all* $Z \quad Z^*$ *a reduction, or no increase, in poverty for all measures in the class (2), where p is continuous, nondecreasing and (weakly) concave in Y, on moving from the distribution F^1 to F is that:*

$$\Delta \Phi(Z) = \int_0^Z \Delta F(Y) \, dY \leq 0 \quad \text{for all} \quad Z \in [0, Z^+].$$ (IIA)

In terms of a diagram, we require that the 'poverty deficit curve' $\Phi(Z)$, lie below (or not above) for all poverty lines less than or equal to Z^+.[5]

The sufficiency of Condition IIA in the case where p is everywhere differentiable on $[0, Z]$ may be seen by integrating the right side of (4) by parts:

$$\Delta G = - p_Y(Z, Z) \, \Delta \Phi(Z) + \int_0^Z p_{YY}(Y, Z) \, \Delta \Phi(Y) \, dY.$$ (5)

More generally, sufficiency may be seen by building on the observation of Hardy *et al.* (1929) that a concave function may be approximated uniformly by the sum of an increasing linear function and a finite number of positive multiples of 'angles', the latter taking the value $-(B - Y)$ for $Y \leqslant B$, zero otherwise, where B is some arbitrary constant. These angles are minus the deficit from an arbitrary line B (and in the present case $B \leqslant Z$). The same angles may be used to show necessity, since the deficit from an arbitrary line B, where $B \leqslant Z$, is a permissible poverty measure.[6]

The statement of Condition IIA takes account of the fact that narrowing of the range of permissible poverty lines to $[Z^-, Z^+]$ does not allow the condition of $\Delta\Phi(Z)$ to be weakened. In order to encompass all non-decreasing and concave functions p, we require that the poverty deficit be no greater at all values of Z below Z^+. Suppose, for example, that we take the measure of Foster *et al.* with the parameter $a = 2$. Then $p_Y(Z, Z) = 0$ and $p_{YY}(Y, Z) = -2/Z^2$. Therefore, from (5), $\Delta G \geqslant 0$ if

$$\int_0^Z \Delta\Phi(Y)\, dY \leqslant 0 \quad \text{for all} \quad Z \in Z^*. \tag{6}$$

It is clearly not sufficient that $\Delta\Phi(Z) \leqslant 0$ for all $Z \in Z^*$. On the other hand, we now have an unambiguous relation between the first-degree and second-degree dominance conditions. Condition IIA is implied by, but does not imply, Condition IA, so that the second-degree condition is clearly weaker.

As we have seen, a second-degree dominance condition is not strong enough to ensure the same ranking by the head-count. What makes the second-degree condition sufficient is that we are willing to assume that p is concave in income; in other words that it satisfies the Dalton transfer principle. The discontinuous p function with the head-count measure does not satisfy this condition. A disequalizing transfer from a poor person to someone richer may reduce the head-count (where the recipient was previously below the poverty line and is raised above by the transfer). Nor is the Dalton transfer principle required by the authors of certain other measures, including that proposed by Sen where the weights on the individual poverty gaps change with the number of poor people. Again a disequalizing transfer from a poor person may reduce measured poverty where the number of poor falls and hence changes the weights.[7]

Do we wish to impose the Dalton transfer principle? Here views may differ. For those who see a minimum income as a basic right, the criticisms of the head-count may not be germane and the transfer principle – at least in its unqualified form – may be irrelevant. On the other hand, those viewing poverty in terms of a continuous gradation may find the transfer principle quite acceptable. It should be stressed that it is quite consistent with giving a specific role to the poverty line. The index may be sensitive to transfers affecting those below the poverty line but neutral with regard to the impact above Z, i.e. the second derivative of p with respect to Y may be strictly negative below Z and zero above Z.[8]

The advantage of assuming the Dalton transfer principle to hold is that we may use Condition IIA, in which case the implications that can be drawn from the poverty deficit curve are much more far-reaching than at first appeared. If the curves do not cross before Z^+, then all of the measures in the Foster *et al.* class with $a \geq 1$, including of course the poverty gap itself, will give the same ranking, as will all measures in the class proposed by Clark *et al.* What is more, the result can be strengthened to include measures which are *s*-concave but not necessarily additively separable, such as the variation on the Sen index proposed by Thon (1979), where the weight attached to the poverty gaps is the ranking in the *whole* population and not just that among the poor. The result may be extended to third (and higher) degrees of stochastic dominance.

The choice of poverty line and the choice of poverty measure have been discussed separately, but it is evident from consideration of Conditions I, IA, and Conditions II, IIA that these issues are intimately related. Agreement on the use of the poverty deficit from among the class of non-decreasing, concave p functions avails us nothing if the poverty line could lie anywhere in the range $[0, Z^+]$. It allows us to apply II rather than IIA, but where $Z^- = 0$ these are identical. Similarly, agreement that the poverty line is Z^+ avails us nothing if the choice of poverty index can give zero weight to those with income Y in some range $Y_0 \leq Y \leq Z^+$. Put more positively, Condition IA and IIA allow for differences of view with regard to the choice of both poverty line and poverty measure, and as such these dominance conditions are powerful tools.

3   POVERTY AND INEQUALITY

At least four schools of thought about the relation between poverty and inequality can be distinguished. These are summarized below, where we denote by I the 'cost' of inequality to be deducted from mean income $\bar{Y}$: the 'equally distributed equivalent income' (Atkinson, 1970; Sen, 1976b) is $\bar{Y} - I$. P similarly denotes the 'cost' of poverty to be subtracted:

1. No specific weight to poverty: maximize $\bar{Y} - I$.
2. Lexicographic approach: maximize $- P$, then $\bar{Y} - I$ where ranking on P identical.
3. Concern only for poverty: maximize $\bar{Y} - P$.
4. Trade-off between poverty and inequality: maximize $\bar{Y} - I - P$.

The first view is that of people who attach no specific weight to poverty, being concerned solely with inequality. If poverty is singled out, then it is simply as a component of social welfare assessment, so that one could adopt a logarithmic social welfare function and decompose the inequality into that due to people having incomes below Z and other components. In this way, the Watts measure of poverty would enter, but only as an interpretation of part of the measured inequality. Such a decomposition into a 'poverty effect' and an 'affluence effect' was indeed discussed by Watts (1968), and is explored by Pyatt (1984), who provides an interesting geometric representation in the case of the Gini coefficient. It should be observed that in such a decomposition the functional form for the poverty component is the same as that for the inequality index.

If, on view 1, the measurement of inequality were to be based on the Rawlsian difference principle (Rawls, 1971), then this might appear to focus attention on the poor. We have however to be careful. The Rawlsian difference principle has usually been presented by economists, myself included, as maximizing the welfare of the least advantaged individual; and this objective is in no way related to a particular income level. Poverty as such has no role. It would be of no significance that people had more or less than Z. All that would matter would be their rank order.

There is, however, more to a Rawlsian theory of poverty than this, although Rawls' own discussion is not explicit (and, incidentally, the word 'poverty' does not appear in his extensive index). To begin with, the popular interpretation in terms of literally the worst-off person is not that which Rawls advocates. He sees his difference principle as concerned with a least fortunate *group*, which in his brief discussion he suggests might be unskilled workers or, alternatively, those 'with less than half of the median income and wealth' (1971, p. 98). Some degree of aggregation over individuals is involved, and the definition of this group may give a role to the poverty line (like half of median income).

Perhaps more importantly, we have to remember that the difference principle is the second of Rawls' two principles, and that concern for poverty may enter through the first of his principles, that which gives priority to basic liberties. It can be argued that these liberties, which include participation in society, are dependent on a specified level of income. This is an approach which has been developed by Barry in terms of 'effective liberty', the idea being that liberty cannot be enjoyed 'unless people reach some necessary level of wealth' (1973, p. 77). This provides one justification for view 2 of the relation between poverty and inequality. This is that we have a *lexicographic approach*, where avoiding poverty has priority in assuring effective liberty, but inequality enters the assessment as a second concern. In this case, there is no reason why the functional form of P should be related to that of I. It would be quite consistent to use the head-count for P and a measure satisfying the transfer principle for I.

In considering the remaining two approaches, it may be useful to think of the assessment of social welfare as involving two stages. First, there is the identification of a particular level of income as being below the poverty line and the evaluation of the costs associated with this deprivation. Second, there is the aggregation across individuals to arrive at an overall social judgement. Again, it may be helpful to draw on the analogy with risk analysis. In the work cited earlier, Fishburn (1977) has shown that the mean-risk model is congruent with expected utility maximization if the utility function takes the value Y for $Y \geq Z$ but the value $T(Y)$ for $Y < Z$ where $T(Y)$ is less than Y and takes account of the cost of a below-target return. This transformation $T(Y)$ is the first of the two stages. The second stage, of aggregation, is linear in the Fishburn case. This leads to a maximand which subtracts the risk measure from the mean; and in the present context this would give a measure in which social welfare is represented by mean income less the 'cost' of poverty: $\bar{Y} - P$.

This situation corresponds to that of concern only for poverty, or the view (3). If the aggregation at the second stage involves social weights, derived from some principle of justice, then we may have a trade-off between poverty and inequality, or view 4. Concern about poverty enters at the first stage and notions of justice come into the second stage. We may, for example, believe that the cost of poverty is best measured by the poverty gap, but be convinced by Sen that distributive justice is best captured by rank order weights, which enter at the second stage. Indeed, the notion of relative position embodied in rank order weights appears much more relevant at this second stage, where the whole income distribution is being considered. The measure obtained by combining these two elements involves subtracting from mean income the cost of inequality as measured by the Gini coefficient (times the mean) and the cost of poverty as measured by the Thon version of the Sen index. This is an example of the trade-off approach, in that an improvement in the value of the Thon index might be held to justify a worsening of the overall Gini coefficient.

CONCLUDING REFLECTIONS

Throughout this chapter, I have tried to show how different views about poverty can be encompassed within a common framework. The aim is to reach some degree of agreement even where judgements differ – whether as to the level of poverty line, the choice of poverty measure, or the relationship between poverty and inequality. To this end, I have in particular argued that dominance conditions may provide tools which are both powerful and easy to apply in empirical research. At the same time, they have not, to my knowledge, been used in this way. As we have seen, the value of the poverty deficit at different poverty lines (say, from 10 per cent to 200 per cent of the official poverty line) provides a lot of information, yet the necessary table is not among the more than 200 published by the US Census Bureau. The sceptics are right in suggesting the need for reconsideration of the basic approach, even if the conclusions reached from such a re-examination may not be palatable to them.

I should like to end with three concluding reflections, prompted in part by reading Bowley's earlier work to which I referred at the outset. First, Bowley asked the question – has poverty diminished? – and concluded that in general it had. I have not attempted to present substantive results here, but the substantive question is an important one and it is a sad commentary on events that the possibility of poverty *increasing* is one that has to be taken seriously.

The second reflection concerns the presentation of results. I referred earlier to Bowley's encounter with Ernest Bevin. Bevin's biographer comments that 'Photographs of the meagre portions of food appeared in half a dozen newspapers over the caption "A Docker's Breakfast". They were worth volumes of statistics in their effect on public opinion' (Bullock, 1960, p. 128). It seems to me that there are lessons here. In this field in particular, economists have remained wedded to volumes of statistics as a means of presenting results and have not been very creative in seeking alternatives. Indeed, since most of the work on poverty is now secondary analysis, we do not even have the case studies which increased the impact of the early research of Bowley and others.

What could we do to enliven the material and improve the effectiveness of communication? One suggestion being pursued at the LSE is to exploit the capacities of microcomputers not just in carrying out research but also in its presentation. Rather than supplying the users with tables, what can be done in this and other fields (such as tax reform analysis) is to supply a disk with data and programs for analysis. These programs contain quite a lot of structure, for example making use of dominance results where appropriate, but they also have the great merit of allowing user participation in the design of the results. The users can specify their own poverty standards, choose their own poverty measures, and look at the position of individual families (suitably anonymized). In this way, the analysis is both more flexible and more immediate.

Finally, I cannot help reflecting that the questions discussed in this Walras–Bowley chapter are ones which did not apparently greatly concern Bowley himself, or other pioneers in the field. In retrospect, this was unfortunate, since important conceptual issues in the measurement of poverty remained undiscussed for too long. What was needed was a greater degree of vertical integration between the statistical measurement of poverty on the one hand and welfare economics on the other. One of the great merits of the Econometric Society is that it brings together these two concerns and I hope that this chapter too has made a contribution to such integration.

NOTES

1. In fact the Bowley family of five had been living on the food budget for the previous three weeks. The *Daily News* carried pictures including one of his ten-year-old daughter with the caption 'The Professor's 47 shillings does not prevent her keeping guinea pigs'. I am grateful to John Creedy for drawing my attention to Bowley (1972).
2. In constructing this diagram, it has been assumed that the poverty lines in different years are comparable. The issue of the adjustment of the poverty line over time is discussed in Chapter 1. No account is taken here of changes in the population size.
3. The significance of the restriction may be seen from the fact that the global first-degree condition ($\Delta F(Z) \leqslant 0$ for all Z) implies the global second-degree condition but that Condition I does not imply Condition II. Suppose that $Z^- = Z^+$ and that $\Delta F(Z) > 0$ for $Z < Z^+$, $\Delta F(Z^+) = 0$. Then Condition I is satisfied, but Condition II is not satisfied.
4. For discussion of the validity of integration by parts, see the stochastic dominance literature; for example, Tesfatsion (1976) and Le Breton (1986).
5. As is noted by Foster and Shorrocks (1984), this is equivalent to requiring that the generalized Lorenz curves do not intersect, although this is a less natural way to state the condition in the present context, since the comparison is made up to a common value of Z, not a common value of F.
6. This method of proof follows that of Karamata (1932). I am grateful to Michael Le Breton for this reference.
7. The measure does satisfy Sen's 'weak transfer axiom': a transfer of income from a person below the poverty line to anyone richer which leaves the number below the poverty line unaffected must increase the poverty measure (see, for example, Sen, 1979, p. 302).
8. Kundu and Smith (1983) have shown that the transfer principle cannot hold simultaneously with two population monotonicity axioms governing comparisons of populations of different sizes. (The same conflict does not arise with the weak transfer axiom.) However, as is noted by Sen, these axioms are 'really very demanding' (1981, p. 193n).

3 · POVERTY IN BRITAIN FROM THE 1930s TO THE 1980s

The starting point for the Beveridge Report of 1942 was a 'diagnosis of want' based on 'social surveys of the conditions of life in a number of principal towns in Britain' (Beveridge, 1942, p. 7). The evidence from these social surveys in the 1930s of the existence of poverty, and analysis of its causes, was used by Beveridge to make the case for his Plan for Social Security.

In 1984, the Secretary of State for Social Services announced a series of major reviews of the social security system, which he intended to constitute 'the most substantial examination of the social security system since the Beveridge Report' (*The Times*, 3 April 1984). (See Parts II and III.) The principal issue I would like to address in this chapter is how our knowledge about poverty in the 1980s compares with that in the 1930s. If, like Beveridge, the Secretary of State's committees were to take as their starting point the evidence about poverty, what would they discover? Would there be a similar diagnosis of the persistence of want? Has the unemployment of the 1980s been accompanied by hardship in the same way as in the 1930s?

I begin in section 1 by summarizing briefly three of the studies in the 1930s, and then take the story up to the 1980s, comparing what we know now with the evidence of fifty years ago (section 2). Any such comparisons raise crucial issues with regard to the definition of poverty and these are the subjects of sections 3 and 4. The lessons to be drawn are summarized in section 5. The appendix contains detailed material on the different studies and their comparison.

1 STUDIES OF POVERTY IN BRITAIN IN THE 1930s

The studies of poverty in the 1930s followed an already well-established approach. This built on the tradition initiated by Charles Booth of the study of particular geographic areas, in his case London, with information being obtained by those familiar with the area and its inhabitants (Booth,

A revised version (with statistical appendix) of the 1984 Roll Lecture delivered at the University of Southampton, May 1984.

1889–1902). It drew on Seebohm Rowntree's pioneering work on the determination of poverty scales and the collection of evidence about earnings and income, as used in his study of York in 1899 (Rowntree, 1901). The investigators, with one notable exception, accepted the validity of random sampling, as developed by A. L. Bowley, first in his study of Reading in 1912 (Bowley, 1913) and applied subsequently to studies of Northampton, Warrington, Stanley and Bolton.

The best known of the three studies carried out in the 1930s considered here is without doubt Rowntree's second survey of York in 1936, which was designed to provide an explicit comparison with 1899, and which in turn can be linked with the study of Rowntree and Lavers (1951) for the postwar period. Rowntree's procedure in 1936 was first to demarcate those areas of the city where 'working-class' families lived and then to interview *all* the families in those streets. The size of this task should be underlined. His enquiry involved interviewing 16,362 households, containing 55,206 people, or 57 per cent of the entire population of York. This is more than twice the size of the present-day *Family Expenditure Survey*. (The main details of the three studies for the 1930s are summarized in Table 3.1; there is further discussion of the studies in the appendix.)

Rowntree's findings in 1936 may be summarized in two ways. He was naturally interested in the comparison with 1899. Applying the same poverty standard as his primary poverty line at that date, adjusted only for the movement in prices, he found that the proportion of the total York population in poverty had fallen – as one might expect – from 9.9 per cent to 3.9 per cent. Rowntree concluded that the percentage living in 'abject poverty' had been more than halved (1941, p. 451).

The second set of findings applied a new poverty standard, based on Rowntree's work on *The Human Needs of Labour* (1937), which he described rather loosely as being the minimum necessary for a 'healthy life' (p. 28), compared with his earlier standard, which was one of 'bare subsistence' (p. 102). It was better put by one of his research workers: 'the second-hand boots and jacket which were adequate in 1899 would not have been entertained by the worker of 1935; a bath and a garden, absent in almost every working class dwelling in 1899, were by now considered essential' (Chapman, 1951, p. 7). His new standard was some £2 a week for a couple with three children, compared with the 1899 figure of £1.45 a week. The percentage found to be in poverty on the basis of this new scale was very much higher: 31.1 per cent of the persons in the sample or 17.7 per cent of the total population. In his analysis, Rowntree gives prominence to the effect of unemployment. He shows that in a quarter of the families below the poverty line the head was unemployed. At the same time, in a larger proportion of cases – over a third – poverty is attributed to 'inadequate' wages or earnings; and there is no guarantee that if the unemployed found jobs these would take them above the poverty line.

Table 3.1 Three studies of poverty in the 1930s

	Population studied	Sample	Measure of earnings	Poverty standard (£ per week)	Incidence of poverty
Rowntree York 1936	'Working-class' streets <£250 a year 57 per cent of York population	16,362 households (response 99.1 per cent) 55,206 persons	Normal (from employers in 60 per cent of cases) estimated (in other cases)	Couple under pension age £1.38 Couple and 3 children £2.02	31.1 per cent of persons in sample; 17.7 per cent of total population; 24.7 per cent of families below poverty line had unemployed head
Tout Bristol 1937	'Working-class' and 'lower middle class' streets 72.5 per cent of Bristol population	1 in 20 sample 4,526 households (response 92.5 per cent) 15,162 persons	Current (or 'full-time')	Couple under pension age £1.01 Couple and 3 children £1.68–£2.18	11.8 per cent of persons in sample; 8.6 per cent of total population; 32 per cent of families below poverty line had unemployed head
Ford Southampton 1931	'Working-class' streets <£250 a year 61.9 per cent of Southampton population	1 in 46 sample 559 households 2,368 persons	Current	Couple under pension age £0.77 Couple and 3 children £1.19–£1.35	21.5 per cent of persons in sample; 13.3 per cent of total population; 63.8 per cent of families below poverty line had unemployed head

As the above description indicates, Rowntree was an exception to the general acceptance of random sampling. His rejection of this approach in the 1936 survey appears to have reflected a suspicion of new inventions. (He also resisted the use of Hollerith punched cards.) As Bowley had argued more than twenty years earlier, a sample of 800 households (in Rowntree's case around 1 in 20) could provide quite reliable results. The simple formula applied by Bowley (Bowley and Burnett-Hurst, 1915, p. 180), gives an estimated standard error for the percentage, p, of $\sqrt{p(1-p)/n}$, where n is the number in the sample. So for a percentage of poverty of 31.1, the estimated standard error with a sample of 800 is 1.6 percentage points. In an attempt to discredit the sampling approach, Rowntree carried out the experiment of drawing samples from his data, so as to see how the conclusions differed. Perhaps to his chagrin, the results bore out Bowley's recommendations. Compared to the full sample figure of 31.1 per cent, a 1 in 20 sub-sample gave a figure of 32.6 per cent, or less than one standard error different.

Other investigators were quick to follow Bowley's lead, and adopt a sampling approach. The second study in the 1930s referred to here is that by Tout in Bristol in 1937. He carried out a 1 in 20 sample survey of incomes, interviewing more than 4,500 households, containing 15,162 persons. The percentage of the population found to be below the poverty line defined by Tout was 8.6 per cent. This is smaller than that recorded by Rowntree in York, but Tout's poverty line was in most cases rather lower, and when account is taken of the difference in scale, the findings seem broadly comparable (see appendix). Like Rowntree, Tout attributed an important part of the poverty to unemployment of the chief wage-earner: 'unemployment is outstandingly the most important reason for family income falling below "needs", and affects nearly a third of the families' (1938, p. 45).

The third survey considered is that by Ford of Southampton earlier in the decade (late 1931). He carried out a 1 in 46 sample of households, covering 2,368 persons, and applied a poverty standard which appears to have been rather lower than that used subsequently in York and Bristol. Yet he found that some 13 per cent of the total Southampton population was in poverty, a finding that he attributes especially to the very high unemployment in 1931, noting that in two-thirds of the families below the poverty line the head was unemployed, and that a return to the level of employment of 1928 would have reduced poverty by a third (1934, p. 118). At the same time, it is a little surprising, viewed from the 1980s, to find such a high incidence of poverty in Southampton. Ford provides a map of Southampton, inspired by Booth's map of London, with each street colour-coded according to its position on the income scale, the coding following the spectrum, commencing with violet for the lowest incomes. It would have been interesting to have had such a map, based on a national survey, for the country as a whole.

These three studies described above, together with those carried out at the end of the 1920s on Merseyside (Jones, 1934, 1948) and the *New Survey of London Life and Labour* (Smith, 1930–35), had a profound influence. Together, they showed the hollowness of claims such as that in 1934 by Sir Kingsley Wood, a Conservative Minister, that 'with old age pensions and unemployment insurance, there was no poverty in the country' (quoted by Branson and Heinemann, 1973, p. 232). The existence of this evidence meant that when Beveridge came to prepare his report, he started from clear evidence of the persistence of poverty: 'the plan is based on a diagnosis of want. It starts from facts as revealed by social surveys' (Beveridge, 1942, p. 8).

2   POVERTY IN BRITAIN IN THE POSTWAR PERIOD

In 1984, the government embarked on what it envisaged as a fundamental re-evaluation of the social security system of the type carried out by Beveridge. This leads one naturally to pose the question – is there evidence about poverty in Britain comparable with that from which Beveridge started? What do we know about poverty, and what light does the evidence cast on the success or otherwise of the postwar welfare state? A former Conservative Minister, Sir Keith Joseph, echoing, no doubt unconsciously, Sir Kingsley Wood, claimed that 'by any absolute standard there is very little poverty in Britain today' (Joseph and Sumption, 1979, p. 27). Does this mean that the Beveridge Report of the 1980s should not concern itself with the question of poverty?

In the early part of the postwar period, there was indeed considerable optimism about the effect of the 1948 national insurance and related legislation. There was a general feeling that the welfare state, coupled with high employment and rising real incomes, had indeed abolished poverty. Striking evidence to support this belief came from Rowntree's third survey of York in 1950 (Rowntree and Lavers, 1951). This was on the same lines as in 1936, except that he had by then come to accept the validity of random sampling, and the study was based on a 1 in 9 sample. (Although the methods by which the sampling was put into practice left quite a lot to be desired – see Chapter 4, and Atkinson, Maynard and Trinder, 1981.) The poverty line was revised upwards in real terms, but the findings still indicated a 'remarkable decrease in poverty between 1936 and 1950' (Rowntree and Lavers, 1951, p. 32). The conclusions were indeed striking. Only 1.66 per cent of the York population were found by Rowntree to be in poverty.

Rowntree and Lavers brought out the impact of family allowances (introduced in 1945), showing that if there had been no allowances the percentage in poverty would have increased from 1.66 to 3.6 per cent

(1951, p. 43). It was however not just social security that was responsible. The fall in unemployment was also crucial. Rowntree and Lavers showed that if unemployment were increased to the level of 1936, affecting workers at random, then the percentage in poverty would have been 4.7 per cent (1951, p. 48). The authors commented that the welfare legislation since 1936 had reduced the severity of the fall in income but 'has certainly not ensured that men can normally be unemployed without their families falling into poverty' (1951, p. 49).

The findings of Rowntree in 1950 were widely publicized. The book appeared in the closing stages of the 1951 general election campaign, and the evidence was used to demonstrate the success of the welfare state. The influence of the findings of Rowntree and Lavers was such that the subject of poverty largely disappeared from the syllabus of economics students. For example, according to Hagenbuch's text on *Social Economics*, 'Rowntree demonstrated the effectiveness of full employment and the social services in the cure of poverty' (1958, p. 175).

This 'consensus' view was questioned by some writers, notably Wedderburn (1962) and Townsend (1962), but it was only in the mid-1960s that public opinion really became aware of the possible persistence of poverty in postwar Britain. In this respect, the publication of *The Poor and the Poorest* by Abel-Smith and Townsend (1965) just before Christmas 1965 had a dramatic impact. It was the first national survey of poverty, being based on the *Family Expenditure Survey* (FES), and it showed that in 1960 some 3.8 per cent of the population had incomes below the national assistance standard. (National assistance was the forerunner of supplementary benefit, which in turn has been replaced by Income Support.)

The publication of *The Poor and the Poorest* led to the setting-up of the Child Poverty Action Group, and more generally to a reawakening of concern about the problem of poverty. The government was not quick to respond, but in the mid-1970s its concern was manifested in the investigation by the Royal Commission on the Distribution of Income and Wealth of 'Lower Incomes' (1978), and the publication of official evidence on the numbers below the supplementary benefit (SB) level, based on regular analyses of the FES. The series of figures in Table 3.2 show around 1.75 million people in families whose incomes were below the SB standard at the start of the 1970s. The number tended to rise in the mid-1970s, and the most recent figure, that for 1981, is over 2.5 million, representing 5.3 per cent of the population (in these figures, heating additions are included in the scale). For families, the estimated percentage is 6.5 per cent. The rise between 1979 and 1981 was particularly marked among those families where the head is below pension age, the number increasing from 1 million to 1,680,000 (where heating additions are not included).

Of particular concern at the present time is the position of the unemployed. Included in the official estimates are nearly 500,000 persons living

Table 3.2 Official estimates of the numbers below
supplementary benefit level

	Families	Persons
1972	1,220,000	1,780,000
1973	1,070,000	1,600,000
1974	920,000	1,410,000
1975	1,090,000	1,840,000
1976	1,350,000	2,280,000
1977[1]	1,260,000	2,020,000
1977	1,190,000	1,900,000
1979	1,420,000	2,130,000
1981	1,620,000	2,640,000
1981[2]	1,760,000	2,810,000

Sources:
1972–77, see Atkinson (1983a), Table 10.2.
1977–79, Department of Health and Social Security (1982).
1981, Department of Health and Social Security (1983).

Notes:
1. The figures 1972–77 represent 'end of year' estimates;
   the subsequent figures are averages over the year.
2. These figures for 1981 include age-related heating additions.

in families where the head had been unemployed for more than three
months. As Rowntree and Lavers had noted, the social security system
cannot, in fact, provide effective income maintenance for the unemployed.
In November 1982, only a third of the registered unemployed were
receiving national insurance benefit (*Second Report of the Social Security
Advisory Committee*, Table 4.1). It is the function of SB to fill the gap, but
there is clear evidence of incomplete take-up: in 1981 some 25 per cent of
the eligible unemployed were not claiming, with an average amount
unclaimed of £19.60 a week (Hansard, 30 November 1983). Beveridge's
diagnosis of the inadequate coverage of social insurance benefits, and the
failure of means-tested assistance to reach all those eligible, appears to
remain valid today.

How does this evidence for the 1980s compare in quality with that from
the 1930s reviewed in the first section? In some respects, our knowledge
is clearly more firmly based. The FES, which is the major source, is a
national survey, whereas the local surveys, excellent though they were,
always faced the problem of extrapolation to the country as a whole.
Moreover, in the case of both York and Southampton, there was the
pre-selection of 'working-class' districts, which must have had the effect of
mis-classifying at least some families. It is indeed scarcely surprising if the
quality of data has improved; we are after all talking about the days of the
Austin 7. However, Austin 7s are private goods, whereas the production
of poverty statistics has really passed beyond the stage where it can be
undertaken by private individuals. The last such venture was the Townsend

survey of 1968–9, but this illustrated the problems of trying to carry out research without adequate funding. The final volume is most impressive, but it appeared only some ten years after the survey (Townsend, 1979).

We are therefore largely dependent on official sources, and – welcome though any official interest is – it can scarcely be said that the official evidence is very extensive. The government produces a handful of tables, every odd-numbered year, based on the FES. It is instructive to compare the situation with that in the United States, where each year the Bureau of the Census produces a large book. That for 1979, for example, consisted of 247 pages – compared with nine pages in the UK – and had more than 60 tables (US Bureau of the Census, 1981). Not only did these tables contain extensive material on the effect of correcting for different shortcomings of the raw data, but also they extended the analysis beyond simple counts of the numbers in poverty. As has been discussed in Chapter 1, the head-count has a number of shortcomings as an indicator; and in practice, it is particularly unsatisfactory when the poverty line coincides with the level at which benefits are paid, since it is then very sensitive to measurement error. In the US report, they also give estimates of the income deficits; and it would naturally be valuable to have such estimates in the official statistics for the UK.

It may be objected that such proposals for a more extensive analysis ignore the limitations of the basic data. Are the numbers involved large enough to bear detailed analysis? Here we should note that, while the US report provides standard errors for all of the main figures, and contains a detailed appendix on the subject, no such calculations are published in the UK. A simple calculation applying the Bowley formula, with an allowance of 25 per cent for the design effect (see appendix), suggests that the overall percentage in poverty may be reasonably well determined (a 95 per cent confidence interval for families in poverty would be some 5.9 per cent to 7.1 per cent), but that there may be difficulties if we come to consider sub-groups of the population. The estimated number of families below the SB level where the head is in full-time work or self-employed is 240,000, but a 95 per cent confidence interval is 175,000–305,000. This leads one to seek methods of increasing the effective sample size, and there are two obvious possibilities. First, the FES data are themselves only used for every alternate year, and it would be quite possible to pool the information, with suitable adjustments for rising money incomes, for two years. A second, more ambitious undertaking, is to combine information from the FES with that collected in the *General Household Survey*.

There is, therefore, little doubt that one could materially improve the available statistical information and that the government *could* be better informed than it was in the 1930s. At the same time, one should not lose sight of the fact that this evidence is purely statistical and that it lacks the qualitative information contained in the local studies of the 1930s. (The incorporation of such qualitative material was one of the strengths of Townsend's 1968–69 study.) In particular, the material sample surveyed in the FES does not allow one to put the circumstances of families in the context of the communities in which they live. The maps drawn by Ford, and earlier by Booth, depicted an aspect which is missing from much modern analysis.

3   COMPARING POVERTY IN THE 1980s WITH THAT IN THE 1930s

What lessons can be drawn from the evidence surveyed above about poverty in the 1980s, and how does it compare with poverty in the 1930s? On the face of it, the official finding that one person in 20 is below the supplementary benefit level suggests the persistence of poverty. The situation is like that from which Beveridge started, with a sizeable minority still living in poverty.

There are, however, those who would disagree. In particular, it is often argued that we are talking about something quite different. The supplementary benefit scale cannot be compared in absolute terms with the poverty lines of the 1930s, and for some people, like Sir Keith Joseph, there is, according to an absolute standard, very little poverty in Britain today.

These writers are clearly correct in arguing that there has been a shift in social values with regard to the definition of poverty. This shift made explicit the view that the definition of poverty should reflect changes in society. As it was put by Titmuss, 'far-reaching changes affecting the structure and functions of social institutions; general improvements in material standards of living; and the growth of knowledge about the causes and consequences of social ills in the modern community, are now forcing on us the task of re-defining poverty' (1962, p. 187). This change in perspective was reflected, for example, in the title of the Royal Commission Report which was on 'lower' not 'low' incomes, and in its claim at the outset that the poverty line 'is now generally accepted as a standard which changes with the general standard of living of society' (Royal Commission on the Distribution of Income and Wealth, 1978, p. 3).

This general acceptance is challenged by those who argue for a return to an absolute approach, with the poverty line being defined in terms of the required consumption of specified goods, uninfluenced by the general living standards of the society. As it has been put by Joseph and Sumption: 'an absolute standard means one defined by reference to the actual needs of the poor and not by reference to the expenditure of those who are not poor. A family is poor if it cannot afford to eat' (1979, p. 27). Set out algebraically, the poverty line is determined by the cost $P.X^*$ of a minimum set of requirements X^* (see Chapter 1).

This approach encounters the obvious question of determining X^*. Joseph and Sumption appear unaware of all the difficulties which this entails (even though they have been discussed at length in the literature, for example, in Townsend, 1970). There is however a weaker version of the absolute argument, to which this objection does not apply with the same force, which suggests that, whatever the level of the poverty line, the comparison over time must be based on the cost of attaining the same basket of goods. (Alternatively, there may be allowance for substitution between goods in response to relative price changes.) This suggests that we should look at the movement of prices over the period. In the appendix there is a detailed discussion of the relevant price indices. Applying two alternative price series to the Rowntree 1936 poverty line, we obtain equivalent figures in 1981 for a couple with three children of £28.65 or £37.37, compared with a SB scale of £56.50–£67.30 (depending on the ages of the children). The real increase over the scale employed by Ford is even greater: the equivalent in 1981 prices of his scale for a couple with three children would be £16.54–£18.81 or £21.57–£24.53.

It appears therefore that the poverty standard has risen significantly in real terms from the 1930s to the 1980s. The question is however more subtle than this suggests. First, there have been changes in the *structure* of the poverty scale, which cast doubt on the value of any simple comparison. These are discussed in the next section. Second, the role of goods in the determination of the poverty criterion needs reconsideration. As noted in Chapter 1 goods should be seen as an input into household activities, with the level of such activities being our concern, not the purchase of goods as such. The significance of this 'household production' view is that changes elsewhere in society now become relevant. Even where poverty is defined in terms of a fixed set of activities, the required bundle of goods may be changing because the input matrix is changing. There are important interdependencies between the circumstances of a particular family and the expenditure of others. A good example, given by Cooper (and quoted in Sen, 1983, p. 162), is that a child may not be able to follow what is happening at school if the family does not have access to a television. Or to take the example quoted earlier with regard to Rowntree's 1936 poverty line, a person without access to a bath might have found it harder to get a job, just as today a person without a telephone may be at a disadvantage.

The approach just described has some similarity with that of Sen (1983), but he goes on to suggest that it closes the gap between the absolute and relative definitions: 'if we view the problem of conceptualising poverty in this light, then there is no conflict between the irreducible absolutist element in the notion of poverty [and] "thoroughgoing relativity"' (1983, p. 161). This is not however evident. The work of Townsend, for example, is concerned with the development of alternative measures of poverty based on the participation of families in the 'community's style of living' (1979, p. 249). This is effectively framed in terms of activities, such as having a week's holiday away, or having a birthday party for children, but the choice of these activities *is* influenced by the living patterns of the rest of society.

A clear distinction should therefore be drawn between measures of poverty based on a fixed set of activities and those where the definition takes account of changing living standards (the set of activities is influenced by what is necessary to participate in a given society). But what appears to be missed by those who advocate an absolute approach is that the former, and not just the latter, may involve a poverty scale which rises in real terms over time if the goods required to carry out specified activities increase with rising standards of living.

4 THE CHANGING STRUCTURE OF THE POVERTY LINE

It is tempting to treat the poverty line as a single number, but this can be highly misleading. In this section, I consider first the treatment of families of different sizes and second the definition of the unit of assessment.

Applying the 'alternative' price series described in the appendix to the Rowntree 1936 scale for a couple with three children yields an equivalent figure of £37.37 a week in 1981, compared with an SB scale (for children aged 5–10) of £56.50, suggesting a 51 per cent increase in real terms. For a couple with no children, where the head is employed, the Rowntree scale is (net of deductions) equivalent to £25.58 in 1981, compared with an SB scale of £34.60, suggesting an increase of 35 per cent. But if the couple had been old-age pensioners, then the increase would have been 110 per cent. There is therefore considerable variation. This is even more marked when we compare the scales for single persons (householders):

| | Increase in real terms 1936–81 | |
	Woman	Man
Over pension age	135 per cent	93 per cent
Under pension age	32 per cent	1 per cent

The structure of the poverty scale has therefore changed quite substantially, with those over pension age being favoured relative to those under pension age, and the scales for men and women being brought into line. As a result, any comparison based on one family type (as with Piachaud's (1981a) use of a couple with three children) may be deceptive. Most significantly, the calculations above suggest that the scale for a single man of working age is effectively no higher in real terms than in Rowntree's poverty scale of 1936.

Changing social values have affected not only the relative scales but also the unit of assessment, in particular the choice between the household and the family as the basis for measuring poverty. Economic textbooks have an unfortunate tendency to talk interchangeably about individuals, families and households, but the distinctions are important. If the poverty calculation is based on the total income of the household, aggregating, for example, the incomes of grown-up children with those of their parents, then a different assessment may be made from that reached if the income is calculated for each family unit. In Rowntree's survey, for example, the unit of assessment was in effect the household, in that he treated as part of the income of the unit the amount contributed by grown-up children and other adults living at home, with a corresponding addition for their needs. As such, his approach was close to that employed under the household means test applied in the 1930s by the Unemployment Assistance Board. This test was highly unpopular, and in 1941 its scope was substantially narrowed in the Determination of Needs Act, so that the 1948 legislation retained only an assumed contribution from non-dependent members to their rent and took no account of the actual transfer of income. This change may appear to be relatively minor, but in earlier years it was of considerable significance, since many more children continued to live at home after reaching the age of economic independence and many households contained lodgers.

So that, while it is tempting to trace a line of descent from Rowntree's poverty line to the present SB scale, via that for NA, not least because of Rowntree's role in the determination of the benefit scale proposed by Beveridge, this misses the important shift in social values with regard to the unit of assessment which was embodied in the postwar NA scale. This is not just of historical significance, since there is evidence that the government today would like to shift back in the direction of the household unit – a move which would, of course, be in the opposite direction from that urged in the field of taxation by those who believe that the individual, not the family, is the appropriate unit.

5   LESSONS TO BE DRAWN

Those who say that the poverty standard applied in the official evidence for the 1980s is not directly comparable with the standards of the 1930s are clearly correct. There have been changes in social values, with regard to both the level and the structure of the scale. This does not however mean that the problem of poverty can be assumed away.

First, we have seen that the concept of a constant 'absolute' standard becomes elusive once we recognize that goods are inputs into activities, and that it may imply a changing real level of expenditure once we allow for the interdependencies which influence the goods required to carry out specified activities (like 'getting a job').

Second, the shifts in social values may be ones which are to be welcomed. It may well be that we want to get away from the household means test. It may well be that differential scales for men and women would find few defenders today. It may be that the needs of the elderly are now given higher priority.

Thirdly, we must not lose sight of the fact that the poverty scale applied in the 1980s is the level of eligibility for benefits, and the fact that people (not in work) fall below is evidence of the inadequacy of social security in terms of its own stated objectives. Whatever the merits or demerits of the SB scale as a poverty criterion, it is clearly a measure of *performance*, and the numbers falling below demonstrate the failure of the 'safety net'. For the unemployed, for example, the limited coverage of national insurance benefits, coupled with incomplete take-up of supplementary benefit, means that the situation is in fact little different from that diagnosed by Beveridge in 1942. This basic ineffectiveness of the system should be the primary concern of those who seek to reform social security.

APPENDIX: STUDIES OF POVERTY IN THE 1930s

The purpose of this appendix is to describe the main features of three major studies of poverty in the 1930s – those of Rowntree (1941) in York in 1936, of Tout (1938) in Bristol in May–October 1937, and of Ford (1934) in Southampton in November–December 1931 – and to compare them with the present-day analyses of poverty based on the *Family Expenditure Survey* (FES), carried out by the Department of Health and Social Security (1983).

A.1 Selection of sample

One feature of all three studies is that they are based on local areas, and the authors accept that this limits the conclusions which can be drawn. In his original study of York in 1899, Rowntree (1901) had been anxious to compare his findings with those of Booth in *The Life and Labour of the People in London*, recognizing that the conditions might be different in the metropolis from those in smaller urban populations. He does, however, suggest that 'the conditions of life obtaining in my native city of York were not exceptional, and ... might be taken as fairly representative of the conditions existing in many, if not most, of our provincial towns' (1901, pp. xvii–xviii). This view appears to underline his subsequent enquiries in 1936 and 1950. Tout, in his study of Bristol, makes a comparison with the evidence from *The New Survey of London Life and Labour* (Smith, 1930–35) in 1929. Ford, in his study of Southampton, makes reference to this and several other studies in the 1920s, including that of Merseyside in 1929–30 (Jones, 1934), and of the 'Five Towns' studies by Bowley (Stanley in 1923; Northampton, Warrington, Reading and Bolton in 1924) in *Has Poverty Diminished?* (Bowley and Hogg, 1925).

The method of conducting the local surveys consisted of taking one or both of the following steps:

1. Demarcating an area of the city as 'working-class', and confining attention to this area.
2. Taking a random sample of all residences in this area.

The first stage characterized the approach of Rowntree in all three studies of York. As it was described in the 1950 report, 'a man who has lived in the city for more than half a century, who knows the city intimately, . . . marked on our list every street where working class families live' (Rowntree and Lavers, 1951, p. 2). (The Rowntree procedure is discussed in Jenkins and Maynard, 1981.) The method was applied more systematically by Ford (1934, p. 103), who drew on his earlier street survey, which had graded all streets in Southampton according to the typical earnings of the occupants, and excluded the top two classes of streets (those typically containing 'supervising and clerical' and 'middle-class' workers, with earnings in excess of £4 a week). The reason given by Ford for omitting middle-class and upper-class families is that they 'are notoriously unwilling to answer personal enquiries of this sort' (1934, p. 103), but the main justification must be that these families are above the poverty line. In view of the undoubted heterogeneity of some streets, it seems likely that this led to some understatement of the number below the poverty line.

Tout's study was similar in that it concentrated on the 'working class', defined as the families of all manual workers and those other workers, including self-employed, with incomes below £5 a week. This selection was, however, made *after* the drawing of a 1 in 20 random sample from the addresses in the Register of Electors. A related criterion was applied by Rowntree, who excluded those living in the streets covered with earnings in excess of £250 a year. This was estimated by Clark to be broadly the top decile of the income distribution in the United Kingdom in 1935 (Tout, 1938, p. 12). Rowntree did not however draw a random sample in 1936 (by 1950 he was converted to sampling methods). Ford took a 1 in 46 sample, and excluded those in the selected streets with incomes of £250 or higher (1934, p. 203).

The effective sample was reduced by non-response, although this was much less than with the present-day FES. Tout refers to a response rate of 92.5 per cent (1938, p. 23). In the York survey, only some 150 schedules had to be left blank (non-response of 0.9 per cent), although in some other cases the information was obtained from neighbours, rather than directly (Rowntree, 1941, pp. 12–13). The high level of response reflects the limited information which was requested, compared with the extensive demands of the FES. It should indeed be noted that Rowntree's survey did not collect earnings data from the households, and he sought to obtain information from employers (see below).

The resulting sample was 16,362 households in York, comprising a population of 55,206. This was estimated by Rowntree to comprise 57 per cent of the total population (59.1 per cent of the non-institutional population) of York (1941, p. 32). (The population figure for the city is affected by the extension of the city boundaries in 1937. This accounts for the difference between the figure of 89,680 given by Rowntree (1941) for 1936 on p. 7, and that of 96,980 used on p. 32.) In Bristol, the sample for whom income could be assessed was 4,526 households, containing 15,162 persons. These households were drawn from an original working-class sample of 4,890 (hence the response rate of 92.5 per cent), which in turn came from a sample of 5,527 on the Register of Electors. On the basis of households, this suggests that the 'working class' accounted for 88.5 per cent of the total. On the basis of population, if we assume that non-respondents had the same family size, the implied total is 327,628, or 72.5 per cent of the population figure quoted by Tout (1938, p. 22) for the survey area. Finally, in Southampton, the percentage of households covered is given as 75 per cent (Ford, 1934, p. 103). The number interviewed was 559, containing 2,368 persons, excluding boarders. Grossed up by the sampling factor of 1 in 46, the latter gives a total of 108,928, or 61.9 per cent of the Census population in 1931 quoted by Ford (1934 p. 25). (In both the Bristol and Southampton figures, the institutional population is included.)

The present-day estimates are based on a national sample, so that there is no problem of extrapolating to a national sample, or of the relationship between the 'working class' and the total population. The sample size for the UK is typically around 7,000–7,500 households: e.g. in 1981 7,525 households, containing 20,535 persons. There is however a sizeable element of non-response (28 per cent in 1981) and there is clear evidence that non-response varies systematically with the characteristics of the family. For this reason, the grossing-up factors applied by the DHSS vary with the age of the head of the family unit (above and below pension age) and the number of children. It should be noted that the official estimates of the number of low-income families exclude Northern Ireland, covering only Great Britain, and that the basic unit of analysis is not the household but the 'family unit', of which there are estimated to be some 27 million in 1981.

The absolute sample size in the FES is therefore considerably larger than that used in Southampton, and about double that used in Bristol. It must however be remembered that the FES is not a simple random sample, being of a multi-stage design, stratified geographically. As is noted by Kemsley, Redpath and Holmes, 'the effect of the multi-stage design is a tendency to increase the true standard error and offset any gain in efficiency derived from stratification' (1980, p. 12). In view of this, allowance has to be made for a 'design effect' when calculating standard errors. No analysis has, to my knowledge, been made of the design effect for measures of poverty in the FES, but the calculations for variables such as mean income or expenditure suggest that a factor of 1.25 would not be an unreasonable first approximation (Kemsley, Redpath and Holmes, 1980, Table 4.11.1).

A.2 Assessment of income and requirements

The basis for the poverty assessment is a comparison of *income*, net of tax, insurance contributions, work expenses, and housing costs with *requirements*, measured according to the poverty scale.

In the case of the Rowntree survey, income consists of earnings, of both husband and wife, old age, industrial, widow's and war pensions, unemployment insurance and assistance payments, public assistance, net rents received from property, net value of vegetables from allotments, free school meals/milk at half-price, and payments by older children and lodgers for board and lodging. The definitions adopted by Tout in Bristol and Ford in Southampton appear broadly similar (although there is no reference to the value of vegetables), but there are two aspects which should be noted.

The first concerns the definition of earnings. Tout made two calculations. The first took the actual earnings in the week of investigation, or previous week, including piecework bonuses; the second was an estimate of normal earnings, averaging bonuses, etc., and treating the unemployed as continuing to receive their normal pay, unless they were 'unlikely to get work again'. Ford was basically concerned with actual earnings during the previous week, although this had to be modified in the case of seamen. Rowntree differed from the other two investigators in that he approached the employers, and for 60 per cent of the wage-earners information was supplied from the wage records (1941, p. 25). These were 'normal' earnings, or in the case of Rowntree Cocoa Works a six months' average. In the remaining 40 per cent of cases, an estimate of normal earnings in the occupation was made.

The second aspect is the treatment of grown-up children and lodgers. In Rowntree's case the income includes their payments (as noted above), and the needs scale includes an element intended to cover their food and household sundries (1941, p. 30). In Bristol, lodgers and grown-up children are treated differently. Lodgers are excluded, and only the 'profit' is included in the family's income. Grown-up children are treated as a full part of the family, their income and needs being counted in full. The definition used by Ford is again similar to that of Rowntree, but he adopts a third approach to lodgers, in that he assumes that they contribute a third of the rent, in addition to an assumed profit from boarders. Grown-up children are treated in the same way as in Bristol.

Table 3.A.1 Poverty scale

	Ford 1931	shillings/pennies (s./d.) Rowntree 1936	Tout[a] 1937
Single man under pension age	9/7	22/9	12/9
Single woman under pension age	8/4	17/6	11/4
Couple under pension age	15/5	27/8	20/3
Couple and 1 child[c]	18/2–19/3[b]	35/-	24/4–27/4[b]
Couple and 2 children[c]	20/11–23/1[b]	38/8	28/8–34/8[b]
Couple and 3 children[c]	23/8–26/11[b]	40/5	33/6–42/6[b]
Each additional child	2/9–3/10[b]	5/4	4/1–7/1[b]
Single man over pension age	6/11	15/3	9/5
Single woman over pension age	6/11	12/6	9/1
Couple over pension age	11/4	22/4	14/8

[a] Plus 1s. for male office workers, shop assistants and commercial travellers, 9d. for female workers in these occupations and 5d. for women aged 16–30 working.
[b] The range reflects the variation with the ages of children.
[c] Under pension age, wife does not work.
Pension age taken to be 70 in the case of Ford, 65 for Tout.
There were 12 pennies in one shilling, and 20 shillings in one pound, in pre-decimal Britain.

The scale of needs applied by Ford is set out in Table 3.A.1. It was a modification of that used in Bowley's *Five Towns* study (Bowley and Hogg, 1925). Tout, writing several years later, took advantage of the British Medical Association's work on diets and the study of George (1937). The result was 'to raise the standard anywhere from 20 per cent to 50 per cent above the traditional one' (Tout, 1938, p. 50). Finally, Rowntree had himself conducted his study of *The Human Needs of Labour* (1937), and this formed the basis for his poverty scale. Rowntree's scale shown in Table 3.A.1 is that for the unemployed; the scale for an employed man includes 1s. 7d. health and unemployment insurance contributions, 6d. trade union subscription, and 1s. for travel to work (so that in terms of net income, it is equivalent). In nearly all cases the Rowntree scale is significantly higher in cash terms than those applied by Ford and Tout.

In comparing the scales applied in the 1930s with that applied in the present-day official studies – the supplementary benefit (SB) scale – it is interesting to note that the provision for pensioners was *lower* than that for those of working age, whereas the SB long-term scale is *higher* (this scale is applied in the official calculations to pensioners only). The lower scale for a single woman than for a single man also appears surprising by the standards of the 1980s.

The SB scale in 1981 is set out in Table 3.A.2. The assessment is similar in principle to that described above but differs in the treatment of the unit of assessment, which is the narrower family, or tax, unit, consisting of man, wife and *dependent* children. Children, who form separate tax units, are treated as separate units, even if they are living at home. Such non-dependent members are assumed to contribute towards housing costs (according to a fixed scale) but otherwise their financial circumstances do

Table 3.A.2 Supplementary benefit scale for householders, 1981

	£ per week
Single man or woman under pension age	21.30
Couple under pension age	34.60
Couple and one child	41.90–45.50
Couple and two children	49.20–56.40
Couple and three children	56.50–67.30
Each additional child	7.30–10.90
Single man or woman over pension age	27.15
Couple over pension age	43.45

Notes:
1. See Table 3.A.1.
2. Where there is a child under 5, or a person 70 or over, a heating addition of £1.40 or more may be payable.

not enter the calculation for the head of the household. It is therefore possible for one member of the household to be above the poverty line and another below.

It should be noted that the official DHSS calculations of the numbers below the SB level are based on normal earnings, where these differ from actual last pay period earnings, and that those off work due to sickness or unemployment for less than 13 weeks are assumed to receive their normal income when in work.

A.3   Comparison of the purchasing power of poverty scales

Some indication of the movement in prices necessary, first, to compare the three studies in the 1930s, which were carried out at different dates, and, second, to compare their purchasing power with that of the present-day supplementary benefit scale. Such comparisons immediately encounter the problem that the measurement of price changes over this period, particularly between 1938 and the postwar period, has been the subject of considerable debate.

The official price series for the period consists of the Cost of Living Index up to June 1947, the Interim Index of Retail Prices from June 1947 to January 1956 and the Index of Retail Prices from January 1956. Recalculating the first of these to exclude housing (*British Labour Statistics 1886–1968*, Table 89), we obtain (July 1914 = 100):

December 1931 (approx. date of Ford's study)	146.9
January 1936 (Rowntree)	144.9
June 1937 (Tout)	150.7
1938 (annual average)	155.6

On the other hand, the index, which had started in 1914, was based on weights derived from a family budget enquiry in 1904, and were likely to be seriously out of date. An alternative calculation may be made on the basis of the consumer expenditure deflator used by Feinstein (1976, Tables 24 and 25). Dividing the current price expenditure series, for all items except housing, by the constant price series yields the following indices (1938 = 100):

1931	98.7
1936	94.8
1937	98.3

These indices differ in being current-weighted, and in relating to the year rather than a specific month. Although there are clearly differences, they confirm that prices in 1936 were rather lower than both before and after. The difference between the Rowntree scale and those of Ford and Tout, with Rowntree's scale typically being higher in cash terms, is therefore likely to be rather larger when measured in terms of purchasing power.

The official cost of living index, recalculated to exclude housing, gives a value for June 1947 of 208.3. The interim index of retail prices which replaced it gives a value for 1955 (annual average, recalculated to exclude housing) of 152.0, where June 1947 = 100 (*British Labour Statistics 1886–1968*, Tables 90 and 91, linking the series at January 1952). Taken together with the earlier figure for 1938, the implied value in 1955, with 1938 = 100, is 203.5. It has however been argued that this seriously understates the rise in prices which took place over this period. Lynes, for example, has argued that for earlier years especially before 1952, the Ministry of Labour indices must be used with the greatest caution (1962, p. 26). He calculates a price index based on the deflator for consumers' expenditure (excluding housing) in the national accounts, which gives a value for 1955 (with 1938 = 100) of 265.3 (1962, p. 22). From the Feinstein series used above, again excluding housing, we obtain a factor for 1955 (with 1938 = 100) of 250.6, linking at 1948 with the series at 1938 prices, or 266.4 if we link with the series at 1948 prices.

In view of this, we base the comparison of the 1981 SB scale with the 1930s scales on two alternative multipliers. The first uses the 'official' price indices (cost of living index, interim index, retail prices index) throughout; the second, 'alternative' multiplier, uses the Lynes deflator for 1938 to 1955, and the official indices prior to 1938 and post 1955. The retail prices index excluding housing rose to (1955 = 100) 648.7 in 1981 (*British Labour Statistics 1886–1968*, Tables 91 and 93; *Department of Employment Gazette*, October 1980, Table 6.6 and October 1983, Table 6.7). The resulting price indices for the period as a whole are (1938 = 100):

	Official indices	Lynes deflator (1938–55)
December 1931 (Ford)	94.4	94.4
January 1936 (Rowntree)	93.1	93.1
June 1937 (Tout)	96.9	96.9
1981	1,320.0	1,721.0

The comparison of the Rowntree 1936 scale with the SB scale is therefore based on a multiplier of either 14.18 or 18.49. On this basis, the scale for a family with three children would be £28.65 or £37.37. These may be compared with the SB scale in 1981 of £56.50–£67.30, depending on the age of the children. For the Tout scale, the comparisons are based on multipliers of 13.62 or 17.76, and the equivalent of the Tout scale for a couple with three children in real terms in 1981 is £22.81–£28.94 on the basis of the official deflator, or £29.75–£37.74 on the basis of the alternative deflator. We have already seen that the Ford scale is lower in money terms, and applying the multipliers of 13.98 or 18.23 yields figures of £16.54–£18.81 or £21.57–£24.53.

The index described above relates to all consumers' expenditure, and it could be argued that it would be more appropriate to base the index on the consumption pattern of low-income households. In recent years, attention has been focused on the tendency for prices to rise faster for the poor: for example, between 1962 and 1981, the index of one-person pensioner households, excluding housing, increased by some 6 per cent more than the general index (*Employment Gazette*, October 1983, Tables 6.6 and 6.7). Similarly, Lynes calculated 'low income price indices', excluding housing, for the period 1948–61, which showed a rise for pensioners of between 76 and 88 per cent, compared with 59 per cent for the official index (1962, Table 5). During the Second World War, the effect of food subsidies should have favoured lower-income groups (Seers, 1956), but, as Lydall has noted, this was in part offset by the rise in the relative price of tobacco (1959, p. 12).

An interesting calculation based on a low-income budget is that of Piachaud (1981). He took the minimum requirements for food, clothing, fuel, light and sundries, which were the basis for Rowntree's poverty line for a family with three children in 1936 and calculated their cost at (May) 1981 prices. Corresponding to 40s. 5d. in Table 3.A.1, he found a 1981 cost of £44.55, or an implied multiplier of 22.05. This does not, of course, allow for any variation in consumption patterns in response to changing relative prices.

Piachaud concludes that the present-day supplementary benefit scale is higher by about a quarter than Rowntree's 1936 scale, comparing £44.55 with £56.50 in Table 3.A.2. Applying our 'alternative' multiplier, the comparable 1936 figure is £37.37, which implies an increase of 51 per cent. As noted in the text, however, the *structure* of the scale has changed, and consideration of only one family type may be misleading. For single pensioners, application of our 'alternative' multiplier yields comparable 1936 figures of £11.56 (single woman) or £14.10 (single man), so that the 1981 scale (£27.15) is more than double for women. On the other hand, for a single unemployed man, the comparable 1936 figure is £21.03, so that the SB scale is virtually the same in real terms.

Two conclusions seem clear. First, the Rowntree 1936 scale is in most cases higher in real terms than the scales applied by Ford and Tout. Second, the change in the structure of the scale, favouring pensioners against persons in work, and bringing the scale for women into line with that of men, means that for some groups there has been a very substantial real increase between the 1930s and the 1980s, whereas for others – such as the single unemployed man – there has been little effective improvement.

A.4 The findings

Bearing in mind the differences in the poverty scales applied, we may now compare the findings of the different studies.

The first in the 1930s, in chronological order, is that of Ford in 1931. Of the 559 households interviewed in Southampton, 120 were found to be below the poverty line, or 21.45 per cent, to which Ford attaches a 99 per cent confidence interval of 17.2–25.8 per cent. The number of people below the poverty line was 510 (232 children plus 278 adults), or 21.5 per cent of the total. If we seek to relate these figures to the whole population, assuming that none of those excluded from the sample were in poverty, then we arrive at a figure of 16.1 per cent (21.45 × 0.75) for households in poverty and of 13.3 per cent (21.5 × 0.619) of the population in poverty.

The Rowntree study of York in 1936 found that 31.1 per cent of the working-class population, or 17.7 per cent of the total population, was below the poverty line. These people lived in 5,088 (31.1 per cent) of the families, so that again – within the 'working-class' population – the percentage in poverty is the same for individuals and for families.

The Tout study distinguished between 'week of investigation' and 'full-time' income. On the former basis, 10.7 per cent of households were below the poverty line; on the latter basis, 7.2 per cent. The percentage of persons below the poverty line is somewhat higher: 11.8 per cent, on the former basis, compared with 10.7 per cent. Applied to the whole population, on the assumption that none of those excluded were below the poverty line, we arrive at 9.5 (10.7 × 0.885) per cent of households and 8.6 (11.8 × 0.725) per cent of the population.

We have therefore a range of results for the 1930s. There is no reason to expect the proportion in poverty to be the same, since the studies relate to different cities and to different dates. Moreover, we have seen that there are significant differences in the scales applied. This latter aspect is illustrated by Figure 3.A.1, which shows the variation in the percentage in poverty, with variations in the level of the poverty line (changing all scales by the same percentage). The alternative figure for the Rowntree study shows the percentage in poverty if the scale is reduced by 22.8 per cent: i.e. from 43s. 5d. for a couple with three children to 33s. 6d., and proportionate reductions for other family types. This group, which constitutes Class A in Rowntree's study, represents 8.1 per cent of the total population. The alternative figures for the Bristol study are in terms of *households*, and

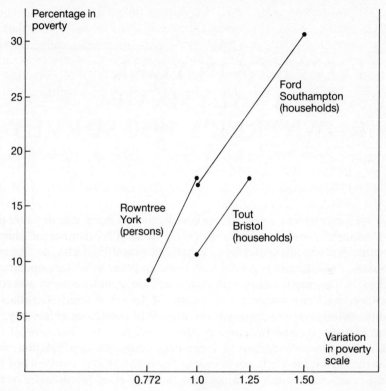

Figure 3.A.1 Variation in poverty percentage with scale

show that an increase of 25 per cent in the scale would raise the percentage of households in poverty to 17.7 per cent. A rise in the Ford poverty scale of 50 per cent would increase the proportion of households in poverty from 16.1 per cent to 30.9 per cent.

If it is the case that the poverty standard applied in Bristol by Tout was rather lower than that applied in York by Rowntree, then it may be that the findings are broadly similar: a 25 per cent increase in the Tout scale would lead to the same percentage for households in poverty as persons in York. On the other hand, poverty in Southampton in 1931 appears to have been higher, reflecting either the different circumstances of the city or the higher level of unemployment. Ford notes that 'if unemployment had been at the level of 1928, the proportion in poverty would probably have been about 13 per cent' (1934, p. 118), where this can be translated to some 10 per cent in terms of the total population.

Turning to the present day, the most recent estimates are those based on the 1981 FES (DHSS, 1983). These show that 6.5 per cent of families containing 5.3 per cent of the population had incomes below the SB level and were not receiving SB. If those in receipt of SB are added, then these percentages rise to 17.7 per cent and 14.3 per cent.

4 · POVERTY IN YORK: A RE-ANALYSIS OF ROWNTREE'S 1950 SURVEY

1 INTRODUCTION

Seebohm Rowntree's surveys of York were pioneering and highly influential. His three large-scale studies in 1899, 1936 and 1950 demonstrated how survey methods could be employed to yield information about poverty and its causes. The findings, together with those of other investigators such as Bowley, led to major changes in public attitudes and in policy towards social security. The opening paragraphs of the Beveridge Report, for example, referred to the impact of the surveys of conditions of life in York and other towns (Beveridge, 1942, p. 7).

The 1950 Rowntree survey is especially significant as a link between Rowntree's work for York, spanning the first half of the twentieth century, and later national studies by academics (notably Abel-Smith and Townsend, 1965) and government statisticians. As such it allows a valuable historical perspective on the changing importance of poverty. The conclusions of the 1950 study (Rowntree and Lavers, 1951), and in particular the small proportion of the population found to be below the poverty line, were widely publicized. According to *The Times* there had been a 'remarkable improvement – no less than the virtual abolition of the sheerest want' (quoted in Coates and Silburn, 1970, p. 14); according to Anthony Crosland, 'primary poverty has been largely eliminated; the "Beveridge revolution" has been carried through' (1956, p. 59); according to W. Hagenbuch, 'the results showed an astonishing improvement ... Rowntree demonstrated the effectiveness of full employment and the social services in the cure of poverty' (1958, pp. 173–75).

The 1950 survey was, however, less satisfactory in certain respects than the two earlier Rowntree investigations, as was indeed recognized by some contemporary commentators. Dobb noted the lack of details provided by

Reprinted from *Bulletin of Economic Research*, 33, 1981. With J. Corlyon, A. K. Maynard, H. Sutherland and C. G. Trinder.
This research was financed by the Joseph Rowntree Memorial Trust, and we are grateful to them for their support. They are in no way responsible for the conclusions drawn. We are grateful to several readers for helpful comments on an earlier version.

Rowntree and Lavers and 'the difficulty which at least one reader has experienced in following their results' (1952, p. 174). Kaim-Caudle (1953) drew attention to the apparent under-representation of children and of married women at work. Townsend (1952) questioned the extent to which York was representative of the country as a whole, and the procedures used by Rowntree.

In this chapter we present a re-analysis of the 1950 data,[1] making use of the 1,363 original survey returns which are still extant in the Rowntree papers (we discuss later the representativeness of the surviving returns, which are approximately two-thirds of the original number). The aim of this re-analysis is to give a more detailed account of the 1950 survey, drawing attention to its shortcomings, to re-analyse the surviving returns, and to put the findings in a form in which they can be related to more recent studies. Most importantly, we have reworked the poverty calculations employing the national assistance method of assessment used in subsequent enquiries rather than Rowntree's own poverty criterion. This not only leads to changes in the conclusions, but also may facilitate easier comparison with more recent estimates of the extent of poverty.

2 THE 1950 ROWNTREE SURVEY

By the time Rowntree came to prepare his 1950 survey of York, he had a clear procedure which drew on the 1899 and 1936 investigations. This restricted attention to the 'working-class population', obtained family composition, occupation and household details from interviews, and relied on employers' wage records (or estimates) for the data on earnings. There was one important departure in 1950. Following the famous supplementary chapter in the 1936 study (Rowntree, 1941, pp. 478–92), in which he examined the reliability of taking samples, Rowntree decided to interview a 1 in 9 sample of the relevant population. This yielded a total of some 2,000 households.

The 1950 study was therefore very much in the tradition of social surveys – a tradition to which Rowntree himself greatly contributed. At the same time, it suffered from a number of shortcomings as a basis from which to draw conclusions about the extent of poverty in postwar Britain. This section discusses the representativeness of York, the selection of the sample, and the quality of the data.

Representativeness of York

In embarking on his 1899 survey, Rowntree expressed the hope that the conditions of life in York 'might be taken as fairly representative of the conditions existing in many, if not most, of our provincial towns' (1901, pp. xvii–xviii). In 1936, he elaborated on this theme, arguing that:

> On the whole, I think, we may safely assume that from the standpoint of the earnings of the workers, York holds a position not far from the median, among the towns of Great Britain. If on the one hand there is no important industry employing a large number of highly skilled and highly paid workers, on the other hand there are no large industries (though unfortunately there are isolated small businesses) where wages are exceptionally low.
>
> (Rowntree, 1941, p. 10)

And this claim was repeated in 1950 (Rowntree and Lavers, 1951, p. 6).

In Atkinson, Maynard and Trinder (1983, Ch. 3) we examine the evidence for this assertion, using data from the 1951 Census of Population and other sources. Although the demographic structure of York was at that time relatively close to that of England and Wales, there are several respects in which York was far from representative. In particular, the industrial structure of employment departed considerably from the national picture. In 1951, some 9,500 men and women were employed in cocoa, chocolate and sugar confectionery. British Railways employed over 5,500 people, and a further 3,000 were engaged on the manufacture and repair of wagons. The categories 'food, drink and tobacco' and 'transport and communication' together accounted for 35.4 per cent of total employment in York in 1951, compared with 10.8 per cent for England and Wales. In contrast, employment in textiles, clothing and agriculture was considerably below the average for England and Wales. The Rowntree survey is likely, therefore, to reflect the characteristics of the dominant industries, and may well not be representative of the country as a whole. Even if it is close to the median, it is quite possible that 'the city would not reflect the "spread" of incomes typical for the country as a whole' (Townsend, 1952, p. 37).

Rowntree's 'working-class' population

The survey concentrated on the 'working-class population', defined as those households with total earnings (husband and wife) of £550 or less per year.[2] The method by which it was selected is described by Rowntree and Lavers:

> We took a list of all the streets of York, and a man who has lived in the city for more than half a century, who knows the city intimately, and has also a wide knowledge of, and sympathy with, our work, marked on our list every street where working class families live. (1951, p. 2)

Although the investigators' local knowledge was no doubt considerable, it is unlikely that all low-income families were located in this way. The proportion of the total population in poverty may therefore be understated, since Rowntree assumes that all those not included in the defined population are above the poverty line.

Selection of the sample

From the defined 'working-class population', a 1 in 9 sample was drawn. This procedure was in principle a perfectly reasonable one, but the execution does not appear to have been closely supervised; and there is evidence of departure from the sample originally selected. Moreover, the response appears to have been considerably less than 100 per cent. These aspects are not described in the published account of the survey, but we have been able to piece together information from the Rowntree papers (deposited at the University of York) and from discussions with those involved. The conclusions drawn involve an element of judgement, but the available evidence seems to tell a consistent story.

The drawing of the sample appears to have been based on the York City Year Book of 1949, taking in general every ninth address in the order listed. This we assume to be the case on the basis of the typed street list, containing 2,177 names and addresses, found among the Rowntree papers.[3]

When interviewing came to be carried out, there was less than 100 per cent response and the sample was extended to include two new estates. This is described in the unpublished report to Rowntree by T. J. Brooke:

> Of the 2,182 interviews contained in the original street-list, 1,893 were carried out. These, together with 102 interviews carried out on the new Gale Lane estate, and 59 on the new portion of the Carr Lane estate, bring the total number of interviews completed in the four weeks to 2,054.[4]

He goes on to say that the reasons for the shortfall from the original list include (a) streets not occupied (e.g. because of slum clearances), (b) streets above the £550 cut-off, (c) streets where it was 'impossible for the interviewer to find the requisite number of households in at the time', and (d) organizational faults. The 289 non-responses from the original list implies a non-response rate of some 13 per cent. This is quite low by the standards of surveys such as the *Family Expenditure Survey*, where it has been of the order of 30 per cent (although this survey does involve a much more detailed questionnaire). None the less, this non-response should have received more attention from Rowntree and Lavers in their report of the results; and it would also have been helpful if they had discussed the implications of adding a further 161 interviews (some 8 per cent of the final total).

More importantly, there appears to have been considerable departure from the original street list. The comment by Brooke about interviewers failing to find the requisite number of households in a street gives the impression that they viewed their task more as finding a specified quota from the street than as being to interview specified households. This impression is supported by discussions we have had with those involved in the interviewing. Further evidence is provided by the typed street list: 1,013 of the 1,363 surviving returns correspond to streets given on the list, and there are broadly the 'right' number in each street. But the proportion which correspond to the actual house numbers on the list is considerably lower. Although in some streets there is 100 per cent correspondence, in others there is none. For example, for Crombie Avenue, all eight schedules are given on the list, whereas for Rowntree Avenue, not one of the ten schedules agrees with the list. This may well reflect the differential success/conscientiousness of different interviewers.

On the basis of the available evidence, it seems reasonable to conclude that the 1950 survey suffered from problems of non-response and of departure from the survey design. The reasons for these shortcomings are easy to understand,[5] but they mean that the results are not necessarily fully representative. Brooke, for example, reported the general conclusions reached by the interviewing team that: 'streets in the centre of the city tended to be too highly represented as against the suburbs and that old-age pensioners and young couples were the most cooperative in answering questions.'

The full number of respondents is nowhere stated explicitly by Rowntree and Lavers (1951). The report by Brooke refers to 2,054 interviews being carried out. On the other hand, it is clear from the Rowntree papers that the published results are based on a multiplier of 9, and working back from the 18,099 working-class families referred to in the report, we arrive at a figure of 2,011. We therefore assume that, although 2,054 interviews were carried out, 43 were not used for some reason.

Quality of the data

The interviewers collected information on the number of occupants, the age, sex and occupation of each member of the household, the rent, and the condition of the house (this description was sometimes highly unflattering). The quality of this information is open to question. The survey was mostly carried out by students, with little previous experience of this kind of work, and there was limited supervision. Rowntree and Lavers themselves felt that the data were adequate, and reported how Lavers revisited some households to verify the data, finding 'no cases in which they furnished inadequate or incorrect information' (1951, p. 2). However, examination of the schedules, and interviewing of the children in our 1975–78 follow-up, suggests that this conclusion was over-optimistic. The schedules contain errors in such details as the Christian names of the respondents, in addresses, and in respondents' ages. From the correspondence between

Rowntree and employers (see below), it is clear that the occupation information was in some cases incorrect. Our discussions with those involved suggest that Lavers did not in fact make any substantial checks.

Such deficiencies of the survey evidence do not necessarily affect the conclusions drawn. They do, however, provide further grounds for carrying out a re-analysis, particularly since in the 1975–78 interviews with the children we have been able to correct a number of the errors (e.g. with respect to family composition).

In his report on the 1936 survey, Rowntree noted that in many cases the interview respondent was a woman who frequently 'only knows what money her husband gives her, not how much he actually receives' (Rowntree, 1941, p. 25). As a consequence, Rowntree went directly to the employers and requested them to supply details of the net earnings of their employees who were in the survey. Where respondents received income from sources such as pensions, unemployment or sickness benefit and public assistance, Rowntree approached the institutions concerned, and acquired and checked relevant data. In 1950, similar methods were used. The description given in the Rowntree–Lavers book is terse, but it is reported that 'altogether we have succeeded in obtaining information from the employers' wage books for over 95 per cent of the heads of the households we called on' (1951, p. 7). In cases where such information was not available, the average earnings of the relevant industries were used to estimate earnings.

From the material in the Rowntree papers, it is possible to form some idea of the reliability of the information. In December 1950, one of the interviewers described how the large firms (e.g. the railways and the confectionery companies) had been most helpful, but that the small firms had been less cooperative. The correspondence indicates how refusals of information were not unusual. For instance, the local authority refused to divulge details of their employees' earnings and, as a result, the authors had to estimate the earnings of 61 of their respondents. Of the 102 respondents in the building industry, 89 had their earnings estimated from basic rates. A further 104 had given incorrect data about their place of work. Altogether from the correspondence it is clear that in nearly 300 cases (14 per cent of the total) the earnings data were not obtained directly from the employers.

The earnings information appears to be less reliable than Rowntree and Lavers suggested.[6] At the same time, there were over 1,100 employees for whom data were collected direct from the employers. Moreover, many seem to have taken a great deal of care in answering the questions, and in correcting and supplementing the interview information: e.g. 'I have taken the liberty of supplying the details on a new form, as on your original list some of the titles, initials, ages and occupations etc. were incorrect.' The earnings data supplied by employers in this way may well be more reliable than those obtained from employees in modern surveys. Moreover, for many of those out of work, detailed information on pensions or social security benefits was supplied by employers or by the National Assistance Board.

Conclusions

The Rowntree 1950 survey seems therefore to fall considerably short of providing a completely adequate picture of poverty in Britain at that time. In the light of this, it now seems clear that undue weight was attached to its findings, and that the criticisms made at the time by Townsend (1952), Kaim-Caudle (1953), and others, should have received more attention.

On the other hand, the 1950 survey has certain valuable features – notably the provision from source of the data on earnings, pensions and social security benefits – and it is one of the few sources of evidence about this period. Moreover, the deficiencies of the methods employed, while weakening the conclusions which can be drawn, do not necessarily mean that the results are completely without value. Finally, from the follow-up study of the children, we have been able to correct a number of the deficiencies. In view of this, a re-analysis of the survey returns appears worthwhile, and this forms the subject of the remainder of the chapter.

3 RE-ANALYSIS OF THE 1950 DATA AND ROWNTREE'S POVERTY CRITERION

As noted earlier, not all of the original 1950 schedules appear to have survived. In the Rowntree papers at the University of York we have only been able to locate schedules relating to 1,363 households (67.8 per cent of the total of 2,011). Moreover, we have not been able to provide a satisfactory explanation why the schedules should be missing.

The loss of a third of the schedules is undoubtedly a major handicap in the re-analysis; we are, however, able to compare the characteristics of the 1,363 schedules with those of the whole sample reported by Rowntree and Lavers (1951). In Atkinson, Maynard and Trinder (1983) we examine the characteristics reported in the book for which a comparison is possible. From this it appears that the average family size is somewhat higher for the surviving schedules. Including lodgers, there are 4,930 adults and children covered by the 1,363 schedules, giving an average family size of 3.6. According to figures given by Rowntree and Lavers, the average family size is 3.5. A direct comparison of the number of families with children is complicated because the definition of a 'child' is not made explicit by Rowntree and Lavers (in particular the treatment of lodgers' children). There appears also to be an under-representation of working wives (5.6 per cent compared with 7.1 per cent reported by Rowntree and Lavers). In other respects the 1,363 schedules appear reasonably representative. For example, the proportion of owner-occupiers is 29.2 per cent, compared with 28.3 per cent in the full survey[7]; the proportion receiving occupational or friendly society pensions is 6.8 per cent compared with 6.9 per cent.

Of particular significance is the distribution of the schedules according to Rowntree's poverty classification, and we turn now to this aspect.

Rowntree's poverty classification

The central feature of Rowntree's analysis of the data was his classification of the 'net resources' of households into five classes[8]:

A below 77 per cent of the minimum requirements,
B below the minimum but 77 per cent or above,
C at or above the minimum but by less than 23 per cent,
D at least 23 per cent but less than 46 per cent above the minimum,
E 46 per cent or more above the minimum.

The minimum was derived applying a similar approach to that in his earlier investigations, although the calculations are not directly comparable (see Townsend, 1952). For a couple with three children, the minimum was £5 a week.

The total income of the household included the net earnings of husband or wife, pensions, family allowances, national insurance benefits, national assistance, value of free school meals/milk and of cheap milk, net value of vegetables grown, and the amounts paid by lodgers and working children for board and lodging. For earnings, the figures given were typically an average for three months. From this total was subtracted the rent and rates paid to arrive at 'net resources', on which the classification was based.

The left-hand part of Table 4.1 summarizes the findings of Rowntree and Lavers for the full sample. These are given in absolute numbers, where we have divided by 9 to obtain the actual sample figures, and in percentages of

Table 4.1 Rowntree poverty standard

Class	Rowntree and Lavers				Re-analysis			
	No. of persons	% of persons[a]	No. of house-holds	% of house-holds[a]	No. of persons	% of persons[a]	No. of house-holds	% of house-holds[a]
A	26	0.37	9	0.41	} 149	3.0	} 70	5.1
B	168	2.40	85	4.23				
C	1,344	19.23	390	19.40	897	18.2	255	18.7
D	1,381	19.76	349	17.38	964	19.6	238	17.5
E	4,065	58.24	1,178	58.58	2,920	59.2	800	58.7
Total	6,984	100.0	2,011	100.0	4,930	100.0	1,363	100.0

Sources:
Rowntree and Lavers (1951), pp. 31, 34, and our re-analysis of 1,363 schedules.

[a] As a percentage of those covered by the survey, i.e. the 'working-class population'.

the 'working-class population'. One point which this brings out, not emphasized by Rowntree and Lavers, is the small absolute number of households involved in certain cases. Most importantly, the bottom class A contained only *nine* households in the full survey, which provides a slender basis for any analysis.[9] In view of this we have amalgamated classes A and B in our re-analysis using the Rowntree classification.

The right-hand part of Table 4.1, headed 'Re-analysis', shows the classification given by Rowntree for the 1,363 schedules in our possession. From the table it appears that there is a slight over-representation of classes A and B: there are 5.1 per cent of 'working-class' households below the poverty line, compared with 4.6 per cent in the original sample. The proportions are, however, in general close to those in the full survey, and suggest that the returns with which we are working are not grossly unrepresentative.

4 POVERTY ACCORDING TO THE NATIONAL ASSISTANCE SCALE

The role played by Rowntree's poverty standards in the development of national assistance may lead to the belief that his approach was similar, in structure, if not in level, to the use of the national assistance/ supplementary benefit scale in more recent studies of poverty. This is not, however, the case. In particular, the Rowntree calculations were based on a different definition of the unit of assessment giving special treatment to the amounts paid by lodgers and adult children, and included income in kind (vegetables grown, free school meals, etc.).

Comparison of Rowntree and national assistance standards

Rowntree's definition of the unit of assessment was effectively the *household* (including non-dependent children and lodgers), whereas the national assistance (NA) scheme was based on the *family*. He did not, however, take total household income and total household requirements. In the case of adult independent children and lodgers ('non-dependants'), he included in household income the amounts they contributed for board and lodging (not their total income) and included in the minimum requirements of the household an amount for food and increment of household sundries (not including, for example, clothing or personal sundries).[10] The assumption in effect made by Rowntree was that the excess of the income of non-dependants over their contribution equalled their requirements for items other than food or household sundries. On this assumption, his classification measures the extent of *household* poverty.

Rowntree's approach was in certain respects close to the household means test employed, for example, under the Unemployment Assistance Act 1934.[11] This test was highly unpopular. As a result, the scope of the household means test was considerably narrowed in the Determination of Needs Act 1941, and this was carried over in the National Assistance Act 1948, which was based on a family unit assessment. This assessment took account of an assumed contribution by non-dependent members of the same household,[12] but considered neither the actual transfer from non-dependants nor their actual income. To the extent that the assumed contribution corresponded to the 'profit' from non-dependants,[13] the NA assessment provided a measure of *family* poverty.

These differences in the method of assessment may lead to different conclusions regarding the extent and composition of poverty. For example, Fiegehen, Lansley and Smith report 7.1 per cent of households to be in poverty in 1971 on a household basis, but 12.5 per cent of families (1977, Ch. 4), and in general we would expect the difference to be in this direction (although it should be noted that Rowntree's treatment of non-dependants is rather different).

In what follows, we explore the consequences of applying the NA standard. This does not mean that we believe the NA scale to be superior or that Rowntree's approach is invalid. Indeed, in that his approach takes account of actual transfers of income within the household, one could argue that it provides a better indicator of 'well-being'. Moreover, for the purpose of comparison with his earlier studies, it was clearly right for him to retain the same method of assessment.

What the Rowntree classification does not capture is the apparent shift in social values between the 1930s and 1950 (see, for example, Ford 1939), according to which the household ceased to be regarded as the appropriate basis for assessment. The NA approach may be seen as embodying the view that incomes should be adequate without recourse to help from other members of the household.

The Rowntree approach also differed in its treatment of income in kind, since he included the imputed value of school meals and cheap milk and of vegetables grown at home, and in the level of the scale. The Rowntree scale was typically about 30–40 per cent higher than the NA scale (except for single women)[14]:

	Ratio of Rowntree scale to national assistance
Single man	1.38
Single woman	1.19
Man and woman	1.31
Man and woman + 1 child	1.34
Man and woman + 2 children	1.36
Man and woman + 3 children	1.36

To sum up, use of a household basis would tend to lead to lower estimates of the extent of poverty, as would the inclusion of income in kind. Working in the opposite direction is the fact that the Rowntree minimum was rather higher than the NA scale.

Applying the national assistance standard

In the re-analysis of the 1,363 schedules, we applied in each case the NA assessment and calculated the family's net resources as a percentage of this scale. Such a classification involved an element of judgement; and the schedules did not in all cases contain the full necessary information. Nevertheless, we have tried to follow the NA provisions as closely as possible (for example, applying where appropriate the special scales for blind persons).[15] The assessment was applied in each case to the family unit of the head of household. This means that other family units contained in the household were not covered – an aspect to which we return below.

The results are shown in Table 4.2, which gives a cross-tabulation of households by Rowntree and NA assessments. This brings out the extent of the differences. Fifty-four families classified by Rowntree as D or E appear on our re-analysis to be below the NA scale. Viewed simply in terms of the classification in relation to the poverty line:

	Below *Rowntree*	Above
Below	37	156
National assistance		
Above	33	1,116

On this basis, there were 14 per cent of cases (189) where the assessments did not agree.[16]

The differences which arise are illustrated by the Terry family (the name is fictional), where the Rowntree classification was E but we assessed the family to be at 75 per cent of the NA level. The family consisted of a husband and wife and 14-year-old son at school. Mr Terry had been off work sick for about a month and was receiving national insurance sickness benefit. There were also two working children, a daughter aged 15 years who worked as a clerk at Rowntrees and a son aged 17 years who was doing an apprenticeship. Rowntree recorded the working children as contributing £1.25 and £1 a week respectively, which was considerably in excess of their addition to the minimum requirements. Under NA assessment neither working child would have been earning sufficient to make a contribution.

An example in the opposite direction is provided by the Cadbury family where the Rowntree classification was B but the NA assessment was 185 per cent. This arose because the family had lodgers (a Corporal in the RAF, his wife and baby) whose contribution was less than the amount added to the Rowntree poverty classification. On an NA basis, the lodgers were treated as contributing 35p, and the requirements were assessed as simply

Table 4.2 Rowntree and national assistance classification compared

Percentage of national assistance scale	Rowntree classification					
	A	B	C	D	E	Total
<80	3	18	49	13	14	97
80–99	3	13	53	16	11	96
100–19	1	26	35	18	9	89
120–39	0	6	35	22	9	72
140–59	0	0	42	27	14	83
160–79	0	0	26	70	17	113
180–99	0	0	5	52	63	120
200–39	0	0	2	14	241	257
240–99	0	0	3	4	241	248
300+	0	0	1	2	164	167
Total	7	63	251	238	783	1,342

Note: In 21 cases it is not possible to calculate the national assistance assessment (mostly because of missing details on income).

those of the Cadbury family. As a result, the Cadbury family were above the poverty line. It is of course possible that the Corporal's family were in poverty, but this cannot be assessed since we do not know their total income.

Extent of poverty according to the national assistance scale

The results in Table 4.2 show that of the 1,342 households which we can classify according to the NA scale, 193 (14.4 per cent) were below that level, and of these 97 were below 80 per cent of the scale. With a higher cut-off (for example, in *The Poor and the Poorest*, Abel-Smith and Townsend (1965), used the NA scale plus 40 per cent), the number in poverty according to our re-analysis of the Rowntree data would have been:

	Number of families (cumulative)	(%)
Below national assistance	193	(14.4)
Below national assistance plus 20 per cent	282	(21.0)
Below national assistance plus 40 per cent	354	(26.4)

These figures need to be adjusted in two respects. First, they relate to the 'working-class population'. If we assume that the remainder of the population were in household units of average size (3.5 persons), then we can apply the same adjustment as used by Rowntree and Lavers (1951, p. 31) for the total population, which involves multiplying the number in poverty by 0.6. To give some idea of the sensitivity of the results to this assumption, if the remainder of the population were in household units of size 2.5, this would imply an adjustment of 0.52 and size 4.5 would imply an adjustment of 0.66. (These calculations assume, as noted earlier, that no one in the remainder of the population was below the poverty line.)

Secondly, we have only considered the position of the family unit of the head of household ('first family unit'). As illustrated by the example of the Cadbury family, we cannot typically assess the position of other family units. We can therefore do little more than indicate the consequences of different assumptions. If the incidence of poverty in other family units is identical to that in the first unit, then the earlier figure applies. On the other hand, if none of the other family units were in poverty – an extreme assumption – we have to reduce the proportion by the ratio of first family units to the total, which we take to be 65 per cent.[17]

Taking these two adjustments together, we obtain a 'low' figure, applying factors of 0.52 and 0.65, of 4.9 per cent of family units in the whole population below the NA level and a figure of 9.5 per cent applying factors of 0.66 and 1.0. The latter is not an upper bound, since the extent of poverty may be greater among other family units. The corresponding figures for the NA scale + 40 per cent are 8.9 per cent and 17.4 per cent. It should be emphasized that these estimates depend not only on the accuracy of the two adjustments just described, but also on the sources of error described earlier. Moreover, in comparing the results with those for a national sample, as in Abel-Smith and Townsend (1965), the representativeness, or otherwise, of York is a crucial question.

5 CONCLUSIONS

The Rowntree 1950 survey of York, like his preceding surveys, was highly influential, and contributed to the widely held view in the 1950s that poverty had been virtually eliminated. However, the argument in this chapter suggests that the weight placed on the conclusions of the survey was not justified. The questions which must be raised include the possible unrepresentativeness of York, the limitation to 'working-class' households, the non-response of a proportion of households, the apparent deviation from the sample design, and the inaccuracies in the information recorded.

At the same time, it should not be concluded that the 1950 survey returns are without value. They contain a great deal of useful information about those in the sample, and the earnings data collected from the employers are of particular interest. Moreover, from the schedules extant, and information collected from the children, it is possible to correct the Rowntree analysis in certain respects.

In our re-analysis of the surviving two-thirds of the original 1950 schedules, we have given particular prominence to the consequences of replacing the Rowntree standard by the National Assistance scale. The Rowntree classification was the natural one to provide a comparison with the earlier York investigations, but it was in effect closer to a household unit than to the family unit assessment embodied in the 1948 legislation.

Although it can be argued that Rowntree's approach had certain advantages as a measure of 'well-being', the national assistance standard was certainly relevant to assessing the performance of the post-war welfare state. If Rowntree had applied the national assistance criterion, then he would – according to our re-analysis – have found 5–10 per cent of families to be below the poverty line, rather than the 2.8 per cent of households in poverty according to *Poverty and the Welfare State* (4.64 per cent from Table 4.1 multiplied by 0.6 to give a percentage of all households).

This leads us to conclude that a more extensive analysis of the Rowntree survey in 1950, geared to postwar concerns rather than to a comparison with the 1930s, would have led to a rather different emphasis. The findings of *The Poor and the Poorest*, published in 1965, might have come to public notice some fifteen years earlier. One can only speculate as to what would have happened if a social investigator of Rowntree's standing had announced in 1951 that a substantial minority of families were below the national assistance scale, but one cannot help feeling that the climate of opinion would have been rather different.

NOTES

1. The re-analysis of the Rowntree data grew out of our use of the survey to investigate the extent of intergenerational income mobility, which involved the tracing of the children of the 1950 respondents. This research has been supported by the DHSS/SSRC Contract on Research into Transmitted Deprivation and is reported in Atkinson, Maynard and Trinder (1983). See also Atkinson, Maynard and Trinder (1981).
2. It should be noted that the institutional population was excluded from the 'working-class population' but included in the total.
3. There is a minor discrepancy with the report to Rowntree in October 1950 by one of those engaged in the survey, T. J. Brooke, who refers to there being 2,182 addresses on the original street list (see below). On the other hand, the most reasonable conclusion in the light of the material in the Rowntree papers is that it is the original list.
4. It may be noted that none of this information was given to the reader of *Poverty and the Welfare State*.
5. By 1951, Seebohm Rowntree was aged 80 and resident in Buckinghamshire. Commander G. R. Lavers was recruited to assist Rowntree with the survey but he seems to have made only weekly visits to York.
6. It is possible that the difference arises partly because the 95 per cent figure quoted by them refers to heads of households.
7. Although there seems to be an under-representation of the higher rent categories among tenants.
8. The percentages refer to the classification for a family of a man, wife and three children, as given on p. 29 of Rowntree and Lavers (1951).
9. For example, Rowntree and Lavers analyse the causes of poverty by different classes. The analysis for class A (Rowntree and Lavers, 1951, p. 34) refers to 36, 36 and 9 families, but these relate in fact to 4, 4, and 1 family in the survey.

10. See Rowntree and Lavers (1951), Chs 2 and 3, and the much fuller account given in Rowntree (1941).
11. See Supplementary Benefits Commission (1977), Appendix A; for a contemporary account, see Ford (1939).
12. The 1948 Act took over the earlier provision of the Determination of Needs Act 1941, under which a contribution of 7s. per member towards household expenses was assumed unless the non-dependant's earnings were below a certain level (70s. in the 1948 Act), with a sliding scale below. In 1959, a new method of calculation was introduced, based on the proportionate share of the rent. (See Supplementary Benefit Commission (1977), Appendix A.)
13. That is, the assumed contribution equalled the actual contribution less the extra expenses (except rent, where this was allowed for in the NA assessment).
14. An exact comparison cannot be made, since the national assistance and Rowntree scales depend on different variables. For example, the former varies with the age of the children (here assumed to be 5–10); the Rowntree scale is different for employed and unemployed families (the figures here are for the employed).
15. More detail of the NA assessment, and an analysis of the 'take-up' rate, is given in Atkinson, Maynard and Trinder (1981).
16. In some cases examination of the schedules suggested that Rowntree's calculations were in error: e.g. for one family it is clear that the earnings were incorrectly recorded as £15 rather than £5. We would not like to suggest that our own calculations are without error, but we have double-checked those where the classification is out of line with that of Rowntree.
17. This figure is based on the number of working adult children and lodgers recorded in the 1950 returns. It may be noted that the ratio recorded in the 1972–73 *Family Expenditure Surveys* is 78 per cent (Royal Commission on the Distribution of Income and Wealth, 1975, p. 39). The proportion could have been expected to rise between 1950 and 1972–73 in view of a decline in the sharing of accommodation by families.

5 · INTER-GENERATIONAL CONTINUITIES IN DEPRIVATION

1 INTRODUCTION

There has been considerable interest in different indicators of deprivation – poor housing, job instability, family breakdown – in addition to economic measures such as low earnings or low income. There has in particular been concern with the extent of 'multiple deprivation', where families are disadvantaged according to more than one indicator. Very little however is known about the association of deprivation, measured by such indicators, across generations. The aim of this chapter is to describe the information which can be derived from the Rowntree follow-up study (see Chapter 4 and Atkinson, Maynard and Trinder, 1983) about inter-generational continuities. It should be emphasized at the outset that this information is limited, and that the restricted scope of the original Rowntree enquiry in 1950 constrains the choice of indicators quite severely. Moreover, the information has to be qualified in several important respects. None the less, even the limited results are felt to be of some value in view of the lack of evidence about inter-generational continuities.

The use of multiple indicators of deprivation is illustrated by the results of the *National Child Development Study*. Wedge and Prosser (1973) report that 23 per cent of 11-year-old children in the survey came from a single-parent family or a family with five or more children, that the same percentage of families suffered from overcrowding (more than 1½ persons per room) or lived in housing where there was not exclusive use of hot water, and that 14 per cent had low income (defined in terms of entitlement to supplementary benefit or free school meals). As Rutter and Madge (1976) point out, if there were no overlap between these disadvantages then ¾ per cent (calculated as 0.23 × 0.23 × 0.14 = 0.0074) of the children would be expected to be deprived on all three counts. In fact 6 per cent were deprived according to all three indicators: 'there was a very marked overlap between different forms of social disadvantage' (Rutter and Madge, 1976, p. 248).

With H. Sutherland.

A more extensive list of indicators has been employed in the Lambeth Inner Area Study report on *Poverty and Multiple Deprivation* (Department of the Environment, 1975). The 'narrow' definition included indicators of housing, income, social life, disability and job instability. Working with a different type of source – the small area statistics of the 1971 Census – Holtermann (1975) used indicators of housing, employment, car ownership, occupational class, pensioner and immigrant populations. Finally, Townsend (1979, Appendix 13) examines a very wide range of factors, including dietary standards, clothing, heating, durables, housing, work conditions, health, education, environment, family, recreational and social amenities.

2   INDICES OF DEPRIVATION

Since our main aim is to compare deprivation in two generations, we are constrained in our choice of indicators by the availability of information for the first generation. This is based on Rowntree's 1950 survey of York, and the limited scope of his questionnaire, coupled with the qualifications surrounding its re-analysis (see Chapter 4), mean that we cannot match the richness of the data collected, for example, by Townsend. We can, however, provide some evidence under the four headings: housing, income, family status and job instability. These may be seen as corresponding to those in the *National Child Development Study* summarized above, plus the indicator of job instability.

In applying standards of deprivation to two generations, we need, of course, to consider the changing extent of disadvantage. Between 1950, when Rowntree studied the first generation (referred to as 'parents') and our survey in 1975–78 of the second generation (referred to as 'children'), there has been a great deal of change. In 1951, 46 per cent of households in Great Britain did not have sole use of a fixed bath and 23 per cent did not have sole use of a toilet; in 1977 only 4 per cent did not have a bath or shower, and 4 per cent did not have an inside toilet (Toland, 1980, p. 28). The implications of changing standards will be considered under each heading, but in general we shall contrast 'absolute' and 'relative' measures.

The evidence on continuities relates to pairs of parents and children, where the latter are those traced in our follow-up study and who provided the required information. In what follows we treat such pairs as units of observation, but it should be noted that parents may appear several times (where more than one child is included in our follow-up). For the purposes of the analysis we have included those where the children are below retirement age, and the maximum sample is 1,397.[1] In some cases the necessary information, for example on income, is missing, so that the sample is reduced.

It should be emphasized that the Rowntree sample was not intended to be representative of the York population, excluding those on upper incomes, and that York certainly cannot be regarded as a microcosm of Great Britain as a whole. In that the children inherit some of the characteristics of their parents, including a tendency to stay in the York area, they too cannot be regarded as representative. The figures given for the absolute incidence of deprivation should not therefore be regarded as estimates for the population as a whole.

Housing

The housing information collected by Rowntree consisted of the number of rooms, relative to the number of occupants, and whether or not there was a bathroom. The latter provides the first index of deprivation (I_1), although as we have just noted, nearly half the households suffered this disadvantage in 1950. Of the 1,317 parents for whom the information exists, 49.4 per cent did not have a bathroom.[2] Applying a similar 'absolute' standard in 1975–78, we have classified as deprived those without sole use of a bathroom and of an indoor toilet. Of the 1,377 children who can be classified, only 62 (4.5 per cent) are in this position.

The second housing indicator, I_2, is that of density of occupation, measured by the number of persons per room (excluding bathrooms and toilets). In 1951, the proportion of households living at a density of 1½ persons per room or higher was 5.1 per cent, but this had fallen considerably by 1971 (*Housing Policy Review*, 1977, Part I, p. 24). This standard was applied by Wedge and Prosser (1973). But as they point out, it is quite stringent, implying that a couple with four children might not be regarded as overcrowded even if there were only two bedrooms. *The Lambeth Inner Area Study* took the lower standard of one person per room. In our analysis we have taken a standard of 1.2 persons per room in 1975–78, and of 1.5 persons per room in 1950, these being broadly double the mean density (*Housing Policy Review*, 1977, Part I, Table I.16). The percentage classified as above this density in 1950 is 5.5 per cent and in 1975–78 is 3.6 per cent.

Income and earnings

The measurement of income in the two generations of the study is discussed extensively in Atkinson, Maynard and Trinder (1983). The indicator, I_3, employed here is based on the national assistance (in 1950) and supplementary benefit (in 1975–78) scale. In each case income net of tax and housing outlays is expressed as a percentage of the NA/SB scale (which varies with family composition). The cut-off applied is the NA/SB scale plus 40 per cent, as in Abel-Smith and Townsend (1965) and other studies. This indicator should be seen as a relative measure in that the scale has risen with incomes, and indeed the standard appears to be rather higher in relation to average incomes in 1975–78. The proportion below the NA scale plus 40 per cent in 1950 is 25.5 per cent; the corresponding proportion in 1975–78 is 23.3 per cent.

In the case of earnings, I_4, we confine attention to male heads of households (and in 1975–78 employees), and to those cases where we can calculate hourly earnings adjusted for age differences. The earnings figures are gross and relate to the last pay period; they are expressed as a percentage of the average earnings for men of that age, using data from the 1976 New Earnings Survey (see Atkinson, Maynard and Trinder, 1983, Ch. 7). As a definition of 'low pay', we have taken the bottom 20 per cent of the national distribution, it being assumed that the distribution in 1950 had the same shape as that in the 1968 New Earnings Survey (on the grounds that there appears to have been considerable stability in the overall distribution over this period).

Family status

The criterion applied by Wedge and Prosser for a 'vulnerable' family structure was that there should be a single parent or five or more children (in the nuclear family). This is the standard used for 1950; for 1975–78, we have defined a 'large' family to be four or more children. This indicator, I_5, takes account of changing family sizes over the generations, and in this sense should be seen as a relative measure. At the same time there has been an increase in the number of single-parent families. On our criterion there are in fact 5.4 per cent of families deprived in 1950 and 5.0 per cent in 1975–78.

Job instability (for families with a male head)

The Lambeth Inner Area Study measure of job instability was based on sickness or unemployment at time of interview, or four or more weeks off in the previous year, or on having had four or more employers in the previous five years. Our information for 1950 provides only current evidence, and the indicator, I_6, for the first generation has to be based on the receipt of state benefits. A family is considered deprived if they were receiving sickness benefit, unemployment benefit, national assistance, disability pension or war pension. For the 1,114 families with a male head in both generations, 40, or 3.6 per cent, fell into this category in the first generation.

For the second generation we collected rather more data on past sickness and unemployment. This means that, in addition to the measure just described based on receipt of benefits,[3] we could use in I_7 the replies to the question about unemployment or sickness experienced over the previous ten years. On this basis a family is classified in the deprived category where there has been at least one spell of unemployment or at least two prolonged spells of sickness in the past ten years. This led to a substantially higher proportion being classified as deprived: 23.6 per cent, compared with 3.8 per cent on the basis of the measure defined using receipt of benefits.

3   INTER-GENERATIONAL CONTINUITIES

In this section we consider the extent of continuity measured by each of the indicators taken separately; the extent of multiple deprivation is discussed in the next section.

We begin with housing deprivation measured by the 'absolute' standard of lack of sole use of bathroom (1950) or bathroom and toilet (1975–78). Excluding the 100 cases for which the information is missing in one or more generations, we have:

| | | 1950 | | | |
		With bathroom		Lack bathroom		Total
1975–78:	with bathroom/toilet	630	(96.9)	617	(95.4)	1,247
(% of column)	without one or other	20	(3.1)	30	(4.6)	50
	Total	650	(100.0)	647	(100.0)	1,297

From this it appears that the children of families without a bathroom in 1950 are somewhat more likely to be lacking in these facilities in 1975–78. The proportion of the children of non-deprived families in 1950 who lacked sole use of bathroom and indoor toilet was 3.1 per cent; the corresponding proportion for the children of families without a bathroom in 1950 was 4.6 per cent. The differential odds are 1.5:1.

The second housing measure is that based on density of occupation, where we have taken a 'relative' standard adjusted for shifts in the average level over the generation. Excluding the 154 cases for which information is missing, we have:

| | | 1950 density: | | | |
| | | | | greater or | | |
		less than 1.5		equal to 1.5		Total
1975–78:	less than 1.2	1,139	(97.1)	67	(95.7)	1,206
(% of column)	greater than or					
	equal to 1.2	34	(2.9)	3	(4.3)	37
	Total	1,173	(100.0)	70	(100.0)	1,243

Again the differential odds are 1.5:1 against the children from deprived families. It is however clear that little weight can be attached to a conclusion based on three cases – the difference is in effect one case. On the other hand, if we take the lower standard and define overcrowding as more than one person per room in 1975–78, as in the *Lambeth Study*, and as more than 1.2 persons in 1950, then 52/254 of the children of families overcrowded in 1950 are themselves in overcrowded conditions, compared with 116/821 of those from families which were living at lower densities. The differential odds are close to that for the more stringent standard: 1.45:1, and it would require 17 cases to be removed for this differential to be eliminated.

It is interesting to compare the continuity in these housing indicators with those for income measured by the NA/SB scale, and for low earnings. For the 1,181 cases which can be assessed, we have:

| | | 1950 Income in relation to NA scale: | | |
		<140%	140% or higher	Total
1975–78 income in relation to the SB scale: (% of column)	<140%	68 (24.8)	191 (21.5)	259
	140% or higher	206 (75.2)	699 (78.5)	905
	Total	274 (100.0)	890 (100.0)	1,164

Again, those from deprived families appear to face rather less favourable chances. The proportion of children below 140 per cent of the SB scale is 24.8 per cent for those where the parents were below 140 per cent of NA, compared with 21.5 per cent for those whose parents were above. The differential odds are, however, smaller than those found for housing deprivation: 1.16:1. This does not seem to be particularly sensitive to small changes in numbers.

The evidence for earnings relates to those families where there was a male head in work in 1950 and a male head who was an employee in 1975–78. The numbers who were low paid according to the criterion of being in the bottom 20 per cent of the earnings distribution were:

| | | Fathers in 1950: | | |
		low-paid	not low-paid	Total
1975–78 sons or sons-in-law (% of column)	low-paid	126 (50.2)	123 (26.5)	249
	not low-paid	125 (49.8)	341 (73.5)	466
	Total	251	464	715

The extent of continuities appear here to be considerably greater. The proportion of children who are low-paid is 50 per cent for those whose fathers are low-paid, compared with 27 per cent for those not low-paid. The differential odds are now greater than for housing: 1.89:1.

When we turn to the other indicators of deprivation we find a rather different picture. The index based on large family size and single-parent families yields the result that deprivation measured this way is found to a greater extent among the families where the parents were *not* deprived in 1950, being 5.1 per cent compared with 3.9 per cent for those whose parents were in this category:

| | | 1950 family status: | | |
		Large family (5+) or single parent	Other	Total
1975–78:	large family (4+) or single parent	3 (3.9)	67 (5.1)	70
	Other	73 (96.1)	1,254 (94.9)	1,327
	Total	76	1,321	1,397

In this case the odds seem to favour those defined as 'deprived'. This finding has a number of possible explanations, but it should also be recognized that it represents a rather crude indicator of likely family stress. What is more, it is based on very small numbers. If ony one child from 'deprived' parents were reclassified as deprived, then the percentage would rise to 5.3 per cent, reversing the conclusion.

The same emerges when we consider receipt of state benefit as an indicator of job instability. The proportion is 3.8 per cent for the children of those not deprived in 1950, compared with 2.5 per cent for those classified as deprived, but in the latter case the absolute number is only one (see the figures below). If there had been two, then the percentage would have risen to 5 per cent, giving a differential disadvantage similar to that found for income. It does not seem possible to base any definite conclusions on these small numbers.

When we turn to the alternative measure of deprivation for 1975–78, based on history of unemployment and sickness, this indicates that the percentages are very close: 23.6 per cent for the children of non-deprived families, against 22.5 per cent for those from 'deprived'. Again, the comparison may be sensitive to the small changes: a switch of one could raise the latter proportion to 25 per cent[4]:

| | | 1950 job status (according to benefits): | | |
		Receiving benefits	Not receiving benefits	Total
1975–78:	receiving benefit	1 (2.5)	41 (3.8)	42
(% of column)	not receiving benefit	39 (97.5)	1,033 (96.2)	1,072
	Total	40 (100.0)	1,074 (100.0)	1,114
1975–78: (% of column)	previous unemployment or sickness (more than one spell)	9 (22.5)	254 (23.6)	263
	not (ditto)	31 (77.5)	820 (76.4)	851
	Total	40 (100.0)	1,074 (100.0)	1,114

Note: Sample is that with male heads of household in both generations.

4   MULTIPLE DEPRIVATION

To look at multiple deprivation within each generation, we have taken three representative indicators which cover the whole sample (i.e. are not confined to the working population). These are the absolute housing indicator, I_1, the level of incomes in relation to national assistance/supplementary benefit, I_3, and family status, I_5.

In the upper part of Table 5.1 we show the joint distribution of these three indicators for 1,314 cases in the first generation who can be classified (for 80 cases information is lacking on housing and for three an NA assessment).[5] In order to assess the results, it may be helpful to calculate the numbers expected to exhibit multiple deprivation if the probabilities were independent. Thus 49.3 per cent have no bathroom and 26.1 per cent were below 140 per cent of the NA scale. If these were independent, we would expect to observe 12.9 per cent with both features – or 169 out of 1,314. In fact we observe 190, so that there does appear to be overlap. The corresponding calculations for other combinations are:

	Expected if independent	Actual
Deprived according to:		
housing, family status	35	18
family status, income	18	25
all three	9	8

These suggest that family status and income go in the same direction, with some degree of overlap, but that the reverse is true for housing and family status. The same applies to deprivation on all three indicators, although the small numbers mean that little weight can be attached to this finding.

Table 5.1 Extent of overlap of deprivation

	Deprived according to family status:		Not deprived according to family status:		
	deprived housing	not deprived housing	deprived housing	not deprived housing	Total
1950 families					
Deprived income	8	17	182	136	343
Not deprived income	10	35	448	478	971
Total	18	52	630	614	1,314
1975–78 families					
Deprived income	1	46	15	196	258
Not deprived income	1	17	34	851	903
Total	2	63	49	1,047	1,161

The lower part of Table 5.1 shows the same information for the 1975–78 families. Again we may compare the number with multiple deprivations with the number expected on the basis of independence:

	Expected if independent	Actual
Deprived according to:		
housing, income	11.3	15
housing, family status	2.9	2
family status, income	14.4	47
all three	0.6	1

Again little weight can be attached to the last line, the numbers being even smaller in this case. The results for the pairwise combinations are similar to those for 1950, the association for family status and income being rather stronger.

5 CONCLUSIONS

The main aim of this chapter has been to examine the extent to which deprivation, according to different indicators, is associated across generations. In pursuit of this aim, we have concentrated on those indicators which can be constructed using the information available for the first generation in our study – that collected by Rowntree in 1950. This constrained the analysis quite significantly, and a study focusing on the 1975–78 generation alone could draw on a wider range of indicators. The 1950 evidence is also restrictive in that the numbers involved are relatively small, and this has qualified the conclusions which can be drawn at a number of points. We have also emphasized that the data must be treated with circumspection.

With these qualifications in mind, we may summarize the conclusions regarding the degree of association across generations:

			Differential odds against children from deprived families	Sensitive to small numbers
I_1	Housing (amenities)	absolute indicator	1.5:1	No
I_2	Housing (density)	relative indicator	1.45:1	No
I_3	Income	relative indicator	1.16:1	No
I_4	Earnings	relative indicator	1.89:1	No
I_5	Family status	relative indicator	0.77:1	Yes
I_6	Job instability (benefit receipt)	absolute indicator	0.66:1	Yes
I_7	Job instability (off work)	absolute indicator	0.95:1	Yes

If any weight can be attached to the last three indicators, which is debatable in the light of the sensitivity of the conclusions to the small numbers involved, then they indicate that there is no positive association, in contrast to housing, earnings and – to a lesser extent – income.

The extent of overlap of disadvantage in a single generation has not been the major focus, but it appears that such overlap exists for housing and income, and for family status and income. The extent of overlap is perhaps less than found, for example, by Wedge and Prosser (1973),[6] but it must be remembered that our sample is much more heterogeneous, covering not just families with children but respondents from 18 to 80.

NOTES

1. In terms of Atkinson, Maynard and Trinder (1983), Chapter 10, this is the sub-samples A and C, but it includes those where the supplementary benefit assessment is not known. In addition, our survey is in part based on a 10 per cent sub-sample; this has been grossed up in the figures reported here.
2. As is explained in Chapter 4, only some two-thirds of the original Rowntree questionnaires still exist; and our re-analysis is based on these. The two-thirds appear to be reasonably representative when compared with the figures in the published report (Rowntree and Lavers, 1951). For example the proportion without bathrooms in the full survey was 48.5 per cent.
3. For 1975–78 we added invalidity benefit to the list.
4. A switch of one from the non-deprived group could only raise the percentage by 0.1 per cent.
5. It should be remembered that a 1950 family is given a weight equal to the number of children included in the follow-up study.
6. In their case the expected proportion with both low income and poor housing is 3.2 per cent on the basis of independence (p. 17); the number with both disadvantages exceeds 6.2 per cent.

6 · POVERTY, UNEMPLOYMENT AND THE FUTURE

In the course of the chapter, I intend to address two main questions. First, what are the implications of the current recession in the labour market for the extent of poverty? In this, I shall be looking particularly at what has happened in the UK, notably since Mrs Thatcher's government took office. What are the mechanisms relating unemployment and poverty? The second question concerns the prospects for the future. Here I shall consider the role of unemployment and employment, and of other important social forces, for the war on poverty. In looking into the future, one is not simply predicting what will happen as the result of unavoidable forces, but also considering what choices there are to be made. I shall argue that there are two different routes which could be followed, both of which could be consistent with the abolition of poverty, but which carry with them important implications, which governments may not find it easy to accept. Before embarking on these two questions, I should emphasize that I am in this chapter concerned principally with the UK, with some glances at the US. This qualification is an important one, since the experience and history of countries is very different. There is a school of thought, especially strong among economists and even more so among US economists, that one can apply the same analysis to all countries. This new form of Anglo-Saxon imperialisam may lead to quite misleading conclusions.

I should also at the outset comment on the interpretation of the term 'poverty'. The meaning of poverty has been much debated and I do not intend to enter into a lengthy discussion here of the concepts involved. I shall be concerned solely with poverty in advanced countries – an important qualification – and I shall in large part take at face value the definitions which have been employed by those studying poverty, in particular the definitions used in the official analyses of poverty in Britain and the US. But there is one conceptual aspect which should be stressed (and which is discussed in Chapter 2). This is the distinction between those who see poverty as concerned with securing a *minimum standard of living* – that is, ensuring access to a minimum level of consumption – and those who are concerned with the *right to a minimum level of resources* – that is,

---

First P. W. Segers Lecture at the University of St Ignatius, Antwerp, 1985.

guaranteeing the right of all citizens to a minimum income, the disposal of which is a matter for them. The difference between these two approaches is important since, in my judgement, there has been a shift in emphasis from viewing poverty in terms of living standards to viewing poverty in terms of minimum rights. For instance, in 1936 Rowntree (1941) could define a poverty line which gave a single woman 18 per cent less than a single man, based on his notion of consumption requirements, but that would scarcely be accepted today, when equal treatment for men and women would generally be regarded as a right.

1   POVERTY AND THE RECESSION

What we would expect – lessons from prewar and from the US

In the five years after 1979, unemployment in the UK, measured according to the OECD statistics rose from 5½ per cent to over 13 per cent (OECD, 1984, Table R12). This nearly 8 percentage point rise has taken the UK well above the OECD average, and brings it to a level reminiscent of the interwar period.

The experience of the 1920s and 1930s leads us to expect that such a rise in unemployment would have led to increased poverty. When Beveridge was writing his report of 1942, he drew on the social surveys which had been carried out in York, London and other towns, which showed the importance of unemployment. Thus, for example, Bowley, and Hogg (1925) concluded in 1924 that if all those workers usually capable of work had been receiving their normal wage, then measured poverty would have been almost halved. The studies by Bowley and others contain a wealth of material and any simple summary is bound to be misleading, but drawing on several of them I have made the approximate calculation that a fall of 1 per cent in the unemployment rate would be associated with a fall of about 5 per cent in the recorded poverty rate.

What this kind of hypothetical calculation shows is the effect of recorded unemployment. This is however only one of several possible mechanisms at work. Recession in the labour market has at least the following effects:

1. More people unemployed.
2. Lower earnings for those at work.
3. Fewer people in the labour force.
4. Changes in living arrangements.

All of these may affect the relationship between recession and poverty. It may be that those in work are getting below-normal wages or that they are forced to accept jobs of a poorer type. It may not just be that the head of the family is unemployed but also that the spouse is discouraged from entering the labour force, so that this source of income is also lost. It may be that people, particularly young people, if they cannot find a job are forced to continue living at home, so as to share in their family's income. What we may call the direct effect of unemployment may only be part of the picture.

If we turn for a moment to the US, we can see that it is the total effect of unemployment which is picked up in the aggregate time-series analyses of the relationship between poverty and macro-variables. One recent study is that by Blank and Blinder (1986), using data for the postwar period (from 1959 to 1983), which estimated that the immediate effect of a 1 per cent rise in the unemployment rate was again approximately an increase in poverty of 5 per cent but that the long-run effect was half as large again. This evidence is interesting in that it takes explicit account of the dynamics. A person who has been unemployed for a relatively short period may not immediately fall below the poverty line, but as benefits are exhausted his position becomes more precarious. It is not just the rise in unemployment which is of concern but also the prospect that it will continue for a decade or more. In this respect, the US, where the old-fashioned business cycle appears to be alive and well, may not be a good guide to what is likely to happen in the prolonged depression of the UK and other European countries.

We have indeed to bear in mind the possibility that high unemployment may leave its scar for many years. Teenagers unable to obtain apprenticeships when they entered the labour force may have low skills and low wages for their entire working lives. On a human capital view of earnings determination, the loss of work experience on its own will reduce earnings for many years. Moreover, the impact of the recession may increasingly show up in increased poverty in old age, and not just among those of working age. Those unemployed in their prime working years may not be able to save to provide adequately for their retirement.

What has happened? The UK in the 1980s

What can we say about the way in which the recession of the 1980s has hit the poor in Britain? Unfortunately, the answer we can give is only a limited one and much of the evidence is piecemeal. The poverty statistics in the UK are in no sense comparable with those in the US. Indeed, in some respects, the information we have today lags behind that which could be obtained from the sample surveys of the 1920s and 1930s (see Chapter 3). The main source of information is the official series for the number of people estimated to live in families with incomes below the supplementary benefit level, or within 40 per cent of it. Supplementary benefit is the income floor of the social security system so that it has the virtue of being also a measure of performance for the social security safety net. On the other hand, it has a number of disadvantages as a measure of poverty.

What is more, one of the decisions of the Conservative government was to cut down on official statistics, and the estimates are now only produced every other year, with the result that the most recent figures are those for 1981. Harold Macmillan once referred to the problems of economic policy-making with out-of-date statistics as like trying to plan a journey with last year's rail timetable; in the case of social policy it appears that the government feels that the timetable from four years ago is quite adequate. From our standpoint, it is particularly a matter for concern, since if unemployment rose 5 per cent between 1979 and 1981, it has risen a further 3 per cent since then.

Taking the official poverty figures at face value, they do indeed show a rise between the 1970s and 1981. The percentage of persons below the SB level was 4 per cent in 1979, but 5.3 per cent in 1981. If we take the more extensive measures which includes those dependent on SB and those on the 'margins' of poverty (less than 40 per cent above the SB scale), then the figure was 21.9 per cent in 1979 and has risen to 28.1 per cent. On the basis of these figures, the prediction that a change in unemployment of 5 per cent would lead to a change in measured poverty of around a quarter (5 per cent for each 1 per cent extra unemployed) does not seem wide of the mark.

Behind the figures

What lies behind these figures? What evidence can we adduce to check that their story is a consistent one? Let us take in turn the four factors outlined earlier.

First, the effect of higher unemployment directly. The consequences for family incomes depends on the replacement rate, that is the ratio.

$$\frac{\text{Benefits} + \text{Other income}}{\text{Earnings} + \text{Other income}}$$

Now it has been argued, particularly by those on the right, that the extent of replacement is much more generous than it was in the 1930s. To begin with, there is the postwar welfare state and the provision of national insurance unemployment benefits. Indeed, some people have suggested that benefits may exceed earnings. However, this argument is usually based on a reading of the rules of the benefits system rather than an analysis of the benefits actually paid. Anyone with experience of advising claimants, or working in welfare rights centres, knows that the reality is different from the hypothetical picture, and this is borne out by the evidence from sample surveys of actual benefit receipt (Atkinson and Micklewright, 1986). The comfortable view that replacement is close to 100 per cent is in fact a myth.

Indeed, the subject of income support for the unemployed is one where there is a great gap between myth and reality. Most people believe that the Beveridge Report brought about significant changes for the unemployed along with other groups. In fact the system we have today is essentially the same as that introduced in 1934 and the recommendations for change in the Beveridge Report were not heeded. In particular, we have a two-tier system, with insurance benefit for some and then a means-tested benefit for the others. The others are now a majority, since only 1 in 3 of the unemployed are (in 1985) in receipt of insurance benefit. In some cases, they have never been eligible (for example because they have not worked for long enough), but in the majority of cases they have exhausted entitlement, which is a year at the maximum. This problem has worsened in that unemployment is increasingly of long duration. In 1979, about a quarter of the unemployed had been out of work for more than a year, in itself a seriously high proportion, but in 1985 it was about 40 per cent.

The situation where only a third get insurance benefit, and the remainder have to rely on supplementary benefit, is far removed from Beveridge's aim that there would be 'a weekly payment continued without means or needs test throughout working age' (Beveridge, 1942 p. 128). It is worrying for precisely the reason that he objected to the two-tier system. This is that the means-tested tier is regarded as stigmatizing, and that as a result a sizeable fraction do not claim. The stigma associated with income-testing appears to have persisted in that the recent estimates suggest that around a quarter of those eligible do not claim. This is a major source of poverty among the unemployed.

The second mechanism is that those who remain in work may have lower earnings opportunities. The impact of the recession may not simply be to make people unemployed: the structure of earnings may shift. For this to happen would be historically surprising. Until recently, one of the unexplained mysteries of the UK labour market was the apparent stability of the distribution of earnings. For example, the lowest decile for all adult full-time male workers was 65.7 per cent of the median in 1968 and was virtually the same (66 per cent) in 1979, despite income policies designed to redistribute towards the low paid and a fivefold increase in cash median earnings. But between 1979 and 1984 the lowest decile fell to 61.6 per cent of the median (Metcalf and Nickell, 1985). Put another way, if median real earnings inceased by some 5 per cent, then real earnings at the lowest decile fell by 2 per cent.

The third mechanism concerns the role of other earnings. Suppose that we consider first the position of the nuclear family. The fact that in two-earner couples earnings are shared is indeed some degree of insurance. We have however to consider the effect of the recession on the participation of the spouse. It is, of course, quite possible that there may be an added worker effect, with for example the wives of unemployed men seeking work to maintain family incomes. The evidence does not however suggest that this has been happening. One of the features of the recent years has been a decline in the activity rate, with early retirement and married women not returning to the labour force. Overall, between 1977 and 1984 the working population grew by 450,000 fewer than if the activity rates had been unchanged (Metcalf and Nickell 1985). If they had entered the labour force and become unemployed, then it would have added nearly 2 per cent to the unemployment rate. Whereas the participation rate for women had been rising up to 1979, it is now lower than it was then, unlike the significant increases recorded in most OECD countries.

What is more, the proportion working full-time has decreased. And when we narrow attention to the wives of the unemployed – there being as far as I know no evidence on the husbands of unemployed women – then the DHSS Cohort Study (1984) suggests that the wives of the unemployed are less likely than the average to be in work: a third rather than more than a half. Given the fact that a high proportion of the unemployed are means-tested on their benefits, there is clearly a sharp financial disincentive to work for their wives. The resulting poverty trap is a second powerful argument against heavy reliance on means-testing.

If we take the household as the unit, then the role of other earners may be important, particularly children living at home after they have reached the age of adulthood. One of the ways in which people can respond to worsening labour market prospects is by moving to live with others who are in work – it is in effect a form of job-sharing, although it may not always be by agreement. This is the fourth mechanism. The consequence for the incidence of measured poverty is that it is reduced, in that the person no longer has to pay independently for housing. But this has other costs. The burden of income support is in effect being borne by those in work, typically the parents. There has been a redistribution within the family. Also it is clear that it cannot be a permanent solution, and that it runs counter to the long-run trends towards greater independence.

2   THE FUTURE

I have tried to describe the current position, piecing together the evidence at our disposal. However, we know lamentably little, and in this respect the move to the second question – what we can forecast about the future – is an exercise different only in degree.

Future prospects

What does the future hold? First, seen from 1985, there is little realistic prospect of a sizeable reduction in the level of unemployment in the course of the 1980s, and there is going to be a rise in the number unemployed. Although there is some rotation, unemployment is random. (If it were random then all academics would be out of work one semester every 2½ years.) Lengthening duration is going to intensify the financial problems of the unemployed. What is more, the government is apparently planning changes in benefits which will transfer even greater weight to the second tier (see Chapter 8). Even if this allows them to improve the level of supplementary benefit, it will not overcome the fundamental problems with means-tested benefits as operated in the UK.

Second, the low-paid are going to be adversely affected by the proposed removal of minimum wage protection (the government plan to end ratification of the ILO convention). We have had such legislation since 1909 (in fact some of the first research at the LSE was into the sweated trades). It is possible that the abolition of the Wages Councils would improve the employment prospects of the adult low-paid, but the jobs created will not necessarily ensure that they are above the poverty line. The current minima are indeed low: some 44 per cent of the median wage, compared with 54 per cent for the SMIC in France (Bazen, 1984). A reduction in the number of the poor unemployed may only be achieved at the expense of an increase in the number of working poor.

The prospects for participation are also not good and again government policy is working in the opposite direction in important respects. For example, the reduction in state-provided services for the elderly or for the disabled means that more of the burden of caring falls on the relatives. This often means that the person providing the care, typically a woman, is unable to participate in the paid labour force.

Finally, the worsening housing situation, and changes in social security benefits for young people, will leave them more dependent on their parents. The long-term trend towards the greater independence of young people is being reversed – not by choice but by coercion.

Choices to be made

In considering the future it is easy to become depressed. In part such depression is rife because we have lost sight of the objectives we are trying to pursue. People are worried not just because of the future but because traditional goals seem to be discredited. In view of this I would like to suggest two possible directions in which we could aim.

The first is to restate the traditional goals, or what I believe to have been the dominant philosophy of the 1950s and 1960s. This sees work in a full-time job as being the basic source of income, and the problems of today as stemming from the absence of this opportunity for a significant number of people. A coherent policy is, on this approach, based on the guarantee of a job to all those able to work. This does not mean *any* job,

...1 respect, and which pays a guaranteed
...ssential prerequisite of this approach is that
... level of earnings. This can be achieved by a
...onal basis prescribed for employers and by the
...g employment at the minimum rate.

...obs guarantee would operate the social security
...plementary to the labour policy. Benefits would be
pr... ...urance basis, for those unable to work through sickness
or tem... ...mployment. (There would in addition be family benefits
to cover th... ...eds of children and pensions.) These benefits should be
non-means-tested, in view of the patent failures of income-testing as
operated in the UK, but they would be *categorical*. Benefits would be
conditional on availability for work, a condition which would have to be
administered and enforced.

The need for employment tests is seen by some as a serious disadvantage
of this approach, coupled with the fact that it assumes – or imposes – a
degree of uniformity on the working population. Everyone is guaranteed a
job – but also expected to take one. Moreover, it emphasizes paid
employment, and the position of people caring for children, or for the
elderly, is not easily accommodated. It forces dependence of wives on
husbands in a traditional family structure. These are some of the reasons
why a second approach has received increasing attention.

The second approach starts from the right to a basic income. Everyone,
regardless of their employment status, would receive a monthly benefit,
which is called the basic income guarantee. If they are in work, then they
continue to receive the benefit, but they pay tax on all their earnings. This
tax rate is likely to be high, and 50 per cent seems a reasonable working
hypothesis.

This approach has the merit of allowing for diversity. If people choose
not to work in the paid labour market, then they will still receive their basic
income. Wives would receive the income guarantee in their own right, and
there would be greater freedom about living arrangements. From the
standpoint of employers, if they wish to offer jobs with low wage rates,
then this would not imply that those choosing them would be in poverty.

The British government appears to favour this second approach, at least
as far as its labour market implications are concerned. The 1985 White
Paper on Employment (Department of Employment, 1985) identifies the
labour market as the 'weak link' and talks about the need for flexibility and
for people not to be prevented from 'pricing themselves into jobs'. But the
government does not seem to have accepted the corollary that if employment cannot guarantee the right to a basic minimum income, then this
becomes the responsibility of the state. The social security and tax systems
have to be reformed, in conjunction, to provide a basic minimum income

for all, including those in employment. And this responsibility has high costs, as my earlier reference to a 50 per cent tax rate demonstrates.

To sum up, there are two routes which could be followed in the search to secure the right of all citizens to a minimum level of resources. The first is to reaffirm the traditional goal of jobs for all, reinforced by minimum wages and complemented by social insurance. The second is to accept that the labour market has changed but to introduce a basic income guarantee for all. The choice is between the right to a job or the right to a basic income. Either would in my view be acceptable, but we must set one of them firmly as our objective if we are to defeat the problem of poverty.

PART II

SOCIAL INSURANCE AND SOCIAL ASSISTANCE

INTRODUCTION

'Social security' is a term which may be used either to denote an objective of government policy or to describe a set of policies. It is in the former sense that it has been applied in the context of developing countries by Drèze and Sen (1988), who point out that the lives of billions are not merely short, but:

> also full of uncertain horrors. An epidemic can wipe out a community, a famine can decimate a nation, unemployment can plunge masses into extreme deprivation, and insecurity, in general, plagues a large part of mankind with savage persistence. It is this general fragility, on top of chronic and predictable deprivations, that makes the need for social security so strong and palpable.
>
> (1988, p. 3)

There are many strategies that may be employed to improve the degree of such security, including asset redistribution, labour market interventions, agricultural reform, food programmes and public works. These go much wider than the set of policies which are usually included under the heading of 'social security' in industrialized countries. When, for example, the United States Department of Health and Human Services publishes its *Social Security Programs Throughout the World* it includes benefits for old age, invalidity and death, sickness, maternity, work injury, and unemployment and family allowances.

It is in the narrower sense of such cash transfer programmes that the term 'social security' is used in this book, and this needs to be borne in mind by the reader. It has also to be remembered that, while transfers are important instruments towards the provision of financial security, they also serve other functions. In addition to securing the living standards of the poor, social security may redistribute resources over the lifetime or within the family. It may be directed at providing insurance against risks, such as sickness or disability, for the population as a whole including those whose existence can in no sense be described as precarious. Some writers have indeed suggested that the case for social security can be made on efficiency as much as distributional reasons:

> The welfare state is much more than a safety net; it is justified not simply by any redistributive aims one may (or may not) have, but because it does things

which private markets for technical reasons either would not do at all, or would do inefficiently. We need a welfare state of some sort for efficiency reasons.

(Barr, 1987, p. 421)

Social security in developed countries typically combines three different elements: income-tested social assistance designed to relieve poverty, social insurance concerned with the provision of security and the spreading of income over the lifecycle, and categorical transfers directed at redistribution between specific groups. The first category is typified in Britain by income support, which traces a direct line of descent from the Elizabethan Poor Law, in France by the *minimum vieillesse*, and in the US by welfare. The second category is illustrated in Britain by national insurance pensions, unemployment benefit and invalidity benefit based on contributions, in France by a similar range of insurance benefits and in the US by OASDHI (Old-Age, Survivors, Disability and Health Insurance). The third category is illustrated by child benefit in Britain; in France, the *allocation familiale* is paid for the second and subsequent children; whereas in the United States there are no general cash benefits for children.

The differences in principle between these three forms of provision are examined in detail in Chapter 7, which is based on a lecture given at the University of Frankfurt in 1986. The chapter traces the historical evolution of the pattern of spending in Britain, showing how the proportion of benefit expenditure accounted for by social insurance increased over the first 40 years of this century. It was the intention of the Beveridge Report that this rise should continue, with basic benefits also growing, and the role of income-tested benefits declining. This has not happened, and, particularly since 1979, there has been a reversal of the historical pattern of development in Britain, with renewed importance of income-testing and cutbacks in social insurance. The chapter goes on to examine the arguments which might underlie such a shift in policy. Is income-tested assistance better targeted? Are there grounds for privatizing social insurance?

The impact of the changes in social security policy in Britain since 1979 on one particularly vulnerable group – the unemployed – is documented in Chapter 8. This lists no fewer than 38 significant changes which have been made to national insurance unemployment benefit and income-tested assistance to the unemployed, the great majority of which have been unfavourable. As result, the scope and effectiveness of unemployment insurance has been seriously curtailed, forcing greater dependence on income-tested assistance, which in turn has become less generous. Some of the changes affected relatively small numbers of people, but the cumulative effect is considerable.

One of the factors which has led to cuts in social security benefits in Britain and other industrialized countries has been the belief that unemployment insurance is one of the causes of unemployment. Those seeking to explain the high unemployment of the 1980s by supply-side considerations have seized on the possible disincentive effects of social security payments. There has been a large literature on this issue, containing a great deal of interesting empirical analysis, much of it involving imaginative use of data, particularly at the micro-economic level, and the development of econometric techniques which allow in sophisticated ways for the subtleties of the problem in hand. Chapter 9 represents one application of this approach, making use of cross-section data for the United Kingdom. Our particular concern is to draw attention to some of the difficulties in obtaining firm results; and we conclude that, while there may be a significant link between benefits and unemployment duration, it does not stand out clearly from the data.

More generally, the measurement of behavioural responses to social security is likely to pose problems. Results in other areas have often proved to be conflicting, even when authors use the source of data, since findings appear often to be highly sensitive to the specification of the behavioural model, to the way in which taxes and benefits are introduced, to the treatment of unobserved variables, and to the choice of sample. For example, Atkinson (1987, Table 5.1) lists seven studies of the effect of pensions on retirement in the US using the same basic source (the Longitudinal Retirement History Survey), of which four conclude that pensions have a significant influence on retirement, but three conclude that the effect is either statistically insignificant or economically unimportant.

Moreover, the interpretation of the results is open to question. For example, the samples studied are typically restricted to a sub-set of the population. This is illustrated by the US literature just cited on the effect of pensions on the date of retirement. If you are a white, married male in employment, then you stand a good chance of being included in the econometric analysis, but if you are black, or female or self-employed, then your retirement decision is much less likely to have been modelled. This severely limits the extent to which the conclusions can be extrapolated to the population as a whole. A second example concerns the use of cross-section survey data, which has been the most active area of recent research. We observe differences in the behaviour of people with different, say, pension levels, but it is not clear what can be inferred from these cross-section differences, since we have to ask what generates the differences in pension levels, which may result from unobserved individual characteristics that are correlated with behaviour. And to the extent that the pension differences are exogenous, it does not follow that we can draw conclusions about what would happen if pensions were to be increased for everyone, since these depend on the general equilibrium of the economy, about which the empirical analysis may not be very informative.

It is for this kind of reason that, in an earlier review of the literature, I concluded, 'the great volume of empirical research in this field in the past decade has not led to robust or widely-accepted answers to the basic question as to how income support affects economic behaviour' (Atkinson, 1987a, p. 880). None the less, it must be recognized that the belief on the part of governments that disincentives are important has been a significant element in the policy debate.

In the current state of knowledge, behavioural responses cannot be incorporated routinely into the modelling of social security changes; for this reason, in our work on the ESRC Programme on Taxation, Incentives and the Distribution of Income we have tended to concentrate on illuminating the way in which the budget constraint is affected. This is the approach adopted to the discussion of the poverty trap in Chapter 10, which is an extract from evidence to a House of Commons Select Committee. The chapter emphasizes that the poverty trap may have several different dimensions, corresponding for example to different work decisions, quantifying their importance in 1980 and the degree to which they would be affected by changes in policy.

One theme which runs through Part II is a concern with the way in which institutions work, and the difference between the form and reality of social security. All too often economists study social security manuals and take for granted that the benefits actually paid correspond to what is prescribed in the legislation. In practice this is frequently not the case, with significant consequences, as illustrated in Chapter 9, where the results obtained using our alternative benefit variable, based on the worker's history, are noticeably different from those obtained assuming a standard benefit pattern.

The difference between form and reality is best exemplified by the problem of incomplete take-up of income-tested benefits, which is the subject of Chapters 11 and 12. The first of these reviews the evidence about take-up in Britain, considering one-parent benefit, family income supplement and supplementary benefit. The evidence about the latter two is particularly important, since the re-named versions of these schemes (they are Family Credit and Income Support, respectively, since April 1988) are central to the Conservative government's anti-poverty strategy. As was pointed out by the House of Commons Social Services Committee, the government was 'extraordinarily silent about take-up'. Certainly, the experience with family income supplement, assessed in Chapter 12, does not provide encouragement to the view that take-up can be radically increased to Sir Keith Joseph's (in itself inadequate) target of 85 per cent.

Low take-up has received particular attention in Britain, but there is evidence from other countries of this problem with income-tested benefits. In the United States, studies have been made of AFDC, of Supplemental Security Income for the aged, blind and disabled, and of food stamps (see Projector and Murray, 1978; Moffitt, 1983; Warlick, 1981; and

MacDonald, 1977). For West Germany, see Hauser *et al.*, 1981; and Hartmann, 1981.

On re-reading these chapters, two aspects seemed to me to be particularly in need of further development. The first is the relation between the design of social security and our view of how the labour market operates. As is noted in Chapter 7, the theoretical literature on tax and benefit structures typically takes no account of involuntary unemployment, of trade unions, of labour market segmentation, or other real-world features. This limits what can be said about the impact of social security. No account is taken, for instance, of the possibility that the existence of unemployment insurance may *encourage* employment in the modern (primary, in the terminology of Doeringer and Piore, 1971) sector of the economy. We cannot properly consider the role of minimum wage legislation or such issues as the role of work.

The second is the 'political economy' of social security. The political acceptability of social security programmes depends on the perceptions by the electorate of the benefits and costs. If, for example, universal schemes of social insurance benefits are seen to be of general benefit, then there may be a higher acceptable share of tax in the economy. Conversely, if the public scheme is seen to be inadequate, with private insurance being necessary to cover deficiencies in state provision, then this may lower the acceptability of taxation. The degree of acceptance may be influenced by the pattern of financing. The social security 'contributions' which individuals make to finance social insurance may have little actuarial relationship with the likely benefits. Instead, they are in reality a hypothecated part of direct taxation. None the less, because they are generally conceived to be a payment for a clearly defined benefit, contributions (and the transfers they fund) may be significantly more acceptable than if general taxation was used. Here, as with other aspects of social security and its financing, perception of how the system works may be more important than its actual functioning, and it is a subject about which firm evidence would be welcome. The same applies to the role of interest groups, where, for example, the 'middle-class capture' thesis of Le Grand and Winter (1987) argues that in Britain under the Thatcher Conservative government the programmes which have survived most successfully are those which have middle-class support, the middle classes being either beneficiaries or suppliers of services. These kinds of consideration must be of central importance to those who are concerned to design reforms of the social security system that can carry political support – the subject of Part III.

7 · SOCIAL INSURANCE AND INCOME MAINTENANCE

1 INTRODUCTION

Social insurance has been widely regarded as the cornerstone of modern income maintenance policy. In most OECD countries social insurance accounts for the greater part of government spending on social security, and it is seen as fundamental to the prevention of poverty. Yet social insurance has come increasingly under attack.

Major attacks have come from two different directions. First, there are those concerned that the present system of income maintenance is failing to provide adequate support to those with low incomes. For example, in the case of the elderly, it is argued that the social insurance system makes generous provision for the pensioners of the twenty-first century but still leaves many of today's old people below the poverty line. What is needed, on this view, is to replace social insurance by a *basic income guarantee* which provides benefits which are linked to old age and not to previous contribution conditions. This line of argument is often linked to a desire to integrate the social security and income tax systems, with attention being drawn to the fact that tax expenditures (e.g. on higher tax allowances for the aged) perform a similar function to that of social security benefits and that the money could be more effectively allocated in a unified system.

The second, quite different, direction of attack is from those, like the British Conservative government from 1979, aiming to reduce state expenditure on income maintenance. If there is a constraint on total government spending, then, it is argued, *income-tested benefits* provide 'better value for money', targeting the payments to those most in need. Similarly, state expenditure could be reduced if social insurance were to be replaced by *private insurance*. Such a switch to private provision would, it is suggested, offer people greater choice and freedom, and provide benefits more efficiently. This is therefore a twin-pronged attack, with both

An earlier version of this chapter appeared as 'Sozialversicherung und Einkommenssicherung', in G. Rolf, P. B. Spahn and G. Wagner (eds), *Sozialvertrag und Sicherung* (Campus Verlag, Frankfurt, 1988). I am grateful to Bernd Spahn, who translated the paper into German and to Frank Cowell, David Piachaud, Jim Gordon, Julian Le Grand and Nick Stern, who provided most useful comments.

income-testing and privatization being advanced to ɪ
ance.

In this chapter, I first describe the essential feature o
of state income support: basic incomes, social insurance
private insurance) and income-tested assistance. The ɪ
chapter reviews the importance of these three methods i
over this century of the income maintenance system i
consider in sections 4–6 the arguments which can be advanced for and
against alternatives to social insurance, considering in turn private insurance, a return to income-testing, and replacement of social insurance by a
basic income scheme.

2   DEFINITIONS

Basic incomes

The definition of a basic income scheme is the simplest. Each person would
receive a basic benefit which would be independent of income and
differentiated according to only a small number of categories. The
distinctions would include age, long-term disability and, possibly, householder status. They would *not* include employment status, the basic benefit
being paid at the same rate to those out of work through unemployment or
sickness as to those in work. It is typically envisaged that the introduction
of the basic benefit scheme would be accompanied by the abolition of tax
allowances. The basic benefits may indeed be seen as the 'cashing-out' of
tax allowances, in just the way that child benefit in the UK replaced both
an earlier social security benefit and income tax allowances for children.
All income apart from the basic benefits would then be subject to tax.

The relatively simple form of the basic benefit provides a benchmark
against which we can compare the two forms which have been used more
extensively in practice: social insurance and income-tested assistance.

Social insurance

Social insurance benefits are similar to basic incomes in that they are not in
general directly related to current income, but they differ in two significant
respects. First, they are usually related to employment status, the purpose
of the benefit being to replace (at least in part) lost earnings. Thus, the
national insurance pension in the UK is a *retirement* pension and (for
the first five years after the minimum retirement age) is conditional on
retirement. The national insurance benefits for contingencies such as
sickness and unemployment are *alternatives* to work income. The second
difference is that payment of benefits is typically linked in some way to
contributions paid (and may in this way be related to past income). Receipt

national insurance pension is conditional on having contributed a minimum period during one's working life; eligibility for NI unemployment benefit depends on previous work history.

This contributory feature brings us to the question of the relationship between private and social insurance, a matter about which there is disagreement. There are those who argue that social insurance is simply private insurance run by the state, and that therefore it could be just as well, or better, run as private insurance (arguments which are discussed in section 4). Others claim that social insurance is a myth and that replacement by income-tested or basic benefits would make no difference.

That social insurance is different in fundamental respects from private insurance was clearly recognized by Beveridge, who said early in his report *Social Insurance and Allied Services* (1942, pp. 12–13) that:

> while adjustment of premiums to risks is of the essence of voluntary insurance
> ... this adjustment is not essential in insurance which is made compulsory by
> the power of the State. . . .
> it is necessary in voluntary insurance to fund contributions. . . . The State with
> its power of compelling successive generations of citizens to become insured
> and its powers of taxation is not under the necessity of accumulating reserves.

That is, social insurance does not necessarily provide an actuarily fair return to each person and there does not have to be funding. As Beveridge observed, the second issue is one 'of financial practice only', an insight which does not seem to be shared by the British Conservative government. (At the same time as it is worrying about the burden of state pensions to future generations it is reducing the net worth of the public sector by selling public-sector assets to finance tax cuts.)

The first distinction – the departure from actuarily fair individual insurance – has two aspects. First, social insurance does not involve a strict matching of contributions and benefits. It may, for example, embody a degree of redistribution *ex ante*, with lower-paid workers obtaining a better deal than the higher-paid. Secondly, the contract may be less tightly drawn. A private-sector insurance policy specifies the contingencies and the benefits and these cannot in general be varied. A social insurance scheme has more flexibility. The government may vary the terms, eliminating or reducing benefits, or adding and improving them, particularly to cover needs which were not previously envisaged. Social insurance offers less certainty, but in recompense it offers the protection of what the French call 'solidarity', a term which was actually used in the Government White Paper on Social Insurance: 'concrete expression is thus given to the solidarity and unity of the nation' (Minister of Reconstruction, 1944, p. 6). Or, as it was put by Beveridge, 'the term social insurance . . . implies both that it is compulsory and that men stand together with their fellows' (1942, p. 13).

Income-tested assistance

Income-tested benefits may, like social insurance, be related to employment status. Thus Income Support in Britain provides for those not in employment; and, conversely, Family Credit is only paid to families in work. But, unlike social insurance, eligibility for assistance, and the amount received, are dependent on current income. Income Support provides for those whose income would otherwise fall below a prescribed level, the payment being sufficient to bring people up to this level. Family Credit is reduced by 70p for each £1 increase in net income above a specified threshold, until entitlement is lost altogether. Housing benefit depends on the amount of housing costs and on family income.

Now it may be argued that this dependence on income is in fact no different from the combination of basic benefit and the taxation of income. Both present the individual or family with a budget constraint, and in principle any such budget constraint may be represented by a basic benefit (intercept) and a tax schedule. Formally, this is correct, but it ignores the differences in the way in which the schedule is affected and perceived – by both government and the citizen. From the standpoint of the government, the basic income scheme presents a clear set of choices with regard to the generosity of benefits on the one hand, and the tax structure on the other. In contrast, discussion of income-tested schemes typically confounds the two aspects (as where variations in the levels of benefit change the marginal tax rates of recipients) and separates the treatment of rich and poor (implicit marginal tax rates are enacted for the poor which would not be acceptable under the income tax).

From the standpoint of the recipient, an important feature of income-tested benefits is that they involve a separate and distinct administrative procedure. Under income-tested assistance, the person has to make a claim and has to provide proof of income; under the basic income neither step would be required. Such a separate administrative machinery may be a regrettable necessity. If many of the intended beneficiaries do not file income tax returns, then information about their incomes may not be available centrally; nor could the government agency identify potential claimants and inform them of their rights. On the other hand, some advocates of income-testing see the separate administration as serving a positive function of deterring claimants, applying the principle of 'less eligibility'. These aspects are discussed in section 5.

3 THE UK EXPERIENCE

What role has been played at different times by these different types of benefit? An ILO Report on the development of social security described a stylized model of its historical evolution:

> First was an era of paternalism: private charity and public poor relief provided for the poor, being often subject to harsh conditions which imposed stigma. Second was an era of social insurance . . . wider compulsory programmes were developed covering more and more occupations and more and more contingencies. . . . In the third stage . . . the range of services is being extended with the aim of maintaining and enhancing the quality of life.
>
> (International Labour Office, 1984, p. 17

How far does such a pattern of development describe the history of the UK? As was noted by Beveridge, 'since the beginning of the present century . . . there has been a strong movement against the form and spirit of the old poor law' (1942, p. 211). In part, this move took the form of replacing the old poor law by more acceptable forms of income-testing. The Old Age Pensions Act 1908 provided old age pensions which were means-tested (and non-contributory) but destitution was not a condition. The Unemployment Act 1934 centralized the administration of assistance to the unemployed in the new Unemployment Assistance Board and the same body took over the payment of means-tested supplementary pensions under the Old Age and Widows' Pensions Act 1940.

But a major part of the change was the replacement of income-tested assistance by social insurance. The introduction of national insurance in the 1911 Act was the first step in Britain – long behind Bismarck's welfare system in Germany – towards replacing the poor law by contributory benefits. These covered unemployment (for certain trades) and sickness benefit administered by the approved friendly societies. The Contributory Pensions Act 1925 brought in contributory pensions of a non-means-tested kind and introduced widows' pensions.

As a result, the proportion of the benefit expenditure accounted for by social insurance increased over the first forty years of this century, as is shown in Figure 7.1, which is derived from the Beveridge Report. In 1900, public assistance accounted for almost all of the expenditure (apart from workmen's compensation). By the end of the period, it accounted for just 10 per cent. If we add the 'new' income-tested benefits of unemployment assistance, non-contributory pensions and blind persons' assistance, then the total reaches 32.6 per cent. The picture is one of a growth of social insurance and a decline of income-testing.

The intention of Beveridge was to take this further, extending the scope of national insurance and making its coverage universal. He stressed the 'strength of popular objection to any kind of means test' (1942, p. 12) and the aim of the Plan was to reduce dependence on assistance. At the same time, Beveridge saw as a precondition for the success of his Plan the introduction of a basic benefit for children – family allowances. So that for the first time, we had on a major scale a form of income support which was neither social insurance nor income-tested assistance (nor war-related).

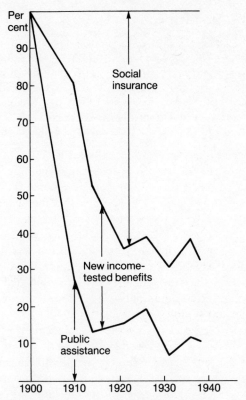

Figure 7.1 Share in social security spending 1900/1–1938/9

Source: Beveridge (1942), p. 214.

Note: The figures do not include war pensions, which I have classified as a basic benefit. These were at their highest after the First World War, when they amounted to £105 million (Peacock and Wiseman, 1967, p. 168). Adding the figures for 1921 to those used in Fig. 7.1 would have shown war pensions as accounting for 46.9 per cent of the total. By 1938, the expenditure had fallen to £39 million, and as a fraction of the total it was 14.3 per cent.

The government did not accept the Beveridge proposals in full, but the broad thrust of a move to non-means-tested benefits was agreed. This is brought out in the table in the 1944 White Paper *Social Insurance* which shows the estimated effects in 1945 of the post-Beveridge proposals (1944, Table V). The share of social insurance was to rise from 66.1 to 74.6 per cent, and the new family allowances would account for 11.9 per cent. As a result, means-tested benefits would fall from 33.9 to 13.5 per cent. Moreover, this fall was projected to continue to 1975, with social insurance accounting for 82 per cent in that year (1944, Table VI).

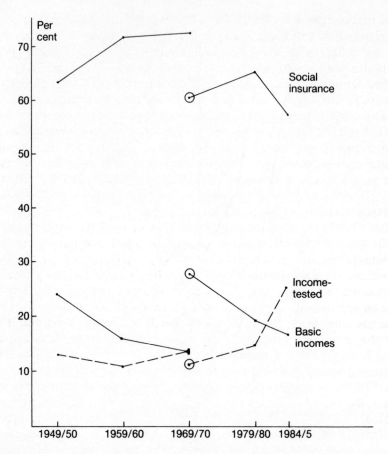

Figure 7.2 Share in total social security spending 1949/50–1984/5

Source: Department of Health and Social Security (1985a), Background Papers, HMSO, Cmnd 9519, Table 2.3, and own calculations.

Notes:
a. There is a break between the figures for 1969/70 and 1979/80 on account of the introduction of child benefit, which replaced both family allowances (previously included) and child income tax allowances (not previously included). The alternative figures for 1969/70 (circled) include estimates of the tax expenditure cost of child tax allowances based on that for 1968/9 (source: Walsh, 1972, p. 217). Other changes in the benefit structure have not been allowed for, but are smaller in magnitude.
b. The figures do not include rate rebates. If these were included, then the percentages for 1984/5 and 1979/80 would become 55.3 per cent and 65.0 per cent for social insurance, 28.3 per cent and 15.7 per cent for income-tested benefits and 16.4 per cent and 19.3 per cent for basic incomes. Figures for earlier years would be little changed. (Source: *The Government's Expenditure Plans 1985–86 to 1987–88*, Cmnd 9428–II, Tables 3.12 and 3.12.5).

The percentages in Figure 7.2 show what in fact happened. They are not fully comparable with those in Figure 7.1, nor with those just quoted, but they are sufficient to show that what transpired, even during the first twenty-five years up to 1969/70, was not entirely according to script. Basic benefits did indeed become sizeable at the outset, but fell over time as a percentage; this was due to the fact that family allowances failed to rise in line with other benefits (and to the reduced importance of war pensions, included under this head, as time went on). There was some expansion of social insurance, as more pensioners became eligible, but the role of national assistance, the means-tested scheme, did not die away. In 1949 there were 1.1 million payments being made each week; in 1969/70 there were 2.7 million. As a percentage of the total expenditure, national assistance increased, rather than fell.

After 1969/70 several things happened. One was that the switch to child benefit made the figures no longer comparable, since a major part of the expenditure on the new child benefit was a cashing out of the tax expenditure on child tax allowances. The latter not being public expenditure was not included in the social security figures. For this reason I have made an approximate estimate of the figure for 1969/70 including the cost of the tax allowances; this is shown by the circled points. From this it is clear that it would be misleading to regard the figures as a continuous series. Taking the circled points and then those for 1979/80, we can see that the gradual upward trend in income-tested benefits became quite marked after 1979/80, when Mrs Thatcher took office. Basic benefits declined, despite the introduction in the 1970s of several new benefits for the disabled, such as the attendance allowance, the mobility allowance and the severe disablement allowance. What is more, after 1979/80 social insurance too began to decline, the rate of fall being quite steep.

What we are witnessing therefore is the reversal of the historical trend. The pattern of social security development in the UK is not moving on to a third stage, but is regressing to the first stage of income-tested assistance.

This regression has taken two main forms. The first is the introduction of new income-tested benefits. The family income supplement (now Family Credit) was a new income-tested benefit introduced in 1971. Rate rebates were brought in in 1966 and substantially extended in 1974. Rent rebates had been available to local authority tenants for many years, but were extended to other tenants in 1973, and the scheme made universal, so that the numbers in receipt increased very greatly. The second form of regression has been the greater reliance on existing income-tested benefits, notably supplementary benefit and Income Support, the successive renamings of national assistance. The restrictions on national insurance benefits, and the abolition of earnings-related supplements to unemployment and sickness benefits – together with the rise in unemployment – have meant that more families have had to rely on income-tested assistance.

This process was further accelerated by the changes in policy following the 1985 review of social security (Department of Health and Social Security, 1985a and b), which has set the course firmly in the direction of greater means-testing. This affects people from cradle to grave. At birth, the universal maternity grant has been abolished and payments made only to low-income families via the Social Fund. For children, from 1988 the income-tested benefit has been extended and renamed Family Credit. The state earnings-related pension scheme, introduced in 1978 with the intention of reducing dependence on income-tested assistance in old age (see Chapter 13), has been scaled down: for example, the additional pension is calculated on 20 rather than 25 per cent of average earnings, and the average is to be taken over the whole of the lifetime rather than the best 20 years. Widows and widowers are to inherit only half of their spouse's pension. The universal death grant has been replaced by payments restricted to those with low incomes.

Finally, the government has also moved further in the direction of *private* as opposed to state pension provision. The scaling down of the state earnings-related pension scheme, for example, has been accompanied by fiscal and other incentives provided to encourage private provision. Similarly, there has been a transfer to employers of the obligation to pay sick pay for the first 28 weeks of illness and to provide maternity pay.

4   ALTERNATIVES TO SOCIAL INSURANCE: (I) PRIVATE INSURANCE

This brings me to the first of the comparisons I want to make – that between social and private insurance. There are, of course, many more issues here than I can possibly cover in this chapter. Part of the message is indeed that the questions are more complex than they are sometimes portrayed. (For discussion of some of the issues not covered here, see, among others, Diamond, 1977; and Creedy and Disney, 1985.)

One of the sources of complexity is that the contingencies covered by social insurance are very varied. This should be borne in mind when considering the simple example chosen to illustrate the analysis. This is the case of sickness, where a worker has a probability p of being unable through illness to work and a probability $(1 - p)$ that he earns a wage w. In both cases he receives income from capital equal to k. We abstract from moral hazard considerations by assuming that malingering is not possible (this may involve administrative costs which I shall come to). Sickness insurance is represented as the person receiving $w(1-\varrho) + k$ if well, where ϱ is the premium rate and $b + k$ if sick, where b is the benefit rate net of the premium. The purpose of taking this highly stylized example is to illustrate some of the issues involved; it is however evident that many important considerations are not captured by its assumptions.

We can plot the incomes in the two states ('work' and 'sickness') in a diagram (Figure 7.3). Starting from the no-insurance point (giving $w + k$ in work and k in sickness), if the insurance is actuarily fair, and there are no administrative costs, then $(1-p)\varrho w = pb$ and insurance allows the person to move along the dotted line with slope $-p / (1-p)$. How much insurance people would buy depends on their preferences. Suppose that people are expected utility maximizers and that the utility of income is the same in both states: i.e. they maximize

$$(1-p) U[w(1-\varrho)+k] + p U[b+k]$$

If the person is risk-averse (i.e. U is strictly concave), then the point chosen will be F on the 45° line, giving full insurance, and this will be true regardless of the precise form of U (for all U the slope of the indifference curve is $-p / (1-p)$ on the 45° line).

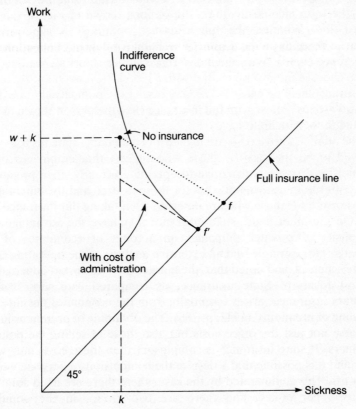

Figure 7.3 Insurance against sickness example

The basis for the argument in favour of privatization of insurance has not always been made fully explicit, particularly the extent of its reliance on the theorems of welfare economics. If the latter are indeed the basis, then the argument is that market competition leads to a Pareto-efficient allocation, an allocation in which it is not possible to make someone better off without making someone else worse off, and government intervention is only justifiable on distributional grounds. One suspects, however, that the case for privatization often has a less 'sophisticated' foundation, resting for example on the view that private companies would be better organized and have lower administrative costs. Or it may be the diversity of choice which is important, such diversity being valued in itself even where there is no gain in allocational efficiency.

The case in terms of administrative costs is important. Even though these considerations are usually ignored in economic analysis, they may be quantitatively as important as the deadweight loss and other elements on which public economics tends to focus. Suppose that there is a fixed cost per policy, denoted by a, collected by deducting a/p from the benefit paid. Then the insurance cover offers the options shown in Figure 7.3 by the dashed line. Whether the full insurance option f' is superior to no insurance depends on the degree of aversion (or degree of curvature of the indifference curve). With the indifference curves shown in Figure 7.3, the person chooses full insurance, but with a less risk-averse set of preferences no insurance may be chosen. We may expect the population to be divided into two groups – those with full insurance (like the person shown in Figure 7.3) and those with none.

If the administrative costs are higher for (voluntary) state insurance, as is believed to be the case by those who suggest that employees of state organizations have less incentive to operate efficiently, then privatization would offer both a saving of costs for those insured and the elimination of the distortion for those who are deterred from taking out insurance by the cost. On the other hand, state insurance may have the advantage over a multiplicity of private companies on account of economies of scale. Beveridge, for example, did an extensive analysis of the operating costs of private schemes, and noted that 'the markedly lower cost of administration in most forms of State insurance, as compared with most forms of voluntary insurance, arises essentially from the economies possible in the obtaining of premiums' (1942, p. 286). The obtaining of premiums includes of course not just the office costs but also those of selling the policies to customers. If state insurance is compulsory then these costs may well be lower and it is possible that – despite the compulsion – everyone would be better off. This is illustrated by the case where there are fixed administrative costs per policy, and there are two groups in the population, characterized by different attitudes towards risk. Suppose that the administrative cost of private insurance is such that the less risk-averse would prefer to opt out, but that the administrative costs of the state scheme are sufficiently lower that they would choose voluntarily to join the scheme. Social insurance could then raise the welfare of all.

The argument regarding diversity may take as its starting point the differences in preferences which we have noted. In our sickness example, suppose that people are identical in all respects except for their attitude towards risk (captured in the diagram by the shape of the indifference curves). They have the same asset income, and the same probability of sickness. Then if state sickness insurance is compulsory, involving full insurance for all, whereas private insurance allows people to opt out, then the latter would offer a freedom of choice which the state sector does not. The value of this extra choice depends on the extent of diversity of preferences, as has been pointed out in a different context by Weitzman (1977). If preferences are sufficiently concentrated that all prefer full insurance, then there will be no loss from compulsion.

Diversity may however refer to the number of suppliers from whom one can choose. Here it is typically taken for granted that a market system has the edge. This however fails to consider whether perfect competition is sustainable in the insurance market, an issue which has been addressed in the work of Rothschild and Stiglitz (1976), Riley (1975) and others (and which brings us back to the welfare economics theorems). To see the difficulties that may arise, suppose that people are identical in all respects except their risk of sickness, there being two classes of people with probabilities p^+ and p^- respectively, where $p^+ > p^-$. The indifference curves of the two types are shown in Figure 7.4. The absolute magnitude of the slope at any point is greater for the high-risk class, as is illustrated at the point B. This point lies on the dashed line AD which shows the locus of contracts which would break even if the whole population purchased insurance (the slope depends on the probabilities p^+ and p^- and on the proportion of the two groups in the population). The line AC^+ shows the locus of contracts which would break even if only the high-risk purchase insurance and AC^- those if only the low-risk purchase. (A 'contract' is a point in the diagram, offering a pair of incomes in the two states.)

The problem is that although individuals know to which group they belong, an insurance company cannot identify the riskiness of any individual customer. This imperfect information leads to problems of non-existence of competitive equilibrium, where an equilibrium is defined as a set of insurance contracts, such that no other contract exists which, if offered, would make a profit. Suppose in our example that the companies offer a contract if it makes a positive profit, and that they assume that their actions have no influence on the contracts offered by others. The equilibrium could consist of a state where all purchase the same contract, along AD. But at a point such as B, it is clear that a contract in the shaded area will attract the low-risk individuals (and not the high-risk individuals) and

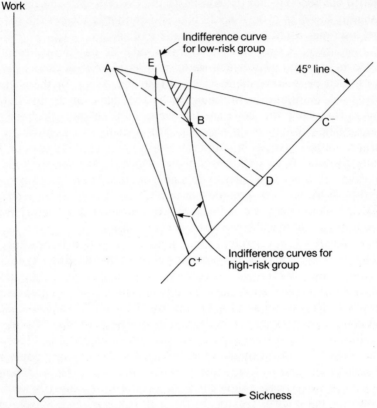

Figure 7.4 Equilibrium in the perfectly competitive insurance market?

be profitable. A 'pooling equilibrium' cannot therefore be stable. The alternative is a 'separating equilibrium' with the high-risk group offered a contract along AC^+ and the low-risk along AC^-. But the latter contract must lie on the section AE, since otherwise the high-risk group would be attracted. This however means that a contract along AD, such as that at B, would be attractive to the low-risk group, who would like to obtain more insurance than can be offered at E, and be profitable.

With this kind of adverse selection in the insurance market, a competitive equilibrium, in the sense defined, may not exist. It is possible to define alternative equilibrium concepts which ensure existence (see, for example, Wilson, 1977; and Riley, 1979), but these do not seem a natural interpretation of what is involved in perfect competition. (It is also possible to consider an equilibrium in 'mixed strategies' – see Dasgupta and Maskin, 1986.) The central message is in fact that the market for insurance is unlikely to be perfectly competitive; and that one cannot make any straightforward statement about there being a large number of suppliers.

By the same token, there can be no simple appeal to the First Theorem of Welfare Economics; there is no guarantee that the market outcome will be Pareto-efficient. As is widely recognized by economic theorists, but less so by practitioners, the conditions for market competition to lead to a Pareto-efficient allocation are restrictive, including the existence of a full set of markets and perfect information. These are unlikely to be satisfied in reality, and their breakdown – in this case the absence of full information – brings into question the performance of the private alternative. (I have not discussed other problems, such as moral hazard, which affect the working of insurance markets – see Barr, 1987, Chapter 5).

Before leaving the welfare economic argument, we should note that the model used here remains within the Arrow–Debreu framework in that it is concerned with *risk* rather than *uncertainty*, using the latter term in the sense of Knight (1921). The insurance is against a well-defined contingency, about which individuals can form probabilities. As suggested earlier, much of the function of social insurance is to provide for contingencies which are unforeseen and to allay fears about events which we cannot forecast. Looking backwards, it is hard to imagine that individuals could have taken out insurance to cover such events as the 1974 fuel price rise, the development of new surgical techniques, or the breakdown of the extended family. A looser form of contract, as with social insurance, may in this respect have significant advantages.

The case for privatization whether in terms of administrative costs, diversity, or welfare economic efficiency, is therefore less straightforward than its proponents tend to suggest. Certainly it cannot be made simply by appeal to general principles. This does not, of course, mean that social insurance is necessarily preferable. What is needed is a careful evaluation of the relative performance of social and private insurance in particular contexts. This must be based on empirical evidence about such matters as the magnitude of administrative costs and the likely market structure. What is important is that this comparison should be even-handed, unlike the British government's analysis behind the *The Reform of Social Security* (Department of Health and Social Security, 1985a and b), which scrutinized the state pension system but failed to investigate in any systematic manner the shortcomings of private provision.

We should however recognize that the economic arguments with regard to private insurance versus state income support are only part of the picture. The detailed weighing of the merits and demerits of the two systems may indeed be regarded as quite irrelevant by some, such as those who attach prior importance to the avoidance of individual coercion. As has been articulated by Nozick (1974), consideration of the end-states may have no role in the judgement; it is the means by which they are brought about that is the sole concern. Providing that individual rights have been acquired in a just manner, and are transferred according to just principles, then justifiable state intervention, according to Nozick, is limited to the prevention of violence, fraud and theft, and the enforcement of contracts. State compulsory insurance, on this view, is a violation of individual liberty, and as such unjustifiable. Social insurance would be rejected even if it could be shown to make everyone better off.

This is an example of the wider social and political factors which may dominate any decision. Although the British government's case for extending private pensions has been couched in terms of economic benefits and individual choice, it seems probable that a more basic political preference for private provision is the main factor underlying their policy.

5 ALTERNATIVES TO SOCIAL INSURANCE: (II) RETURN TO INCOME-TESTING

We turn now to the consideration of alternative forms of state income support. As we have seen in section 3, there was a historical pattern of development by which earlier means-tested programmes were supplanted by the introduction and expansion of social insurance, but that this has tended to be reversed in recent years in Britain.

The case for such a reversal of the historical trend is often made in terms of the 'target efficiency' of benefits in combating poverty, or the concentration of benefits on those with low income. The Institute for Fiscal Studies in presenting their proposed reform of social security argued that 'if our principal objective is to boost low incomes to an acceptable level, this could be done much more cheaply, and/or we could afford to be considerably more generous to the poor, if payments to those who do not strictly "need" the money were curtailed' (Dilnot, Kay and Morris, 1984, p. 55).

The issue concerns in part the shape of the budget constraint. The provision of a uniform benefit shifts the constraint in a parallel manner, leaving the marginal tax rate zero below the tax threshold. The introduction of income-testing, with a rate of withdrawal t, tapers the benefit and makes the marginal tax rate t up to the point where the benefit is totally withdrawn. In order to explore the implications in the context of the sickness example, let us suppose that there is no private insurance and simply a state benefit, at rate b, financed by a tax on those in work at rate ϱ. People are now assumed to be identical in all respects apart from their income from savings, denoted by k. Should the state benefit be income-related, in the sense that the amount paid becomes $b - tk$, falling to zero if $b \leq tk$? If the government is assumed to maximize the integral of expected utilities subject to a revenue constraint, the revenue released by income-testing being used to raise the level of benefit (the contribution rate ϱ is taken as fixed), then, not surprisingly, the introduction of income-testing raises social welfare; and this continues until the withdrawal rate is set at

100 per cent, as with Income Support in Britain.

The argument against such a 100 per cent tax rate on benefits is o
We have taken no account of the disincentive to save which woul
generated. In order to allow for this, we need to extend the model to
incorporate the savings decision. The optimum choice of the rate of
withdrawal then involves balancing the efficiency costs of the savings
distortion against the gain from greater target efficiency. In general, the tax
rate t will be strictly positive, so that in this sense income-testing is
desirable; and it could still be that a 100 per cent rate of withdrawal is
optimal, even with a non-zero substitution elasticity for savings, since
savings would be taxed at 100 per cent only in the state of the world where
the person becomes sick.

It is in these terms that the public economics literature has tended to
approach the issue of income-testing, building on the literature on optimum taxation. For example, Kesselman and Garfinkel (1978) examine the
choice between a negative income tax and a basic income scheme in terms
of the desirability, or otherwise, of having a higher marginal rate of tax
over the range where the person is a net beneficiary. However, our
representation in terms of the shape of the budget constraint only comes to
grips with the first element of income-testing: that concerned with the
tapering of benefit. The second feature of income-testing – the fact that it is
administered separately – must also be brought into the analysis. Although
proposals have been made to administer income-tested benefits through
the tax system, they typically require the provision of further information,
or other actions, by those who wish to claim (as was the case with the
Institute for Fiscal Studies scheme). This is important in view of the
argument that this separate treatment is at best costly in time and at worst
stigmatizing. There are costs of time involved in informing oneself about
the benefit, in claiming, in attending the relevant office, obtaining the
necessary documentation, and in appealing against erroneous decisions.

The costs associated with the receipt of separate income-tested benefits
mean that people do not always claim the assistance to which they are
entitled. Where it is a matter of information and time, then modest
amounts of benefit may not appear worth claiming. Others find the
procedure demeaning and stigmatizing, and refuse to claim even if the
sums involved are sizeable. They may be fully informed of their rights but
still not claim. The problem of incomplete take-up is a serious one (see
Chapter 11). On several occasions, the effort has been made to improve
the take-up rate of benefits, for example via extensive advertising. These
have not in general achieved a lasting increase in take-up (see, for
example, Atkinson, 1969).

For some people, the existence of such incomplete take-up is actually
seen as desirable. Nichols and Zeckhauser (1982) argue in favour of
'ordeals', which is how they label the 'demeaning qualification tests and

cedures'. They suggest that 'ordeals may en-
82, p. 376), a view reminiscent of the New Poor
never considers only one aspect of efficiency. As
sbrod (1969), when he introduced the notion of
s both accuracy in assisting *only* those in the target
covering *all* of those in the group. A take-up rate
as much evidence of failure as is the provision of
le the target group.

In order ... ne case for income-testing in place of social insurance,
we have therefore to extend the model to incorporate the take-up decision.
The most straightforward way in which this can be done is to introduce the
time costs into a household production model. (The use of waiting time
as a rationing device has been examined by Nichols *et al.*, 1971.) An
income-tested benefit which involves H hours in claiming may be seen as
providing a benefit equal to $b - \omega H$ in terms of 'full income', as defined by
Becker (1965), where ω is the opportunity cost of time. It might, for
example, be suggested that income-testing is desirable since the poor have
lower wage rates, and hence a lower opportunity cost of time, but this
ignores the possibility that they are also 'time poor' (Vickrey, 1977) and
constrained in their labour market choices. The problems in incorporating
stigma are less tractable, although some interesting suggestions were made
by Weisbrod (1970). One important consideration is that behaviour may be
interdependent, as has been analysed by Cowell (1985). The probability
that a person claims a given benefit may depend positively on the fraction
of the population in receipt. If that is the case, then extension of means-
testing might make it more socially acceptable and raise the rate of take-up.
Conversely, a more efficient targeting of benefits on the poor may reduce
still further their rate of take-up.

Finally, it may again be the case that economic arguments are not
decisive. Income-testing may be rejected on account of a basic objection to
policies which are inherently divisive: 'services specially designed for poor
people ... divide society, creating second class citizens who get second
class treatment' (Donnison, 1982, p. 12). Or, more positively, primary
importance may be attached to social integration and a sense of common
identity: 'the principle that public services should provide a range of
common experience that all citizens undergo' (Weale, 1983, p. 153).
Solidarity may be an overriding goal just as much as liberty.

6 ALTERNATIVES TO SOCIAL INSURANCE: (III) BASIC INCOMES

Both basic incomes and social insurance are likely to be consistent with a
goal of solidarity, but there are two major differences between them. First,

there are the contribution conditions for social insurance, which raise a number of important issues, not least the way in which the programmes are perceived. Secondly, social insurance benefits are linked to work status. In my sickness example, the person receives under social insurance $w(1-\varrho)$ + k if in work and $b + k$ if sick. Under a basic income scheme, the person would not receive any additional benefit for being sick; the amount would be, β say, in both states. So he receives $w(1-t) + k(1-t) + \beta$ if well and $k(1-t) + \beta$ if sick.

There are two evident advantages to the basic income approach. First, there is no need to determine a person's employment status, with a consequent saving in administrative costs. The second advantage is that, by providing an adequate income regardless of employment circumstances, it deals with the problem to which social insurance as such has no answer – that of people who are low paid even though they are in work. This brings us to the important question of the relation between social security and the labour market. The Beveridge Plan was based firmly on the assumption of the maintenance of employment: 'it should be possible to make unemployment of any individual for more than 26 weeks continuously a rare thing in normal times' (1942, p. 164). This in itself would not have been enough, without some guarantee that the employment would be at a reasonable level of wages. Here Beveridge would no doubt have flinched at the thought of a minimum wage, but it is seen by many as the natural partner in the social insurance approach. The establishment of a minimum wage, at some premium over the benefit level, with guaranteed state employment at that rate, together with social insurance, would provide a coherent policy towards both the interruption of employment and low pay while at work. As argued in Chapter 6, this is one possible 'vision' of the relationship between social security policy and the labour market.

Such a plan would of course represent a major change in labour market policy – at least as far as Britain is concerned – and it is scarcely surprising that income support policies which do not depend on full employment have been advocated. Here the basic income approach offers an alternative vision of the relationship. This starts from the right to a basic income, to which everyone is entitled, and to which earnings would be an addition, although they are all taxed, quite probably at a high rate, like 50 per cent. This approach allows diversity. If people choose not to work in the paid labour force, then they still receive the basic income. There would be no minimum wage, and the basic income scheme is consistent with the policy of the British Conservative government of seeking to create low-paid jobs. If employers wished to offer such jobs, then they could do so in the knowledge that those taking them would not be in poverty and that their income would be higher than if not at work.

What can economic analysis say about the choice between these schemes? If we consider first the design of the basic income scheme, we can see that the choice of β and the tax rate t is that which has been investigated in the literature on the optimum linear income tax. Suppose that in our sickness example people differ in their wage rate per hour, having identical preferences, and no income from capital ($k = 0$). There is assumed to be a perfectly elastic demand for any type of labour at the specified wage rate. Workers are assumed to choose their hours of work, utility being derived from net income and from leisure. There will be a critical wage rate, denoted by w_0, such that people with wages below this level choose not to work even if well, living from the basic income. The level of w_0 is governed by β and t. The choice of t, and hence from the revenue constraint β, depends on the form of the social welfare function (see for example, Atkinson and Stiglitz, 1980, Lecture 13), but the optimum solution involves one of two possibilities: either (Type A) the critical wage w_0 is below the lowest wage in the economy, denoted by w^-, which means that all choose to work, or (Type B) $w_0 > w^-$, in which the level of basic income is such that some people choose not to work.

Suppose that we have derived the optimum basic income scheme, balancing the benefits from a higher basic income against the costs of raising taxes (the balance depends of course on distributional judgements), and that we now consider the introduction of social insurance, paying an additional benefit b to the sick, who are correctly identified. (Diamond and Mirrlees, 1978, examine a theoretical model of social insurance where the government cannot distinguish between those unable to work and those who choose not to.) If the basic income optimum was of type A, then it can be shown that raising b marginally above zero (with offsetting adjustments) would raise social welfare where leisure is a normal good. This is because the sickness benefit, unlike β, is targeted to the lowest income group, and has no adverse income effect on labour supply. This result is parallel to the analysis of 'tagging' by Akerlof (1978). A categorical social insurance benefit can raise social welfare, providing that the extra administrative costs are not too great. (The same argument may apply to categorical income-tested schemes.)

This suggests that we have to balance the better targeting of social insurance against the cost of imposing the employment test. But we have not yet considered the minimum wage and the relation between benefit levels and net incomes in work. The optimum taxation models as developed to date are not very helpful in this regard, since the treatment of the labour market is insufficiently developed. In particular, they incorporate none of the elements which have been put forward to explain involuntary unemployment, such as implicit contracts, efficiency wages, or insider–outsider relations and trade unions. This is an area where further theoretical research is needed.

And again the welfare economic calculus may have to defer to wider considerations. There may be doubts about social arrangements which provide some people with no financial incentive to work. Ellwood and Summers refer to 'the value society places on self-reliance. We expect those who can to help themselves' (1986, p. 104). Gueron, writing about workfare in the US, refers to 'the now prevailing view that employable women – as well as men – have a responsibility to work and support their families' (1986, p. 2). It may therefore be imposed as a prior constraint that everyone should derive a financial gain from working. If this is the case, then solutions to the basic income design problem which are of Type B will be ruled out. The basic income scheme may then be constrained to offer a level of β which on other grounds would be regarded as inadequate. The social insurance system can overcome this problem, providing that it can be accompanied by a minimum wage. However, this too may be rejected on ideological grounds.

7 CONCLUDING COMMENTS

One theme running through this chapter has been the need to recognize that economic arguments may only play a limited role in deciding such questions as the privatization of social insurance or the return to means-testing or the introduction of a basic income. Before the 1970s, the economic aspects of social insurance received little attention. In the 1970s and 1980s, this changed, not least because of the writing in the US which has stressed the impact of social insurance on the economy, such as the effect on incentives to work and save. In my view, there is a danger that too much weight may now be given to the economic arguments. The non-economic arguments – such as those concerned with liberty, solidarity, or divisiveness – require more attention. This is not to suggest that the economic arguments are unimportant. They can illustrate the advantages and disadvantages of different approaches, but they must be seen in perspective.

The second concluding reflection which is suggested by the analysis is that the determination of government policy has been considered in a classical public finance manner, without benefiting from the insights of the more recent public choice approach. In choosing the structure of income support, we have to consider the possibility that the government may follow its own objectives without regard for any notion of social welfare. The public choice theory has tended to emphasize the propensity of governments to expand state activity beyond the socially optimal level, but the reverse may also be true, with governments cutting back state provision. (For an analysis of the changing political forces determining the degree of redistribution, see Lindbeck, 1985.) Would income-tested benefits, being more focused, be more likely to escape the cuts made by right-wing governments? Or would these benefits, lacking a broad political base, be more easily cut, as would be suggested by Director's Law (Stigler, 1970)? Would a basic income, by linking taxes and benefits so directly, be more exposed to political forces? These are interesting and important questions.

8 · TURNING THE SCREW: BENEFITS FOR THE UNEMPLOYED, 1979–1988

1 INTRODUCTION

The high level of unemployment in Britain in the 1980s has put the benefit system for the unemployed under a degree of strain not previously experienced in postwar years and not envisaged by those who drew up much of the relevant legislation. It would be natural therefore to expect that the system has been subjected to detailed scrutiny. However, this is not the case. Notably, the 1985 Green Paper on the reform of social security, which preceded the benefit changes introduced in April 1988, devoted very little space to the problems of coping with high unemployment and simply proposed 'to leave the present arrangements for unemployment benefit as they are' (Cmnd 9517, para. 10.2). In contrast to the interwar depression, there has been no Royal Commission on unemployment insurance, no new machinery such as the Unemployment Assistance Board, and certainly no collapse of a government over failure to agree on a cut in benefits for the unemployed.

If there has been little public debate about the adequacy of income support for the unemployed, this does not mean that the system has remained untouched. As we show in this chapter, there have in fact been many changes in the benefit system for the unemployed over the past ten years. Some of these are well known, such as the abolition of earnings-related national insurance benefit and the taxation of short-term benefits. Others have been given less publicity and the cumulative impact of the different changes does not seem to have been widely recognized. Although many of the measures are limited in their individual impact, the great majority have made the system less generous and have weakened the role of unemployment *insurance* as opposed to unemployment *assistance*. The total effect of the Conservative government's action is such that the structure of benefits for the unemployed in 1988 is quite different from that in 1979. It is a matter of concern that little by little the system has

With J. Micklewright. The research reported in this chapter has been carried out as part of the ESRC Programme on Taxation, Incentives, and the Distribution of Income. We are grateful to Holly Sutherland for her help with the data, and to Andrew Dilnot and Ian Walker for their comments.

undergone major changes of principle without any widespread public recognition. As was noted by the Social Security Advisory Committee in its first report, 'a major shift from contributory to means-tested non-contributory benefit appears to be taking place without public debate on its implications' (*First Report of the SSAC 1981*, para. 3.6).

Our first purpose in this chapter is simply to catalogue the changes over the last ten years and to place them in their historical context. The mere length of the list of measures affecting the benefits of the unemployed between 1979 and 1988 is in itself indicative. Our appendix, which may not be comprehensive, itemizes 38 significant changes. In examining this catalogue, we consider first (in section 2) national insurance unemployment benefit, and then (in section 3) the income-tested assistance provided by supplementary benefit (now Income Support) and housing benefit.

Our second purpose is to quantify the effect of the changes on the incomes of the unemployed. Just how much has the screw been tightened? Discussion of the effect of the benefit system frequently employs hypothetical calculations of the entitlement of people with particular family and household characteristics. These calculations cannot however capture the myriad of characteristics that exist in the population nor, crucially, do they reflect the fact that entitlement itself may be changed by policy. Changes in the contribution conditions or in the administration of benefit may have a substantial effect, with the result that looking only at the hypothetical levels of benefit for those that do receive may be quite misleading. Similarly, aggregate statistics on numbers in receipt in different years cannot give the full story, since it is not clear whether any changes reflect changes in the benefit system or changes in the composition of the unemployed between the two dates.

Our approach is to take a sample of actual unemployed people and to compare their incomes under the benefit system as it was in 1979 and as it is after the introduction of Income Support in 1988. This approach is similar in spirit to earlier studies by Dilnot and Morris (1983) and Mallender and Ramsden (1984). However, our analysis differs from these in several respects. Dilnot and Morris concentrated on the incentive for the employed to become unemployed, and most of their results related to the position of those in employment (comparing their income with that if they were to quit their jobs). In contrast, we are concerned exclusively with the position of those already unemployed. Mallender and Ramsden looked at the effects of changes between 1978 and 1982 using a sample of the male inflow into unemployment, focusing on the impact in the early months of unemployment. In our analysis we consider a sample of the stock of the unemployed, including both men and women and covering all durations of unemployment. Moreover, in contrast to both these studies we look solely at incomes out of work and do not compare these with incomes when employed. This allows us to concentrate on the effects of changes in unemployment benefits without the analysis having to take account of changes to incomes in work.

The methods by which these calculations are carried out, using a version of the LSE Tax-Benefit model TAXMOD, are described in section 4. The findings with regard to unemployment insurance and the erosion of national insurance are given in section 5. Section 6 shows the total effect of both national insurance and income-tested benefits. The main conclusions are summarized in section 7.

2   CHANGES IN UNEMPLOYMENT INSURANCE 1979–88

The present 'two-tier' structure of benefits for the unemployed – a flat-rate insurance benefit paid subject to contribution and other conditions, supported by a second tier of income-tested assistance – is essentially the same as that introduced in the Unemployment Act 1934. Although it is widely believed that the Beveridge Report led to major changes in unemployment benefit, his principal recommendation of an unlimited duration for insurance benefit was not accepted. Although a third, earnings-related, tier was introduced in 1966, this was one of the first casualties of the Thatcher government. The basic structure in 1988 is therefore little different from that half a century earlier.

What has changed are the details of the schemes. The last decade has seen many changes in both insurance and income-tested benefits for unemployed workers – many more than we realized when we began to list them. What began as a relatively short appendix turns out to include 17 significant changes for national insurance unemployment benefit (UB) alone. Some of the changes have received a lot of attention, such as the abolition of the earnings-related supplement (ERS) and the taxation of benefits. Others may be less familiar, such as the change in the linked spells rule, the abolition of reduced rates of benefit, the abatement for occupational pensions, the introduction of the equal treatment provisions required by the European Community, and the change in the contribution conditions contained in the Social Security Bill 1988.

The changes affecting national insurance UB are listed in Table 8.1. Where possible, we indicate the direction of the effect of the measures on the net incomes of the unemployed. We highlight below those that we consider to represent major changes in emphasis.

1. The abolition of ERS has meant that Britain is the only member of the European Community with no element of unemployment benefits linked to past earnings and one of only four OECD countries in this position (the others are Australia, New Zealand and Iceland).

Table 8.1 Changes in national insurance unemployment benefit, 1979–88

Measure[1]	Indication of quantitative importance[2]
Measures favourable to the unemployed	
Equal treatment provisions (7)	
Definition of voluntary redundancy (12)	
Measures whose effect may be positive or negative	
Basis for up-rating of benefit (3)	See text.
Linked spell rule (8)	
Earnings rule (9)	
Payment of benefits (14)	Postal charges affect 195,000 claimants, saving £0.6m (H, 10 June 1986, col. 145).
Measures unfavourable to the unemployed	
End of earnings-related supplement (1)	Saving in 1978/9 some £95m (see text).
Taxation of NI unemployment benefit (2)	Tax yield on benefits paid to unemployed (NI and SB) £375m in 1986/87 (UUB 24).
Suspension of statutory indexation (4)	See text.
Abolition of child additions (5)	In Nov. 1984 123,000 men had child dependency additions (SSS, 1987, Table 1.40).
Abolition of lower rate benefits (6)	Estimated savings £27m. (SSAC Fifth Report, 1986/7). 57,000 without SB affected (UUB 19).
Abatement for occupational pensioners (10)	Saving to NI Fund £65m. in 1989/90 (SSB 1988).
More stringent administration (11)	
Disqualification period (13)	Extension from 6 to 13 weeks estimated to save £25m–30m (H, 1 March 1988, col. 849).
Students (15)	
Full extent normal rule (16)	
Contribution conditions (17)	Saving to NI Fund £380m in 1990/1 (SSB 1988).

Notes:
1. The numbers in brackets refer to sections in the Appendix.
2. The references make use of the following abbreviations: H (Hansard), SSS (Social Security Statistics), SSB (Social Security Bill), SSAC (Social Security Advisory Committee), UUB (Unemployment Bulletin).

2. The abatement of UB for occupational pensions has introduced an element of personal means-testing into national insurance unemployment benefit for the first time.

3. The abolition of reduced rate NI benefit taken with that of ERS ends the principle of better benefit for better contributors embodied in legislation since the introduction of national insurance in 1911.

4. The equal treatment provisions means that UB now treats husbands and wives symmetrically with respect to claiming for a dependant.

5. The more than four-fold increase in the maximum disqualification period from NI benefit (and reduction in SB) in the case of voluntary quitting, industrial misconduct or refusal of a job offer, has changed a

parameter of the benefit system that had been in operation for much of the century (the original 1911 Act, the two major inter-war Acts of 1920 and 1934, and the post-Beveridge 1946 Act all stipulated a six-week figure).

6. The new contribution conditions contained in the 1988 Social Security Bill mean that benefit entitlement depends on paid (rather than paid or credited) contributions in the two preceding tax years; this strikes at the system introduced by Beveridge, and returns us to a situation similar to that of fifty years ago.

Considering the individual measures in Table 8.1, we see that in certain cases they have improved the position of the unemployed. The equal treatment provisions extend the range of choice open to unemployed couples. The redefinition of voluntary redundancy in 1985 was designed to make sure that workers are not regarded as having left their job voluntarily even when they volunteer or agree to be made redundant.

In other cases, the effect may have been positive or negative. An example is provided by the change in the linked spells rule, which reduced the period of linking from 13 weeks to 8 weeks. This disadvantaged a worker who lost his job again after, say, 9 weeks in that he had a further three waiting days before he could receive benefit, but it was an advantage in that a person could 'start a fresh run of unemployment benefit after only eight weeks back at work, instead of thirteen' (Social Security Advisory Committee, First Report, 1982, p. 9). (It is not clear whether this was widely appreciated at the time since the change also applied to NI sickness benefit where the intention was to reduce the number of people qualifying for invalidity benefit paid at a higher rate.) Another example is the sequence of changes in the method of payment of benefits, particularly following the Rayner Report in 1981, some of which made life easier for the unemployed as well as the DHSS, and some of which – such as the liability to pay postal charges – were to the disadvantage of claimants.

We have also included in this indeterminate category changes which initially had a positive effect, but which were later eroded or reversed. The change in the earnings rule, increasing the permitted earnings to £2 a day from 75p in 1982, represented a distinct improvement at the time, but the figure has not changed. So that, whereas it was then possible for an unemployed person to earn up to 53 per cent of the UB daily amount, by 1988 it had fallen to 37 per cent.[1] This is an example of a 'hidden constant' of the social security system, i.e. a parameter which is not regularly updated and which erodes benefit entitlements without people being aware. Another example is the abatement rule for occupational pensions, which was introduced at the level of £35 in 1981 and has remained fixed in money terms. (The introduction of this abatement had, of course, a negative effect which has now worsened.)

Turning to the uprating of benefits, we may note that the effect of the change in basis from 'forecast' to 'historic' depends on the path of inflation. We have however recorded the suspension of indexation as a negative entry in the balance sheet. Whatever the actual outcome, the suspension of inflation-proofing of UB represented a loss of certainty for the unemployed. This has been reinforced by government statements. In July 1983, the Prime Minister was asked to give a guarantee that UB would be increased in line with inflation like other NI benefits and refused to do so. A similar position was taken by the Chancellor of the Exchequer, who in his reply referred to concern about voluntary unemployment. The new provision in the Social Security Act 1986 means that the level of benefit in

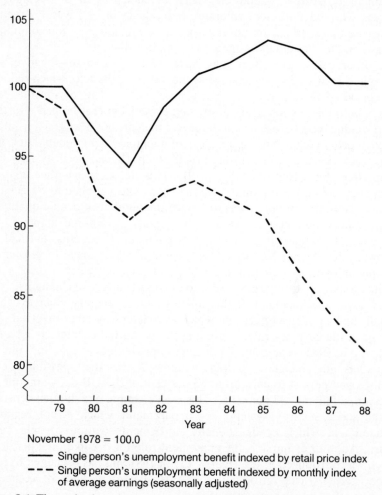

November 1978 = 100.0

——— Single person's unemployment benefit indexed by retail price index
--- Single person's unemployment benefit indexed by monthly index of average earnings (seasonally adjusted)

Figure 8.1 The real value of unemployment benefit, 1978–88

real terms is now permanently at risk. Even if *ex post* the purchasing power has been maintained (see below), *ex ante* there has been uncertainty.

The movement over time in the real value of UB for a single person is shown by the solid line in Figure 8.1, where the dates plotted are those of up-ratings, so that these represent the *maximum* real values for the periods in question. Taking the decade as a whole, we see that NI UB increased more or less in line with the retail price index: between November 1978 and April 1987 UB for a single person rose by 99.7 per cent, compared with a rise of 98.3 per cent in the retail price index (Public Expenditure White Paper, January 1988, p. 274). However, the position in individual years displays some variation – the solid line in Figure 8.1 is not horizontal. In particular, there was a fall in the real value in the early years, reflecting the 5 per cent withdrawal in advance of the taxation of benefit, restored in November 1983. The dashed line in Figure 8.1 shows the movement in the same UB figure when indexed by movements in average earnings. Viewed in this way, the level of benefit has declined markedly, in particular in later years when real wage rises have been large. By the end of the period, the value of a single person's UB indexed by earnings had fallen by almost a fifth.

The majority of the measures listed in Table 8.1 were quite clearly unfavourable to the unemployed. The abolition of ERS is a prominent example. Although it was not widely lamented due to the somewhat arcane mechanics of the scheme, the sum of money involved was substantial, and if reallocated to an increase in the flat-rate UB could have allowed a significant improvement. In November 1978, 156,000 men were receiving ERS with an average of £9.34 and there were 53,000 women with an average of £6.49 (*Social Security Statistics*, 1982, Table 1.50). This corresponds to expenditure at an annual rate of some £95 million, compared with total expenditure on NI unemployment benefit in the year 1978/9 of £632 million (same source, Table 44.04). If the money had been allocated to raising the flat-rate UB then it appears that the latter could have been raised by 17.5 per cent without changing the total spent on NI benefits for unemployment. In the calculations in sections 5 and 6, we show the effect of such a 17.5 per cent increase in flat-rate UB. A second reason for considering such an increase is that it would restore UB to approximately the same proportion of average earnings as in 1978 – see Figure 8.1 – thus preserving the historical pattern. (Of course, consideration would have had to have been given to the relativity with other short-term benefits, and to the effects on total social security spending including SB.)

The amount of UB being paid has been reduced by the abolition of child additions, by the abolition of the ½ and ¾ rates of benefit, and by the abatement for occupational pensions. The abolition of child additions has meant that since the Conservative government took office the payment per child in families in receipt of UB rose by 85p a week less than for other families. In 1984 the additions were being received for some 230,000 children (*Social Security Statistics*, 1987, Table 1.40), so that this would correspond to some £10 million a year. The abolition of the reduced rates of benefit mean that those with incomplete contribution records now receive no insurance benefit at all, rather than a fraction of the benefit. This change was estimated to save some £27 million. The abatement for occupational pensions[2] reduces the amount of UB paid to those over the age of 60 pound for pound over £35 a week, and hence extinguishes entitlement for those with sufficiently large pensions.[3]

It is not widely appreciated that many people fail to qualify for insurance benefit on account of insufficient contributions (*Social Security Statistics* gives no information on the reasons for non-receipt). In May 1986, over 800,000 of the 3 million people unemployed had insufficient contributions to receive any UB, a figure not much less than the 1.07 million who had exhausted their period entitlement (Hansard, 28 November 1986, col. 405).[4] The new contribution conditions introduced in 1988 will substantially worsen this position. The estimated saving to the NI fund in 1990/1 is £380 million. Those affected will include people with lengthy contribution records. A man may have been employed for 30 years and still not qualify for UB during a second spell of unemployment, since the crediting of contributions during the first spell will not now count towards the relevant condition for UB.

Entitlement may also be lost as a result of the extended disqualification period, set in 1911 at 6 weeks, which has been increased to 13 weeks and then, only 18 months later, to 26 weeks. The Social Security Advisory Committee comments on the recent extension to 26 weeks that:

> disqualification from unemployment benefit for 6 months, with reduced income support entitlement, is a harsh penalty and one which should therefore be applied with care. We regret that voluntary unemployment is an area in which claimants may be assumed 'guilty' until they can prove their 'innocence' in that where the benefit officer suspects voluntary unemployment he or she may suspend payment of benefit pending a decision by the adjudication officer on disqualification.
>
> (Sixth Report, 1988, p. 14)

The way in which disqualification works in practice has been described by Rowland:

> The issues in these cases are never as clear cut as the legislators would wish, as employers and employees usually have different views about the reasons for dismissals or resignations. Cases are investigated by the writing of letters which takes a long time and during that time benefit is suspended and any income support paid at a reduced rate. ... Even if the decision to disqualify has been made by the date of the tribunal hearing, the tribunal are invariably unable to consider that question as the adjudication officer does not have the right set of papers at the hearing. The end result is that many people are disqualified for much longer than should be the case because they are not

sufficiently articulate on paper, and then tribunals only consider their cases some months after the events have happened if the claimants can keep their enthusiasm going for long enough to make a second appeal.

(1988, p. ix)

Some of the changes listed in Table 8.1 affected relatively small numbers of people. For example, the announcement of the abolition of the reduced rates of UB said that the number without SB eligible for the ¾ rate was 36,000 and the number eligible for the ½ rate was 21,000. As we emphasized in the Introduction, the cumulation of such small changes may however have a sizeable impact. Moreover, the different measures interact. For example, the tighter contribution conditions mean that more people will have incomplete contribution records in the relevant periods and hence that the removal of the reduced rates of benefit will be more significant.

The measures that have been taken in recent years are one of the reasons why the number of UB recipients has fallen and is predicted to fall in the next few years. This is not of course the only explanation, but it is noteworthy that the Public Expenditure White Paper projections (HM Treasury 1988, Table 15.6) show the number of recipients as falling from 755,000 in 1988/9 to 635,000 in 1990/1 on the basis of the conventional assumption of *constant* unemployment. Administrative data show that UB recipients as a *proportion* of the total benefit recipients has fallen. Again there are other factors in operation, including the changing duration mix of the unemployed. This is one reason why the calculations in sections 5 and 6 have been undertaken, since they hold constant the composition of the population.

3   CHANGES IN INCOME-TESTED BENEFITS FOR THE UNEMPLOYED, 1979–88

Income-tested assistance to the unemployed, unlike that in many other countries, is not a separate scheme but forms part of the general programme of income support. It is intended to act as a 'safety net', and hence it is often suggested that any cuts in NI UB are simply offset by a corresponding increase in the safety net payment under SB/IS. So that for those receiving SB, the abolition of ERS may not have entailed any overall loss of net income (12.5 per cent of male ERS recipients in November 1980 were also receiving SB (*Social Security Statistics*, 1985, Table 1.32)). There are however important reasons why this is too optimistic a view:

1. In some cases the cuts in NI are complemented in SB/IS: for example, where a person is disqualified from NI UB there is a 40 per cent voluntary unemployment deduction in SB/IS.

2. SB/IS is assessed on a family basis rather than an individual basis and the total family income may be such that the person is not eligible. Families with incomes not far above the SB/IS level will therefore lose from reductions in UB.
3. A sizeable fraction of those entitled to SB do not claim their entitlement. The official figure quoted in the Public Expenditure White Paper (HM Treasury 1987, p. 244) is that the take-up rate for the unemployed in 1983 was 81 per cent. This means that some 1 in 5 are not receiving their entitlement, and even though take-up measured in value terms may be higher, the safety net evidently has holes.

It is also the case that changes have been made to SB/IS over the period 1979–88 – including, of course, the renaming – and that the majority of which have reduced the effectiveness of the safety net. These measures are summarized in Table 8.2. In addition to the two major reforms in the past decade, there have been a series of less sweeping measures, some of them specifically directed at the unemployed.

The effects of the reform of supplementary benefit in November 1980, and of the replacement of supplementary benefits by Income Support in April 1988, are not easily summarized in that there were many different changes, some of which operated in different directions as far as the unemployed are concerned. The reduction, in 1980, in the number of scales for children, for instance, represented a real improvement for

Table 8.2 Changes in supplementary benefit/Income Support affecting the unemployed, 1979–88

Measures favourable to the unemployed
Long-term SB rate (19)
Equal treatment provisions (21)

Measures whose effect may be positive or negative
1980 reform of SB (18)
Part-time study (27)
Introduction of IS in 1988 (30)

Measures unfavourable to the unemployed
Taxation of benefit (2)
Students (15)
More stringent administration (20)
Non-householder housing cost addition (22)
Voluntary unemployment deductions (23)
Disqualification period (24)
Board and lodging (25)
School-leavers (26)
Heating additions (28)
Mortgage interest (29)
Social fund (31)
16–17 year olds (32)

Note: The numbers in brackets refer to sections in the Appendix.

younger children in the new ranges. On the other hand, the introduction of an absolute capital cut-off meant that a number of the unemployed lost their entitlement to SB. In 1988, the raising of the capital limit, accompanied by the reintroduction of a tariff income for capital between £3,000 and £6,000, is to the benefit of a number of potential claimants. On the other hand, the limitation of rates assistance to 80 per cent, and the loss of water rates, have not been compensated in all cases by the new IS scales.

The measures introduced at other dates are also mixed in their effects. The extension of the long-term rate to unemployed men aged 60 and over provided substantial benefit to this group, estimated to number 40,000 (SSAC First Report, p. 27) benefiting from the extension in 1981, coupled with the later extension of automatic entitlement to the lower rate heating addition. But the majority of the measures are unfavourable to the unemployed: for example, under SB, there has been the raising of the age for the non-householder housing cost addition, the measures taken to limit board and lodging payments, and the fact that, for owner-occupiers aged under 60, only 50 per cent of the interest is taken into the calculation for the first 16 weeks on benefit, a change introduced in January 1987 and retained in the Income Support scheme. In addition, there were a number of measures parallel to those described for NI benefit; these include the taxation of SB with effect from 1982, and the lengthening of the disqualification period. The last of these has been just one of a number of measures that represent a continuing attempt to administer the receipt of both benefits more stringently. In this the government's response to high unemployment has been similar in nature to the interwar period. The 1988 White Paper, *Training for Employment* (Cm 316), highlights the government's view that 'significant numbers of benefit claimants are not genuinely available for work' and this is labelled as one of the 'three major problems' to be faced if unemployment is to be reduced (p. 4). Availability testing has concentrated on closer scrutiny of the initial claim, which now involves an additional questionnaire on availability,[5] and use of the Restart scheme. From April 1988 all unemployed people are called to Restart interviews every six months.

Like supplementary benefit, housing benefit has been through two major sets of changes – the new scheme legislated in the Social Security and

Table 8.3 Changes in housing benefit affecting the
unemployed, 1979–88

Introduction of new HB in 1982 (33)
Non-dependant deductions (34)
Changes in tapers (35)
Changes in needs allowances (36)
Minimum payments (37)
Social Security Act 1986 (38)

Note: The numbers in brackets refer to sections in the Appendix.

Housing Benefits Act 1982 and introduced in November 1982/April 1983, and the reforms made in the Social Security Act 1986 which came into effect in April 1988 along with the introduction of Income Support. In addition there have been a series of cuts in housing benefit via increases in the tapers and non-dependant deductions, which have not been fully offset by changes in the opposite direction, such as the increase in the real value of the child's needs allowance. These changes have to be seen against a background of substantially faster increases in levels of rents and rates than in the retail prices index.

In describing the changes in this section we have not considered the payments made by such 'special employment measures' as the Youth Training Scheme or the Community Programme. It is certainly the case that large numbers of people without work are dependent on the income that these schemes provide and that the increase in the coverage of these schemes has been a prominent feature of the labour market in the 1980s. However, as we describe in the next section, we exclude persons on these schemes from the definition of unemployment that we use.

Finally, we have concentrated on the position of the unemployed, but a number of the measures described above have major implications for other groups in the population

4   MODELLING THE EFFECTS ON THE UNEMPLOYED

In the rest of this chapter we are concerned with modelling the effects of the policy changes between 1979 and 1988 described above on the incomes of families containing an unemployed person. For this purpose we use the TAXMOD model constructed at LSE (for further details see Atkinson and Sutherland, 1988). The data we use are a sample of actual families drawn from the 1982 UK Family Expenditure Survey (FES). We take those families interviewed in the 1982/3 tax year before the November benefit uprating.

An important preliminary is to make clear our definition of 'unemployed'. The definition adopted here is intended to approximate, as far as possible, the ILO/OECD definition, which requires that people are:

1. Without a paid job.
2. Available to start work in the next two weeks.
3. Have either looked for work at some time in the past four weeks or are waiting to take up a job.

In terms of FES definitions, this can be approached most closely by taking those who are 'out of employment but seeking or about to start work' excluding those who are receiving a TOPS or YOPS (in 1982) allowance. This excludes a number of those (in 1982) in receipt of NI unemployment benefit, and it is well known that the ILO/OECD definition leads to a different classification from the Department of Employment's claimant count (see, for example, the *Employment Gazette*, January 1988, p. 30).

Our concern is with the effect of the changes on the net incomes of the unemployed families measured at one date. Our calculations are therefore for the current position, not for income over the course of a year (for discussion of this aspect, see Nolan, 1987). The focus on *family* incomes means that we may be including in the 'unemployed families' those where the husband is unemployed but the wife has high earnings (or vice versa), so that the family as a unit is in one of the top income ranges (evidence about this is provided by Nolan, ibid.). We should also note that there is a sizeable number with no recorded income at all in the current period.

Calculations are made first of the net incomes arising from the benefit system in October 1988 (taken as representing the tax year 1988/89)[6]; we then put history into reverse and ask how the incomes of the unemployed families would be changed if we were to introduce in 1988/89 the measures that were in force in 1978/79. The aim of this comparison is to show the effect, for a constant population, of the policy changes over the decade.

There are a number of aspects of this exercise that need to be emphasized. First, the data that we use are drawn from neither of the two tax years we focus on: 1978/79 or 1988/89. However, we update the characteristics of the 1982 sample of unemployed families that influence benefit entitlement. Thus, housing costs, wages and other income are updated by appropriate retail price sub-indices and indices of earnings, pensions, etc. Secondly, when modelling the 1978/79 benefit system we hold fixed the characteristics of the unemployed sample of families as predicted for 1988/89; the only variables being changed are the policy parameters. We are not investigating what would happen if we returned to 1978/79 levels of unemployment. Thirdly, we should stress that we are not attempting to predict any changes in behaviour that would be induced by the policy changes (this applies equally to our calculations for 1988/89 and 1978/79). Fourthly, the calculations at both dates clearly depend on a number of assumptions about benefit receipt, an aspect of the analysis on which we now elaborate.

Our strategy is to take as much account as is feasible of the information on benefit receipt recorded in the 1982 FES data. For example, if an unemployed person is not recorded as receiving national insurance UB in 1982 then we do not assume receipt in 1988, unless there is reason to believe that there would be eligibility as the result of the policy changes (an example would be the equal treatment provisions, although these are not covered by the model). But if reduced rate UB is identified as being received in 1982 then we do not allow receipt in 1988, this being one of the changes that has occurred. Our assumptions about take-up of means-tested benefits use information recorded on receipt in 1982, together with a random element, but of course we are hampered where there was no eligibility at that date. We assume that the take-up rates for the new benefits to be the same as for SB in the case of IS and the same as FIS in the case of Family Credit.

The TAXMOD model uses a system of grossing-up factors to produce an estimate of the population from the FES sample data (the sample has 538 tax units containing an unemployed person). The results of the calculations with the 1988/89 system are shown in Tables 8.4 and 8.5 in two different ways. In Table 8.4 we show in column 2 the distribution of unemployed families by range of total net income (i.e. income including all benefits, including housing benefit, minus income tax and NIC); and for comparison the distribution of all families is given alongside. This makes no adjustment for differences in family size; it also takes no account of housing costs. In Table 8.5 we show the distribution of net resources, defined as net income minus housing costs, the latter including water rates. Net resources are then expressed relative to a scale obtained by taking £31.70 a week for a single person (the SB scale for 1987/88 uprated by 4.2 per cent) and using the following equivalence scale:

Couple   1.6
+ per child   0.4

(these being based broadly on the SB equivalences).

These calculations of the position in 1988/89 provide a base against which we can compare the effects of a return to the 1978/79 policy parameters. It is clear that the net incomes of the unemployed are typically much lower. The median net income is some £50 a week, compared to a figure of £130 a week for the whole population (which includes the unemployed). Put another way, half the unemployed families have net incomes of less than £50 per week compared to only 1 in 8 in the population as a whole. The proportions below £40 show an even more marked comparison, being 43.7 per cent for the unemployed and 7.5 per cent in the whole population. However, the table does show that a significant number of unemployed families have much higher incomes, where for example there is one partner in work or substantial income from another source. This illustrates the variety of circumstances faced by the unemployed. For example, nearly 1 in 10 tax units have incomes above £200 per week although the figure for the population as a whole is not surprisingly much higher (a quarter).

Turning to the calculations of resources relative to the equivalence scale described above, we see from Table 8.5 that a third of the unemployed families are at only 90 per cent of the scale or less compared to only 7 per cent in the population as a whole. Two-thirds are below 110 per cent of the scale (many of those close to the scale are likely to be receiving IS). The comparison further up the distribution is now more marked: only 2 in 10 unemployed families have net resources greater than 160 per cent of the scale compared to 7 in 10 in the whole population.

Table 8.4 Calculated distribution of net income in 1988: unemployed and whole population

Range of net income (upper limit in £ per week)	Unemployed %	Unemployed cumulative %	Whole population %	Whole population cumulative %
25	14.1	14.1	2.7	2.7
40	29.6	43.6	4.8	7.5
55	9.6	53.3	6.9	14.4
70	7.1	60.3	8.7	23.2
85	4.7	65.0	7.3	30.4
100	6.0	71.0	7.7	38.1
115	4.8	75.8	6.4	44.5
130	3.8	79.6	5.9	50.3
145	3.6	83.1	5.4	55.8
160	2.0	85.1	5.0	60.8
175	2.1	87.2	4.1	64.8
190	2.8	90.1	4.5	69.3
205	2.2	92.2	3.9	73.2
220	1.9	94.1	3.6	76.7
235	1.5	95.6	3.2	79.9
250	0.6	96.2	2.8	82.7
—	3.8	100.0	17.3	100.0

Table 8.5 Calculated distribution of equivalent net resources in 1988: unemployed and whole population

Range of equivalent net income (upper limit as % scale)	Unemployed %	Unemployed cumulative %	Whole population %	Whole population cumulative %
80	21.3	21.3	4.4	4.4
90	13.6	34.9	2.4	6.8
100	5.7	40.6	1.3	8.1
110	26.4	66.9	4.1	12.2
120	5.3	72.2	2.6	14.7
130	3.2	75.4	3.3	18.0
140	2.5	77.9	6.7	24.7
160	2.8	80.6	5.8	30.5
180	1.3	81.9	4.3	34.8
200	1.3	83.3	3.9	38.7
240	4.4	87.7	8.6	47.3
—	12.3	100.0	52.7	100.0

Note: The scale is based on net resources of £31.70 a week for a single person, £50.72 for a couple, plus £12.68 per child.

5   THE EROSION OF NATIONAL INSURANCE BENEFIT

In this section we concentrate on the effects of the changes that have taken place in national insurance benefit. What would be the incomes of the unemployed in 1988/89 if national insurance benefit were paid under the rules prevailing in 1978/79 (with benefits uprated by the rise in the retail price index) but assuming the *current* system of means-tested benefits, i.e.

Income Support/post-April 1988 housing benefit? We should stress at the outset that we do not provide a full answer to this question. Several of the changes described in Table 8.1 are very difficult to model adequately, such as the treatment of voluntary redundancy. Notably, we have not attempted to recreate the workings of the now defunct earnings-related supplement (this being a much harder exercise than several observers have appreciated; see Micklewright, 1985). Instead, we have increased the real value of flat-rate benefit payable in 1978/79 by a uniform 17.5 per cent. This is the amount we identified in section 2 as being possible if the total ERS being paid at the time had been redistributed to all unemployed NI benefit recipients and would restore the level of flat-rate UB in relation to average earnings. Finally, we have not included measures which took effect after October 1988, including the lowering of the age for the occupational pension abatement and the tightening of the contribution conditions which will have a major impact.

The measures covered by our calculations (together with their reference number in Table 8.1) are: the taxation of benefit (2),[7] the abolition of child additions (5), the abolition of lower rate benefits (6), the abatement for occupational pensioners (7), and the lengthening of the disqualification period (13). While we account for neither of the two measures in Table 8.1 which we labelled as being definitely favourable to the unemployed, we also exclude a number of changes that have been unfavourable and as a result we do not think that we have over-stated the comparison.

We calculate the gross cost of reversing these changes in NI benefit to be £417 million. This cost refers to the unemployed sample studied here. As noted earlier, some NI recipients are not covered, so that the total cost is higher. However, increases in NI benefit lead to some saving in means-tested benefits. There is also the loss of income tax revenue. Taking these into account the net cost is £365 million for the unemployed sample studied here. (The net cost of the measures apart from the 17.5 per cent rise is £153 million).

No net gain in income (or in 0.4 per cent of cases, a loss[8]) is experienced by 77.5 per cent of unemployed families, this occurring where there is no NI benefit entitlement or where the increases in NI benefit are insufficient to extinguish the receipt of IS. A gain of up to £6 per week accrues to 14 per cent of the unemployed while 8 per cent gain more than this figure. Table 8.6 shows the average gain (taking zeros and losses into account) and the percentage of families which gain in each of the ranges analysed in Tables 8.4 and 8.5 (we have combined the higher ranges), where the results are shown separately for net income and equivalent net resources. Looking at net income, we see that one of the largest proportions of gainers is to be found in the highest income range, but that the largest average gain is experienced by families in the lowest range. One of the smallest average gains and lowest percentage of gaining families is in the range £40–55 which

Table 8.6 Effect on unemployed of returning UB system from
1988 to 1979

Range of net income in 1988 (upper limit)	Average gain £ per week	Percentage of gainers
25	3.85	13.2
40	1.71	30.3
55	1.00	13.9
70	1.87	20.6
85	1.91	18.8
100	2.78	19.2
115	3.76	15.3
130	0.78	13.5
145	2.05	11.2
—	2.83	28.8
Average	2.29	22.1

Range of equivalent net resources (upper limit as % of scale)	Average gain	Percentage of gainers
80	3.48	20.0
90	0.44	3.9
100	1.08	13.9
110	2.01	31.0
120	2.08	9.6
130	1.09	18.2
140	1.09	17.5
150	3.61	56.6
160	1.56	22.1
—	3.47	31.0
Average	2.29	22.1

Table 8.7 Effect on unemployed of returning UB system from 1988 to 1979:
breakdown of average gain by family and household characteristics

	Average gain £ per week		
Head of household	2.53	1.96	Non-head of household
Owner	3.41	1.78	Tenant
Married	3.14	1.74	Single
Children	2.02	2.38	No children
Wife works	6.07	1.95	No working wife

contains the median. The impression of the greatest gains being at both
ends of the distribution is reinforced by the results for equivalent net
resources.[9]

Table 8.7 analyses the average gain in a different way, distinguishing
between different family and household characteristics. It shows that in
terms of net income, a return to the 1978/79 NI benefit system would
benefit householders more than non-householders, owners more than
tenants, couples more than single persons, and those with no children
slightly more than those with none (it should be remembered that there is
no adjustment for family size in these calculations). The average gain for
those units with a working wife is particularly notable.

Our concern in this chapter is with the effect of policy changes on the levels of income of the unemployed. We should however note one – no doubt unintended – consequence of the shift away from insurance benefits since 1979, which is the rise in the marginal tax rate faced by working wives where their husbands are unemployed. The independent basis inherent in NI UB does not lead to the family being penalized if the wife earns more (unless the dependant's addition is thereby lost), whereas the family assessment under SB means that she faces a high tax rate. Moreover, the marginal tax rate was raised when NI UB became taxable, since this reduced the allowances which could be set against the earnings of breadwinner wives. Our calculations show that 8 per cent of wives in paid work would have faced a lower marginal tax rate if the 1978/9 NI system had been in force, and that the average marginal tax rate would have been some 2 percentage points lower. This may well have affected work decisions – which we assume here to be unchanged. (See Dilnot and Kell, 1987, for discussion of male unemployment and women's work.)

6   THE TOTAL EFFECT

The erosion of insurance benefit has been accompanied by changes in the income-tested benefits which also affected the incomes of the unemployed. In this section we show the additional effects of the changes that have taken place in SB/IS and housing benefit. As before, we cannot model all of the changes that have taken place. Those included (with their reference numbers in Tables 8.2 and 8.3) are: taxation of SB (2), 1980 reform (18), long-term SB rate (19), non-householder housing cost addition (22), voluntary unemployment deduction (23), disqualification period (24), heating additions (28), mortgage interest (29), Income Support (30), 1982 housing benefit (33), tapers (35), needs allowances (36), minima (37) and 1988 measures (38). In a number of cases these relate to only a small number of cases in the sample, and this should be borne in mind when considering the results.

There are certain people who would be worse off with the 1978/9 system. This applies, for example, to unemployed men aged 60 and over who benefited from the long-term scale. It applies to families with children in the younger part of the post-1980 age ranges who enjoyed a real increase as a result of that reform. Both of these measures mean that the SB paid would have been lower. On the other hand, the payment of rates and mortgage interest in full, the payment of water rates, the restoration of the housing costs addition for non-householders aged under 25, and the return to the 1979 treatment of capital income, would all have increased the SB in payment. Netting out the amount transferred from certificated housing benefit, SB payments are estimated in the model to be some £150 million higher for the families covered. The total effect is that the unemployed covered in our analysis would have received £510 million more than under the present policy, or an average of £3.21 a week. It should be noted that a return to the 1978/79 system would have implications for other groups besides the unemployed, and that the overall cost would be very much larger.

The effect of the total package on families in different ranges of net income is given in Table 8.8. This shows that those losing from a return to the system of 1978/79 (as modelled here) are a minority – about 1 in 5. The majority would have gained. One in three would have gained more than £4 a week – see Table 8.9. The percentage of gainers is above average in most of the lower ranges of net income (below £85 a week) and there are fewer losers in the ranges of equivalent resources below 100 per cent of the scale. It is not surprising that there are no losers among families with equivalent resources in excess of 140 per cent of the scale, since they are not affected by the changes in income-tested benefits. There is also a smaller percentage of gainers (a third) in the top group.

It should be re-emphasized that the coverage of these calculations is incomplete and subject to qualifications. We have covered only 20 out of

Table 8.8 Effect on unemployed of returning UB and SB/IS from 1988 to 1979

Range of net income in 1988 (upper limit) £ per week	% families in range	Average gain £ per week	Percentage of gainers	Percentage of losers
25	14.1	5.27	55.6	5.7
40	29.6	2.83	77.5	19.5
55	9.6	4.24	78.0	12.7
70	7.1	2.76	70.3	14.4
85	4.7	3.11	67.7	27.0
100	6.0	2.96	51.8	40.7
115	4.8	3.59	29.6	47.4
130	3.8	−0.47	25.3	67.4
145	3.6	1.73	32.9	27.9
—	16.9	2.88	31.0	3.2
Average		3.21	58.3	18.8

Range of equivalent net resources (upper limit as % of scale)	% families in range	Average gain £ per week	Percentage of gainers	Percentage of losers
80	21.3	6.69	62.6	6.2
90	13.6	4.13	100.0	0.0
100	5.7	3.24	76.8	10.5
110	26.4	1.40	58.3	41.1
120	5.3	2.83	45.9	48.1
130	3.2	−1.49	33.5	57.7
140	2.5	−7.61	30.8	69.2
150	0.7	5.13	74.6	0.0
160	2.1	1.56	22.1	0.0
—	19.4	3.54	33.0	0.0
Average		3.21	58.3	18.8

Table 8.9 Extent of gains and losses in returning UB and SB/IS from 1988 to 1979

Limit of range £ per week	Percentage of families
Losses	
>10.00	1.7
4.00–10.00	8.0
<4.00	9.1
No change	22.9
Gains	
<4.00	28.1
4.00–10.00	22.4
>10.00	7.7

the 36 measures listed in the Appendix which are in force in 1988. We have not, for example, taken account of the Social Fund and the fact that in 1986 2 million exceptional needs payments were made to the unemployed with an average rate of £82 (Social Security Statistics, 1987, p. 216). We do not allow for the changes affecting the benefit entitlement of 16–17-year-olds currently being debated, or those to be introduced in October 1988 or later, such as the change in contribution conditions. Moreover, there are features which are not modelled or only approximated. These include the effect of exceptional circumstances additions, which are not included in the 1978/79 SB calculations and hence understate the gain from a return to this system: the average value of these additions per unemployed person in 1978 indexed to 1988 is £0.37 (*Social Security Statistics*, 1978, Tables 34.43 and 1.32). They include the problem of take-up, where the model needs to be refined. None the less, we feel that the calculations provide a useful guide to the orders of magnitude involved in the changes covered.

7 CONCLUSIONS

The Green Paper on the reform of social security which preceded the April 1988 benefit changes was presented by the government as 'the most extensive reform of social security since Beveridge'. In the case of the unemployed, however, the Green Paper paid scant attention to the financial problems of coping with unemployment, problems that concerned Beveridge throughout much of his professional life. Notwithstanding, the government has felt able to borrow from Beveridge to provide justification for some of its policies towards the unemployed. His proposal that benefit after a certain duration of unemployment should be made conditional on attendance at a work or training centre has seen considerable airing in relation to the denial of Income Support to 16- and 17-year-olds. In its recent White Paper *Training for Employment*, the government quoted Beveridge's support for the 'enforcement of the citizen's obligation to seek and accept all reasonable opportunities of work'.

In citing Beveridge in support of their policies, the government must have hoped that readers would not go back to the original source, since this makes clear that Beveridge envisaged a quite different system of benefits for the unemployed from that we see today. The paragraph concerned (§130) refers explicitly to insurance benefits being made adequate for subsistence *without other means*; and indeed the paragraph opens with the trenchant statement that:

> To reduce the income of an unemployed or disabled person, either directly or *by application of a means test*, because the unemployment or disability has lasted for a certain period, is wrong in principle.
>
> (1942, p. 57, our emphasis)

The postwar national insurance benefit for the unemployed has never incorporated this recommendation, and there has always been a substantial proportion of the unemployed who have exhausted their entitlement to insurance benefit or who have been debarred by the contribution conditions. None the less, the period prior to 1979 did represent a time when there was a presumption in favour of a contributory system paying benefit as of right. Since 1979, however, there has been a major shift away from insurance benefit towards reliance on income-tested assistance for the unemployed. Without public debate, there has been a shift in principle underlying income support for the unemployed. The role of insurance benefits has been eroded by the tightening of the contribution conditions, the extension of the disqualification period, the restriction of benefits to students, the abolition of the lower rate benefits, and the abatement for occupational pensioners; their value has been reduced by the taxation of benefits; and the abandonment of statutory indexation has made the position of recipients insecure. As we have seen, these measures add up to a substantial reduction in the amount of national insurance benefit paid to the unemployed. At the same time, the generosity of income-tested assistance has been reduced in a number of respects, and the overall loss to the unemployed covered in our analysis for 1988 – from just the measures included in the modelling – is some £500 million or around 7 per cent of the predicted total benefit expenditure for the unemployed (HM Treasury, 1988, Table 15.8).

We have not considered the reasons why these changes have been made,[10] but it is clear that most have stemmed from the government's belief that the benefit system it inherited in 1979 constituted a major disincentive to work and that the generosity of benefit needed to be reduced (e.g. Department of Employment, 1985). In our view this belief is misguided and is not supported by the evidence, which does not in general indicate a large and significant disincentive to return to work, as we and others have argued elsewhere (see Chapter 9, Narendranathan *et al.*, 1985; and Micklewright, 1986). And the disincentive most likely to be serious is that concerning the labour supply of the wives of unemployed men, and here we have seen that recent policy has worsened rather than improved the position.

There has been a major change in emphasis, amounting to the covert abandonment of the insurance principle as far as the unemployed are concerned. However, it is not our intention to fight the corner of particular pieces of earlier legislation. Rather, we are concerned that the change in policy towards income support for the unemployed appears to have taken place without any serious discussion of the relative merits of social insurance and the income-tested alternative. Social insurance is clearly different in that there is no significant problem of non-take-up, so that the benefit is effective in reaching those for whom it is intended. Social insurance is based largely on individual entitlements, rather than a family means-test, and hence is in line with the trend towards independence in the field of personal taxation. The contribution conditions for social insurance provide an incentive for labour force participation and for people to take 'regular' as opposed to 'marginal' employment (Atkinson and Micklewright, 1988).

APPENDIX

A catalogue of changes in benefits for the unemployed, 1979–88

This appendix describes the changes affecting the unemployed which took place between 1979 and 1988 in national insurance unemployment benefit, referred to as UB, in Income Support (IS), which was previously supplementary benefit (SB), and in housing benefit (HB). Only a brief account is given of the individual measures; we do not, for example, give a blow-by-blow account of the controversy surrounding SB payments for board and lodging. It should be emphasized that the coverage is not intended to be exhaustive. We do not include measures affecting job training schemes, but it should be noted that the payments made under such schemes may be basically similar (indeed when the new Job Training Scheme supplement was introduced, it was technically SB and participants continued to be entitled to passport benefits).

The order of the measures is broadly chronological.

The references for each change include the following abbreviations: SSAC (Social Security Advisory Committee), SSN (Social Security Notes, published by the Department of Health and Social Security), Tolley's (Social Security and State Benefits, published by Tolley's), WRB (Welfare

Rights Bulletin published by the Child Poverty Action Group) and UUB (Unemployment Bulletin published by the Unemployment Unit).

National Insurance (NI)

1. Abolition of earnings-related supplement (ERS)
The Social Security (No. 2) Act 1980 abolished ERS. The 15 per cent rate of ERS was reduced to 10 per cent in January 1981, and from January 1982 no new claims could be made for ERS. As a result, no ERS was payable after June 1982.

2. Taxation of UB and SB
The income tax treatment of the unemployed has been changed in two respects: tax refunds are not paid till after the resumption of work, or the end of the tax year if that is sooner, and UB and SB have become taxable. The first was implemented with effect from April 1982. The taxation of benefits was announced in the 1980 Budget as coming into effect at this date, but it was deferred to July 1982, partly on account of civil service industrial action. The provisions are included in section 27 of the Finance Act 1981 and the details are given in Income Tax (Employments) No. 13 Regulations 1982. On the termination of the benefit claim, or the end of the tax year if that comes sooner, the claimant's tax position is calculated, taking account of the benefit received, and any net refund due is made. Where there is a net liability this would normally be collected by an adjustment of the PAYE code. The taxable benefits are the UB for the claimant plus the addition for one adult dependant, and any SB (for the claimant and adult dependant) paid in lieu of UB. Additions for children are not taxable. In the case of a breadwinner wife, the tax office will only transfer the balance of the married man's allowance after subtracting UB at the standard rate for the rest of the tax year (WRB 49, August 1982).

3. Basis for uprating of benefit
The uprating of short-term NI benefits has been modified in two important respects. The first concerns the calculation of the inflation rate. The Social Security Act 1975 required the Secretary of State to forecast the inflation rate, a forecast which naturally was not always accurate. As a result, in November 1981, there was a clawback of a 1 per cent overestimate of the inflation rate for the previous period; a 2 per cent underestimate was made good in November 1982. In the March 1983 Budget it was announced that there would be a reversion to an historic basis, with the uprating announced in June on the basis of inflation up to the end of May. The 1985 Social Security Act gave provision for a move to an April uprating from 1987, with a transitional uprating in July 1986.

4. Suspension of statutory indexation

The second change to uprating concerned the extent to which NI short-term benefits would in fact be inflation-proofed. The Social Security (No. 2) Act 1980 suspended for three years the duty of the Secretary of State to index link short-term NI benefits, giving power to increase them by up to 5 percentage points less than the rate of inflation. In 1980 there was indeed a 5 per cent withholding of UB pending taxation of UB, which was restored in November 1983. The Social Security Act 1986 provides for the Secretary of State to vary the amount of any increase 'if he considers it appropriate, having regard to the national economic situation and any other matters which he considers relevant' (Matthewman and Calvert, 1987, p. 103).

5. Abolition of child additions

In November 1980 there was a change in the method of calculating the inflation adjustment for the child's addition; and this addition was abolished from 26 November 1984, except for claimants over pensionable age.

6. Abolition of lower rate benefits

In January 1986 it was announced that the ¾ and ½ rates of NI benefit for those not meeting the full contribution conditions were to be abolished and it was implemented under the Social Security Act 1986 from October 1986.

7. Equal treatment provisions

In accordance with a 1978 European Community directive, in November 1983 regulations were introduced to ensure 'equal treatment' of men and women. These allowed married women to claim NI dependency additions. The payment of an addition for a dependent husband is conditional on the husband earning less than the amount of the addition.

8. Linked spell rule

From September 1980, the linked spell period was reduced from 13 weeks to 8 weeks if there was unexhausted entitlement to national insurance benefit (Social Security (No. 2) Act 1980). If entitlement had been exhausted then the period remained at 13 weeks. The significance of the linking is that a person does not have to wait a further three waiting days, but the total period of receipt in the linked spells is limited to 52 weeks (SSAC First Report, p. 9).

9. Earnings rule

From March 1982 the regulations were amended to increase from 75p to £2 the amount that an unemployed person could earn per day without losing UB providing that he/she is still available for full-time work on that day (WRB 47, April 1982). This remains at £2 in 1988. The rules were also eased to allow certain types of voluntary work.

10. Abatement for occupational pensioners

From April 1981, a person over the age of 60 and receiving an occupational pension of more than £35 has UB (including increases for dependants) reduced by 10p for every 10p above this level (Social Security (No. 2) Act 1980). The occupational pension abatement is the same in 1988, but the Social Security Bill 1988 reduces the age from 60 to 55 (introduced in January 1989).

11. More stringent administration

The operations of Unemployment Review Officers (UROs), responsible for finding out what the claimant is doing to get a job, traditionally based on the supplementary benefits side, were extended to cover those receiving NI unemployment benefit supplemented by SB in 1980. From October 1982, registration for work at a Job Centre became voluntary for unemployed people aged 18 and over. At the same time, unemployment benefit offices took over from Job Centres the task of testing 'availability for work'.

In August 1983 the Department of Employment set up Regional Benefit Investigation Teams. In 1984 the DHSS ordered a major drive in 59 areas into social security abuse: UROs questioned 18–25-year-olds about why they had left their jobs; Social Security Policy Inspectorate interviewed young people not joining a YTS scheme. Restart scheme introduced nationally in July 1986 with benefit monitoring function (UUB 21). More stringent availability-to-work test introduced in October 1986 involving new questionnaire for new claimants (UUB 22). Revised questionnaire for new claimants and new questionnaire for claimants called to Restart interviews were introduced from April 1988 (*Employment Gazette* January 1988, p. 3). All unemployed to be invited to Restart interviews every six months for duration of claim and all new claims to be handled by more senior staff than before (White Paper *Training for Employment* Cm 316, pp. 38–9).

12. Definition of voluntary redundancy

The Social Security Act 1985 amended the disqualification provisions to ensure that they are not applied to those who volunteer or agree to be made redundant within the meaning of the Employment Protection (Consolidation) Act 1978. Such workers were no longer liable to disqualification from NI benefit from July 1985 (SSN, 15, October 1985).

13. Disqualification period

The Social Security Act 1986 extended the maximum period of benefit disqualification from 6 to 13 weeks, with effect from October 1986 (SSN, 17, July 1986). This applies where there is quitting without just cause, or loss of job through industrial misconduct, or refusal to take suitable work or training offers (the voluntary unemployment deduction). The extension was made 'in view of concern at the number of people leaving their job voluntarily' (*Public Expenditure White Paper*, 1987, Vol. II, p. 246). The Act gave the Secretary of State the power to alter this period and from 11 April 1988, there was a further increase to 26 weeks. The Act also allows the Secretary to make regulations which will provide that days of disqualification count towards the entitlement to a total of 312 days of benefit (SSN, 17, July 1986). As is noted by the SSAC, this would mean for the UB claimant 'a longer maximum period of disqualification during which no benefit is paid, followed by a shortened entitlement to UB' (Fifth Report, p. 36).

14. Payment of benefits
In September 1979 the Social Security (Claims and Payments) Amendment Regulations became effective: UB to be paid fortnightly, except for those on short-time working or who chose to be paid weekly. The Rayner Report on Payment of Benefits to Unemployed people was published in March 1981. In June 1984 it was announced that all new claimants would be paid fortnightly in arrears instead of one week in advance/one week in arrears (Hansard, 18 June 1984, col. 20). In April 1986 postal claimants of UB became liable to pay their own postal charges. In April 1987 new rules were introduced governing overpayments. Whereas previously benefit could only be recovered if the claimant failed to use 'due care and diligence', now it may be recovered if due to any misrepresentation or failure to disclose a material fact, even where this was entirely innocent (e.g. where the fact was unknown to the claimant).

15. Students
From September 1986 regulations were made to remove entitlement by full-time students to UB and SB during the 'grant-aided period', effectively removing entitlement for most students in the short vacations (SSN, 18, October 1986, WRB 70, February 1986).

16. Full extent normal rule
This rule prevents those who do not normally work on every working day in the week from claiming UB on their 'off' days. This has caused particular difficulties with part-time Community Programme (CP) workers. Following a decision by a tribunal of Commissioners that such persons were not precluded from claiming UB, regulations were introduced with effect from March 1987 preventing such people from claiming UB for days on which they are not employed on a CP scheme (WRB 79, August, 1987).

17. Contribution conditions
The Social Security Bill 1988 tightens the contribution conditions for NI benefit, with the change planned to take effect from October 1988. The

entitlement will depend on the contribution record for the *two* tax years before the start of the benefit year, as opposed to the present one tax year. Class 1 contributions on earnings of at least 50 times the lower weekly earnings limit must have been paid or credited in both tax years; and, for unemployment benefit, Class 1 contributions must have been paid (i.e. *not* credited) on earnings of at least 25 times the weekly lower earnings limit in one of the two tax years (as opposed to *any* tax year). Moreover, the rule permitting the aggregation of contributions paid in more than one tax year in order to satisfy the second condition is abolished.

Income support supplementary benefit and the unemployed

(See also (2.) and (15.) above.)

18. 1980 Reform
On 24 November 1980 the SB scheme was revised, with the changes including (introduced in Social Security Act 1980):

1. Alignment of SB and NI rates.
2. Reduction in number of age ranges for children from 5 to 3 (previously there had been scales for ages 0–4, 5–10, 11–12, 13–15 and 16–17; these became 0–10, 11–15 and 16–17).
3. Changes in earnings disregards, and introduction of tapered earnings disregard for single parents.
4. A capital limit of £2,000 (in place of £1,250), which became absolute (rather than tariff income assumed).
5. School-leavers denied the right to claim benefit until the end of the vacation following their last term in full-time education (see (26) below).
6. Introduction of standard rent share deduction for non-dependent members of the household.
7. Extra Circumstance Additions (ECAs) became part of the legal entitlement for those meeting specified conditions.
8. Introduction of new powers to recover overpayments retrospectively.

19. Long-term SB rate
In November 1981 the long-term SB rate was extended to unemployed men aged 60 or over, provided that they ceased to register for employment, so that if unemployed for more than one year, and no longer registering for work, they received the higher long-term rate (SSAC First Report, pp. 11 and 27). From May 1983, all unemployed men aged 60 and over were no longer required to be available for employment and became entitled to the long-term rate of SB (WRB, 54, June 1983). From November 1985, people in this position qualified automatically for the lower rate of heating addition (WRB 67, August 1985).

20. More stringent administration

The number of Unemployment Review Officers, responsible for finding out what the claimant is doing to get a job, increased from 300 in 1978 to 880 in 1981 (*Payments of Benefits to Unemployed People*, p. 26). In February 1980 the Social Security Minister announced deployment of 1,050 additional staff to carry out a drive to expose social security fraud. Specialist claims control teams controlled by Regional Fraud Section to deal with specific areas including the 'workshy' were introduced nationally in November 1981 (SSN, 7, July 1983). Total DHSS staff allocated to fraud work increased from 2,044 in 1980/1 to 3,674 in 1986/7 (Hansard, 19 June 1986, col. 591, 20 Feb. 1986, col. 315, 24 Feb. 1986, col. 589, and 15 May 1986, col. 533).

21. Equal treatment

As with NI benefit, 'equal treatment' provisions were introduced in November 1983. These allow for one of a couple to be the claimant, according to qualifying conditions and restrictions on the dates at which changes in roles are permitted (SSN, 8, October 1983 and WRB, 56 and 57).

22. Non-householder fixed housing cost addition

The non-householder fixed housing cost addition was abolished for those aged 16–17 in April 1983 (WRB, 12th edition, p. 41), for those aged 18–20 in 1984, and for those aged 21–24 in 1986 (this representing a step towards the Income Support scheme with its lower rates for those aged under 25) (WRB, 17th edition, p. 49).

23. Voluntary unemployment deductions

In 1983 the Social Security Policy Inspectorate reported on voluntary unemployment deductions, disclosing widespread misapplication of these rules. These rules apply to those persons disqualified from NI benefit and reduce the SB payable by either 40 or 20 per cent of the personal scale rate (no deduction being made with respect to payments for a partner or children). The lower 20 per cent rate was applied where the full cut would cause hardship (the so-called 'compassion clause'). From August 1983 the application of the 20 per cent deduction, as opposed to 40 per cent, was restricted to families where someone in the family was pregnant or seriously ill and the claimant's capital is less than £100 (£220 from April 1988) (SSN, 8, October 1983).

24. Disqualification period

The extensions of the disqualification period in 1986 and 1988 described for NI benefit also applies to SB where there is a 40 per cent (or 20 per cent) deduction.

25. Board and lodgings

In September 1984 DHSS announced a six-month freeze on amounts of SB paid to people in board and lodgings. With effect from April 1985, a system of national maxima was introduced, the general discretion to disapply the maxima was removed, and restrictions were introduced to limit the length of time an unemployed person under the age of 26 could claim benefit as a boarder in given locations. Certain parts of these regulations were found by the High Court to be *ultra vires*; they were remade in October 1985 but were subsequently withdrawn. A further set of regulations was produced in November 1985 (SSAC, Fifth Report, Chapter 7, WRB 76, February 1987, WRB 78, June 1987).

26. School-leavers

Prior to 1980, school-leavers could claim benefit as soon as they left school. In 1980 the concept of a 'terminal date' was introduced, under which benefit could not be claimed until approximately the first Monday of the following term. Easter leavers entered for a summer examination were deemed to be ineligible for benefit until September (SSAC, Second Report, p. 13, Fifth Report, p. 30).

27. Part-time study

The conditions for students taking part-time courses which do not prevent them being available for work have been the subject of a number of changes in regulations. The '21-hour' rule allows people to undertake up to 21 hours of part-time study without prejudice to their entitlement to SB. In 1982 a regulation made clear that the 21 hours referred to supervised study and did not include private study or non-teaching time such as lunch-breaks, but this regulation also introduced a qualifying period, requiring that the person had for the previous three months been in receipt of SB, UB or sickness benefit (or an alternative condition during the previous six months) (SSAC, Second report, p. 16, WRB, 49, August 1982). This condition did not apply to 16–18-year-olds whose course was not deemed to be 'full-time'. The definition of the latter was changed in August 1984 to more than 12 hours a week of supervised study excluding homework and meal breaks (WRB, 61, August 1984).

28. Heating additions

No awards for central heating additions for SB were made from August 1985 (WRB, 67, August 1985).

29. Mortgage interest

Those aged under 60 receive only 50 per cent of the mortgage interest eligible for SB during the first 16 weeks on benefit (WRB, 76, February 1987 and 78, June 1987). Claimants have to make an appropriate application within four weeks of the end of the period (or else start a new claim again). This provision was introduced for SB from January 1987 and is retained in the Income Support scheme.

30. Income support

The replacement of SB in 1988 by IS has meant major changes. It replaces the system of short-term and long-term rates, and distinction between householders and non-householders, by personal allowances determining benefit on the basis of age and marital status. There is a flat-rate premium paid to all families with children in addition to age-related scales for children. It replaces the variety of extra payments under SB designed to cater for different dimensions of need (for heating, laundry, special diets, etc.) by premia for different groups: lone parents, pensioners, the disabled, and other groups. Exceptional needs payments are replaced by the social fund (see below). In addition there are the following changes:

1. Those with capital in excess of £6,000 are not eligible for IS or housing benefit; capital between £3,000 and £6,000 is assumed to produce a weekly income (equal to £1 for each £250, or part thereof, in excess of £3,000) which is taken into account in assessing entitlement.
2. The IS payment no longer includes water rates or residual housing costs (such as maintenance or insurance for owner-occupiers).
3. The definition of net earnings is changed (for example, only half of contributions to occupational pension schemes is deducted and there is no provision for work expenses) and higher earnings disregard for couples unemployed for two years (and lone parents).
4. Persons working 24 hours or more are defined as being in 'remunerative work' and ineligible for IS.
5. Couples have a free choice as to which claims where neither works 24 hours or more a week (where one works 24 hours or more then there is no entitlement).

In determining the scales for IS, 'the Government has had regard to the previous levels of supplementary benefit . . . as well as trends in the number of beneficiaries of different types, to the overall support available for various groups from public funds, and to the need to restrain public expenditure. The rates of these benefits include the average amount that the Government expect householders who are income support claimants will have to meet as their minimum contribution to domestic rates in 1988–89' (*Public Expenditure White Paper*, 1987, Vol. II, p. 274).

There is transitional protection for existing SB claimants in April 1988 who would qualify for a lower level of IS. Their benefit is frozen at its current level in money terms until the IS entitlement has been uprated to a higher level.

31. Social Fund
In April 1988 the new Social Fund replaced supplementary benefit single payments (SSN, 20, February 1988). (In 1987 the Social Fund had begun to make maternity and funeral payments in place of the maternity grant, the death grant and single payments for these contingencies.) Payments are at the discretion of the Social Fund officers; there is no legal right to help nor to an independent appeal if help is refused. The payments are in most cases loans, not grants, the only exception, apart from maternity and funeral payments, being grants being paid for certain community care needs. To repay loans, a claimant's weekly benefit is reduced, normally by 15 per cent. Payments, apart from those for maternity or funeral expenses, are subject to a cash limit on total expenditure.

32. 16–17-year-olds
The Social Security Bill 1988 and the Employment Bill 1988 make major changes in the income support for school leavers aged under 18. The former removes the general entitlement to IS of 16- and 17-year-olds, allowing only for IS to be awarded on a discretionary basis where 'severe hardship' might occur (this may include those with disabilities and single parents). The Bill also allows parents to continue to receive child benefit for a period after their son or daughter leaves school. The Employment Bill provides for a 'bridging allowance' to be paid to 16- and 17-year-olds who leave jobs or YTS and are waiting for a YTS place, on condition that the claimant has registered for a place on the scheme. The Bill extends the circumstances in which benefit may be withdrawn or reduced for unemployed people leaving or refusing places on job training schemes.

Housing benefit

33. Social Security and Housing Benefits Act 1982
Under the system in force in 1979 an unemployed person could receive either supplementary benefit (SB) or housing benefit (HB), with the possibility of an overlap at the beginning of a spell of unemployment where HB continued to be paid. The choice between SB and HB gave rise to the 'better-off' problem. Whereas an unemployed person with no other source of income would be better off on SB, a person in receipt of NI benefit, or with a working spouse, could be treated more favourably under HB. This added a major source of complexity and there is little doubt that many claimants received the less advantageous benefit (see Atkinson and Micklewright, 1985, p. 37). The better-off problem was eliminated by the 1982 legislation. This transferred the payment of rent and rates assistance to the local authorities, although payments for water rates and for owner-occupier's mortgage interest (and other costs) continued under SB. Where the unemployed person's resources fell short of his or her SB

calculation of requirements (not including rent and rates), there was entitlement to SB and to certificated HB, paying (normally) 100 per cent rent and rates. Where the resources exceed requirements, so that the person was not eligible for SB, then standard HB could be claimed. If after receiving HB the net rent and rates was greater than the excess of resources over requirements, then HB supplement could be claimed equal to the difference. There were therefore after 1982 four types of payment for housing: SB payments for water rates and owner occupier's costs, certificated HB, standard HB and HB supplement. There were in addition changes in the tapers, non-dependent deductions, and other parameters of the scheme.

34. Changes in tapers
The tapers determine the amount of HB payable where income is above or below the needs allowance. With effect from April 1983, the tapers for claimants below pension age with incomes above the needs allowance were 21 per cent for rent rebates and 7 per cent for rate rebates. These tapers were increased to 26 per cent and 9 per cent from April 1984 and to 29 per cent for rent rebates from November 1984. The taper for rate rebate was further increased to 13 per cent from November 1985, and the rent rebate taper to 33 per cent in April 1987.

35. Non-dependent deductions
From April 1984 changes were made in the non-dependent deductions, extending these to persons aged under 18 and increasing their level. In consequence of the abolition of the fixed housing cost addition to SB for non-householders aged under 21, the deduction was set at zero for persons aged under 21 (25 from 1986) and either receiving SB or attending YTS.

36. Changes in needs allowances
There have been changes in the real value of the needs allowances, including a 50p increase in the real value of the needs allowance for a child in November 1984 and a 95p increase in November 1985 (H, 20 May 1986, col. 169).

37. Minimum payments
The minimum payment has been increased to 50p a week (H, 20 May 1986, col. 169).

38. 1988 changes
The Social Security Act 1986 introduced a common basis of assessment for housing benefit and IS (with the exception that HB has a higher single-parent premium) and abolished HB supplement. Where a person's income is below the IS level then HB is paid in full, where this is 100 per cent of

rents (unless these are considered 'unreasonable') and 80 per cent of rates, less deductions for non-dependants. Where the income is above the IS level then the rate rebate is reduced by 20 per cent of the excess, not being payable where the net amount falls below 50p a week, and the rent rebate is reduced by 65 per cent of the excess, not being payable where the net amount falls below 50p a week. One major implication of the alignment of HB and IS is that HB has become subject to a capital condition. The fact that the claimant has to meet a minimum of 20 per cent of the rates payment represents a major departure, and has to be judged in conjunction with the introduction of the poll tax.

NOTES

1. In Hansard (6 November 1986, col. 589) the government gave a figure for the approximate hours of work for a person on half national average earnings represented by the earnings limit. In 1956 this was 2½ hours; in 1965 and 1975, 1½ hours; and in 1985, 1 hour.
2. It should be pointed out that previous governments had considered this change which was suggested by a report of the National Insurance Advisory Committee in 1968 (Cmnd 3545).
3. The meaning of 'occupational pensions' is open to interpretation. According to Rowland, 'arrangements are widely interpreted as occupational pensions. The term has been held to include payments not actually made out of an occupational pension fund' (1988, p. 37).
4. In Atkinson and Micklewright (1985, Chapter 4) we provide an analysis of unpublished administrative data on reasons for non-receipt of UB for unemployed men in each year 1972–79.
5. The problems that claimants may face are described by Rowland (1988, p. ix): 'those least articulate are at a disadvantage and administrators do not seem to realise that the completion of forms does not always give a realistic picture of events. Thus parents may well not have made detailed arrangements for the care of their children in the event of their obtaining employment but they may also know that in the short term arrangements can be made informally with friends and family and longer-term arrangements can be sorted out then. The lack of precision does not appeal to administrators.'
6. The version of TAXMOD used is 6.4.
7. Although we do not take account of the effect on weekly incomes of tax refunds that might be payable during unemployment.
8. A loss may arise where entitlement to SB ceases and, as a result, passport benefits are lost.
9. If we had modelled the entitlement to ERS as such, the gains at the upper end would probably have been greater.
10. The political economy of unemployment insurance is discussed in Atkinson (1988b).

9 · UNEMPLOYMENT BENEFIT, DURATION AND INCENTIVES IN BRITAIN

How robust is the evidence?

1 INTRODUCTION

> The theory of job search suggests that subsidized benefits of a general
> unemployment insurance system ... create substitution effects in favor of
> greater frequency and longer duration periods of unemployment. ... Indeed,
> empirical studies do indicate a statistically significant effect of this type.
>
> (Lindbeck, 1981, p. 38)

Assar Lindbeck's statement is a good summary of the prevailing wisdom
concerning the relationship between the behaviour of the unemployed and
the unemployment insurance system – that higher benefits lead to longer
durations. The search theory model provides a clearcut qualitative prediction, and the empirical evidence, it is claimed, confirms that the effect is
both of the expected sign and statistically significant. The review of the US
literature by Danziger, Haveman and Plotnick concluded that: 'despite the
problems, a positive relation between UI and duration of unemployment
appears robust' (1981, p. 992). Hamermesh similarly summarized 'nearly
two dozen studies' as indicating 'fairly consistently that a 20 per cent
increase in UI benefits induces between one-half and one extra week of
measured unemployment (3 to 6 per cent)' (1982, p. 238). In Britain, which
is our particular focus, Lancaster and Nickell, reviewing their separate
work, concluded that: 'the effect on unemployment durations of the
relative level of unemployment benefit is consistent both with theoretical
reasoning and a number of previous studies ... We would regard the size of

Reprinted from *Journal of Public Economics*, 23, 1984. With J. Gomulka, J. Micklewright
and N. Rau. This chapter describes results from a project carried out with support from HM
Treasury. It forms part of the SSRC programme on Taxation, Incentives and the Distribution
of Income (Grant HR 4652). Neither HM Treasury nor the SSRC is responsible for the views
expressed in the chapter. In revising the chapter, the authors have benefited considerably
from the comments of the discussants, A. Lancaster and I. Byatt, of other participants in the
NBER/SSRC Conference on Micro-Data and Public Economics, Oxford, 1982, and of the
referees.

the effect of benefits as being now a rather firmly established parameter' (1980, p. 151).

In the present political and economic climate, it is scarcely surprising that such conditions have received a great deal of attention and that they have been used – and misused – in public debate about the conduct of policy.[1] Those seeking to explain the present level of unemployment from the supplyside have seized on the role of social security benefits (for example, Minford, 1982). There have been calls in the United Kingdom for reductions in unemployment benefit. In this context, it is important to assess the robustness of the conclusions which have been reached. In this chapter we provide such a reassessment, from which we conclude that the evidence – at least that from household surveys in Britain – is far from robust, and that the size of the effect of benefits cannot be regarded as 'firmly established'.

In our reconsideration of the evidence about unemployment duration and benefits, we concentrate on the cross-section approach, and we confine attention to the evidence for the United Kingdom, seeking to build on the earlier work of Lancaster and Nickell (separately Lancaster, 1979; Nickell, 1979a, 1979b; and Lancaster and Nickell, 1980). These studies have made a major contribution.[2] They have drawn on models of search behaviour, relating theory and economic specification more closely than is often the case. They have shown how micro-data can be used to throw light on issues where the aggregate time-series evidence, is, at best, difficult to interpret. They have developed econometric techniques to handle the estimation problems which arise as a result of the way in which the sample is established and of the form of the data. At the same time, there are several features which seem to warrant further examination.

The first concerns the link between theory and specification. As we show in section 2, even the simplest search theory framework does not lead to a convenient functional form and the role of the theory has been mainly to suggest possible candidates for right-hand variables. Moreover, certain key elements of the problem, notably the effect of the British cumulative income tax system, cannot be handled within this framework.

The second aspect is the treatment of unemployment benefits. Much of the aggregate time-series analysis in Britain has used a 'representative' level of benefits to characterize the impact of social security: for example, Maki and Spindler (1975) take a hypothetical married man with a non-working wife and two children, in weeks 3–28 of unemployment, with no previous spell out of work, who earned average earnings in the relevant contribution year. One of the criticisms of the time-series literature is that such representative calculations bear little relation to the reality of benefit receipt and are misleading even as an indicator of the trends over time. It is a merit of the cross-section studies that benefit receipt may be related to individual characteristics. However, the limitations of the source (the *General Household Survey*) employed by Nickell (1979a and b) mean that he had to calculate benefits largely by applying the rules for a 'standard case', and the resulting variable is inconsistent with other evidence about benefit receipt. In contrast, the data set used in our work,[3] the *Family Expenditure Survey* (FES), contains richer information about actual benefits, allowing us to capture more fully the range of variation in individual circumstances – especially the time-path of receipt. Section 3 describes the FES data and the calculation of a benefit variable which corresponds more closely with the evidence from administrative records; section 4 shows how the data are used to estimate the model of re-employment probabilities.

The third aspect which warrants further attention is the role of varying labour market conditions. The studies by Nickell and Lancaster relate to 1972 and 1973, respectively, when average unemployment in the United Kingdom was 850,000 (3.7 per cent) and 610,000 (2.6 per cent). Our own data span the period from 1972 to 1977. These years do not cover the very high levels of the early 1980s, but they do include the rise to over 1.5 million in 1977 (5.7 per cent). It has also been suggested that the size of the benefit effect may depend on the overall level of unemployment. In its evidence to a House of Commons select committee, the Treasury noted that: 'it is likely that the effect on unemployment of a change in the ratio will depend overall conditions in the labour market, and numerical estimates calculated for one period should not be translated to another when circumstances are very different' (Treasury and Civil Service Committee, The Structure of Personal Income Taxation and Income Support, Minutes of Evidence, 12 May 1982, p. 204).

The main part of the chapter is concerned with the estimation of a model of re-employment probabilities using the FES data. For purposes of comparability, the model used is of the same form as that of Lancaster and Nickell, and in section 5 we show that it yields rather similar estimates of the effects of benefits to those in the earlier studies. However, in section 6 we demonstrate that the use of our alternative benefit variable, more closely related to actual receipt, leads to quite different findings. In section 7 we present results based on different concepts of the replacement rate, relevant in different tax/benefit situations, and taking account of the cumulative nature of the tax system. The implications of our research are discussed in section 8.

As will be apparent, we are only considering certain aspects of the effect of unemployment insurance. We concentrate, like Lancaster and Nickell, on the probability of return to work, conditional on being unemployed; we do not consider any impact on the flow into unemployment (see Nickell, 1980; and Stern, 1982). We do not examine the incentives for employers, emphasized in the United States by Feldstein (1976); nor do we investigate the possible effect of social security benefits on wage bargaining.

2   THE MODEL

The studies of Lancaster and Nickell, like those of Kiefer and Neumann (1979a and b, 1981) in the United States, make an impressive attempt to draw on theories of search behaviour when specifying the model of re-employment probabilities. For convenience, the essentials of the model are summarized below.[4]

1. The person maximizes the expected present value of income over an infinite horizon, discounted at rate ϱ.
2. While unemployed, the person receives a constant level of unemployment benefit, b, and other income, y.
3. Job offers arrive randomly at a constant average rate, λ, per unit of time.
4. A job offer is described by a constant wage, w, with a stationary cumulative distribution function $F(w)$, where $w \geqq w_0$ and has mean $\bar{w}$. The wage lasts forever, giving total income in work of $(w + y)$.
5. The person is free to accept or reject job offers (there is no risk of disqualification from benefit).

Individual behaviour can be represented in terms of the choice of reservation wage, w^*, with the person accepting the job if and only if $w \geqq w^*$. The probability of an unemployed person being re-employed, θ, is therefore given by

$$\theta(w^*)\,\mathrm{d}t = \lambda[1 - F(w^*)]\,\mathrm{d}t. \tag{1}$$

It can then be shown that the choice of w^* must satisfy the condition (where $w^* \geqq w_0$):

$$w^* - b = \frac{\lambda}{\varrho} \int_{w^*}^{\infty} (w - w^*)\,\mathrm{d}F = \frac{\theta}{\varrho}(\bar{w}|_{w^*} - w^*), \tag{2}$$

where $\bar{w}|_{w^*}$ is the expected wage conditional on $w \geqq w^*$.

The search theory formulation has not typically been used to derive explicit functional forms for the re-employment probability, θ. Even with relatively tractable wage offer distributions such as the Pareto, no simple functional form emerges. We do not therefore have a situation like that in consumer demand analysis where the standard theoretical model leads straightforwardly to explicit – if restrictive – functional forms. There is no apparent analogue of the Cobb–Douglas. The role of the theory has therefore been the more circumscribed one of indicating the variables to be included. Even here, the link is at best tenuous.

The limited nature of the link between the theoretical framework and the empirical work is illustrated by the variable which is the main focus of this paper – the level of benefit income. If, to begin with, we accept the simple search theory framework, then, with the additional assumption that the wage offer distribution shifts proportionately as we consider different individuals (Nickell, 1979a), we can deduce that the relevant variable is $b/\bar{w}$, where $\bar{w}$ measures the 'location' of the wage offer distribution. The actual variables employed have however been different. In the case of Lancaster (1979), the numerator is benefit income, but the denominator is net earnings in last job. If the job search decisions are made on the same basis each time, then the latter may be seen as having an expected value of $\bar{w}|_{w^*}$. Since, other things being equal, those who are more selective about jobs have on average higher earnings in their last job, actual last earnings do not seem the appropriate variable to use.

The endogeneity of last job earnings is stressed by Nickell (1979a), who uses in the denominator predicted earnings, based on an estimated earnings function. In this respect, his denominator corresponds to $\bar{w}$. On the other hand, in both the numerator and the denominator he adds other family income, so that the replacement variable is in effect of the form $(b + y)/(\bar{w} + y)$. Given the formulation described above, y should not in fact enter the determination of the reservation wage. With the expected present value objective, we are concerned only with the marginal additions to cash income, and other income which is independent of employment status, such as investment income, is not relevant. The analysis may be seen as parallel to the 'constant marginal utility of wealth' supply functions of Heckman and MaCurdy (1980). If, as is quite possible, we do not like the implication that a millionaire will search as hard as a pauper, then the theoretical formulation needs to be modified. This is not difficult to do, via the introduction of leisure or risk-aversion, but the need to do so underlines the relatively weak link between the theory and the empirical specification.

We need however to go further, and to leave the simple framework of eq. (2) if we are to take account of one important aspect of incentives not adequately treated in earlier studies – the interrelation with the income tax system. In calculating net income, it has typically been assumed that the income tax deducted is that applicable in a full year, whereas it has been argued by Atkinson and Flemming (1978), Kay, Morris and Warren (1980), and others, that it is *marginal* net earnings that may be relevant, not the *average* net earnings over a full tax year. The cumulative tax system in operation in Britain means that the marginal net earnings from returning to work a week earlier may be considerably less than the average net earnings. If the tax system[5] has a constant marginal rate, u, on all income in excess of the exemption level, x, then the marginal net earnings where a person is liable for tax in this tax year is $(1 - u)w$ compared with average net earnings $(1 - u) w + ux$.

The theoretical framework described above cannot be applied directly to this problem, in view of the intertemporal dependence of the budget constraint with a cumulative tax system. As is shown in Atkinson and Rau

(1981), the marginal gain from returning to work depends on a variety of factors, including the date of entry into unemployment, relative to the tax year, past earnings in the tax year, the perceptions of the probability of securing a job, the length of time a job is expected to last, and the rate of discount. There is an obvious analogy with the theory of the firm, where the cost of capital depends on the relevant margin at which the firm is operating (and may or may not be affected by profit taxation). As in the literature on investment and the cost of capital, we proceed empirically, considering the effect of alternative specifications for the 'replacement rate'. These are:

$$R_A = \frac{b + y}{(1 - u)(w + y) + ux}, \qquad \text{'average' after tax,}$$

$$R_B = \frac{b + y}{w + y}, \qquad \text{'average' after tax,}$$

$$R_C = \frac{b}{(1 - u)w}, \qquad \text{'marginal' after tax,}$$

$$R_D = \frac{b}{w}, \qquad \text{'marginal' before tax,}$$

Each of these may be relevant to the re-employment probability in different sets of circumstances, or with different representations of the decision-making by the unemployed, including use of rules-of-thumb rather than explicit maximization. There are not, as is sometimes suggested, grounds for concentrating on only the 'marginal' rates (see Atkinson and Rau, 1981).

3 THE FES DATA AND BENEFIT RECEIPT

The *Family Expenditure Survey* (FES) data used in this chapter are drawn from the surveys carried out over the period 1972–77.[6] Taking the data from several years not only increases the sample size but also means that we have observations spanning a range of labour market conditions. The observations relate to men aged 16–64 who were in the category 'out of employment and seeking work', a definition which may include some people not registered as unemployed and may exclude certain people receiving unemployment benefit (e.g. those on short time or temporarily laid off). It should be noted that men may leave the category by returning to work, either employed or self-employed, *or* by becoming sick or injured *or* by leaving the labour force. The probability θ of leaving unemployment covers therefore, transitions to several possible states and not just 're-employment'. It is quite possible, for example, that increases in unemployment insurance benefits might provide people with an incentive to remain registered as unemployed rather than retire.

The full sample for the period is 1,231 men, which may be compared with 447 men and 32 women in the case of Lancaster (1979) and 426 men in the case of Nickell (1979a). These men had been away from work for up to five years (the maximum recorded in the FES; those unemployed more than five years are not included in the category we are considering). In parts of the analysis, we restrict attention to the 'One Year Sample' of 845 men unemployed for a year or less at the date of interview and for whom previous earnings are recorded (thus excluding, for example, school-leavers), or the 'Two Year Sample, of 1,140 men out of work for two years or less. Our information on the spell of unemployment is considerably more precise than that of Nickell in that we have the exact number of weeks rather than broad ranges (such as 26–52 weeks).[7]

The receipt of social security benefit depends on the parameters of the national insurance and supplementary benefit schemes, on the person's previous employment record and earnings, on the income of other family members, on housing expenses, and on duration. The FES records receipt of different types of benefit over the 12 months prior to the date of interview, the number of weeks the benefit was received, the amount of the last payment, and whether the benefit is received at present. It does not, however, provide all the information that we require. In the estimation procedure we need to calculate the relevant variable for all weeks that the person has been unemployed, and to extrapolate to other possible entry dates. We have therefore to make assumptions – as in virtually any study. But we have departed from earlier work in that we have tried to relate our assumptions closely to the information recorded in the FES, whereas the main benefit variables employed by Nickell are 'imputed using the rules current at the appropriate date' (1979a, p. 1265). In what follows, we describe the implications for two key elements: the type of benefit received and the calculation of the earnings-related supplement to national insurance benefit.

The *type of benefit* is characterized by five possible regimes through which a person may pass during a spell of unemployment:

1. No national insurance (NI) benefit; there may be entitlement to supplementary benefit (SB).
2. NI flat-rate benefit received, with possible entitlement to SB.
3. NI flat-rate benefit and earnings-related supplement (ERS) received (maximum duration 26 weeks), with possible entitlement to SB.
4. NI flat-rate benefit received (maximum duration in (2), (3) and (4) 52 weeks), with possible entitlement to SB.
5. SB entitlement only.

In much of the work on replacement rates, it is assumed that people follow the 'standard' pattern of three waiting days, followed by two weeks flat-rate benefit, 26 weeks with ERS, a further 24 weeks flat-rate benefit, and entitlement to NI benefit exhausted after a year. There are however a number of reasons why actual benefit receipt does not follow this pattern. Where, for example, the person has previously been unemployed, the spells may be 'linked'; if he has previously used up his entitlement to ERS, then he goes straight to regime (4), and NI benefit is terminated before the end of 52 weeks. A person may have received sickness benefit during part of his spell off work, which may extend entitlement to NI benefit beyond 52 weeks. There may be a lag in the commencement of payment of benefit: e.g. where he has been disqualified for 'voluntary' leaving. The person may be ineligible for NI benefit because of an incomplete contribution record. And so on.

The FES does not contain full benefit histories, but from the available data we conclude that in about two-thirds of cases the 'standard' pattern of benefit receipt does not seem to apply. We have produced for each observation a 'calculated' pattern of benefit receipt (for details, see Atkinson et al., 1981). These calculations are subject to error, but they seem more likely to be realistic than the approach adopted by Nickell (which was forced on him by the limited data on income contained in the *General Household Survey*).

The effect of our alternative assumptions may be illustrated by the results for the One Year Sample (845 cases). On the standard assumptions, all would be supposed to be receiving NI benefit, whereas the recorded pattern on which our calculations are based shows a proportion of 65.3 per cent. This latter figure is close to the figures obtainable from the administrative records. According to the DHSS figures, the proportion of men unemployed for 52 weeks or less who received NI benefit varied between 55 and 60 per cent over the period 1972–77. The FES figure for all those unemployed less than a year (i.e. including those with no previous earnings) is 60.5 per cent.

The *calculation of the earnings-related supplement* (ERS) is of some importance, since this element of the unemployment insurance system attracted a lot of attention in debate about the incentive effect. The introduction of ERS in 1966 was held to be responsible for a substantial rise in unemployment (e.g. Maki and Spindler, 1975); and the Conservative government's decision to abolish it, with effect from January 1982 was undoubtedly influenced by the belief that it acted as a disincentive to work. On the other hand, the typical treatment of the supplement in empirical work is unsatisfactory. This is not perhaps surprising, in that the calculation is complex, being based on total annual earnings in the relevant past contribution year: e.g. in the calendar year 1977, the ERS depended on earnings in the tax year ending in April 1976 (see Micklewright, 1984b and

1985). The amount of entitlement depended therefore on the level of weekly earnings and on the employment record in a period some distance in the past.

The 'standard' assumption in the calculations of ERS is that the person was employed for the entire year at an estimated level of earnings. (Nickell uses the same predicted earnings equation as in the denominator of the replacement rate.) This makes no use of the information on earnings in the last job, and ignores periods of interruption of employment, which may reduce ERS or mean that there is no entitlement (where the annual total falls below the lower limit). Following Nickell (1979b), we examine the effect of 'alternative' assumptions. These involve first replacing predicted earnings in the calculation of the amount of ERS by the reported normal earnings in the previous job (this information is only available for the One Year Sample) deflated to the relevant contribution year.[8] Secondly, the amount of ERS is adjusted according to the estimated relation between calculated and predicted amounts in the FES. Finally, on the basis of an analysis of the cases calculated to be receiving ERS in the FES, we assign zero receipt where the probability falls below a critical value chosen to give approximately the national proportion. The probability is significantly lower for unskilled workers, for those not married, and those not reporting receipt of redundancy payments (see Atkinson and Micklewright, 1986).

The need for adjustments of this kind may be illustrated by the comparison with the DHSS administrative figures. In May 1977, the proportion of men unemployed for less than a year receiving ERS was 25.1 per cent. With the 'alternative' assumption, the calculated proportion in the FES is 23.7 per cent, whereas with the 'standard' assumption it would be 37.3 per cent. The mean payment of ERS in 1976 recorded by the DHSS was £7.02 a week. With the 'alternative' assumption, the mean amount in 1976 is £7.18 a week, compared with £8.68 without the adjustment of the amounts. There are therefore some grounds for believing that the alternative assumptions may be closer than the standard assumption to the reality of benefit receipt.

In addition to the NI benefit described above, we have also allowed for supplementary benefit, family allowances/child benefit, and rate and rent rebates. All except supplementary benefit are also relevant in work, and are taken into account, together with family income supplement, when calculating net income in employment. The latter is based on predicted earnings functions estimated separately for five occupational groups using data for the employed population in the FES 1970–77 (see Micklewright and Rau, 1980). In the case of means-tested benefits, we assume 100 per cent take-up. This assumption is the same as that of Nickell, but may be unsatisfactory in view of recent evidence that the take-up of benefits available when at work by unemployed men is particularly low (Millar, 1982). We also assume that no tax refunds are received; in this case, the assumption may be closer to reality than the opposite extreme assumption that refunds are received as they accrue. Finally, we should note that the wife's earnings are assumed to be independent of the man's employment status. This is an aspect which deserves more investigation (see Smee and Stern, 1978).

4   ESTIMATION OF THE MODEL

As we have seen, the search theory formulation does not provide clear indication of the appropriate choice of functional form. In view of this, we have followed Lancaster in assuming that the conditional probability, θ, of returning to work after a spell, s, given that the person has been out of work since τ and has characteristics x_i, is given by:

$$\theta = \alpha s^{\alpha-1} e^{\beta \cdot x_i(s, \tau)}, \quad \text{where } \alpha > 0. \tag{3}$$

This introduces duration dependence via α. If x_i were constant for all s, eq. (3) would imply a Weibull distribution for the duration of unemployment, given entry at τ.[9]

In the FES, like the GHS used by Nickell, a person is interviewed only once, and we observe only uncompleted spells. To form the likelihood, we define the survivor function, $F(s|\tau)$, which is the probability that the spell is s or greater, conditional on entry at τ:

$$F_i(s|\tau) = \exp\left[-\int_0^s \theta(\sigma, x_i)\, d\sigma \right]. \tag{4}$$

It may be noted that F depends on the timepath of characteristics x_i for $0 \leq \sigma \leq s$. The contribution to the likelihood function from individual i, with characteristics x_i, who has duration s_i, having entered at τ_i is (where $t_i = \tau_i + s_i$):

$$\frac{\text{Prob}\,[s \geq s_i|\text{entry at } \tau_i \text{ and } x_i]\,\text{Prob}\,[\text{entry at } \tau_i|x_i]}{\text{Prob}\,[\text{unemployed at } t_i|x_i]}$$

$$= \frac{F_i(s_i|\tau_i)u_i(\tau_i)}{\sum_{z = t_i - T}^{t_i} F_i(t_i - z|z)u_i(z)}. \tag{5}$$

In this expression, $u_i(\tau)$ denotes the probability of person i entering unemployment in week τ. Following Nickell, we assume that $u_i = k_i u(\tau)$, where $u(\tau)$ is the ratio of the aggregate flow into unemployment in week τ to aggregate employment, and k_i is a fixed individual effect. With this assumption, the individual effects cancel in (5) and u_i is replaced by $u(\tau)$, which we base on the monthly inflow divided by total male employed and unemployed. The summation in the denominator of (5) is taken over the relevant range.

It should be noted that in the likelihood function we have, in contrast to Nickell, allowed for the time dependence of θ. He effectively assumes that θ depends on duration but not on calendar time. With the changes in the macro-economic position over the period considered, this does not seem a particularly reasonable assumption, and we have relaxed it here. On the other hand, we have not treated unobserved differences between individuals. The incorporation of unobservables poses major difficulties, including the relation between the assumptions made for the subpopulation (i.e. the unemployed) and those for the whole population (Chesher and Lancaster, 1981; Lancaster and Chesher, 1981), and the specification of the distribution of the unobserved characteristics (Heckman and Singer, 1982, 1984a, b and c), where theoretical considerations provide little guidance. If we were concerned to develop positive conclusions, then the failure to treat unobservable effects would be a serious drawback; however, our purpose is rather different. In the earlier studies (e.g. Lancaster and Nickell, 1980, Tables 2 and 3), the estimated coefficients for the replacement variables and other characteristics are similar with and without allowance for omitted variables; and the introduction of unobservables does not seem necessary in order to demonstrate the sensitivity to other aspects of their analysis (although reference is made to the possible implications of heterogeneity).

In addition to the replacement variable already discussed, the vector x_i in eq. (3) incorporates the factors governing differences in the discount rate, in the probability of a job offer, and in the wage offer distribution. Some variables immediately suggest themselves for inclusion: for example, age is likely to affect all three elements. But in general the theory as such gives little in the way of assistance, and investigators are typically reduced to drawing on fragments of *a priori* evidence. This is illustrated by the family composition variables introduced by Nickell, based for example on the statement that 'the lack of a wife is known to be correlated with undesirable employee characteristics such as mental instability and alcoholism' (1979a, p. 1254). In what follows we have deliberately remained close to the earlier studies, but we comment on the sensitivity of the findings to the specification of the x variables.

5   RESULTS FOR STANDARD TREATMENT OF THE REPLACEMENT VARIABLE

In presenting the results, we begin in column 1 of Table 9.1 with the case where no x variables are included apart from a constant, this providing a

Table 9.1 Estimated re-employment probability function: standard treatment of the replacement variable[a]

	Full sample			Two year sample			One year sample		
	(1)	(2)	(3)	(4)	(5)	(6)	(7)	(8)	(9)
Constant	-1.57 (0.12)	0.749 (0.242)	1.900 (0.289)	-1.64 (0.17)	0.560 (0.336)	1.54 (0.428)	-1.83 (0.287)	0.118 (0.564)	1.24 (0.589)
α	0.494 (0.033)	0.490 (0.039)	0.483 (0.039)	0.516 (0.057)	0.505 (0.059)	0.495 (0.058)	0.601 (0.111)	0.687 (0.109)	0.691 (0.107)
Log replacement rate	—	-0.577 (0.129)	—	—	-0.492 (0.199)	—	—	-0.635 (0.299)	—
Replacement rate	—	—	-1.360 (0.258)	—	—	-1.170 (0.382)	—	—	-1.310 (0.540)
U/V	—	-0.036 (0.006)	-0.036 (0.006)	—	-0.043 (0.007)	-0.042 (0.007)	—	-0.060 (0.012)	-0.060 (0.012)
Log age	—	-0.736 (0.076)	-0.746 (0.079)	—	-0.649 (0.099)	-0.654 (0.099)	—	-0.594 (0.153)	-0.602 (0.152)
Married	—	0.361 (0.089)	0.427 (0.087)	—	0.278 (0.118)	0.334 (0.118)	—	0.104 (0.169)	0.156 (0.169)
Log-likelihood	5,460.1	5,361.4	5,356.0	4,684.5	4,628.4	4,626.2	3,074.7	3,041.4	3,040.5

[a] Coefficients (asymptotic standard errors in brackets).

useful benchmark. The re-employment probability is then proportional to $s^{\alpha-1}$. The estimated value of α is close to a half, and the implied re-employment probability is halved between weeks 1 and 4, and down to a fifth after 24 weeks. Columns (4) and (7) show the similar equations for the restricted samples. (The higher value of α in the one year sample suggests that an alternative functional form for s might be more appropriate.)

The x variables introduced in columns (2) and (3) are the replacement rate, with the 'standard' assumptions, in the average after tax form R_A, age, marital status, and a measure of the state of the labour market, taken to be the ratio of unemployment to vacancies (U/V), which varies over time and across regions. As may be seen, there is a substantial increase in log-likelihood from the benchmark model. Twice the difference in the log-likelihood is 197.4 which may be compared with a χ^2 critical value at the 1 per cent level of 13.3. The effect of all variables appears to be quantitatively significant. In order to show the implications of the co-efficients, let us take as a 'base situation' a married man of 36, with a replacement rate of 60 per cent and $U/V = 10$, these latter characteristics being fairly close to the mean for the sample. The predicted effect on the re-employment probability of variation in these characteristics is shown below.

	Re-employment probability [from col. (2) in Table 9.1] base situation = 100 per cent
	%
Replacement rate rise to 80 per cent	85
U/V rise to 15	84
Age 46 rather than 36	84
Single rather than married	70

As may be seen, the first three variations have rather similar effects on the re-employment probability, reducing it by about 15 per cent. If we contrast the effects with the findings of Nickell (1979a, Table 1, eq. 1), then the effect of the age variable is close, that of marital status quite a lot smaller here, but that of the labour market variable definitely larger (the comparable effect in Nickell is a reduction in the re-employment prob-ability of some 4 per cent).[10] Our data, allowing more variation across different states of the labour market over time, indicate that individual re-employment probabilities do vary significantly with the pressure of demand.

In the case of the replacement variable, the evidence from the FES in Table 9.1 appears to provide considerable support for the earlier con-clusions. The estimated elasticity of the re-employment probability with respect to the replacement variable is around 0.6 – which is the figure often quoted. Our findings may therefore be seen as corroborative of the earlier studies. However, they also corroborate another, less noticed, feature.

The coefficient of the replacement variable was not particularly well determined in the earlier studies, and the same is true here. Lancaster's estimated coefficient (1979, Table 1) has a two standard error confidence interval of 0.01–0.85; Nickel's estimate of 1.69 has a two standard error confidence interval of 0.73–2.63. In Table 9.1, the similar confidence intervals for the logarithmic specification are 0.32–0.84 (full sample) and 0.04–1.23 (one year sample). The confidence intervals for the linear equations are shown by the solid lines in Fig. 9.1 (the dashed lines are discussed in the next section).[11] Even, therefore, with a considerable increase in sample size (our full sample is more than 2½ times as large) we are not able to estimate the effects of benefits at all precisely.

Our main concern is with the specification of the benefit variable, and this is discussed in the next section, but we should note at this point that the estimated replacement rate coefficients vary considerably with changes in the specification of the family composition variable and with changes in the

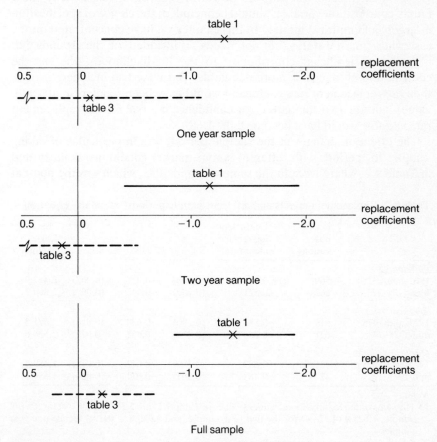

Figure 9.1 Confidence intervals for replacement coefficients

time period of estimation. The former is illustrated by the following results for the two year sample with a linear specification for the replacement rate.

Specification (variables included)	Estimated coefficient of replacement rate (asymptotic standard error)	−Log likelihood
Marital status [col. (6) in Table 9.1]	−1.170 (0.382)	4,626.2
Marital status and 'needs' (defined as 1+0.6 × wife+0.4 × dependent children)	−0.880 (0.406)	4,624.2
'Needs'	−0.341 (0.367)	4,630.5

As we have seen, there is no powerful theoretical reason why these family composition variables should be included; the choice of specification is largely an empirical matter. In this chapter we have concentrated on the case where marital status, but not 'needs', is included, on the grounds that it makes a significant contribution to the log-likelihood, whereas the contribution of 'needs' is more debatable. But if we had included 'needs', then the replacement rate coefficient would have been smaller (in absolute value), and the two standard error confidence interval for the replacement rate variable would have become 0.08–1.68.

The effect of changes in the sample period, and in particular of taking samples for periods with different labour market conditions, is illustrated in Table 9.2, where we split the sample in mid-1975, which was the point at

Table 9.2 Replacement effects and different sample periods: 'standard' equation

	No. of obser- vations	Coefficient log replace- ment rate	S.E.	U/V	S.E.	Log- likelihood
Full sample						
1972–mid-1975	569	−0.566	(0.180)	−0.027	(0.007)	2,467.9
Mid-1975–77	662	−0.571	(0.200)	−0.047	(0.009)	2,890.2
Two year sample						
1972–mid-1975	519	−0.587	(0.290)	−0.030	(0.010)	2,071.3
mid-1975–77	621	−0.286	(0.301)	−0.052	(0.011)	2,554.6
One year sample						
1972–mid-1975	421	−0.689	(0.399)	−0.042	(0.015)	1,480.7
mid-1975–77	424	−0.483	(0.505)	−0.077	(0.024)	1,559.3

Notes:
1. The sums of the log-likelihood values (values in Table 9.1) are 5,358.1 (5,361.4) for the full sample, 4,625.9 (4,628.4) for the two year sample, and 3,040.0 (3,041.4) for the one year sample.
2. S.E. denotes asymptotic standard error.

which the overall unemployment rate began to rise above 5 per cent. The coefficient of the labour market variable, U/V, is higher in the second period in all cases, and indicates that labour market conditions came to play a more important role in the second half of the 1970s. In contrast, for the replacement rate the findings are conflicting: in the full sample, the coefficients are virtually identical for the two sub-periods, but in the one year and two year samples the coefficient is lower for the period mid-1975–77. The latter provides some support for the view that there has been a shift over time, but the former warns us against reading too much into the shift. Once again, the results are best seen as pointing to the lack of robustness. With the two year sample, an investigator using the 519 observations (a quite respectable number) for 1972–mid-1975 would have found a benefit elasticity of close to 0.6. If he had failed to heed the warning of the estimated standard error, which indicated a two standard error confidence interval of 0–1.2, then he might have advertised this as a well-established finding This 'finding' would have been overturned by subsequent research using the 621 observations for mid-1975–77, but of course this 'new' estimate of 0.3 is significantly different neither from 0.6 nor from zero.

6 THE USE OF AN ALTERNATIVE BENEFIT VARIABLE

The results in Tables 9.1 and 9.2 are based on a set of assumptions concerning the construction of the replacement rate which do not seem to accord with the recorded benefit information in our sample nor with the administrative statistics. In Table 9.3, we show the consequences of replacing the 'standard' pattern of benefit receipt by the 'calculated' pattern, based on information recorded in the FES. The *amount* of benefit is still calculated according to the standard assumptions and we retain for the present the specification R_A.

Comparing the results with those in Table 9.1, we can see that the coefficient of α is now rather higher, as is the magnitude of the labour market coefficient, whereas the age coefficient is virtually identical. The most dramatic difference, however, is in the coefficient of the replacement variable, which is estimated to be around zero rather than -0.6 or -1.3. Indeed, four of the six estimates are actually positive.

This finding can be given several different interpretations. The first is that changes in the method of calculation make a substantial difference to the results, and that the choice between them is an empirical matter. If we take the likelihood values as a basis for such a comparison, then the standard assumptions of Table 9.1 are not challenged by our alternative variable. The difference in log-likelihood is 9.2 for the full sample (logarithmic version) and 2.1 for the one year sample. On the other hand,

Table 9.3 Alternative assumptions about pattern of benefit receipt[a]

	Full sample		Two year sample		One year sample	
	(1)	(2)	(3)	(4)	(5)	(6)
Constant	0.991	1.070	0.867	0.654	0.537	0.512
	(0.253)	(0.255)	(0.356)	(0.376)	(0.589)	(0.573)
α	0.561	0.557	0.591	0.584	0.752	0.753
	(0.039)	(0.039)	(0.061)	(0.061)	(0.116)	(0.115)
Log replacement rate	0.023	—	0.186	—	0.067	—
	(0.112)		(0.169)		(0.252)	
Replacement rate	—	−0.206	—	0.136	—	−0.122
		(0.213)		(0.330)		(0.486)
U/V	−0.040	−0.039	−0.049	−0.048	−0.067	−0.066
	(0.006)	(0.006)	(0.007)	(0.007)	(0.013)	(0.013)
Log age	−0.719	−0.724	−0.692	−0.640	−0.610	−0.604
	(0.075)	(0.075)	(0.097)	(0.097)	(0.157)	(0.156)
Married	0.072	0.143	0.034	0.024	−0.166	−0.105
	(0.085)	(0.083)	(0.111)	(0.113)	(0.166)	(0.173)
−Log-likelihood	5,370.6	5,370.2	4,630.8	4,631.4	3,043.5	3,043.5

[a] Coefficients (asymptotic standard errors in brackets).

there appear to be two objections to such an interpretation. First, it is not clear that any justification can be given for comparing the likelihood values, given that the models are not nested. Secondly, and more seriously, this interpretation ignores the fact that the standard assumptions are inconsistent with the administrative data on benefits referred to above. There is extra-sample information in support of our alternative variable. People are simply not getting the benefits hypothesised with the standard assumption.

The second interpretation is that[12] our benefit variable, by taking account of certain aspects of employment history, is (negatively) correlated with unobserved characteristics of the worker which reduce his re-employment prospects. For example, the person with a previous spell would both get lower benefit and be less likely to get a job, causing the coefficient possibly to be biased towards zero. It may be argued that the standard variable is a better instrument, not being contaminated in this way (the objections in the previous paragraph do not apply). On the other hand, the details of the reasons for the differences between the variables do not necessarily support this interpretation. The example of linked spells, used above, only applies to some 1 in 13 of the cases which depart from the 'standard' assumptions. Where there is 'delay in receipt', which accounts for one-half the 'non-standard' cases, this *may* be related to characteristics which reduce the chance of a new job (e.g. where a person was sacked because of misconduct), but the reverse may apply. The person who is (correctly) confident that he can get another job soon may not sign on for benefit at once. If the unobserved characteristic is willingness to live off benefits and turn down jobs, this may well be correlated *positively* with benefit receipt. This interpretation rests therefore to a considerable extent on supposition.

The third interpretation – and in our view the safest one – is that the replacement coefficient was in any case poorly determined. Given the wide confidence intervals for the estimates with the standard variable, it can scarcely be claimed that we are starting from a precisely determined coefficient. This is illustrated in Figure 9.1, where the dashed lines are the two standard error confidence intervals for the coefficients in Table 9.3, linear equations (calculated independently).

In Table 9.4, we present the results of two further variations. The first replaces the calculation of the amounts of ERS by the 'alternative' procedure described in section 3, but retains the 'standard' pattern of benefit receipt. Comparing columns (3) and (1), we can see that this *alone* reduces the coefficient of the replacement rate to insignificance, but that the other coefficients are little changed. If we use last reported earnings in the denominator, as in column (5), the estimated coefficient of the logarithm of the replacment rate rises to 0.77 (with a standard error of 0.19). The log-likelihood, of $-3,037.0$, is the highest for this series of estimates.[13]

Table 9.4 Different assumptions about replacement rate – one year sample[a]

			Assumptions:		
	'Standard' (1)	'Calculated' (2)	As (1) but alternative ERS (3)	As (2) but alternative ERS (4)	As (1) but last reported earnings (5)
Constant	0.118 (0.564)	0.537 (0.589)	0.374 (0.600)	0.490 (0.613)	0.351 (0.537)
α	0.687 (0.109)	0.752 (0.116)	0.744 (0.114)	0.753 (0.115)	0.689 (0.124)
Log replacement rate	-0.635 (0.299)	0.067 (0.252)	-0.103 (0.260)	0.018 (0.261)	-0.772 (0.188)
U/V	-0.060 (0.012)	-0.067 (0.013)	-0.066 (0.013)	-0.067 (0.013)	-0.066 (0.013)
Log age	-0.594 (0.153)	-0.610 (0.157)	-0.603 (0.156)	-0.607 (0.156)	-0.675 (0.157)
Married	0.104 (0.169)	-0.166 (0.166)	-0.077 (0.196)	-0.146 (0.203)	0.120 (0.139)
$-$Log-likelihood	3,041.4	3,043.5	3,043.5	3,043.6	3,037.0

Note: Col. (1) is the same as col. (8) in Table 9.1; col. (2) is the same as col. (5) in Table 9.3.
[a] Coefficients (asymptotic standard errors in brackets).

7 MARGINAL AND AVERAGE REPLACEMENT RATES

The replacement variable used to this point can be criticized on the grounds that the strict application of the search theory model would indicate that the relevant comparison is of benefits and wages, ignoring other income, and that we need to take account of the marginal rather than average tax rate on earnings.

In Table 9.5, we show the effects of replacing R_A by the marginal net of tax form, R_C. The latter takes account of the *marginal* rate of income tax (as opposed to the average tax rate that takes into account tax allowances), and employee's national insurance contributions, both of which varied over the period, for those who are calculated to be liable for tax. For those not liable for tax, the national insurance contribution alone applies. In general, the marginal tax exceeds the average tax rate, and this tends to reduce the denominator. On the other hand, the marginal form excludes other income from both numerator and denominator, which tends to reduce the replacement rate. The fact that the numerator now consists only of benefit income means that the replacement rate is zero in some cases, and we therefore concentrate on the linear specification. This has the consequence that, in comparing the implications for the elasticities, we need to allow for the differences in the means: the means for the marginal variable, R_C, is some 10 per cent higher than for the average variable, R_A.

The results are summarized in terms of the replacement rate variables, their standard errors, and the likelihood values. (There is not in general any significant change in α or the coefficients for U/V and age.) The replacement rate coefficients are all negative, and references to their size are concerned with the absolute value. From Table 9.5, it appears that use of the marginal form of the replacement variable, R_C, rather than R_A, leads to larger coefficients with the 'calculated' benefit pattern. For example, in eq. (5), with the 'alternative' assumptions about ERS, the estimated coefficient is -0.57, although it is still not large in relation to its estimated standard error. In contrast, with the 'standard' benefit variable, the coefficient is little changed (one year sample) or is reduced (full sample); multiplying by 1.1 to allow for the difference in the means, the estimated elasticities are identical (eq. (3)) or reduced.

The lower part of Table 9.5 shows the effects of using the before-tax replacement rates R_B in average form and R_D in marginal form. Again, we have to take account of the differences in the means when interpreting the coefficients. The variable R_B has a mean about 20 per cent lower than R_A, so that the coefficient in eq. (6) implies a considerably smaller elasticity (0.5 against 0.85) than that in eq. (1). Even therefore for the 'standard' assumptions, the choice of specification appears to affect the conclusions drawn, underlining our earlier conclusions about the lack of robustness.

Table 9.5 Different forms of the replacement variable: marginal versus average

Equation	Average form			'Marginal' form		
	Coefficient	S.E.	–Log-likelihood	Coefficient	S.E.	–Log-likelihood
Full sample (1,231 observations)	R_A			R_C		
(1) 'Standard' benefit pattern	−1.36	(0.26)	5,356.0	−0.76	(0.12)	5,352.8
(2) 'Calculated' benefit pattern	−0.21	(0.21)	5,370.2	−0.29	(0.10)	5,367.2
One year sample (845 observations)						
(3) 'Standard' benefit pattern	−1.31	(0.54)	3,040.5	−1.21	(0.32)	3,036.6
(4) 'Calculated' benefit pattern	−0.12	(0.49)	3,043.5	−0.46	(0.29)	3,042.1
(5) 'Calculated' benefit pattern and 'Alternative' assumption about ERS	−0.18	(0.52)	3,043.5	−0.57	(0.31)	3,041.5
	R_B			R_D		
(6) 'Standard' benefit pattern *pre-tax*	−1.05	(0.64)	3,042.0	−1.80	(0.52)	3,037.7
(7) 'Calculated' benefit pattern and 'Alternative' assumption about ERS *pre-tax*	−0.06	(0.57)	3,043.6	−0.81	(0.49)	3,042.0

Note: S.E. denotes asymptotic standard error.

8   CONCLUSIONS AND IMPLICATIONS

In the design of public policy, the use of empirical evidence on behavioural reactions is crucial – the alternative being reliance on anecdote and prejudice. Yet it is essential that the empirical evidence be robust. 'Robustness' does not mean that all estimates with different data must be identical, nor that simplifying assumptions are ruled out, nor that all sources of bias must be eliminated. Feldstein has rightly emphasized the value of estimating 'false models':

> judgements must be formed by studying the results of several studies, each of which focuses on part of the problem and makes false assumptions about other parts ... a finding that the results of several quite different studies all point to the same conclusion suggests that the specification errors in each of the studies are relatively innocuous.
>
> (1982, p. 830)

But he goes on to say that:

> Not all issues can be resolved in this satisfying way. For many problems, different plausible specifications lead to quite different conclusions.... In these cases, estimating alternative models to study the same question can be a useful reminder of the limits of our knowledge.
>
> (1982, p. 831)

In this chapter we have argued that the evidence about unemployment benefit and unemployment duration in Britain is far from robust. Despite the claims quoted at the beginning that the effect of benefits is 'firmly established', the coefficient turns out to be poorly determined – even within the framework of the earlier studies. There is considerable variation in the estimated elasticity when we consider alternative benefit variables, different specifications of the replacement rate, different time periods, and the inclusion/exclusion of family circumstances. With some combinations of assumptions, it is possible to reproduce the earlier finding of an elasticity around 0.6; with other, quite reasonable, formulations the estimated elasticity is not significantly different from zero.

There is, therefore, substantial scope for the conclusions drawn to be influenced by prior beliefs. The person who expects to find a significant disincentive of unemployment insurance will no doubt reject our 'alternative' benefit variable, would prefer the results for the early 1970s, would regard the inclusion of marital status/exclusion of 'needs' as correct, and would – if he could overcome his qualms about endogeneity – plump for last normal earnings in the denominator, rather than predicted earnings. The person who does not believe in a disincentive is likely to accept the 'alternative' benefit variable, to point to the results for the mid-1970s, to note that marital status has little more (or less) theoretical justification than 'needs', and to argue that the 'average' specification is more relevant to actual behaviour than the 'sophisticated' calculations underlying the 'marginal' specification.

In sum, we are in the second of the situations described by Feldstein, and the main aim of the chapter has been to emphasize 'the limits of our knowledge'. There may be a significant link between benefits and duration, but it does not stand out strongly from the, quite large and extensive, microdata set that we have been using. In order to establish any relationship, we are going to need a combination of richer data, a more fully specified theoretical framework, and the development of the statistical treatment.

NOTES

1. The study by Hamermesh (1982) of the knowledge of economic research by members of the National Commission on Unemployment Compensation in the United States showed a quite high degree of awareness of this research.
2. For a review of this evidence, see Atkinson et al. (1981, 1983).
3. The chapter draws on a series of detailed research reports, circulated as Unemployment Project Working Notes 1–13, in which there is a more extensive account of a number of aspects. These reports contain full information about the definition of variables and sources.
4. The models used by individual authors differ slightly from that described below: for example, Lancaster and Chesher (1983) allow a constant probability of termination of the job.
5. The income tax system in Britain is of this form for all except the top income group.
6. For a description of this survey, see Kemsley, Redpath and Holmes (1980). Among the points which should be noticed is the substantial rate of non-response (around 30 per cent) but our comparison (Micklewright, 1984a) of the FES sample with Department of Employment statistics does not suggest that it is seriously unrepresentative with respect to characteristics such as duration, region or industry.
7. An alternative source which has recently become available is the 1978–79 DHSS Cohort Study of the Unemployed (see Narendranathan, Nickell and Stern, 1983). This data set has considerable advantages: for example, information on benefits is obtained directly from the computer records. At the same time it has certain disadvantages, including the limited timespan and the fact that the duration data relate to the period since registration as unemployed rather than the total period away from work.
8. It should be noted that the *normal* earnings variable is used, on the grounds that 'last pay' is often unrepresentative for the unemployed (Moylan and Davies, 1981).
9. Where $\alpha < 1$, the re-employment probability falls with duration. It might appear that individuals could 'reset the clock' by, for example, leaving the labour force, but it is really time since last job that is relevant.

10. This is calculated at a duration of one week, with the ill-health dummy set at 0, and assuming that he has a wife and one other dependant.

11. As a check on the estimation of the asymptotic standard errors, we also applied the approach of White (1981). The 'robust' standard errors for col. (9) in Table 9.1 are given below, together with those calculated in our standard estimation procedure: (0.615, 0.589), (0.118, 0.107), (0.508, 0.540), (0.013, 0.012), (0.163, 0.152), and (0.163, 0.169). These seem reassuringly close.

12. We are grateful to A. Deaton, M. Feldstein and J. A. Hausman for discussion on this point.

13. It has been argued that it is the real level of benefits, rather than the replacement ratio, which is the relevant variable. In Atkinson *et al.* (1982), we enter the logarithm of real benefits and of real work income separately. With the two year sample, the 'standard' assumption gives estimates of -0.462 (0.206) for benefits and 0.580 (0.217) for work income, and the alternative assumption gives 0.214 (0.171) and -0.015 (0.200) respectively.

10 · THE POVERTY TRAP IN BRITAIN

1 THE DEFINITION OF THE POVERTY TRAP

The phrase 'poverty trap' is used in a variety of ways and it requires careful definition. Some commentators see the poverty trap as arising in any situation where a family is both in receipt of means-tested benefits and liable for income tax. In this case, the trap can only be removed by increases in the tax threshold or by reducing the scope of means-tested benefits (e.g. by increasing other sources of income such as child benefit).

Others see the poverty trap as being concerned with situations where families face high marginal rates of tax on additional earnings, where the tax arises from income tax, national insurance (NI) contributions and from the withdrawal of income-related benefits. It is on this aspect that we concentrate here. It should however be noted that the poverty trap defined in this way may have several different dimensions, depending on the way in which a family may consider increasing its earnings. The standard assumption (e.g. *Social Trends*, 1981, Chart 6.15; and HM Treasury, 1982, p. 198) is that there is a marginal £1 increase in the earnings of the family head, but this is not the only nor even necessarily the most realistic possibility. The household head may face the decision as to whether or not to take a second job, for which the increase in earnings is likely to be considerably more than £1. In the case of a married couple, the wife may consider going out to work, either part-time or full-time. The percentage lost through taxation and the withdrawal of benefits may be quite different in these cases: for example, because of the tax treatment of the earnings of married women.

These examples bring out two factors which are missing from the calculations made by the government of the significance of the poverty trap. First, consideration needs to be given to non-marginal increases in earnings, allowing for the fact that the relevant work decision may involve a discrete either/or choice. Second, the implications for other members of the family need to be taken into account. In the calculations presented

With M. A. King and N. H. Stern. Section A of a memorandum submitted to the House of Commons Treasury and Civil Service Committee Sub-Committee on 'The Structure of Personal Income Taxation and Income Support', published as an appendix to their Report, 11 May 1983, HMSO, London.

below, based on the *Family Expenditure Survey* (FES) for 1980, we consider the following range of variations in earnings:

1. £1 increase in earnings of head of tax unit (standard assumption),
2. 15 per cent increase in earnings of head of tax unit (e.g. half day's overtime at time and a half),
3. £1 increase in earnings of wife where she is at work,
4. £15 ⎫ earnings by wife where
5. £30 ⎬ she is not at present in
6. £75 ⎭ work and takes a job.

What we want to calculate in each case is the relation between extra tax paid/benefits withdrawn and the increase in earnings, or what we may call the tax ratio on extra income, or 'tax ratio', for short.

2   SOURCES OF INFORMATION

To estimate the number of families facing high tax ratios in Britain, we need information on the characteristics of actual families in the population. Although widespread use is made of hypothetical examples, as in the DHSS Tax/Benefit Model, they cannot be employed to measure the extent of the poverty trap. The diversity of household circumstances found in reality cannot be adequately represented by a hypothetical model, even with a range of assumptions.

The evidence about actual circumstances is however limited. The administrative records on the operation of particular benefits (e.g. FIS) do not provide enough information on other characteristics to allow the tax ratios to be calculated at all accurately. Reliance has to be placed mainly on household survey information, such as that employed here from the *Family Expenditure Survey*. We have devoted considerable attention to the reliability of the data collected in this survey, and have reached the conclusion that some of the more common criticisms are not warranted. For example, our analysis (Atkinson and Micklewright, 1983) of the income data suggests that for earnings, social security benefits and pensions, the FES compares well with the national income accounts. What cannot be denied, however, is that the numbers in the relevant groups covered by the survey are small. For example, the 50,000 families reported by HM Treasury (1982) to have marginal tax rates of 100 per cent or higher in 1977 correspond to some *20* families in the original survey. This is a small number on which to base firm conclusions, and in particular to draw inferences about changes from one year to the next. If the government wishes to use survey information to monitor the poverty trap, and especially the trends in its importance over time, then richer sources of information are necessary.

3 THE CALCULATION OF TAX RATIOS

The calculations given below are concerned with family units (as defined for tax purposes) in the United Kingdom where the head is a man or single woman in full-time employment paid in the current pay period. There are 5,160 such tax units in the FES 1980. In order to obtain figures corresponding to the whole household population, we gross up by a factor of 2,913 based on the ratio of the total UK non-institutional population to the FES population. The figures cover therefore some 15 million tax units, made up as follows:

single without children	5.1m
single-parent families	0.5m
married couples without children	3.8m
married couples with children	5.6m
	15.0m

The calculations take account of income tax, NI contributions, rent and rate rebates and family income supplement. The higher rates of income tax are not taken into account, but are discussed briefly below. Our calculations therefore include the main elements typically discussed in connection with the poverty trap, but there are other means-tested benefits which we have not covered, including free school meals and welfare milk (these being the other benefits covered in the DHSS Tax/Benefit Model), free prescriptions, free dental treatment, dentures and glasses, fares to hospital, school uniform grants, educational maintenance allowances and legal aid. To the extent that a rise in earnings would reduce the benefits under these schemes, the tax ratios are understated by our calculations.

There are two further aspects of our calculations to which we should draw attention. First, we have not at this stage allowed for the non-take-up of means-tested benefits; the calculations assume that all those eligible are in receipt. Second, it is assumed that benefits are immediately adjusted, e.g. no account is taken of the fact that FIS may continue unadjusted for up to 52 weeks. This may well be the appropriate assumption for someone considering changing jobs, but would not apply to temporary changes in, for example, overtime earnings.

The rates of taxation and benefit are those ruling at the relevant date in 1980, so that the basic rate of income tax is 30 per cent, NI contributions (taken to be contracted in); 6.5 per cent (prior to 6 April 1980) or 6.75 per cent (April 1980 onwards), the withdrawal rate for rent rebates 25 or 17 per cent, and that for rate rebates, 8 or 6 per cent.

In Table 10.1, we show the tax ratios on the standard basis of an increase of £1 in the earnings of the head of the tax unit. In order to help identify the different elements, the results are shown where possible as actual tax ratios (rounded to the nearest whole number), rather than as broad ranges.

Table 10.1 Tax ratios on £1 additional earnings by head of tax unit, 1980

Tax ratio (tax paid + benefits lost)	Number in FES	(%)	Estimated number of tax units in whole population[a]
zero	67	(1)	200,000
1–7	13		40,000
8–26	13		40,000
30 (income tax only)	729	(14)	2,120,000
31–2	43	(1)	130,000
33–6	21		60,000
37 (income tax + NI contribution)	3,844	(74)	11,200,000
38–42	3		10,000
43 (income tax + NI contribution + rate rebate)	185	(4)	540,000
44–9	2		10,000
50–9	66	(1)	190,000
60 (income tax + NI contribution + rent and rate rebate)	105	(2)	310,000
61–9 ⎫	15		40,000
70–9 ⎪ For these households the	21		60,000
80–9 ⎬ calculation involved FIS	6		20,000
90–9 ⎪	14		40,000
100– ⎭	13		40,000
Total	5,160		15,030,000

[a] Rounded to the nearest 10,000. For this reason, the figures do not add exactly to the total.

We show the absolute numbers in the FES to highlight the small sample size: the estimate of 40,000 families with tax ratios of 100 per cent or higher is based on 13 actual families in the FES.

According to these estimates, 239 families faced tax ratios of 50 per cent or higher, or some 700,000 in the population as a whole. Given the much larger number of units involved, we can have more confidence in these estimates than those for the number in excess of 100 per cent. The official evidence (HM Treasury, 1982, p. 254) refers to 220,000 families in 1979. Our figures differ in that the calculation is done assuming 100 per cent take-up, and in that they cover tax units without children (as well as relating to a more recent year). Expressed as a percentage, our figures are 4.5 per cent of total tax units, compared with 'about 3½' in the official estimates.

The inclusion of families without children would not make much difference if the primary source of the poverty trap were FIS. However, it is clear from Table 10.1 that FIS is of rather less significance than housing rebates in generating high tax ratios. A family paying tax, NI contributions and receiving FIS and both rent and rate rebates could have a tax ratio of 103 per cent (higher taper for housing rebates) or 98 per cent (lower taper). There are very few families in Table 10.1 in this bracket.

The relative contribution of FIS and housing rebates to the estimated numbers of those facing high marginal tax ratios may be seen if we consider the effect of abolishing the two schemes in turn from the calculation (grossed-up figures):

	Number with tax ratios of 50 per cent or higher In FES	Estimated in population
Table 10.1	240	700,000
Without FIS	217	630,000
Without housing rebates	40	120,000

Although it is FIS that has received most attention in public discussion of the poverty trap, it is clear that housing rebates affect many more people. Although they do not, on their own, generate tax ratios of 100 per cent or higher, they mean that a sizeable minority of families face a tax ratio of 60 per cent.

A rate of 60 per cent corresponds to the top marginal income tax rate on earned income. The higher rates of tax are not included in the calculations described above, but it is interesting to compare the numbers with those estimated by the Inland Revenue to be facing marginal income tax rates of 50 per cent or higher in 1980/1:

	Number of tax units facing higher rates of income tax
50 per cent or higher	270,000
60 per cent	70,000

Source: HM Treasury, 1982, p. 212.

The numbers involved are, therefore, quite a lot smaller than those at the lower end, as indicated by Table 10.1.

4   EFFECT ON ALTERNATIVE WORK DECISIONS

To this point, we have concentrated on the effect on decisions of the family head to earn an extra £1. More relevant may be the effect on an either/or choice, such as working a half day a week overtime. To represent this, we show in the first column of Table 10.2 the tax ratio for a 15 per cent increase in earnings. In this case a person may pay tax, or lose benefits, for *part* of the increase; so that the ratios are less easily identified with the rates of tax or taper. We present in this case, therefore, the results in terms of ranges. As is to be expected, the estimated number facing high tax ratios, 50 per cent or above, is reduced, from 700,000 to 530,000. From this point of view, the effect on work incentives may be less than the standard calculation suggests.

The tax ratios faced on the wife's earnings are shown in columns 2–5 of Table 10.2. There are some 2,000 families in the 1980 FES where the wife is at work (employed or self-employed), corresponding to 6 million in total. The table shows first the tax ratio on an increased £1 in her earnings.

Table 10.2 Tax ratios for different earnings decisions, FES 1980

	1. Earnings of head of tax unit increased by 15%	2. Wife at work[a] earns extra £1	3. Wife not at present at work earns: £15	4. £30	5. £75
zero	170,000	1,680,000	2,090,000	—	—
1–9%	10,000	100,000	280,000	—	—
10–19%	20,000	50,000	110,000	2,410,000	—
20–9%	10,000	50,000	—	70,000	2,340,000
30%	2,230,000	4,190,000	—	—	40,000
31–9%	11,400,000	30,000	—	—	70,000
40–9%	640,000	20,000	—	—	—
50–9%	240,000	10,000	—	—	—
60–74%	220,000	—	—	—	—
75% or more	70,000	—	—	—	—

[a] Excluding in this case NI contributions.
— less than 5,000.

Since the wife's national insurance position is not known, the calculations do not include NI contributions. Even allowing for this, it is clear that very few face high tax ratios. If the NI contribution rate is added in all cases, then there are still only 30,000 with tax ratios of 50 per cent or higher. (Again attention should be paid to the small numbers in the FES underlying some of the entries in the table.)

In the case of around 850 families, corresponding to some 2.5 million in the population, the wife is not in paid work and is not in receipt of NI benefits (pension, sickness benefit, etc.). In columns 3–5 of Table 10.2, we show the tax ratios for the following possible levels of earnings if she went out to work: £15 (part-time job); £30 (part-time job that takes her over the income tax and NI thresholds); and £75 (full-time job).

In the first situation, about 85 per cent have a tax ratio of zero; the remaining 15 per cent are those affected by the withdrawal of means-tested benefits, but in virtually no cases does the loss exceed a fifth of the extra earnings. In the second and third situations, the principal considerations are income tax and NI contributions, the modal rates being 10 per cent for an increase in earnings of £30 and 26 per cent for an increase in earnings of £75.

The tax ratio faced by the wife is therefore largely governed by income tax and NI contributions, and this must clearly be taken into account in considering any reform.

5   ILLUSTRATIVE CHANGES IN POLICY

To illustrate the points made above, we consider three variations in policy, which are intended to be broadly revenue-neutral in 1982–3 terms:

Policy I   An increase in single, married and single-parent tax allowances of 20 per cent, and in the basic rate of income tax of 3 percentage points.

Policy II   No change in allowances, child benefit (including single-parent addition) doubled, and an increase in the basic rate of income tax of 3 percentage points.

Policy III   Child benefit doubled, and abolition of married man's allowance and single-parent addition

In the case of both Policy II and Policy III, the increase in child benefit is taken into account when assessing entitlement to housing benefits but not FIS (as at present).

The effects of these changes on the tax ratios relevant to two different earnings decisions are shown in Table 10.3. If we consider first Policy I, in the case of earnings by the head of the tax unit, the modal tax ratio rises in line with the increase in the basic rate. But for those at present facing high tax ratios, the change may represent an improvement to the extent that it releases them from the payment of tax (we are not considering here the implications for net incomes). This may be partly offset, in terms of the overall numbers with high tax ratios (say 50 per cent or higher), by the effect on those who remain within the tax net of the rise in the basic rate of tax. It may be seen in fact that there is little reduction in terms of the numbers with ratios of 50 per cent or higher, but a 20,000 fall in the numbers facing 75 per cent or higher (although it should be remembered that this is based on a small number of actual families).

Table 10.3 Effect of policy changes on tax ratios

	Present position	Policy: I	II	III
		Threshold increased by 20%/basic rate increased by 3p	Child benefit doubled/basic rate increased by 3p	Abolish married allowance/child benefit doubled
Tax ratio on £1 extra earnings by head of unit				
Modal tax ratio	37	40	40	37
Number of tax units with tax ratio of:				
50% or higher	700,000	690,000	570,000	570,000
75% or higher	100,000	80,000	110,000	120,000
Tax ratio on £75 earnings by wife (not at present at work)				
Modal tax ratio	26	26	28	26

The effect of an increase in child benefit, introduced in Policy II, differs from that of raising tax thresholds in floating families off dependence on housing benefits, although not FIS (with the present FIS rules, child benefit is not taken into account). We should not expect Policy II to contribute, therefore, to reducing the number of the very highest tax ratios, and in fact there is a slight increase, arising from the increased basic rate, in the numbers with ratios of 75 per cent or higher. On the other hand, the reduced dependence on rent and rate rebates means that the number with tax ratios of 50 per cent or higher is reduced by nearly a fifth. (For the reasons explained earlier, we can have more confidence in this latter figure, which is based on some 200 families in the FES.)

Policy III, in contrast to the other changes, leaves the basic rate unaltered, but in this case the beneficial effect of the rise in child benefit has to be balanced with the impact of the reduction in the threshold for married couples. It appears that this policy increases the number with ratios of 75 per cent or higher (the reduction in the threshold being more serious than the increase in basic rate with Policy II), but that the effect on those with ratios of 50 per cent and above is as great as with Policy II.

In the lower part of Table 10.3 we show the influence on the potential earnings decision by a married woman, considering a job at £75 a week. The modal tax rate, applying to some 60 per cent of cases, is unchanged by Policy I, the effect of the basic rate increase being offset by the increase in the earnings allowance for married women. But with Policy II, the modal tax rate rises to 28 per cent from 26 per cent. This illustrates the kind of trade-off which is involved in attempts to reduce the poverty trap. A policy which improves the position with regard to the tax rates on additional earnings by the husband may worsen it with regard to the incentive faced by the wife.

Finally, we should note that in considering these policy changes, no account has been taken of the fact that if families vary their work decisions as a result of the tax and benefit changes, then this could mean that they face a different situation from that shown in Table 10.3.

6   SUMMARY OF MAIN CONCLUSIONS

The first main conclusion is that inferences about the number of people facing high tax ratios tend to be based on a small number of families. To obtain more reliable estimates, and particularly to monitor trends over time, we need to obtain larger samples. It would be possible to do this by 'splicing' the data in the FES with those in the *General Household Survey* (GHS), an approach which may now be possible as a result of the changed wording of the income questions in the latter since 1979. Alternatively, there could be more frequent special-purpose surveys, such as the *Family Finances Survey*.

The second lesson is that examining only the effect of marginal increases in earnings by the family head may conceal significant dimensions. In particular, the tax ratios relevant to the decisions of married women (for example, considering taking a job, be it part-time or full-time) appear to be surprisingly low. Given that the evidence on labour supply suggests that such decisions may well be quantitatively more responsive to the tax ratios than marginal decisions on hours, this is of some importance.

The third conclusion is that an increase in benefits, such as child benefit, appears to be more effective in reducing the number of people with tax ratios in excess of 50 per cent than an increase in the tax threshold.

11 · THE TAKE-UP OF SOCIAL SECURITY BENEFITS

1 INTRODUCTION

The 'take-up' problem is concerned with those people who are entitled to social security benefits but do not in fact receive them. Incomplete take-up is, on the face of it, evidence that the social security programme is failing fully to meet its objectives. Benefits are not reaching some of those for whom they are intended. In the case of means-tested benefits, such as supplementary benefit or family income supplement, this typically means that people are living on incomes below the minimum which the income maintenance provisions seek to guarantee. The existence of incomplete take-up of social security benefits in Britain has therefore led to considerable concern.

Most of the current evidence about the extent of non-take-up in Britain comes from official sources. In the case of supplementary allowances, the government estimate is that 25 per cent of those eligible were not receiving benefit in 1981, and that for supplementary pensions the figure was 33 per cent (Hansard, 30 November 1983, cols 539–40). For family income supplement, the government estimate of take-up is around 50 per cent (*Social Security Statistics 1983*, p. 261). The apparent failure to reach between a quarter and a half of those eligible has cast serious doubt on the effectiveness of means-tested benefits.

The estimation of the extent of take-up is, however, a complex matter. It depends on being able to identify those families who would receive the benefit if they were to claim, and this is not easy. The experience with a succession of new social security benefits has been that it is difficult to estimate the size of the eligible population. When supplementary pensions were introduced in 1940, the number applying was over three times that expected by the government (Deacon and Bradshaw, 1983, p. 37). Less dramatically, but more recently, in the second reading debate on the Family Income Supplement Bill (10 November 1970), the Secretary of State gave an estimate of 164,000 eligible families, but this was later

Revised version of paper prepared for the Comptroller and Auditor General. I am grateful to Ruth Hancock for helpful discussions.

replaced by an estimated range of 110,000–170,000 (Stacpoole, 1972). This degree of uncertainty is relevant to the take-up, since the difficulty of estimating the number of eligible non-claimants remains after the scheme has been introduced.

The aim of this chapter is to assess the information which is available to assess the extent of non-take-up in Britain and the reliability of the conclusions which may be drawn. In section 2, a general framework is set out for the measurement of take-up, and some of the conceptual issues are discussed. Sections 3–5 examine in turn three categories of social security benefit; one-parent benefit, FIS and supplementary benefit. Although these three benefits account for less than 20 per cent of total social security expenditure, they are those where non-take-up has attracted most attention: for example, in its evidence to the House of Commons Social Services Committee (31 March 1982), the DHSS concerned itself with these benefits (plus attendance/mobility allowance). Section 6 draws together the main conclusions and makes recommendations for steps which could be taken to improve knowledge about take-up.

2 THE MEASUREMENT OF TAKE-UP

What we are trying to measure

It may be helpful to distinguish first between the measurement of non-take-up as *an indicator of the lack of effectiveness of* a particular benefit and non-take-up as *a cause of low incomes*. In the former case, the failure to achieve a satisfactory level of take-up is in itself a matter for concern – the benefit is not doing what it should. In the latter case, take-up is an intermediate objective, a means to the end of securing a desired level of income support. As an illustration of a situation where the distinction may be useful, suppose that families not claiming supplementary benefit (SB) receive housing rebates which close most of the income gap. Non-take-up of SB is in this case evidence that the programme is not working fully, but the income maintenance consequences may be less serious.

Let us start with *non-take-up as an indicator of effectiveness*. One has at once to confront the issue that non-claiming of the benefit may be a matter of choice. If a person is informed of his or her entitlement but does not claim, then it is sometimes argued that this is not a matter for concern. If a wealthy lone parent chooses not to claim one-parent benefit because of the time involved, then, it is argued, there is nothing that the DHSS can do. However, the very fact that people are seen as making a choice means that there must be non-trivial costs which have to be set against the benefits (in our example, the cost of time). The existence of such costs reduces the value of the benefit. Moreover, this applies not just to those who do not claim but also to those who *do* claim. If claiming one-parent benefit involves a significant investment of time, then it may be just as serious to a hard-pressed working single parent. She may claim, but the effective help provided by the benefit may be reduced. In the same way, if stigma is one factor causing a third of pensioners not to claim a supplementary pension, then we need also to take account of the possible cost in terms of loss of dignity for the two-thirds who do claim.

The existence of non-take-up is therefore grounds for concern about the effectiveness of the programme. At the same time, the cost–benefit calculation suggests that the seriousness of the problem may be related to the amount of unclaimed benefit. This has been recognized in the official analyses:

> Take-up tends to be higher as the amount of entitlement increases. The estimated proportion of benefit take-up in 1981 – 85 per cent – was higher than the proportion of those entitled at any one time who actually claimed – 71 per cent.
>
> (Hansard, 30 November 1983, cols 541–2)

In addition to measuring the proportion not claiming, we need to consider its relation with the amount of entitlement, including other benefits from claiming (e.g. the 'passport' to other benefits). In particular, it seems reasonable to exclude from the category of 'non-claimants' those who would derive no benefit (financial or other) from claiming.

There are several possible reasons for non-take-up. People may be unaware of the benefit. They may be aware of its existence but believe that they are not eligible. This may happen, for example, where they had previously claimed and been deemed 'ineligible', but there has been a subsequent benefit uprating which makes them eligible. People may be aware of their eligibility but not claim on account of the costs of doing so, discussed earlier, including any perceived loss of dignity ('stigma'). They may claim but their claim be rejected through administrative error. The last of these reasons would be manifest evidence of ineffectiveness, and the same applies to the lack of information. In these cases, there is no spillover to those in receipt: there is no cost to those who do get the benefit. On the other hand, as discussed, the time and other costs may apply also to recipients and the significance of these costs may be greater than measures of non-take-up indicate.

The dynamics of the process must be considered. If the problem were one of the diffusion of information, then we would expect the probability of claiming to increase the longer a person had been eligible. In this context, the rapidity with which family circumstances may change is an important element: for example, one-parent families may be in transition. This is also relevant if non-take-up is a matter of decision, since there may be fixed costs in claiming, which would only make a claim worthwhile if the eligibility is likely to last for some time.

We need, therefore, ideally to have information on (i) the number of non-recipients, (ii) the amount of benefit not claimed, (iii) duration of eligibility, and (iv) the reasons for non-take-up. The last of these is, in addition, important in judging what measures could improve take-up.

If we turn to the *income support implications* of non-take-up, it is interesting to note that the estimates of take-up of SB are typically based on a similar analysis to that of *low income families*, produced every two years by the DHSS. There are, however, significant differences in the approach to this formulation of the take-up problem.

If we are concerned about non-take-up as a cause of low incomes, then the proportion not claiming benefit is not in itself a particularly relevant measure. Nor is the amount of unclaimed entitlement necessarily the right variable. As the earlier example suggested, the amount of SB unclaimed is not of direct concern if part of the shortfall is made up by housing rebates. In the case of FIS, it is not just the FIS entitlement but also the passport to other benefits (which *increases* the loss) and the repercussions for housing rebates (which *reduce* the loss). Put this way, the question we want to ask is:

If take-up were 100 per cent (or some other target level), how far would this contribute to reducing the problems of those with low incomes?

This is, of course, a much more complex question. Not least it requires a specification of the low income objective. This has several dimensions, as may be illustrated by two aspects. First, there is the duration of non-claiming, referred to earlier. Suppose that non-claiming among pensioners is concentrated among those newly eligible, who take some time to become aware of their entitlement. This may be regarded as a less serious shortcoming than if some of those eligible do not claim at all in their old age. Or, in the case of family income supplement (FIS), suppose that a person's earnings temporarily fall to a low level for five weeks, and then recover. We may be less concerned about this failure to claim than where a family is persistently low paid. (This is an example where the administrative procedures may have failed to capture the original intention of the scheme.) The second example concerns whether non-claimants are heads of households or whether they are living with others. The government has drawn attention to the fact that 'non-take-up of benefit may be due to the fact that potential claimants . . . are living in reasonably well-off households' (Hansard, 30 November 1983). Whether or not this leads us to be less concerned depends on whether one is judging the adequacy of incomes in terms of *households* or of *family units*. The assessment for supplementary benefit is firmly based on the family unit, with the presence of non-dependants in the same household entering the calculation of housing costs but not otherwise affecting the assessment. On the other hand, it is sometimes suggested – as implicitly in the passage just quoted – that the position of the household should be considered as a whole (an issue which has been discussed in Part I).

The second formulation of the take-up problem, in terms of its income support implications, involves us therefore in judgements of value about the appropriate objective. It also imposes greater requirements on the empirical data. In what follows, I concentrate on the first formulation (non-take-up as an indicator of ineffectiveness), but this should not be taken as implying that I consider the income support implications to be unimportant.

Empirical difficulties

This section considers the major empirical difficulties in trying to quantify the aspects identified above: the extent of non-take-up, the amounts not claimed, and the importance of different reasons for not claiming. In each case, we may distinguish between those difficulties which arise in measuring the *level* and those concerned with *changes over time*. This distinction is important, since it is not uncommon for governments to admit that the problem is serious but to argue that there are signs of improvement over time.

In order to be eligible for a particular benefit, a person has to satisfy certain conditions. These may include demographic conditions (e.g. having a child whose age falls in a certain range), marital status (e.g. single), employment status (e.g. working 24 hours or more a week), income or 'resources', and indicators of 'needs' (such as housing costs). In some cases, the conditions may be relatively straightforward to check (e.g. age), but in others, they may involve quite complicated calculations (e.g. resources), or a significant degree of ambiguity (e.g. whether two people are cohabiting).

How can we identify those people who are eligible but not claiming? One possible approach would be a sample survey of the population at risk (e.g. families with children) to screen out potentially eligible persons, who are then asked to put in a claim for benefit, with this being taken to appeal if there were grounds to suspect that eligibility had not in fact been correctly determined. A procedure of broadly this type has been implemented in the study by OPCS of a small sample of pensioners (Broad, 1977), but this study indicated that there are serious problems in securing agreement to put in a claim (only 12 out of 41 agreed to do so). Indeed, only if lack of information was the main reason for non-claiming would we expect it to be easy to secure agreement.

For this reason, the studies of take-up have typically had to rely on determining eligibility from information supplied directly by the respondents. The reliability of this approach depends on the benefit in question. For one-parent benefit, the list of qualifying conditions is quite short (although some are not easily determined). For FIS, the calculation of the prescribed amount is relatively straightforward, much more so than the determination of needs for supplementary benefit purposes. Reliability also depends on whether the survey questions are well constructed, and here we must draw a distinction between the specially-designed surveys and the use of multi-purpose surveys such as the *Family Expenditure Survey* (FES) and the *General Household Survey* (GHS). For some purposes, such as exploring the reasons for non-claiming, special surveys are obviously the only way. For others, the FES or GHS can be used, but the fact that the questions are not tailored to the purpose means that the calculation of entitlement is likely to involve more approximations. An example is provided by FIS. In the specially designed *Family Finances Survey*, the questions asked for earnings in the previous five weeks, or two months, which is the basis for entitlement. In the FES, the question only asks about last pay period earnings and in the calculation of eligibility for FIS it has to be assumed that this is representative. To take another example, the 'capital resources' variable necessary to assess SB is not recorded in the FES and has to be estimated from the recorded investment income. Similarly, the calculation of additional requirements cannot readily be made for items such as special diets or laundry.

In any sample survey, the information obtained will be subject to recording error. This may take the form of incorrectly reporting receipt of benefit: for example, supplementary benefit received by the unemployed may be reported as national insurance unemployment benefit. If the errors tend to be in the direction of not acknowledging receipt of a means-tested benefit, then take-up may be understated. Take-up may also be understated if eligibility is overestimated on account of under-reporting of income. It is sometimes suggested that the FES income data are seriously deficient. Detailed examination of the data shows in fact that the FES performs quite well for all except investment and self-employment income. In the case of earnings, for example, a comparison may be made with the *New Earnings Survey*, and the conclusions reached (Atkinson, Micklewright and Stern, 1982) are relatively reassuring. At the same time, account must be taken of the likely under-recording of investment and self-employment income.

When we move from the individual to the population as a whole, there arises the question of the representativeness of the sample. First, the small numbers involved in surveys such as the FES mean that there is likely to be substantial sampling error. This is not easily estimated in view of the multi-stage design of the FES, and the calculations given by the DHSS are based on the assumption of a simple random sample (Supplementary Benefits Commission, 1978). They conclude, in the case of SB, that a 95 per cent confidence interval for the percentage take-up by pensioners would be ±3 percentage points, i.e. 71 to 77 per cent in 1975. This means that any year-to-year changes must be treated with considerable caution. For example, the estimates for 1973–77 are 74 per cent, 76 per cent, 74 per cent, 74 per cent and 73 per cent (Supplementary Benefits Commission, *Annual Report 1978*, Table 12.8), which all lie within this range. It is an interesting question whether other measures of non-take-up, such as the amount of unclaimed benefit, are more or less sensitive to sampling fluctuations.

Second, cooperation is voluntary and non-response in the FES is typically around 30 per cent. Studies of the characteristics of non-respondents indicate associations with age and family composition (Kemsley, Redpath and Holmes, 1980), and it is possible that it is related to income or employment status. Clearly, if there is differential non-response, it may affect the conclusions drawn with regard to the rate of take-up, or the scale of the problem.

An alternative source of information to sample surveys is that derived from administrative records. This, by its very nature, cannot tell us about eligible non-claimants, but it can be used to supplement survey data in two ways. First, it is sometimes employed to draw conclusions about trends over time. In this case, evidence about non-take-up is necessary for a base date, with the administrative data being used to extrapolate over time. They have the advantage of a much larger sample size than typically found in sources such as the FES, but they must be interpreted with great care. The accuracy of the inferences drawn depends crucially on controlling for other factors which may have affected the (observed) receipt or the (unobserved) eligibility. It has been known for governments to acknowledge that surveys have shown incomplete take-up but to cite a rising level of claims as evidence that the problem was becoming now less serious. This is only valid if there are not factors, such as an uprating of the benefit scales, which could be expected to lead to an increase quite independently of any improvement in take-up. One has therefore to construct a 'counterfactual' position against which to assess the observed increase. This can be done by a time-series analysis of past changes in benefit receipt, levels, etc., as in Chapter 12 below for the one of FIS. An alternative approach, not discussed here, is to examine variation in benefit receipt across geographical regions. This approach has been used by Bradshaw (1977) in studying rent rebates.

The administrative data are also combined with survey evidence in a different way. The official estimates of the take-up of SB have been calculated as follows:

Numbers receiving (from annual statistical enquiry of SB claimants)

———————————————————————————————————————

Numbers receiving (as above) + numbers eligible but not receiving (estimated from FES)   (1)

This combination of evidence from two sources introduces a number of problems. For one thing, it complicates the calculations of sampling error. More serious is the relation between (i) receipt, (ii) receipt recorded in the FES, and (iii) calculated entitlement in the FES. In terms of receipt, the FES appears to give a reasonably similar picture to that obtained from the administrative records. The calculations of Atkinson and Mickelwright (1983) of the number of current claimants of SB for the period 1970–77 were close to administrative totals (100.2 per cent when adjusted for differential non-response by age), although there was some year-to-year variation (from 93.3 per cent to 107.7 per cent). But if recorded receipt in the FES is compared with calculated entitlement, then quite a number of cases record SB receipt who are not calculated to be eligible (Altmann, 1981a). This may well reflect the approximate nature of the entitlement calculations, but it may also reflect errors in the administration of the benefit. In the latter case, if we are concerned with the percentage of 'true' eligibles who claim, then those incorrectly receiving should be deducted from both top and bottom of expression (1).

There are therefore serious difficulties in the measurement of take-up. These difficulties should not however be seen as implying that we can say *nothing*. The argument is for caution, not nihilism. In particular, we can hope to put bounds on the different sources of error, a procedure which has been used to good effect by the DHSS (Supplementary Benefits Commission, 1978). Moreover, there are steps which can be taken to improve our knowledge. To the extent that the difficulties result from small sample sizes in the FES, it would be possible to make greater use of pooling data over years (with appropriate adjustments) or to consider combining data from the FES and GHS. Special surveys, designed specifically to measure take-up have an important role to play, since they can ensure that the questions asked are those necessary to assess eligibility, and the sample can be selected to give adequate representation of the relevant groups. Such special surveys do not overcome all difficulties (for instance, there would remain problems of non-response and under-recording of income), but the past examples demonstrate their potential, as is discussed in more detail in the context of individual benefits.

3 ONE-PARENT BENEFIT

One-parent benefit (OPB) is the simplest in structure of the three benefits considered, there being no means test and the key conditions being:

1. The person is not married and not living with anyone as man and wife.
2. He or she is receiving child benefit for at least one child.

3. The person is not already receiving child's special allowance, guard-ian's allowance, a higher rate industrial death benefit for the child, or an increase for the child paid with industrial disablement benefit, invalid care allowance, retirement pension, war or service widow's pension, widow's allowance or widowed mother's allowance.

The official estimate of take-up in Great Britain is 70 per cent in 1981 (Social Security Advisory Committee, *Second Report*, 1982/3, p. 8). The earlier figure of 66 per cent in 1980 was given by the DHSS in evidence to the House of Commons Social Services Committee (31 March 1982), together with an estimate of the unclaimed benefit of £20 million for 1980/1. For 1979, the estimated take-up was 60 per cent (*Social Security Statistics*, 1981, p. 253). The benefit was previously called child interim benefit and child benefit increase. The change in name to one-parent benefit in April 1981 was intended, with other advertising measures, to raise take-up, and some commentators have concluded from the figures quoted above that there has been an improvement (e.g. Hansard, 15 November 1983, col. 710).

Although relatively straightforward in conception, the case of OPB illustrates a number of the difficulties in assessing take-up described above. The basis for the 1980 calculation was explained by the DHSS (evidence to House of Commons Social Security Committee, 31 March 1982):

$$\frac{438,000 \text{ recipients of OPB} - 128,000 \text{ also receiving SB}}{900,000 \text{ single-parent families} - 434,000 \text{ not entitled or receiving SB}} = 66 \text{ per cent}$$

Accepting the number in receipt of OPB as correct, there are three possible sources of error:

1. The take-up rate is defined in terms of 'those who stand to gain by claiming the benefit'. This leads the DHSS to deduct all those in receipt of supplementary benefit, in the assessment of which OPB is taken fully into account. Of the 336,000 one-parent families on SB in November 1980, 120,000 were receiving OPB. The latter number is deducted from the top, and the former number is deducted from the bottom, of the take-up calculation. It should however be noted that some of those in receipt of SB might gain from claiming OPB, if their SB entitlement were less than the OPB (plus any advantage from passport benefits or single SB payments), so to this (minor) extent the take-up rate is overstated. More importantly, it is not clear that one should simply consider the cash gain. One of the merits of OPB from the point of view of the recipient is that it constitutes a more certain income, not subject to the, perceived or real, vagaries of SB. There might be a number of SB recipients eligible for, but not receiving, OPB who would welcome this alternative source, even if it brings no cash gain. To this extent take-up is overstated.

2. There are a number of families not entitled to claim (this can be obtained as a residual from the earlier figure, as 98,000), which is presumably based on administrative records for those in receipt of benefits such as the widowed mother's allowance.
3. The total number of one-parent families is the subject of considerable debate. The estimate of 900,000 was supplied by the OPCS (for end-1981, the comparable figure is 950,000), but their own study draws attention to the difficulties involved:

> estimates for years after 1971 must rely on many disparate data sources, none of which is ideal ... only a few of the many ways of becoming (or ceasing to be) a lone parent are monitored through internal registration.
>
> (Leete, 1978, p. 9)

Moreover, even the Census of Population figures, which will supply a firmer basis for 1981, are subject to limitations and need to be adjusted. The original estimate prepared for the Finer Committee on the basis of the 1971 Census was, for example, reduced from 620,000 to 570,000 (Leete, 1978, Table 1). It should be noted that a one-parent family may be defined in a variety of different ways, both with regard to the 'lone-parent' status and to the definition of a 'child'. What we need are definitions comparable with those applied in the administration of OPB, but the Census does not correspond in either case in a completely satisfactory manner (see Hamill, 1978).

There are therefore problems with even this relatively simply benefit. Moreover, these may be of some quantitative significance. Suppose that the estimated total of one-parent families in 1980 was in fact 875,000. This corresponds to an overstatement (e.g. because some of the children are not in fact eligible for child benefit) of only 2.9 per cent, but the take-up rate would become 70 per cent rather than 66 per cent. Such errors could have at least as much impact as the year-to-year changes in the reported take-up.

The amount not claimed under OPB is easily calculated given the estimated numbers, but the available evidence throws little light on the characteristics of non-recipients, the reasons why they do not claim, or the duration of their eligibility. In order to investigate these questions, evidence from surveys seems necessary. One possible source is the *Family Finances Survey*, covering some 1,123 one-parent families. This promises to provide valuable evidence (see Millar, 1983), although it has limitations (for example, the type of family – widowed, divorced, separated, unmarried – is not recorded explicitly). A specially designed survey would be a valuable addition. This would require very careful design, but it would offer the opportunity to explore in interviews such aspects as the value placed on one-parent benefit contrasted with supplementary benefit.

4 FAMILY INCOME SUPPLEMENT

Family income supplement (FIS) is payable to all families with children, so that there is no question of defining one-parent families, but it is a means-tested benefit with all the attendant difficulties of determining eligibility. There is moreover the condition that the claimant must be normally engaged in full-time work (30 hours per week for a married couple, 24 hours for a single parent).

The take-up of FIS has been surrounded by controversy since its inception, when the government referred to a target take-up of 85 per cent (Hansard, 10 November 1970, col. 227). In 1972, the take-up was estimated to be around 50 per cent; and this estimate increased to 'about two-thirds' in 1972 and 'about three-quarters' in 1974 and 1975 (*Social Security Statistics 1976*, Table 32.15). These estimates were based on the FES. Subsequently, a reconsideration of the method employed led to their being revised downwards to 'about one-half' (Hansard, 10 June 1981, cols 133–4). *The Family Finances Survey* conducted from October 1978 to September 1979 led to an estimate for Great Britain of 51 per cent. For Northern Ireland, the figure from December 1979 to November 1980 was a take-up rate of 65 per cent (Social Security Advisory Committee, *Second Report*, 1982/3, p. 8).

There are two fundamental difficulties in estimating the take-up of FIS: the proportion of the population affected is extremely small, and entitlement to benefit for 52 weeks is based on income in a five week or two month period.

It is the latter of these points that led to the reconsideration of the method employed. At any one time, families receiving FIS are those who qualified on the basis of qualifying income below the minimum at some point in the preceding 12 months. They may well not qualify on the basis of their current income; indeed there is evidence from surveys that a substantial proportion of recipients would not qualify at the date of interview. For example, in 1972, when FIS was paid for 26 weeks, rather than 52 weeks, a study of two-parent families receiving FIS found 'that more than one in five of the sample would not have qualified for a FIS award at all, had they applied at the time of interview' (Knight and Nixon, 1975, p. 72). This suggests two possible calculations:

1. Those receiving FIS at date of interview

   TOP + those non-claimants who would have qualified
        at any point in past 52 weeks

2. Those receiving FIS whose claim would have
   succeeded at date of interview

   TOP + those non-claimants whose claim would
       have succeeded at the date of interview

where in each case, TOP refers to the numerator in the expression.

In order to apply measure 1, one needs to obtain income data for families over the past 12 months and this is not typically collected in sample surveys. The feasibility of collecting such information was examined by the OPCS who concluded that 'moving to a 12 months income period would not be feasible if consultation of records was an important assurance of accuracy' (Kemsley, Redpath and Holmes, 1980, p. 72). The earlier method used in calculating take-up may be seen as an attempt to approximate 1, taking the estimated position 12 months earlier, but this was recognized in the re-evaluation to produce 'a misleadingly high figure for take-up' (Department of Health and Social Security, 1981, Appendix C).

In view of the problems with measure 1, it is measure 2 on which recent estimates have concentrated. Even here there are obstacles. The income information in the FES does not even allow last five weeks or last two months income to be calculated accurately, and this has to be approximated from last pay period earnings.

Estimation of take-up from the FES brings with it the second basic problem – that of small numbers. In broad terms, there are some 175,000 families receiving FIS; the effective sampling fraction in the FES is approximately 1 in 2,800; so we would expect to find 62.5 families in the survey receiving FIS. In the 1970s, when the numbers in receipt were around half this level, we might expect only some 30 in the FES. When we eliminate those whose claims would not have succeeded at the date of interview, this number would become even smaller, and it is apparent that the sampling error would be quite sizeable. Certainly it is going to be difficult to draw conclusions about changes over time in the rate of take-up from the FES. Nor is it easy to describe at all reliably the characteristics of non-claimants.

The need for a larger sample of low income families was one of the main motivations for the DHSS carrying out the *Family Finances Survey* (FFS), which was explicitly intended to provide information about the take-up of income-tested benefits (Knight, 1981, p. 3). The first hurdle faced by this study was that there is no sampling frame from which low-income families can be identified. The investigation consisted therefore of two stages: an initial screening of a sample of families drawn from the child benefit records, followed by a main interview with those who appeared to fall below the low-income threshold (140 per cent of the supplementary benefit scale). The response to the first sift was 75.2 per cent, and at the second stage usable income data were obtained for 71.2 per cent of those eligible, giving a final sample of 3,214 low-income families (Atkinson and Rahmatulla, 1983).

The FFS asked questions explicitly designed to check eligibility for FIS (for example, asking about the earnings for the last five weeks or two months) and probably provides as good a basis as any sample survey for assessing take-up, according to measure 2. There are however the following shortcomings:

1. The calculated take-up figure excludes the self-employed, who in December 1979 constituted 7 per cent of FIS recipients. The DHSS (1981) note the difficulties in obtaining appropriate income information for the self-employed, and the possible understatement of income. Accepting the information supplied in the FFS at face value, it appears that take-up is very low, and, taking account of the qualifications, the DHSS conclude that 'although it is not possible to produce a reliable take-up from the survey for the self-employed, the evidence points strongly to a lower take-up than for the employed' (1981, para. B9).

2. The total numbers are still quite small, there being only 69 employees in the FFS with apparent unclaimed entitlement to FIS. The DHSS estimate a 95 per cent confidence interval of 43–59 per cent (1981, para. 6). The small numbers undoubtedly limit the usefulness of the survey in exploring the characteristics of non-claimants as a possible guide to reasons for not claiming. For example, it would be interesting to examine the relation between current and 'normal' income.

3. There are problems in extrapolating to the population as a whole, particularly because of the complicated sample design and the high degree of non-response (some 37 per cent overall). The DHSS draws attention to the exclusion at the second stage of possible or actual recipients (with incomes above 140 per cent of the SB scale) and correct for this, and they note that at the first stage (the sift of child benefit records) there is an apparent under-statement of FIS recipients, compared with the administrative statistics. The implications may be seen from the following numbers for measure 2:

$$\frac{69,000 \text{ (in receipt/current claim would succeed)}}{69,000 + 66,000 \text{ (eligible non-claimants)}} = 51 \text{ per cent}$$

According to the administrative records, the number 69,000 should be 78,000. This in itself would raise estimated take-up to 54 per cent, which would be correct if the understatement were due to higher non-response amongst recipients. But if the understatement were due to respondents to FFS failing to declare receipt of FIS, then the number of eligible non-claimants would be overstated. If we deduct the 9,000 from 66,000, then the estimated take-up becomes 58 per cent. It may be noted that it is a feature of FIS that a person in receipt will still be calculated to be eligible, even if FIS is being paid and accurately recorded as part of other income. This could not happen with SB, since the other income (i.e. SB) would raise the person to the SB level, if calculated accurately.

There is therefore a considerable margin of uncertainty surrounding the estimated take-up of FIS. At the same time, it is unlikely to exceed 66 per cent (the upper end of a 95 per cent confidence interval centred on 58 per cent), particularly if the self-employed were included. One can conclude that the take-up falls well short of the 85 per cent target. The FFS contains useful information about the characteristics of non-claimants and, in conjunction with the follow-up *Family Resources Survey* a year later, may be used to examine the dynamics of claiming and its relation to changing family circumstances.

Since these surveys were carried out, there has been a very substantial increase in the receipt of FIS, and the government has drawn encouragement from this. In April 1979 (the midpoint of the FFS sample period) the number of families receiving FIS was 78,000, by April 1981 this had increased to 112,000, and by April 1983 to 186,000. Receipt had more than doubled, and for two-parent families the increase was even more marked: from 40,000 in April 1979 to 108,000 in April 1983.

Analysis of changes over time in the number receiving benefits is an important source of information, when linked with a base figure for take-up derived from survey evidence. But, as we have seen, its validity depends on controlling for the other factors which affect eligibility and receipt, as is discussed further in Chapter 12. This suggests that one needs to exercise considerable caution in drawing conclusions from the number of claimants. In order to establish whether the position has changed, it would be very desirable to repeat a special survey of the *Family Finances Survey* type, modified to take account of the lessons described above.

5 SUPPLEMENTARY BENEFIT

The take-up of supplementary benefit is the aspect which has been most discussed, although it was a number of years after the introduction of the postwar national assistance that the problem came to public awareness. In 1954, the Phillips Committee on the Economic and Financial Problems of the Provision for Old Age commented, 'we have had no evidence to suggest that the present arrangements for national assistance are not fully capable of playing their essential part of preventing distress among the old by securing a basic minimum' (Phillips, 1954, p. 77). (Although, as discussed in Chapter 4, evidence *could* have been obtained from Rowntree's 1950 survey of York.)

It was only in the 1960s that evidence began to be published which showed the incomplete nature of take-up. The survey by Cole and Utling (1962) of the elderly in 1959–60 found that over 10 per cent of all people over the retirement age appeared to be entitled to national assistance but were not claiming. Abel-Smith and Townsend (1965) concluded that about one million people were in this position. These academic enquiries led to the setting up of the Ministry of Pensions and National Insurance (1966) study, which was intended to establish the number of retirement pensioners who were not claiming assistance and the reasons why they did not apply. This study was carefully designed and conducted, and in many respects is a model of its type. Moreover, some of the problems which we have noted in the case of FIS and the *Family Finances Survey* do not apply. The retirement pension records provided a ready sampling frame, although it should be noted that it excluded those not entitled to national insurance pensions (more important in 1965 than today). The population 'at risk' in the case of pensioners is considerably higher, and this, coupled with a sample size of over 10,000, and a response rate of 90 per cent, meant that it was possible to give quite reliable and detailed results. It is in the nature of SB that entitlement is less easily calculated, but this aspect, and the reliability of the data, were examined in depth, including test checks of the information with the National Assistance Board. As a result, corrections were made, and the resulting estimate of 700,000 pensioner households who could have received national assistance in 1965 if they had applied is one in which one can have considerable confidence.

Following the 1965 enquiry, the government made major changes in national assistance, renaming it supplementary benefits, with the intention of improving take-up. These changes were claimed by the government of the time to be a 'remarkable success', a claim based on the substantial increase in the number of old people receiving assistance. Again, however, we have to allow for the improvement in the scale rate, which increased the number eligible. In Atkinson (1969), I examined how much of the increase could be attributed to the improved scale, using two approaches. From the ministry enquiry, it was possible to estimate the number then above the scale who would become entitled. From the past time-series of aggregate numbers in receipt, it was possible to estimate the relationship with the scale rate (relative to the national insurance pension). These sources led to the conclusion that between a half and two-thirds of the increase in the number of recipients could be attributed to the more generous scale.

Non-take-up remained, therefore, a problem, and in the 1970s the government began publishing estimates of the take-up rate based on the FES. The most recent are those quoted earlier from 1981, and the series is summarized in Table 11.1.

These estimates are surrounded by a number of qualifications, and these have been examined in detail by the Supplementary Benefits Commission (1978). The aspects which they consider are:

1. Differential non-response in the FES.
2. Under-recording of income.
3. Exceptional circumstance additions.
4. Treatment of capital.

5. The interdependence with housing benefits.
6. Availability for work in the case of the unemployed.
7. Sampling error.

As they show, a number of these could lead to noticeable variation in the estimates. For example, if all above pension age had failed to report income of £1 a week, the take-up estimate becomes 80 per cent, rather than 74 per cent. On the other hand, if those not claiming had additional requirements equal to the average of SB recipients (rather than zero, as assumed), then the take-up for pensioners would fall from 74 per cent to 70 per cent. At the same time, one should not exaggerate the impact. Making quite extreme (and clearly unrealistic) assumptions about the characteristics of non-respondents to the FES leads to the range 62 per cent to 81 per cent – a wide range, but one which still means that virtually 1 in 5 are not claiming.

Refinement of the figures is not likely, therefore, to lead to a reversal of the broad conclusion that there is significant non-take-up. The same cannot however be said about the conclusions regarding trends over time. As already noted, the changes year-by-year are of the same order of magnitude as the effect of adjustments on the estimates. If the errors remained constant over time, then of course the measurement of the trends would not be affected, but there are reasons to suppose that they *have* changed. Most important is the role of additions to the basic scale. Over the 1970s there was a definite increase in the extent of such additions, so that the

Table 11.1 Estimated take-up of supplementary benefit

	Head of family over pension age		Head below pension age	
	%	unclaimed benefit (£m)	%	unclaimed benefit (£m)
1973	74	55	70	110
1974	76	60	72	120
1975	74	65	75	175
1976	74	80	79	170
1977 original	73	100	76	245
1977 revised	72	100	79	165
1979	65	145	78	210
1981 excluding heating additions	72	—	—	—
1981 with heating additions	67	210	75	550

Sources: Supplementary Benefits Commission, *Annual Report 1978*, Tables 12.8 and 12.9. Hansard, 5 April 1982, cols 249–50, 30 November 1983, cols 539–42.

Notes: The reason for the break in the series in 1977 is that the 'original' estimate (and those for earlier years) included a number of unoccupied people whose entitlement to benefit was in doubt. Two-thirds of this group are excluded in the revised estimate, and the remaining third reclassified (Hansard, 5 April 1982).

failure to take them into account led to an increasing overstatement of take-up. With the 1980 recasting of SB, the treatment of additional payments changed, and the 1981 estimates take account of heating additions where provided on grounds of age. The figure of 67 per cent for pensioners in 1981 in Table 11.1 cannot for this reason be compared with 65 per cent in 1979.

A further factor is the interdependence with housing rebates. In the official estimates, people are not treated as non-claimants if they are not claiming SB but would be better off if they claimed rent and rate rebates. While it is useful to distinguish between these people and those better off on SB, it is not apparent that they should be excluded. It is a failure of SB if people fail to claim, irrespective of whether they would be better off on another benefit. (The official practice also means that measured take-up depends on the level of housing rebates.) The Supplementary Benefits Commission (1978) consider the effect of excluding from claimants those who in fact would be better off on housing rebates, but the appropriate procedure seems to be to add to those eligible the people who do not claim SB but would be better off on housing benefits. This is quantitatively quite important, as is shown in Altmann (1981a and b), who calculates a take-up rate of SB for male pensioners of less than 60 per cent over the period 1970–77. Furthermore, it affects the measured trend over time, since the housing benefit system has changed over the period.

6 CONCLUSIONS

The existing evidence tells us quite a lot about the *level* of non-take-up. For all three of the benefits considered, it is evident that a significant minority are not claiming the benefit to which they are entitled. A number of the sources provide estimates of the amount of entitlement not claimed and an indication of the main characteristics of the non-claimants. And, in the case of specially designed surveys such as that of retirement pensioners in 1965, there is evidence about the reasons for not claiming.

At the same time, there is considerable scope for improving the reliability of the estimates. In the case of supplementary benefit, the *Family Expenditure Survey* provides a reasonable basis for the estimates, but it would be possible to narrow the margin of uncertainty by:

1. Pooling the information for more than one year (particularly since the estimates are only now produced for odd-numbered years).
2. Doing parallel calculations using the *General Household Survey* (for those years with housing cost information), which has a larger sample size and, since 1979, broadly comparable income data.
3. Treating explicitly the relationship with housing benefits.

4. Adding questions on capital resources.
5. Adding questions designed to elicit information about additional requirements.

For one-parent benefit and FIS, the FES is not going to provide a sufficiently large sample (although it would be helpful if one-parent benefit were separated from child benefit in the FES income questions). Here the role of special surveys is critical, and there is a strong case for a repeat of the *Family Finances Survey*, preferably with a larger sample size. This should particularly probe take-up by the self-employed and the recorded receipt of FIS, both of which we have seen to cause problems in the FFS. It would ideally be linked with a detailed investigation of the reasons for non-claiming.

The need for a further benchmark survey of this kind is all the more pressing when we consider how little can be said about the *trends* over time for all three benefits. Administrative data on the numbers in receipt need to be interpreted with care and, without more sophisticated analysis, cannot be used to determine how far take-up has changed. The FES estimates of take-up of SB would need to show a dramatic, and sustained, shift for one to be confident that take-up had improved. A repeat of the 1965 Ministry of Pensions and National Insurance enquiry would be extremely valuable. Moreover, it would be useful to explore, in interviews, the experience of *recipients* and the costs, such as time, which are involved in claiming.

These suggestions all involve additional work or expense. They require, as a minimum, additional statistical resources for the analysis of existing data, and ideally they involve the mounting of major new surveys. But if the government seriously wishes to be in a position to assess the effectiveness of these expenditure programmes, then such costs are inevitable.

12 · FAMILY INCOME SUPPLEMENT AND TWO-PARENT FAMILIES, 1971–1980

Question: Did you ever know of a practice in your parish of paying a part of
the wages of labour out of the poor rate?
Answer: They do at this time.
Question: Have you ever applied to them for any addition to your wages?
Answer: No I never did; I always try to do without.
(Evidence of Thomas Smart to Select Committee on Labourers'
Wages, 1824 in Rose, 1971, pp. 63–4)

1 INTRODUCTION

The family income supplement (FIS) scheme, which received Royal Assent
in December 1970 and came into effect in Britain on 3 August 1971,
represented a major change in the direction of postwar social policy,
although it could indeed be seen as a return to the principles of an earlier
age. The FIS scheme provided a means-tested benefit for families with
children headed by a full-time worker. As such, it differed from family
allowances, now child benefit, which are paid at the same rate for all
families irrespective of income, and from supplementary benefit, which is
a means-tested benefit, but only paid to families where the head is out of
work.

The main elements of the scheme remained unchanged from its introduction to its replacement by Family Credit in 1988. There is a qualifying
level, which varies with the number of children, and FIS is payable where a
family's gross income is less than this qualifying level, being equal to half
the difference, subject to an overall maximum. The assessment is based on
earnings for five weeks (two months for monthly paid workers). The
benefit is then paid for 52 weeks (26 weeks prior to October 1972) and
is not affected by changing circumstances, although it is adjusted if the
scheme is uprated.

Throughout its short history, the scheme has been the subject of
controversy. From the outset, doubts were expressed as to whether it

---

With B. Champion.

would succeed in reaching all those entitled – a contrast being drawn between the new means-tested scheme and the universal family allowances, where the receipt is close to 100 per cent. It soon appeared that in fact the numbers claiming fell short of those expected and that there was a serious 'take-up' problem. Opinions continued to differ, however, as to whether this was a temporary problem, likely to die away as the scheme gained wider acceptability, and as to the effectiveness of advertising and government publicity in increasing the rate of take-up.

These issues are of central importance for social security policy. The future shape of income maintenance depends very much on the weight to be attached to means-testing as a strategy. The FIS scheme, although small in scale, provides for this reason a valuable case study. In this chapter we analyse the experience of the period 1971–80 and the evidence about numbers receiving as recorded in the monthly administrative statistics. The next section (section 2) describes the history of the scheme and the main issues which have figured in political and public debate. Section 3 examines the factors influencing the number of recipients and provides a simple framework for the analysis of the data. Section 4 presents a statistical analysis of the monthly time-series from August 1971 to January 1980, investigating the sensitivity of the numbers receiving FIS to variation in the qualifying levels and other changes. The main conclusions are summarized in section 5.

2 THE HISTORY OF FIS, 1970–80

The idea of a means-tested benefit for low-paid workers with children had been under consideration during the 1964–70 Wilson government (see, for example, Banting, 1979, Ch. 3), but the impetus for its introduction came from the Conservative Party's pledge in the June 1970 election to 'tackle the problem of family poverty'. Although Edward Heath, the Prime Minister, had given the clear impression that this would be achieved through an increase in family allowances, the incoming government rejected this approach on the grounds of cost and that a relatively small fraction of the expenditure would go to low-income families. As it was argued by Sir Keith Joseph, Secretary of State for Social Services, 'an increase in family allowances . . . could not provide the scale of help which the very poorest of wage earning households desperately need, that is, not without going into astronomic figures' (House of Commons, 10 November 1970, Hansard, vol. 806, col. 218). Moreover, family allowances were not payable to families with one child, and the extension of the scheme to cover this group would, it was felt, have been very expensive.

The FIS scheme restricted the cost by paying benefits only to those families below the qualifying level (referred to in the legislation as the prescribed amount). This meant that, even though the scheme covered one-child families, the number of beneficiaries was expected to be relatively small. In the second reading debate (10 November 1970), the Secretary of State estimated that 110,000 two-parent families and 54,000 single-parent families would receive benefits.[1] This may be compared with over four million families receiving family allowances at that date. The expected cost was correspondingly small. The Family Income Supplement Bill (Financial Memorandum) estimated that the cost would be £7 million in a full year,[2] which may be compared with an expenditure of £339 million on family allowances in the financial year 1970–1.

Against the lower outlay on benefits must be set the greater administrative complexity of the means-tested scheme – even though it was designed with a view to minimizing administrative costs (see Stacpoole, 1972). The benefit is administered by post from a single office in Blackpool. The assessment of income is based on a short period (five weeks for weekly paid workers, two months for monthly paid), and takes gross rather than net income. The benefit does not depend on the ages of the children nor on whether there are one or two parents. It is only revised within a payment period if the scales are changed. Despite these simplifications, the administrative expenses were expected from the outset to be high. According to the Memorandum accompanying the Bill, the annual cost was expected to be £600,000, or 9 per cent of the expenditure on the supplement, and about 200 additional staff would be needed. For family allowances in 1972–3, the corresponding administrative cost was 3 per cent on the benefit paid and 2,100 man-years were required (House of Commons, written answer 18 July 1974).

The difference in terms of administrative costs is clearly much smaller than the difference in the cost of the benefits; the administration of the scheme is however crucial in another respect – the success of the scheme in reaching those eligible for benefit. From the outset, concern was expressed about the take-up problem. In the second reading debate (10 November 1970), Mrs Shirley Williams for the Opposition criticized the 'extension of complex means-testing in which the burden rested . . . on those least able to cope with this extension of bureaucracy'. A *Guardian* editorial (11 November 1970) expressed scepticism: 'we know from experience of other means-tested relief schemes that people are reluctant to identify themselves as "poor"'; and carried articles by Professor Titmuss (29 October 1970) and Professor Townsend (30 October 1970), criticizing the FIS proposals. For the government, Mr Paul Dean, Under-Secretary at the DHSS, accepted that 'take-up of the new benefit was vital to its success' (House of Commons, 10 November 1970). Similarly, Sir Keith Joseph stated that the government would initiate an elaborate campaign to reach as many families as possible, and referred to a target take-up rate of 85 per cent (House of Commons, 10 November 1970; Hansard, vol. 806, col. 227).

The information at the disposal of the government in planning the scheme, and in assessing take-up, was very limited. The estimates quoted in the second reading debate by the Secretary of State were based on the *Family Expenditure Survey*, but the sample for one year contains small numbers of families with children in the relevant income ranges. He later revised the figure from 164,000 to 140,000 (21 December 1971, written answer), although this appeared to be based on a range of 110,000–170,000 (Stacpoole, 1972). There was therefore a considerable margin of uncertainty.

The scheme started operation on 3 August 1971, with claims being received from May 1971. The parameters of the scheme at the start of operation, together with details of the subsequent upratings, are shown in Table 12.1. The key features are that the head of the family must be in full-time work, defined as 30 hours or more a week (reduced to 24 hours a week for single parents from April 1979), that there must be at least one child, defined as under 16 or 16 and over and still undergoing secondary education, and that gross income must be below the prescribed amount. Gross income is defined to include all earnings from full-time or part-time work of both husband and wife, self-employment income, family allowances (but not child benefit), other allowances or benefit, maintenance payments, profit from boarders or sub-tenants, interest on savings, and any other regular income. The supplement is equal to 50 per cent of the difference between the prescribed amount and gross income, subject to a maximum (see Table 12.1) and a minimum payment (20p). FIS recipients have the further 'passport' facility, which automatically entitles them to free prescriptions, dental treatment, welfare foods, etc.

The number of awards built up steadily in the early months, from 47,000 in August 1971 to over 100,000 in June 1972 and September 1973.[3] As may be seen from Figure 12.1, this was a peak, the number falling to 52,000 in June 1975, and varying around 80–90,000 in the latter half of the 1970s. At the outset, two-thirds of the recipients were two-parent families, but by 1974 one-parent families had become a majority.

Seen in terms of the earlier targets, the take-up of FIS in the early years appears to have been disappointing. On the basis of the revised figure of 140,000 given by Sir Keith Joseph in December 1971, the take-up rate was estimated to be approximately 50 per cent. The same figure was given by Mr Paul Dean (House of Commons, 21 March 1973, col. 148) for the take-up rate at the end of January 1973.

The low initial response could be seen in part as a transitory problem. In July 1971, when claims were coming in, but no benefits had yet been paid, the Secretary of State said, 'I had hoped that the take-up at this stage would be bigger. But my experienced advisers warned me that the take-up of a brand-new benefit would tend to be slow' (House of Commons, 13 July 1971, cols 191–4). In this respect it should be noted that subsequent estimates of take-up indicate that the proportion rose from 50 per cent in 1972

Table 12.1 Rates of family income supplement, 1971–80

Date	Prescribed amount: Number of children				For each additional child	Maximum payable: Number of children			For each additional child	Changes in scheme
	1	2	3	4		1	2	3		
3.8.71	18.00	20.00	22.00	24.00	2.00	4.00	4.00	4.00	—	
4.4.72	20.00	22.00	24.00	26.00	2.00	5.00	5.00	5.00	—	
3.4.73	21.00	23.50	26.00	28.50	2.00	5.00	5.00	5.00	—	Annual awards introduced
2.10.73	21.50	24.00	26.50	29.00	2.50	5.00	5.00	6.00	—	Maximum differentiated by family size
23.7.74	25.00	28.00	31.00	34.00	3.00	5.50	5.50	7.00	0.50	
22.7.75	31.50	35.00	38.50	42.00	3.50	7.00	7.50	8.00	0.50	
20.7.76	39.00	43.50	48.00	52.50	4.50	8.50	9.00	9.50	0.50	Child benefit introduced
5.4.77	39.00	42.50	46.00	49.50	3.50	8.50	9.00	9.50	0.50	and disregarded for FIS
19.7.77	41.50	45.00	48.50	52.00	3.50	8.50	9.00	9.50	0.50	
15.11.77	43.80	47.80	51.80	55.80	4.00	9.50	10.50	11.50	1.00	
13.11.78	46.00	50.00	54.00	58.00	4.00	10.50	11.50	12.50	1.00	
12.11.79	56.00	60.50	65.00	69.50	4.50	13.50	14.50	15.50	1.00	
24.11.80	67.00	74.00	81.00	88.00	7.00	17.00	18.50	20.00	1.50	

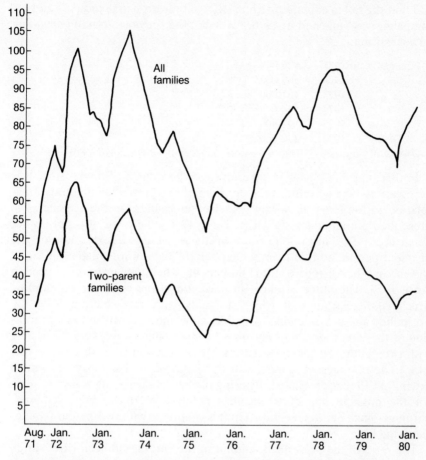

Figure 12.1 Numbers receiving FIS August 1971–January 1980 (in thousands)

Note: The data are taken from Department of Health and Social Security, *Social Security Statistics 1977*, Table 32.10, with more recent figures supplied by the Department.

to 'about two-thirds' in 1973 and 'about three-quarters' in 1974 and 1975 (*Social Security Statistics 1976*, Table 32.15).

The level of response may also be affected by the publicity given to the scheme, and a number of MPs urged that the government take active steps to advertise the new benefit. The initial campaign involved sending leaflets to potential claimants, letters to social workers and local authorities, and press and TV advertising. The expenditure on advertising was of the order of £300,000 for the first two years, but then dropped. It was argued by Mr Kenneth Clarke, MP, that a continuing advertising effort was necessary, and that the fall in expenditure had led to a reduction in take-up. A further campaign was launched in 1976, reversing the previous trend in spending on advertising:

Financial year 1971	£326,000
1972	309,000
1973	161,000
1974	124,000
1975	91,000
1976	172,000

(House of Commons, Written Answer, 6 December 1976, cols 79–80).

In assessing the changing take-up, and the impact of advertising, it is necessary to take account of the uprating of FIS prescribed amounts, their relation to the level of earnings, and other changes in the scheme. The prescribed amounts are shown in Table 12.1, where we also note other departures. The most important of these were the extension of the payment period, so that from 9 October 1972 all awards made ran for 52 weeks, and the 'disregard' for child benefits when they were introduced in April 1977. The latter is taken into account in the indicator we employ, which is the earnings at which a family with two children is at the prescribed amount, allowing for family allowances, expressed as a proportion of the lowest decile of earnings for male manual workers.[4] A family with two children is taken as reasonably representative of those receiving FIS.[5] The earnings of manual workers is taken as that most relevant to potential FIS recipients, and, by using the lowest decile, allowance is made for the possible impact of incomes policy.[6] We have employed *male* earnings, since our main concern in this chapter is with two-parent families receiving FIS.

The ratio of the prescribed amount to the earnings indicator has varied considerably over the period. Between each uprating ('peak') the ratio falls, but in addition the upratings have not maintained any consistent relationship with earnings. The ratio of prescribed amount (less family allowance) to the earnings index at each of these 'peaks', together with the succeeding 'trough', was:

	Peak		Trough following
August 1971	1.021		0.974
April 1972	1.066	A	0.938
April 1973	0.996		0.904
October 1973	0.913		0.802
July 1974	0.912	B	0.744
July 1975	0.908		0.803
July 1976	1.002		0.926
July 1977	0.980	C	0.955
November 1977	1.002		0.884
November 1978	0.904	D	0.756
November 1979	0.900		—

There are broadly four sub-periods. Initially (period A) the peak ratio was around 1.0, and this was maintained until 1973 when the effect of inflation was not restored. The peak was then maintained (in period B) around 0.9, with the depth of the trough depending on the rate of inflation, reaching 0.74 in 1974. In July 1976, the peak was again restored to around 1.0 (period C), but this was not sustained beyond 1978, when it fell once more to 0.9 (period D), and with the rapid increase in earnings the trough was once more around 0.75.

These changes in the parameters of the scheme are likely to have affected the number of recipients. Taking the period as a whole, the qualifying level has fallen relative to the earnings indicator,[7] and other things equal this would have reduced the potential number of beneficiaries. We have moreover to allow for the possible impact of increased unemployment, which may also have reduced the potential number. These factors need to be taken into account in considering the changes over time in the number of beneficiaries.

There are therefore several questions which need to be asked about its success in reaching those entitled.

- Has there been a gradual acceptance of the scheme, with take-up improving over time?
- Has the number of recipients remained small because the scheme has become less generous in relation to the level of earnings?
- What has been the impact of increased unemployment?
- Is there any sign that advertising and publicity campaigns have been successful, and does their effect die away?

In the next sections we see what light can be thrown on these questions from an examination of the monthly time-series of numbers receiving FIS.

3 FACTORS INFLUENCING THE NUMBER OF RECIPIENTS

The first important factor influencing the number of recipients is the relation between the prescribed amount and the level of earnings; and this clearly formed the basis for the government's estimates of the number potentially eligible. Abstracting from differences in family size, if the distribution of earnings, Y, has a density $f(Y)$ and the prescribed amount is Q, then the eligible population is

$$E(Q) = \int_0^Q f(Y)\, dY \tag{1}$$

(see Figure 12.2). Moreover, if we suppose that the proportion claiming is a function of Y and Q, given by $\lambda(Y, Q)$, then the number receiving awards of benefit is given by

$$A(Q) = \int_0^Q \lambda(Y, Q) f(Y)\, dY$$

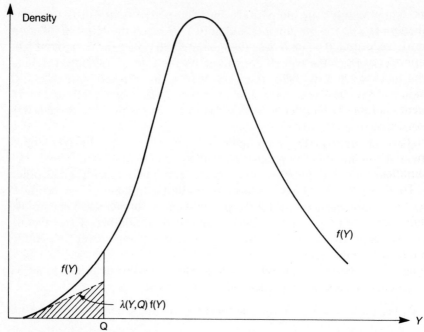

Figure 12.2 Model of FIS receipt

Figure 12.2 illustrates the case where the take-up rate, λ, increases with the amount received $(0.5 \times (Y - Y))$; the number receiving is given by the shaded area.

Over time, the distribution of earnings shifts because of changes in money earnings, even if the relative shape is maintained; and periodically the prescribed amounts are adjusted. A simple way in which to treat this is to assume that the relevant part of the earnings distribution shifts according to a proportionate index, θ_t at time t, and to express the number of awards at time t as a function of the ratio Q_t/θ_t, defined to be q_t.

The number of recipients will also depend on the size of the relevant population, i.e. families in work with one or more children. If the changes over time simply added proportionately to the number at each earnings level, then the adjustment would in principle be straightforward. The implementation is more difficult in that there are no firm figures for the number of families in work with children; and the adjustment would in practice involve a substantial degree of estimation. Moreover, there is no reason to suppose that the numbers at each earnings level would be proportionately affected. With higher levels of unemployment, it is quite possible that those with low-paid jobs have been particularly adversely affected. A study by the Department of Health and Social Security found the incidence and length of unemployment to be clearly above that for the working population as a whole (1975, p. 52). It is possible therefore that the numbers receiving benefit may be a declining function of the level of unemployment.[8] Working in the opposite direction is the possibility that more widespread short-time, and reduced overtime, may increase the numbers of workers with low earnings. We have also to allow for the fact that the relevant variable is total income and that other components apart from the husband's earnings may be affected by the level of unemployment, notably employment opportunities for the wife. In the empirical work we consider, therefore, the effect of unemployment, where this is taken to be the seasonally adjusted rate, on the grounds that we want to measure the secular trend in unemployment rather than month-to-month variations.

To this point we have considered the determinants of the numbers receiving FIS on the basis of current incomes; the timepath is however influenced by the benefit period. Taken together with the differing intervals between up-ratings, this induces a rather complex pattern of lags. Suppose that the benefit period is m, then the number receiving benefit at time t, N_t, depends on the awards, A_t, in the preceding m periods:

$$N_t = \sum_{i=1}^{m} A_{t-i+1} \tag{3}$$

The number of awards may be divided into 'new' awards, G_t, to those who had not previously claimed or whose award had not been renewed on a previous occasion but who had now become eligible (e.g. because of an uprating), and 'renewal' of awards running out. The former depend on the qualifying level in relation to incomes, q_t;[9] the latter will depend on the number expiring and the qualifying level when they become eligible:

$$A_t = G_t(q_t) + g(q_t, q_{t-m})A_{t-m} \tag{4}$$

In terms of the history of the FIS scheme, this lag structure has three main implications. The first is that during the initial months, and during the period when the 12-month benefit period was introduced (April–September 1973), the number of recipients was bound to increase, since there were no expiring benefits.[10] The second is that a concentration of new awards in particular months may lead to an 'echo' effect. For example, a substantial number of the awards were made in August 1971, which then came due for renewal in February 1972, August 1972, February 1973, February 1974. . . . If the qualifying level tends to fall, or there is variation in the earnings of the families, then a smaller proportion will be eligible; and the numbers receiving benefit will move down by an amount which may be large in relation to other movements in the series. In fact the changes for these months were quite noticeable: e.g. the fall from 65,000 to 60,000 in August 1972. Thirdly, the number of new awards, G_t, is likely to be particularly high in the months when the FIS scale has been uprated.

Those who had previously claimed and had been ineligible may become eligible at this juncture.[11]

In what follows we adopt two main approaches. First we take an *ad hoc* specification, which relates the number of recipients to the average value of q_t over the relevant benefit period, which considers also the effect of the current value of q_t, and which incorporates a time trend to allow for the build-up of awards over the initial period (August 1971–January 1972) and when the benefit period was extended (April–September 1973). Secondly, we have calculated the number of awards and estimated equation (4) directly (although assuming g to be a constant). This procedure is more satisfactory in terms of the specification but appears more subject to problems arising from errors of measurement, particularly when working with the rounded data available in published sources.[12]

4 A STATISTICAL ANALYSIS

In this section we consider the extent to which the factors described above can explain the variation in the number of two-parent families receiving FIS over the period August 1971–January 1980.

We begin with the first specification, relating the number of awards to the average value, $\bar{q}_t$, over the relevant benefit period of the qualifying level (taken to be that for a family with two children) divided by the earnings index (taken to be that for the lowest decile of adult male manual workers). We allow for a time trend over the initial six months ($TR1$) and when the benefit period was extended ($TR2$). The functional form of the relationship between N_t and $\bar{q}_t$ is taken to be log-linear.

The results for this equation are shown in the upper part of Table 12.2. The first equation, estimated by ordinary least squares, indicates the presence of serial correlation. The remaining equations are estimated using the Cochrane–Orcutt procedure for first-order auto-regressive errors, and the estimated values of ϱ (the correlation between successive errors) are close to unity. (Alternative assumptions about the auto-regressive structure are the subject of further work.) The coefficients of the independent variables are relatively little affected – see lines 1 and 2.

All the equations indicate a strong relationship between the average qualifying level and the numbers receiving. The estimated elasticity with respect to $\bar{q}_t$ lies between 3.7 and 4.2. This suggests that a fall of 10 per cent in the qualifying level, as occurred between the peaks of period A, C and those of B, D (see page 214), could be expected to lead to a fall in numbers receiving of 32–6 per cent. In line (3) of Table 12.2 we introduce the current value of the qualifying level, and this appears to have a definite, but much smaller, effect. To see the implications, we consider the period 1978–79. The uprating in November 1978 was not sufficient to maintain the

Table 12.2 Regression analysis of numbers receiving FIS

A. Dependent variable: log numbers receiving

	Constant	$\log \hat{q}_t$	TR1	TR2	$\log q_t$	other variables	$\bar{R}^2$	SE	DW (serial correlation coefficient ϱ)
1.	10.21	3.932 (0.166)	0.112 (0.013)	0.023 (0.005)	—	—	0.882	0.084	0.283
2.	10.38	4.216 (0.444)	0.085 (0.032)	0.034 (0.015)	—	—	0.968	0.043	$\varrho = 0.890$
3.	10.22	3.658 (0.464)	0.103 (0.022)	0.046 (0.015)	0.583 (0.092)	—	0.977	0.037	$\varrho = 0.941$
4.	10.10	3.711 (0.478)	0.108 (0.023)	0.046 (0.016)	0.581 (0.092)	0.0016T (0.0024)	0.977	0.037	$\varrho = 0.946$
5.	10.38	4.214 (0.444)	0.085 (0.032)	0.034 (0.015)	—	0.00026U (0.02430)	0.968	0.044	$\varrho = 0.890$

B. Dependent variable: number of awards (thousands)

	Constant	$\log \hat{q}_t$	$\log q_t$	No. expiring awards (thousands)	$\bar{R}^2$	SE	DW
6.	1.97	—	12.867 (2.672)	0.807 (0.035)	0.875	2.07	1.574
7.	0.80	3.551 (3.812)	—	0.833 (0.040)	0.843	2.31	1.368

Figures in brackets are standard errors.

Notes:
1. Equations 1–5 estimated over whole sample period (August 1971–January 1980). Equations 6 and 7 exclude the first six months and the six months following the extension of the benefit period (when there were no expiries).
2. Equations 2–5 are estimated using the Cochrane–Orcutt iterative procedure.
3. The variables are defined as follows:

$\hat{q}_t$ and q_t – see text
TR1 – 1, 2, 3, 4, 5, 6, 6 thereafter
TR2 – 0 for 20 months, 1, 2, 3, 4, 5, 6, 6 thereafter
T – trend 1, 2, 3, ….
U – percentage unemployment rate for males in Great Britain, seasonally adjusted and excluding school-leavers (*source: Department of Employment Gazettes*).

prescribed level in relation to earnings, and the value of q_t was some 10 per cent lower for the subsequent 12 months. From equation 3, we can calculate that the predicted effect of a 10 per cent reduction would be an initial fall of 9 per cent, but that by the end of the 12 months the total reduction would be 36 per cent.[13] In fact, the number of recipients fell from 47,000 in October 1978 to 32,400 in October 1979, a fall of 31 per cent.

The estimated equations examine the effect of possible trends over time. As we have seen, the awards took time to build up, and the initial trend over the first six months ($TR1$) is estimated to be around 10 per cent per month. Similarly, there appears to have been a significant trend during the period when the benefit was extended from 6 to 12 months. The coefficient of $TR2$ indicates a total increase of some 32 per cent (from equation 3) on this account. This appears quite large, and suggests that there was a substantial number who would have lost their entitlement if reassessed after six months and who have benefited from the extension. The Department of Health and Social Security study (1978) found that over half the sample would have been entitled to less FIS if assessed at the time of interview, and that 20 per cent would have had no entitlement.

It is possible that there has been a more long-term upward trend in the numbers receiving FIS, as the scheme became more widely known and accepted. In order to explore this, we included in equation 4 a time trend. This does not however prove to be significant, and does not suggest that there has been a long-term improvement. We also examined in equation 5 the possible relation with the level of unemployment, U, but this is insignificant and provides no indication of a cyclical response.

The effect of advertising and publicity campaigns is more difficult to handle in the econometric equations. The figures given for expenditure (see page 214) indicate a falling-off up to 1975, and then a renewed campaign in 1975–76. If we examine the actual values for the logarithm of numbers receiving, and the fitted values using equation 3 in Table 12.2, then they do not indicate any clear tendency for the numbers to exceed the predicted values in that period. Figure 12.3 shows the plot of actual and fitted values. For example, a national advertising campaign was launched at the time of the July 1976 uprating (House of Commons, 20 May 1976). The residuals (actual−fitted) are:

1976		(percentage effect)
July	−0.0043	−0.43%
August	+0.0567	+5.20%
September	+0.0160	+1.02%
October	−0.0063	−0.63%
November	+0.0419	+4.28%
December	−0.0278	−2.74%

There appears to be no systematic pattern.[14]

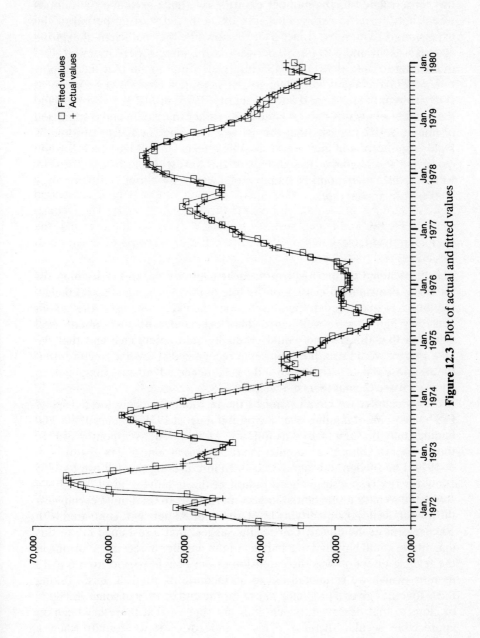

Figure 12.3 Plot of actual and fitted values

Finally, in the lower part of Table 12.2, we show the equations for awards (new awards + renewals). As explained earlier, we would expect this to be related to the number expiring (we have excluded the periods when there were no expiries because of the initial start-up period or the extension to 12 months). Lines 6 and 7 show that the coefficient of expiring awards was around 0.8, i.e. 80 per cent at the margin were renewed. It is interesting to note that the DHSS interview study found that the proportion of FIS recipients intending to put in a new claim was 80 per cent (Department of Health and Social Security, 1975, p. 74). We also expected the number of awards to be related to q_t, rather than to $\bar{q}_t$, and comparison of lines 6 and 7 suggests that this is the case. The coefficient of log q_t is highly significant and indicates a sizeable effect. On this basis, a fall in the qualifying level relative to earnings at the lowest decile from 1.0 to 0.9 would reduce the monthly number of awards by about 1,350, or over 16,000 at an annual rate.

5 CONCLUSIONS

The FIS scheme has been surrounded by controversy, and raises many of the issues central to discussion of the role of means-testing in social policy. Doubts were expressed at the outset about the likely take-up of the benefit and early figures were well below those expected. The government itself expected that the scheme would gradually gain acceptance and that the take-up rate would rise. It has however recognized at several junctures that the response was unsatisfactory and has launched advertising campaigns to try to increase the numbers in receipt of FIS.

In this chapter we have examined the factors influencing the receipt of FIS by two-parent families over the period August 1971–January 1980. The findings may be summarized as follows. After the first six months of FIS, the number of two-parent families in receipt was around 50,000; by the end of 1979 it had fallen to around 35,000. In interpreting this fall, we have to allow for the response to the variation in the qualifying level, which we estimated to have a substantial impact on receipt. In relation to earnings at the lowest decile, the qualifying level was some 83 per cent, compared with 100 per cent at the outset. Our results suggest that a sustained fall of this magnitude could have led to a halving of the number in receipt. Working in the reverse direction was the extension of the benefit period from 6 to 12 months, which we estimated led to an increase of about a third. Taking these together gives a predicted figure for the end of 1979 of some 33,000,[15] or close to that observed, which does not suggest that there has been an appreciable secular increase. This is indeed what we found: when a time-trend was included, it proved to be insignificant. Moreover, there is no evidence that advertising campaigns have led to an appreciable increase.

These conclusions must be qualified, in that it is difficult to draw firm inferences from such data, and that the analysis needs to be refined in several respects. The latter include the specification of the time-path of errors in the econometric equations, and construction of indicators of advertising 'effort', and the introduction of other explanatory variables (although in one obvious case – unemployment – we did not find a significant effect). None the less, we feel that the experience with this scheme provides some useful evidence about the wisdom, or otherwise, of returning on a wider scale to social policies reminiscent of the nineteenth century.

NOTES

1. A further 24,000 unemployed workers would have benefited through an easing of the wage stop.
2. A further £1 million was expected to be spent on supplementary benefit following the easing of the wage stop provisions.
3. The estimated number of recipients was revised in March 1974 following discovery of bias in the sample on which previous estimates were based (Hansard, 22 March 1974, vol. 870, col. 211).
4. The earnings figure is taken from the *New Earnings Survey* for April of each year and interpolated using the index of average earnings, seasonally adjusted, from the *Department of Employment Gazette* for all classified occupations on the basis of the monthly enquiry.
5. In December 1977, the distribution of two-parent families receiving FIS was:

one child	10,000	four children	8,000
two children	15,000	five children	4,000
three children	12,000	six or more	2,000

   (*Social Security Statistics 1977*, Table 32.30)
6. It was suggested by Mr B. George, MP (House of Commons Debate, 20 May 1976) that the numbers eligible for FIS had been reduced by the pay policy directed at the low paid.
7. Put in terms of the index of average earnings

	August 1971	November 1979
FIS prescribed amount (minus family allowance)	100	316.8
Index of average earnings (older series)	100	338.0

   This may appear a quite modest shortfall, but it would require a £4 increase in the FIS to restore the relationship.
8. To the extent that the unemployed are drawn disproportionately from the lowest earnings ranges, this will increase, other things equal, the bottom decile relative to the median. This effect is however of a smaller order of magnitude than the possible impact on the numbers receiving FIS.
9. It may also depend on the qualifying levels in earlier periods, which influence, for example, the number who had not been eligible at the time of earlier claims.
10. Thus benefit awarded on 2 October 1972 expired on 1 April 1973, but benefit awarded on 9 October 1972 expired on 8 October 1973.

11. The timing and duration of awards clearly have implications for the error structure in the equations estimated.
12. The numbers are typically given to the nearest thousand, whereas the number of awards in a month could be of the order of a thousand or smaller.
13. The initial effect is calculated from $(0.9916)^{3.66}$ $(0.9)^{0.58}$; the final effect from $(0.9)^{3.66}$ $(0.9)^{0.58}$. (The first of these takes 1/12 of the 10 per cent reduction.)
14. The fact that advertising campaigns coincided with dates of uprating may lead one to suspect that we are (wrongly) attributing their effect to the q_t variable; there were, however, a number of occasions on which q_t changed discretely without any associated advertising campaign.
15. i.e. $50,000 \times \frac{1}{2} \times \frac{1}{3}$.

PART III

REFORMING SOCIAL SECURITY
AND INCOME TAXATION
IN THE UNITED KINGDOM

INTRODUCTION

The chapters in Part III are concerned with the reform of social security, and its relation to personal income taxation, in the United Kingdom. The details of the different schemes discussed are therefore applicable to one specific country, with its institutional idiosyncrasies and its particular political problems (the shadow of Mrs Thatcher may be seen to fall heavily over several of the chapters). It is hoped however that the chapters will be of interest to readers from other countries, in that the methods of analysis are of more general applicability.

Two of the chapters are indeed more concerned with methods than with the substantive policy issues. Chapter 15 describes the approach adopted by the ESRC Programme on Taxation, Incentives and the Distribution of Income, emphasizing the need to look at the impact of reforms on actual families rather than relying on hypothetical examples, as is common in policy debate. It goes on to examine the use that can be made of information from sample surveys, notably the *Family Expenditure Survey* in Britain. The availability of micro-data from this very high-quality survey via the ESRC Data Archive at the University of Essex has transformed the possibilities for research in this field. This survey has been the basis for the tax-benefit model TAXMOD that we have constructed as part of the work of our ESRC Programme. The model, results from which are used in Chapters 14, 15 and 17, is described in Chapter 18, which tries to bring out both the strengths and weaknesses, and illustrates its application to a reform that doubles child benefit financed by the abolition of the married man's extra income tax allowance (the married couple's allowance from April 1990). This is indeed an area where techniques developed in one country have proved of value elsewhere. A model similar in conception to TAXMOD has been constructed by Bourguignon, Chiappori and Sastre-Descals (1988) in France, and interest in building similar models has been expressed in Eire, Italy, West Germany and other countries.

The concrete policy situations discussed in other chapters are also specific to the date at which they were written, and for this reason I have included a note of this date in brackets [] at the beginning. In several cases policy has moved on, but I have not attempted to revise the chapters to take account of subsequent developments.

This applies to Chapter 13, which is concerned with alternative approaches to state pensions and retirement up to the year 2031. It explores some of the aggregate arithmetic, and the likely evolution of state support for the retired under different policy choices. Given its fifty-year timespan, it does not make use of micro-data as such, but it does emphasize the distributional aspects. Particular attention should be drawn to the role of the state earnings-related pension (SERPS) in reducing dependence on means-tested benefits, a role which was lost from sight when the Conservative government came to review SERPS, and the issue of *inter-generational* redistribution, which lies at the heart of much debate about pensions but is rarely analysed explicitly. The important policy changes which have taken place in this area stemmed from the Fowler Review of 1985 (Department of Health and Social Security, 1985a) and the legislation was embodied in the Social Security Act 1986. The principal change affecting Chapter 13 is the scaling-down of SERPS. Having originally proposed its abolition, and encountered a great deal of opposition, the government made the following major changes with effect from 1988:

1. Benefits to be calculated on the basis of lifetime average earnings, rather than on the best 20 years.
2. Pensions to be calculated as 20 per cent rather than 25 per cent of average earnings.
3. The amount of pension that can be inherited by a spouse to be a half, rather than the full amount.
4. Additional encouragement of occupational and personal pensions, including an extra rebate for those becoming contracted-out from the state scheme.

It was predicted by the government (Department of Health and Social Security, 1985b) that the changes would almost halve the cost of SERPS in the year 2033.

Chapter 14 takes a shorter time-horizon – the ten years from 1983 – and concentrates on the working population. The chapter was prepared for a seminar at Leeds Castle attended by no fewer than six permanent secretaries, and it was very much directed at the policy preoccupations of the government. It did, however, seek to indicate how one could ease the constraints under which social policy was being planned and to stress that there *are* alternatives. The chapter considers a range of policy options, beginning with those described as 'incrementalist', in that they develop the existing structure rather than representing radical reforms. Again, the details have to some extent been overtaken by events, and the reader should bear in mind that, from April 1988:

| income support | replaced | supplementary benefit |
| family credit | replaced | family income supplement |

The chapter then goes on to more sweeping proposals, including a reformed social insurance scheme financed by a graduated schedule of income tax rates, a basic income guarantee, and the extension of income-testing via a negative income tax. These proposals may be seen as making concrete the different approaches identified in Chapter 7.

The basic income scheme is examined in greater depth in Chapters 16 and 17. The first of these investigates the cost of these radical reforms, taking the basic income guarantee scheme devised by Hermione Parker (also discussed in Chapter 14) and the tax credit scheme drawn up by Philip Vince for the Liberal Party (as it then was), also discussed in Chapter 15. These schemes involve the replacement of personal tax allowances (as well as all social security benefits) by a basic income or tax credit, with all income being subject to tax, a single rate being applicable to the bulk of income. A crucial issue is therefore the rate of tax which would be necessary, and Chapter 16 examines the underlying arithmetic. Although it is tempting to reach for the national accounts and do a back-of-the-envelope calculation, this in fact turns out to be misleading, and careful consideration needs to be given to the size of the likely tax base. The conclusion reached is that the necessary tax rate is probably significantly higher than the 43–4 per cent suggested and might exceed 50 per cent. This is one of the major reasons why interest has been shown in a *partial* basic income, which is the subject of Chapter 17. This would mean that basic incomes replaced part but not all of existing benefits and could be introduced with less extensive redistribution.

Schemes such as the basic income guarantee force one to consider the interrelation between social security and other areas of policy. The interdependencies are however all too often forgotten. For example, the cost of increasing the basic pension is usually calculated without taking account of the additional income tax that would be collected. Of particular note is the failure to consider the impact of 'tax expenditures'. As is noted in Chapter 13, there has been a rapid growth in the cost of the age allowance, a figure which is rarely put alongside that for the cost of pensions. Equally, the government expressed great anxiety about the projected expense of SERPS and has sought to encourage private provision, but without any calculation being presented of the cost in terms of income tax revenue forgone.

One of the aims of the chapters here is to bring out the interrelation between the social security and tax systems, an interrelation that has become even more important as a result of the April 1988 changes. Income-tested benefits such as family credit and housing benefit are now calculated on the basis of income net of tax. This means, for example, that an increase in tax allowances is worth less to low-income taxpayers (since part of the gain in take-home pay is clawed back via reduced benefits). Similarly, in assessing the effect of abolishing the married man's allowance and using the revenue to double child benefit, the example taken in Chapter 18, the calculation is now more complicated, since the increased tax bill means that family credit and housing benefit may rise.

Interdependency between benefits and taxes is one of the factors leading to complexity in this field; and there can be little doubt that this is a barrier to effective public debate. This was borne in on me during the period I spent as a specialist adviser to the House of Commons Treasury and Civil Service Committee (see Atkinson, 1984b). It is however important that discussion of policy reform in this area should not be confined to a small circle of academics and other specialists. It is for this reason that a primary aim of the ESRC Programme has been increasing the *accessibility* of the tools necessary to explore alternatives. The TAXMOD model in particular has been designed to be used by those without detailed knowledge of the present system and to help them devise possible reforms. I have included Chapter 18, describing the model and illustrating its use, not just to explain the basis for some of the calculations in earlier chapters but also as an invitation to readers to try their hand. Do-it-yourself tax and social security reform is indeed possible. If the chapters in Part III have made more accessible the tools necessary for policy analysis, then they will have served their function.

13 · STATE PENSIONS, TAXATION AND RETIREMENT INCOME, 1981–2031

1 INTRODUCTION

The aim of this chapter is to explore some of the policy alternatives open to the government with regard to pensions, retirement and taxation over the next 50 years (as seen from 1981). There are clearly a number of critical issues which have to be resolved in the immediate future but which have implications extending to the year 2031 and beyond. The earnings-related pension scheme, in operation since 1978, will lead to a substantial increase in state pensions, with the build-up of expenditure continuing well into the next century. Some people have argued for modifications to the scheme, which could be made before the transition period is completed in 1998. At the same time, the new scheme is creating pressure for improvements in the basic pension for those already retired or retiring before 1998 and there has been a longstanding campaign to reduce the number of pensioners dependent on supplementary benefit by an increase in the national insurance pension. Other policy reforms, such as changing the retirement age, or introducing a tax credit for pensioners, have major implications for the elderly.

In exploring policy alternatives in this area, we are not seeking to reach definitive conclusions or to recommend particular measures. Our aim is to provide a framework within which policy can be discussed, and which allows the key elements in the analysis to be identified. It should be made clear at the outset that this framework is highly simplified, and that we have not attempted to construct an elaborate simulation model covering the next 50 years. Not only does the uncertainty surrounding the movement of central variables over this period mean that such an exercise would be of limited value, but also we feel that it is helpful to the reader to have a

With R. M. Altmann. This research forms part of the SSRC programme on Taxation, Incentives and the Distribution of Income, directed by A. B. Atkinson, M. A. King and N. H. Stern. We are grateful to John Creedy, Richard Hemming, Colin Stewart and David Ulph for their helpful comments on the first draft. Reprinted from M. Fogarty (ed.), *Retirement Policy: the Next Fifty Years*, Heinemann, London, 1982. [Written in 1981.]

model sufficiently simple to allow the implications of alternative assumptions to be relatively transparent.

The analysis of different policies concentrates on three main aspects. These do not cover all matters which occupy policy-makers, but may be representative of the concerns typically expressed. The first is the impact on public expenditure. This reflects the current preoccupation of the government, but it should be noted that we have taken a relatively broad definition, including 'tax expenditures', which may depart from some of the indicators employed in popular debate. The second is the traditional concern with the effectiveness of income support in ensuring a minimum standard of income. How do different policies contribute to the prevention of poverty, measured according to a specified definition, among the elderly? The third indicator is one less commonly made explicit, but often lying behind public discussion. This is the extent of redistribution between generations. Are we being 'fair' to the generation retiring today relative to those retiring in the next century?

In the second section we describe the main areas of policy considered in the chapter, giving a brief account of the provisions as in 1981, and outlining six variations in policy. In the third section, we set out the framework for the analysis, indicating the assumptions made with regard to demographic structure, retirement behaviour, the calculation of earnings-related pensions, take-up of supplementary benefit, and so on. This framework is then employed in the next three sections to investigate the three aspects identified in the previous paragraph. The main conclusions are brought together in the last section.

2 POLICY ALTERNATIVES

Our focus in the chapter is on four main areas of government policy:

1. state pensions (the basic national insurance pension and the earnings-related 'additional pension'),
2. supplementary benefit,
3. retirement age and state benefits for those retiring before the minimum retirement age,
4. income tax treatment of the elderly and tax credits.

(To avoid any possible misunderstanding, the term 'state pension' does not cover the occupational pensions of employees in the public sector; it refers solely to national insurance.)

From this list, it is obvious that there is a number of serious omissions. We do not discuss such issues as policy towards occupational pensions, or indexed bonds and the tax treatment of savings, or job opportunities for the elderly; nor do we consider the important question of state support to the elderly in the form of expenditure on health, social services, and so on.

National insurance pension

In this section, we describe the policy parameters considered. We begin with the national insurance pension. Briefly, there are two main elements. The first is the basic pension, which is approximately 20 per cent of gross average earnings (for adult men) for a single person, with an addition of approximately 10 per cent for a wife on her husband's insurance record. (Throughout the chapter we use rounded figures of this kind, since they ease the exposition and nothing essential is lost). We shall assume that, unless a specific policy decision is taken to the contrary, the basic pension will maintain this relationship with gross average earnings. Although the Social Security Act 1980 abolished the formal link with earnings, there are good reasons to suppose that governments will in the long run keep the basic pension more or less in line with earnings (as was the case before any formal guarantee).

The second element is the additional component payable under the new state earnings-related pension scheme, which requires a rather fuller description. If we begin with a single person, not contracted out of the scheme, who was never married, then he or she receives an additional pension at retirement which depends on (indexed) earnings over the best 20 years of working life, which we denote by $\varepsilon\bar{E}$, where $\bar{E}$ is the current level of average earnings. The pension is then equal to a fraction $\theta_1\theta_2$ of the earnings $\varepsilon\bar{E}$ which lie in the band between the lower limit (broadly equal to the basic pension) and the upper ceiling (which we take to be $1.4\bar{E}$). The parameters θ are:

θ_1 the pension fraction, at present set at 25 per cent;

θ_2 the transitional element, whereby a person retiring x years after the start of the scheme receives $x/20$ of the pension, up to $x = 20$, after which $\theta_2 = 1$.

After retirement, the additional pension is adjusted in line with prices. Where the person is contracted out, the employer takes over responsibility for one element of the pension, known as the guaranteed minimum pension.

From the formula, it may be seen that a person with average earnings ($\bar{E} = 1$) retiring when the transition period is complete ($\theta_2 = 1$) would receive, with a pension fraction (θ_1) of 25 per cent and a lower limit of $0.2\bar{E}$, an additional pension equal to 20 per cent of average earnings. The total, including the basic pension, would be 40 per cent of average earnings. A 'low-paid' worker, with 60 per cent of average earnings, would receive at retirement a pension of 30 per cent of current average earnings (or 50 per cent of his own average).

For a married couple where the wife has never worked, the same formula applies for the additional pension, so that the person with average earnings would receive 50 per cent of current average earnings at retirement. If the husband dies and the widow is aged 50 and over, she is entitled to the single basic pension plus the additional component calculated as above. If the wife also has pension entitlement in her own right, the couple receive two single basic pensions plus two earnings-related elements (provided contribution records are complete). There are provisions for the transfer of the additional pension to the spouse on death, subject to an overall maximum.

It is clear that there is a wide variety of parameters in the national insurance pension scheme which could be changed. We concentrate on two main variations on the state pension. The first reflects the widespread concern that the scheme is offering benefits for the future but doing little for current pensioners or those retiring in the early years of the new state scheme (Fogarty, 1980, pp. 26–7). We therefore consider:

Variation 1   Basic pension raised to 25 per cent of current gross average earnings for a single person (37½ per cent for a married couple) for all those retiring up to 1988, with a tapered withdrawal of the 5 per cent increase up to 1998. (It is assumed that the lower limit in the additional pension formula would be unchanged.)

The second, rather different, concern is that the level of benefits offered to future pensioners is too high, and we consider:

Variation 2   Pension fraction (θ_1) reduced to 12½ per cent, with the transition provisions modified so that each year of service 1978/79–1987/88 is treated as two years.

This means that pensions awarded up to 1988 are identical to the present formula, but that the transition process will cease at this point, with the ultimate level of pensions being half that under the present scheme.

Supplementary benefit and other benefits

At present a substantial proportion of pensioners, about a quarter, receive supplementary benefit (SB) in addition to the state pension. SB is a means-tested benefit, payable where a pensioner's resources (treating a couple as a unit) fall short of their 'requirements' calculated according to a fixed scale plus an allowance for housing and certain other items. The resources include the state pension (in full) and all other major sources of income (subject to certain, limited, disregards). There is also a limit on the amount of capital. There were major changes in SB in November 1980 (Allbeson, 1980).

The SB scale rate for pensioners (the long-term rate) is taken to be aligned with the basic state pension at 20 per cent of current average earnings (30 per cent for married couples). The number of pensioners eligible for SB depends therefore on the relation between other income in excess of the basic pension, and requirements in excess of the scale rate.

The effect of the new additional pension, and of the increase in the basic pension referred to under Variation 1, would be to reduce the number dependent on SB. The magnitude of 'other requirements' depends particularly on housing costs, and on the rent/rate rebate schemes. The latter are not treated explicitly here, and it should be noted that this is an area where a major change in policy is under consideration.

The SB scheme is designed to provide a safety net, but evidence over the past 20 years has shown that the take-up rate is considerably less than 100 per cent, since a substantial proportion of those apparently entitled to SB do not in fact claim (see Chapter 11). This phenomenon is examined further by Altmann (1981a and b), where attention is drawn to the fact that the treatment of housing rebates in these calculations causes the official estimates of SB take-up to be *over*stated.

The level of take-up is an aspect of the social security scheme which may be influenced by government policy, although the experience of earlier changes, such as the introduction of SB in place of national assistance in 1966, does not suggest that progress can easily be made (Atkinson, 1969). In order to bring out the role played by non-take-up, we consider the (possibly infeasible) case:

Variation 3   Take-up of SB raised to 100 per cent.

Retirement age and benefits below retirement age

Thus far, we have considered the position of people over the minimum retirement age (65 for men, 60 for women). Clearly one policy option which needs to be considered is that of a change in the retirement age. The various possibilities have been widely discussed (for example, *Department of Employment Gazette*, March 1978, and Fogarty, 1980, pp. 18–33); here we take one of these to illustrate the implications of earlier retirement for men, permitting equalisation of the retirement age:

Variation 4   Minimum retirement age 60 for men and women from 1984, with full entitlement to basic and additional state pension.

The implications of a change in the retirement age depend very much on the position of those who currently retire before 65. The circumstances of the 'early retired' have in fact been little studied. From the evidence which is available (Altmann, 1981a and b; Parker, 1980), it appears that about half of such men retired with an occupational pension but that as many as three-quarters receive either invalidity benefit or another form of state benefit associated with ill-health. This suggests that we should consider the possibility of permitting retirement for men at the age of 60 with the basic pension. The additional pension would remain payable at age 65, thus decreasing the cost of reducing the retirement age (equalizing it for men and women). This is:

Variation 5 National insurance benefit paid to all men aged 60–4 who have retired, at same level as basic retirement pension (20 per cent of current average earnings, 30 per cent for a couple).

It would mean a small increase in benefit for those currently receiving an invalidity benefit (in November 1981 equal to 96 per cent of the basic pension) and a larger increase for those receiving sickness benefit (76 per cent of the basic pension). Account has of course to be taken of the possibility that, with both Variations 4 and 5, the numbers retiring at 60–4 would rise, and this is discussed in the next section.

Income tax age allowance and tax credits for the elderly

The age allowance applies to tax units where either the taxpayer or his wife is 65 years of age or over. It provides a higher personal allowance for all those with incomes below a ceiling (£5,900 in 1981–2), with a tapered withdrawal of the benefit above that point. For 1981–2, the allowances are:

	Single	Married
Age allowance	£1,820	£2,895
	(25)	(40)
Ordinary personal allowance	£1,375	£2,145
	(19)	(29)

The figures in brackets indicate approximate percentages of average earnings. It should be noted that the age allowance does not apply to single women aged 60–4.

The rationale for the age allowance in its present form is hard to discern. A number of proposals have been made for alternative tax treatments. Here we restrict ourselves to consideration of the introduction of a tax credit scheme (Fogarty, 1980, p. 27):

Variation 6 Introduce tax credit of 10 per cent of current average earnings for single persons (15 per cent for couples), payable where the taxpayer or his wife is aged 60 or over, with all social security benefits, apart from SB, subject to tax.

We have described above the present provisions, and six variations in policy. In later sections we examine their likely implications over the next half-century, using the framework set out in the next section.

3   A FRAMEWORK FOR ANALYSIS

Demographic structure

The first element in the analysis is the demographic structure over the period in question. For ease of presentation, we confine attention to four dates (1986, 2001, 2016 and 2031), which span the next 50 (at the time of writing) years and correspond to certain phases in the evolution of pension provision. For example, in 2001 the transition period for the additional pension will be complete (although the scheme will not, of course, be fully mature). Population projections have been published by the Government Actuary covering 1986, 2001 and 2016, so that for three of the four dates considered here we have official demographic estimates. For the year 2031, we use the projections by Ermisch (1981). In each case we consider the age groups 60–4, 65–9, 70–4, 75–9 and 80+, and treat separately married couples (by age of man), single men and single women. The numbers (Table 13.1) are deliberately rounded since greater accuracy does not seem

Table 13.1 Demographic structure (Great Britain), 1981–2031

	1981	1986	2001	2016	2031[a]
			Millions		
Married couples (age of man)					
60–64	1.1	1.2	1.0	1.2	1.3
65–69	1.0	0.9	0.9	1.1	1.2
70–74	0.7	0.7	0.7	0.8	0.9
75–79	0.4	0.4	0.5	0.4	0.5
80+	0.2	0.2	0.3	0.3	0.4
Total	3.4	3.4	3.4	3.8	4.3
Single men					
60–64	0.2	0.2	0.2	0.3	0.3
65–69	0.2	0.2	0.2	0.3	0.3
70–74	0.2	0.2	0.2	0.2	0.3
75–79	0.2	0.2	0.2	0.2	0.2
80+	0.2	0.2	0.3	0.3	0.3
Total	1.0	1.0	1.1	1.3	1.4
Single women					
60–64	0.5	0.5	0.4	0.5	0.5
65–69	0.7	0.6	0.5	0.7	0.7
70–74	0.8	0.8	0.7	0.7	0.8
75–79	0.8	0.8	0.7	0.6	0.8
80+	1.0	1.1	1.2	1.2	1.3
Total	3.8	3.8	3.5	3.7	4.1
Total number of people[b]	11.6	11.6	11.4	12.6	14.1

Source:
1981–2016 from Office of Population Censuses and Surveys, *Population Projections 1977–2017*, London, HMSO, 1979, pp. 68–9.

[a]   2031 based on estimates kindly supplied by John Ermisch which we have split according to marital status, applying the proportions of 2016.
[b]   Married couples count as two.

warranted in view of the uncertainties surrounding the calculations. These figures show the familiar U-shaped projections, with the year 2001 corresponding approximately to the turning point. It may be noted that we do not attempt to estimate the size of the working population, which clearly depends crucially on trends in fertility (Ermisch, 1981; and Hemming and Kay, 1981).

Retirement

The second element concerns retirement. This can be defined in a variety of ways. We can, for example, take the national insurance pension retirement condition, which is the relevant variable when predicting expenditure on benefits. This definition may not however be applicable to those below minimum retirement age, since it permits a level of earnings which would be precluded by the receipt of short-term benefits. Moreover, we have to tailor the definition to the available data, and surprisingly little is known about the labour force participation of the elderly. Information derived from the *Family Expenditure Survey* for the years 1970–77 (Altmann, 1981b) shows for men a decline in labour force participation by age, with a sharp drop at age 65. Over time, the findings for men aged 65–9 indicate an annual downward trend of some 0.6–1.0 percentage points, no significant impact of the level of the pension relative to average earnings, and (in most cases) a negative effect of increased unemployment. For men aged 60–4, the results were more mixed, with a significant positive trend in the case of some ages and not for others. Towards the end of the period, however, there is evidence of a decline for this group, and account has to be taken of the introduction of the Job Release Scheme in January 1977. The figures from the *General Household Survey* for the age group 60–4 show a decline from 82 per cent economically active in 1974 to 76 per cent in 1978 (*Employment Gazette*, April 1980, p. 367).

These findings suggest that the participation rate at age 65 and over is likely to continue to fall, and that by 1986 only a small proportion (of men, at least) will be at work. For simplicity, we assume that all those over the minimum retirement age are in fact retired. It may be noted that the Government Actuary (1975) forecasts that the proportion at work in the five years after the minimum retirement age will fall ultimately to 3 per cent for men, 2 per cent for women. The treatment of those aged 60–4 is more problematic, and is likely to depend on policy changes. We assume that 20 per cent of men aged 60–4 are retired, but that this rises to 50 per cent with Variations 4 and 5. It is interesting to note in this context the differences in the proportion of men aged 60–4 who are retired in different countries. The 1977 Labour Force Survey shows that the average rate for the European Community is 43 per cent, whereas it is only 20 per cent in the UK (Office of Population Censuses and Surveys, 1980 Table 6.2).

Contribution records

The third element concerns the assumptions made about past contribution records, where there is very little in the way of data to guide us. As we have seen, the entitlement of a married couple depends on the wife's contribution record as well as that of her husband. The entitlement of a single woman depends on her own contribution record and, if she was previously married, on that of her husband. We cannot attempt to deal with this complex pattern in its entirety, and we ignore, for example, situations where there may be overlapping of basic benefit or where there is divorce/separation.

In making projections, we assume that the proportion of single women previously married is 80 per cent (70 per cent for single men). Clearly the percentage of married, or previously married, women with entitlement in their own right is likely to increase, as a result of the withdrawal of the married women's option to pay reduced contributions. It is difficult to form any accurate estimate of the likely impact in 50 years' time, so the reader should regard with due caution our assumption that the proportion will be 22 per cent in 1986 (in line with present figures), rising to 30 per cent in 2001, 40 per cent in 2016 and 50 per cent in 2031. It may well be thought that these figures are too low, and extrapolation of the trends of the past 30 years suggests that the proportion could be substantially greater by 2031. In our view, such extrapolation appears open to question in the light of recent developments in the labour market (including, for example, the cutting back of public-sector employment), but it is open to the reader to replace the assumption by an alternative (the sensitivity of the calculations is discussed later).

Earnings formula for additional pension

The additional pensions formula introduces several complexities into the calculation of entitlements, notably the use of averaged earnings, the effect of the ceiling, and the provision for choosing the best 20 years. The implications are discussed in some detail by Creedy (1980), whose results have influenced the assumptions made here. In calculating the average additional pension at retirement, we make assumptions about the value of ε (correcting for the 20-year averaged earnings relative to average earnings at retirement), about the proportion affected by the contribution ceiling, about the earnings of women relative to men, and about the rate of real earnings growth. In each case, the assumption represents a compromise between conflicting considerations, and for this reason alone the resulting calculations can only be regarded as illustrative. We take, for example, a real earnings growth rate of 5 per cent per five years, which may be considered optimistic by some and pessimistic by others. The value of ε, assumed to be 1.0 for those retiring up to 1998, and 1.2 thereafter, is probably too high in the early stages (when those retiring cannot benefit from the 20 'best' years provision) but some writers (for example, Creedy (1980) suggest that it should be higher when the scheme reaches maturity. The assumption that the average earnings of women are $0.7\bar{E}$ may make insufficient allowance for part-time working; on the other hand, it must be noted that this relates to women with entitlement in their own right (assumed to be 50 per cent or less of married women).

Contracting out

The effect of contracting out is to reduce government expenditure by the amount of the guaranteed minimum pension, which is paid by the employer (and, of course, to reduce receipts of national insurance contributions). The calculation depends on a number of elements, and here we make the approximate assumption that it is equal at retirement to the average additional pension. This again represents a compromise between the factors which led the guaranteed minimum pension to be less than the additional pension (such as the absence of a 'best' 20 years rule) and the tendency for those contracted out to have higher earnings. After retirement, no indexation is provided, and we assume that the guaranteed minimum pension falls relative to current average earnings by a factor of two-thirds per five years. The proportion contracted out is assumed, on the basis of the Government Actuary (1981), to be 45 per cent. It may be noted that the absolute number, some 10 million, is larger than the upper end of the range (8 million) taken in the calculations of the Government Actuary.

Benefits for early retired

In the light of the information described earlier, it is assumed that 75 per cent of men aged 60–4 who are retired receive a state national insurance benefit at present, and this is taken to be at the rate of $0.18\bar{E}$ for a single man (see earlier calculations for invalidity benefit and sickness benefit), and $0.27\bar{E}$ for a married man.

Income taxation

The level of the standard tax allowances in recent years means that a person with a basic national insurance pension is more or less on the margin of being taxed. If it were not for the effect of the age allowance, therefore, all other income, including the additional pension, would be subject to income tax. (We assume that in the future the threshold, and the age allowance, will be increased proportionately with average earnings – an assumption which is a triumph of hope over experience.) The first element in the calculation of the effects of income tax is, therefore, the tax forgone as a result of the age allowance. In projecting the cost, we have made the (approximate) assumption that pensioners have on average other taxable income of $0.015\bar{E}$ (single) or $0.03\bar{E}$ (couple), where this remains a constant proportion of average earnings. The income tax paid will change as a result of the policy options which affect basic or additional pensions. In the case of those aged 60–4, who do not benefit from the age allowance, we assume that the entire increase is taxable; in the case of those aged 65+ the tax is based on the average amount, allowing for other taxable income as described above.

Supplementary benefit

Entitlement to SB depends on other sources of income and on requirements. We have adopted an approximate procedure to calculate the effect of changes in the amounts of pension. From the evidence on the amounts of SB in payment (for example *Social Security Statistics*, 1977, Table 34, 38), and on amounts to which non-claimants are entitled on the basis of the *Family Expenditure Survey*, we make assumptions about the effect of an increase in pensions, or other income, on entitlement to SB. We distinguish here between SB recipients and those who are entitled but do not claim. The assumptions imply a mean amount received of $0.087\bar{E}$, and a mean SB unclaimed of $0.04\bar{E}$. The average take-up rate is taken to be 66 per cent. This is below the official estimates. However, the latter exclude from non-claimants those who would be better off receiving a housing rebate. For our purposes we are concerned with all those not claiming their entitlement, and adjustment to the official estimates for this factor indicates a lower take-up figure, as do direct calculations from the *Family Expenditure Survey*, (Altmann, 1981a).

In calculating the effect of changes in policy on the amount of SB, and the numbers below this level, we make several simplifying assumptions. First, the proportion of pensioners who have incomes apart from the additional pension (and from any variations in policy), which are below the SB level, is assumed to be constant at 22½ per cent for married couples and 45 per cent for single pensioners. There are reasons, such as the increase in occupational pensions, to expect the proportion to fall, but this is in part taken into account in the guaranteed minimum pension element of the additional pension. Moreover, it has to be borne in mind that other elements of income, such as that from savings, may be eroded, and 'requirements' such as those for heating may increase in relative terms. Second, we make two alternative assumptions about the additional pension received by those otherwise below the SB level: 'low AP' based on 60 per cent of average earnings (broadly the bottom decile of the annual distribution), and 'average AP' based on average earnings. These two assumptions seem likely to bracket the true range. Finally, we have not allowed for any effect on average SB payments of the 1980 legislation.

4   THE COST OF STATE INCOME SUPPORT FOR THE RETIRED

Armed with the assumptions described in the previous section, we can explore the implications of different policy variations for the cost of state income support. As we have emphasized, the assumptions are strong ones, and the calculations are undoubtedly sensitive to changes in them. Our aim is to produce a broad guide to the likely evolution of expenditure over the next 50 years, rather than detailed estimates, and for a number of items – for instance, the gross expenditure on state pensions – there are bodies (like the Government Actuary's Department) much better equipped to make such estimates. Our intention is to illustrate the interaction of different elements within the framework outlined above, and we consider in turn the basic pension, the additional pension, other benefits, income tax and supplementary benefit.

Cost of basic pension

The results of the calculation of the cost of the basic pension are shown in the first part of Table 13.2. They are expressed in terms of average earnings (for adult full time men) at a January 1982 level (taken to be approximately £148.00 a week). Although this item depends less on assumptions than other elements, there are a number of simplifications. For example, the assumption that all those over minimum retirement age are retired leads to an over-statement of expenditure. On the other hand, no allowance has been made for any additions for children, for deferred retirement, for those aged over 80, and so on.

The figures indicate that a substantial increase in expenditure on the basic pension is to be expected in the next century. In part, this arises because of our assumptions about the proportion of married women with entitlement on their own insurance. However, even if this were assumed unchanged at 22 per cent, rather than rising to 50 per cent, the estimate for 2031 would still be £15,400 million. The bulk of the rise in the predicted expenditure is associated with the rise of more than 20 per cent in the number above retirement age.

A number of the policy variations involve the basic pension, and their implications in the years 1986–2031 are given in lower sections of Table 13.2, where in each case we show the *change* in cost. Variation 1 involves an immediate increase in the pension and the extra expenditure would be substantial in 1986. The cost would fall steadily, until it would be around

Table 13.2 Items of cost of state support for retired in Great Britain (January 1982 earnings levels)

	1981	1986	2001	2016	2031
Standard model		£ million			
Basic pension	12,800	12,500	12,900	14,000	16,100
Additional pension (AP)	—	500	4,000	8,600	10,400
Other national insurance benefits	400	400	350	450	450
Income tax:					
cost of age allowance	300	400	900	1,000	1,250
tax paid on AP	—	−150	−1,200	−2,600	−3,100
Supplementary benefit:					
'low AP'	1,200	1,100	650	400	400
'average AP'		1,050	450	100	100
Variation 1					
Basic pension	—	+3,100	+2,050	+200	0
Income tax:					
cost of age allowance	—	+550	+100	0	0
tax on national insurance benefits	—	−950	−600	−50	0
Supplementary benefit:					
'low AP'	—	−550	−300	−50	0
'average AP'	—	−550	−300	0	
Variation 2					
Additional pension	—	0	−1,300	−4,100	−5,200
Income tax:					
cost of age allowance	—	0	−150	0	0
tax on national insurance benefit	—	0	+400	+1,200	+1,600
Supplementary benefit:					
'low AP'	—	0	+100	+350	+400
'average AP'	—	0	+50	+250	+300
Variation 3					
Supplementary benefit:					
'low AP'	—	+250	+100	0	0
'average AP'	—	+200	+50	0	0
Variation 4					
Basic pension	—	+1,500	+1,300	+1,600	+1,700
Additional pension	—	+200	+400	+1,000	+1,150
Other national insurance benefits	—	−400	−350	−450	−450
Income tax on national insurance benefits	—	−200	−400	−600	−600
Supplementary benefit:					
'low AP'	—	+50	+50	−50	0
'average AP'	—	+50	0	−50	−50
Variation 5					
Basic pension	—	+1,500	+1,300	+1,600	+1,700
Other national insurance benefits	—	−400	−350	−450	−450
Income tax on national insurance benefits	—	−100	−100	−100	−100
Supplementary benefit	—	0	0	0	0
Variation 6					
Income tax	—	+3,350	+2,600	+2,800	+3,000
Supplementary benefit:					
'low AP'	—	−450	−250	−100	−150
'average AP'	—	−450	−150	0	0

zero in 2016. There would be a consequential rise in income tax receipts, although this is substantially reduced by the operation of the age allowance. Variations 4 and 5 have identical implications for the basic pension. The estimated gross cost of extending the basic pension to men aged 60–4 is considerable – more than a tenth of the total cost. This figure is clearly highly sensitive to the assumption made about the proportion retired (taken to be 50 per cent), and the reader can see the effect of alternative assumptions by varying the estimate proportionately. Thus a retirement rate of 90 per cent, closer to that found for those aged 65–9, would imply a cost of £2,800 million in 1986.

Cost of additional pension

It should be stressed at the outset that the estimates of the cost of the additional pension depend critically on a number of assumptions, and that the figures should be regarded with considerable caution. There are a number of reasons why our estimates may overstate the cost, including the possible overestimate of the average earnings of women, and the fact that ε may initially be below 1.0. At the same time, there are arguments in the opposite direction, such as the possibility that a higher proportion of married women are entitled in their own right, and that the 'best 20 years' provision causes ε to exceed 1.2 towards the end of the period. Indeed, our figures are not greatly out of line with the 'steady state' results of Hemming and Kay (1981).

The estimates in Table 13.2 indicate a relatively slow build-up, with the total reaching a third of that for the basic pension in the year 2001. At this point the 20-year transition has just ended, but the cost continues to rise as a larger proportion of pensioners retire with a full 20 years in the new scheme, as the 'best 20 years' provision has increased effect, and as more married women are entitled to pensions on their own insurance. Thus, by 2016, additional pensions amount to about two-thirds of the total for basic pensions.

With Variation 2, the pension scheme reaches the end of its transition period 10 years earlier but the benefits are scaled down by half at maturity. Thus, in 2031, when we assume that no one is affected by the transition provisions, the cost is simply halved. (This illustrates the kind of simplification made in our calculations. A woman retiring at 60 in 1997 would not receive a full pension and could well still be alive in 2031.) Variation 4 involves the payment of pensions to men aged 50–64, which adds considerably to the cost, and after 1986 has consequential effects for older age groups, who will now have been retired longer. The expenditure will be less by virtue of the assumption that additional pensions are indexed in line with prices, not earnings, but will be greater because of the indexation of guaranteed minimum pensions. The latter effect dominates and the total cost is therefore larger than the amount paid to men aged 60–4. Thus in 2031 the estimated cost of the pensions to single men and married couples aged 60–4 is some £950 million, the consequential effects being about £200 million. From the same calculation, it can be seen that, if all 60–4 year-olds retired at the minimum age, the cost would rise by £950 million.

Cost of other national insurance benefits

This item refers to the payment of other national insurance benefits to men aged 60–4 who have retired. In relative terms, the cost is small. Variations 4 and 5 assume that these other benefits would be replaced by retirement pensions.

Income tax

The 'income tax' calculation in the first part of Table 13.2 is broken down into two elements. The first is the cost of the age allowance: that is, the extra tax that would have been paid if those aged 65 and over had received the standard personal allowance. The second element is the tax payable on the additional pension (the basic pension is assumed equal to the standard personal allowance), where this is shown as a negative item, reducing the 'cost' of income support. As the additional pension builds up, the tax liability (broadly 30 per cent) increases proportionately but in part this is offset by the age allowance, so that the cost of this provision is increased. In other words, the gross expenditure on additional pensions in 1986 of £500 million attracts a tax liability of some £150 million but for a substantial number of pensioners part or all of their additional pension is covered by unused age allowance, so that the cost of the latter rises (by £100 million).

The rising cost of the age allowance should be emphasized, since this 'tax expenditure' is often overlooked. According to the government Expenditure White Paper 1981–2 to 1983–4 (Cmnd 8175) the estimated cost is £370 million for 1980/81. (This indicates that our estimates may be on the low side.) Recent years have seen rapid growth in expenditure on this 'programme': a rise of 28 per cent between 1979/80 and 1980/81, compared with an increase of less than 20 per cent in cash outlay on basic pensions. Our projections suggest that this will continue, so that the cost will be some four times larger in the year 2031.

The different variations we have suggested in the national insurance benefits will have implications for the tax liability and for the cost of the age allowance. An increase in the basic pension will attract tax, thus reducing the net cost, but it also means that more people benefit from the age allowance. Variation 6 is explicitly concerned with the tax system, involving the introduction of a tax credit in place of the present personal allowances, and age allowance, with a net cost to the Inland Revenue of some £3,000 million.

Cost of supplementary benefits

With the development of the additional pension, the expenditure on SB is likely to fall, so that by the year 2001 the amount is about half its present level. The precise impact of the scheme does, however, depend on the earnings record of those who would otherwise fall below the SB level; this is illustrated by the two assumptions shown in Table 13.2. In 2031, for example, if the additional pension is calculated on the basis of average earnings then virtually all over minimum retirement age are predicted to be above the SB level. On the other hand, if it is more realistic to use a base of 60 per cent of average earnings, then a significant minority (45 per cent) are predicted to be still in receipt of SB.

All the Variations have consequential implications for SB, and these are shown in the lower sections of Table 13.2. Variation 3, however, is explicitly directed at SB, and shows the effect of 100 per cent take-up. The predicted effect on total expenditure in 1981 would be an increase, given the assumptions described earlier, of

$$\underset{\substack{\text{non-}\\\text{claimants}}}{\frac{34}{64}} \times \underset{\substack{\text{average amount unclaimed}\\\text{(relative to average payment)}}}{0.46} = 23.7\%$$

This would imply a rise of some £300 million. For other years, we allow for the effect of the higher additional pensions, and the cost is less.

Cost implications: summary

Our calculations are not in any sense intended to provide an absolute measure of the cost of income support for the retired, and indeed the proper definition of such a concept is debatable. We have for this reason not totalled the different items in Table 13.2.

At the same time, the Variations are intended to measure the main financial consequences for the state of changes in policy. Interpreted in this way, we can summarize the net cost, or saving, of different policies (where the range corresponds to alternative assumptions about the effect on SB):

	1986	2001	2016	2031
		£ million		
Variation 1	2,150	1,250	100 to 150	0
2	0	−950 to 1,000	−2,550 to 2,650	−3,200 to 3,300
3	200 to 250	50 to 100	0	0
4	1,150	950 to 1,000	1,500	1,750 to 1,800
5	1,000	850	1,050	1,150
6	2,900	2,350 to 2,450	2,700 to 2,800	2,850 to 3,000

Of the policy alternatives, only one would reduce the total outlays – Variation 2. In this case, the gross expenditure on additional pensions is halved, but the offsetting loss of tax and extra expenditure on SB reduce the net saving by about £2 billion. This illustrates the need to consider the consequential effects, via income tax and SB, when discussing the cost of the new state pension scheme. The gross cost, in terms of contribution rates required, is only part of the picture. Variation 1 involves a substantial expenditure over the next 25 years, with the net impact being again some two-thirds of the gross increase in pensions; Variation 3 affects the same time period, on a much smaller scale. Variations 4, 5 and 6 all involve continuing substantial net costs in the long term, of the rough order of £2 billion, £1 billion and £3 billion, respectively.

5   A GUARANTEED MINIMUM INCOME?

The White Paper *Better Pensions* (Cmnd 5713) took as its starting point the failure of the past system 'to guarantee all pensioners more than a low standard of living, or to prevent large numbers of them from having to rely on means-tested supplementary benefits' (p. 1). In this section we examine the likely effectiveness of the new scheme in raising the incomes of pensioners above the SB scale, and the implications of possible changes in policy. We do not enter into any discussion of the appropriate definition of a minimum income (for example, of the treatment of different types of need). We simply accept the SB Standard, and assume that it remains unchanged at 20 per cent of average earnings, for a single person, and 30 per cent for a married couple. Clearly, other indicators could be employed, and the same framework applied.

As explained earlier our calculations are necessarily approximate. For the years for which we are making projections, the predicted numbers receiving SB, and eligible but not claiming, in the absence of additional pensions are shown in the first line of Table 13.3. These figures do, of course, reflect our assumptions about the other income of pensioners. If, for example, occupational pensions were to add to the incomes of those below the SB level by $0.04\bar{E}$ (some £6 a week at 1981 levels), then the numbers receiving SB would be lower, on our assumptions, by 20 per cent and the number of non-claimants would be halved. In the case of men retired before 65, on our assumptions there would be some 40,000 receiving SB and 20,000 non-claimants, although it should be emphasized that our estimates for this group are highly uncertain.

Our main concern is with the effect of the alternative policy options on the numbers receiving SB and the numbers below the SB level. The first question is therefore the impact of the new state additional pension. Our estimates are shown in Table 13.3, where we have a higher figure, with the pension based on 60 per cent of average earnings, and a lower figure based

Table 13.3 Estimated numbers receiving supplementary benefit and eligible but not claiming (Great Britain)[a]

	1986	2001	2016	2031
		millions		
In absence of				
additional pension:				
Receiving SB	1.7	1.7	1.8	2.0
Below SB	0.9	0.9	0.9	1.1
With additional				
pensions[b]:				
Receiving SB	1.6–1.7	0.8–1.2	0.2–0.9	0.1–1.0
Below SB	0.8–0.8	0.3–0.4	0 –0.1	0 –0
Variation 1:				
Receiving SB	1.1–1.1	0.5–0.8	0.1–0.8	0.1–1.0
Below SB	0.2–0.2	0.1–0.1	0 –0	0 –0
Variation 2:				
Receiving SB	1.6–1.7	1.1–1.5	0.8–1.4	1.0–1.6
Below SB	0.8–0.8	0.2–0.6	0 –0.4	0 –0.5
Variation 3:				
Receiving SB	2.4–2.5	1.1–1.6	0.2–1.0	0.1–1.0
Below SB	0	0	0	0
Variation 4:				
Receiving SB	1.7–1.8	0.9–1.3	0.2–1.0	0.1–1.0
Below SB	0.8–0.9	0.3–0.4	0 –0.1	0
Variation 5:				
Receiving SB	1.7–1.7	0.9–1.3	0.2–1.0	0.2–1.0
Below SB	0.8–0.9	0.3–0.4	0 –0.1	0.1
Variation 6:				
Receiving SB	1.2–1.3	0.7–1.0	0.2–0.7	0.2–0.8
Below SB	0.3–0.4	0.1–0.2	0	0

[a] All figures rounded to nearest 100,000; 0 denotes less than 50,000
[b] Range corresponds to different assumptions about additional pensions.

on average earnings. These bring out the important contribution that the additional pension scheme will make as it reaches maturity. By 2031 the number estimated to be receiving SB is, on the more pessimistic assumption, half that predicted in the absence of the new scheme. If the alternative average earnings assumption is made, then the number of recipients would be about a twentieth. The number of non-claimants is predicted to be small in both cases.

These calculations, albeit approximate, illustrate the potential of the new scheme. They also show that a scaling-down of the scheme, as in Variation 2, would significantly reduce its effectiveness from the standpoint of reducing the numbers below the SB level. This policy option, attractive in terms of the reduction in cost, would, on the more optimistic assumption, leave half on SB; and the figure could be as high as 1½ million – or not far short of the present number.

The estimates in Table 13.3 also show the time required for the new scheme to have effect. In the year 2001 there are still a considerable number dependent on SB or eligible but not claiming. These are predominantly the older pensioners retiring with little entitlement under the new scheme. Variation 1 is designed to help this group. The immediate impact is to reduce the number on SB to 1.1 million, with a larger proportionate reduction in non-claimants. This improvement in the basic pension would make a substantial contribution to reducing the dependence of pensioners on SB over the next 20 years; and would be broadly comparable in effect with that of the 'low' additional pension when that scheme reaches maturity.

The effect of Variation 3 is, by definition, to ensure that all are at or above the SB level. As we noted at the outset, the problem with this variation is whether it is, in fact, feasible.

Variations 4 and 5 both concern the group of 'early retired': single men aged 60–4 and couples where the husband is in this age range. In both cases we assume that the number retired increases as a result of the extension of benefits, thus increasing the size of the population 'at risk' of being below the SB level. Reducing the minimum retirement age to 60 for all men and women would, on our assumptions, increase the number of pensioners (counting couples as two) in 1986 by 14 per cent and the number retired by 12 per cent. The improvement for those previously retired, with higher benefit reducing dependence on SB, works in the opposite direction, but the net effect, on our assumptions, is a rise in the numbers receiving SB or eligible and not claiming. Interestingly, Variations 4 and 5 have a similar effect, their implications being much the same for those with low incomes.

Finally, the tax credit (Variation 6) is estimated to have a substantial impact, reducing the number receiving SB to around 1¼ million in 1986. The effect does however appear to be rather smaller than that of the increase in basic pension (Variation 1).

The results described above give some impression of the effect of different policies on the circumstances of pensioners with low income. The principal conclusion, however, is that the calculations are heavily dependent on the assumptions made, and that this is an area where more detailed analysis has a high priority. This is well illustrated by the alternative figures for additional pensions. The correlation between additional pension and other income (net of requirements) is critical to predicting the success of the new scheme in reducing dependence on SB.

6 REDISTRIBUTION BETWEEN GENERATIONS

The development of expenditure on state pensions over the next 50 years makes clear that there are going to be significant differences in pension provision for different generations. Treating our five-year age groups as cohorts, with the group 60–4 taken as age 62, etc., the first cohort to retire after completing the transition period will be those 65–9 (60–4 for women) in 2001, and the expenditure will continue to build up after this date. The average amount of state pension, including the guaranteed minimum pension, per person in the different cohorts aged 60–4 (women) and 65–9 (married couples and men) will be (at January 1982 earnings levels):

Average amount of state pension

Year	1986	2001	2016	2031
£p.a.	1,600	2,400	2,500	2,600

The figures are affected by any changes in the balance between married and single, but these have a relatively minor effect. Thus the average amount will rise by two-thirds. Or, put another way, without the additional pension, the average amount in 2031 would have been only slightly over half the figure shown above. At any particular point in time, the disparities between pensioners of different ages will be marked. For example, in 2001 the position is estimated to be (on the same basis as in the previous table):

Average amount of state pension

Age: 65–9 Age: 60–4 (Single women)	70–4 65–9	75–9 70–4	80+ 75–79	80+
		£ per annum		
2,400	2,100	1,900	1,800	1,600

The cohort retiring with full additional pensions will, on average, receive 40–50 per cent more than the 80-year-olds.

The pension scheme raises therefore, in an acute form, issues of inter-generational fairness; and in this section we present some simple calculations of lifetime incomes intended to illuminate this controversial area. These calculations are extremely crude, but do allow for the differing earnings experience of different generations.

The concept of lifetime income is a difficult one. First, the standard approach is to take the present discounted value of the income stream. However, the implicit assumption of a perfect capital market, with unlimited borrowing or lending at a fixed interest rate, is an unattractive one. We should ideally take account of differences in borrowing and lending rates, and of restriction on borrowing opportunities. Even with the assumption of a perfect capital market, the choice of discount rate is a difficult one. Secondly, there is the problem of differences in survival probabilities, if lifetime income is measured on an *ex ante* basis, and of differences in actual lifetimes if it is measured *ex post*. As emphasized by Creedy (1980), differential mortality tends to offset the redistributive nature of the pension formula.

In the calculations below we make no attempt to resolve these issues, and present the simplest of possible calculations. We take the undiscounted sum of real incomes (that is, a real interest rate of zero), and consider the total income received to date by the surviving members of cohorts of the same age (that is, we compare the position of the 60–4 cohort in 1986, 2001, 2016 and 2031). We consider only earned income before retirement, and pensions and other income (including SB) after retirement, in each case summed over five-year periods. We make no allowance for unemployment, sickness or other interruption of earnings. Real earnings are based on the average ruling at the relevant date, with an assumed growth of 5 per cent per five years in the future. Earnings are taken from Feinstein (1972), (Table 65) and prices from London and Cambridge Economic Service (1970), (Table E). It is assumed that participation is 100 per cent for men and single women, and that the participation of married women rises from 10 per cent in 1926 to 60 per cent in 1981, following the historically observed path. The average earnings of women are taken to be 50 per cent of those for men until 1971 and 60 per cent thereafter. It is assumed, as above, that 80 per cent of single men and women were previously married and that their spouses were alive up to the previous five-year period. For simplicity, early retirement (of men aged 60–4) is ignored in these calculations, and for the additional pension we take the case of a couple/wife not entitled on own insurance as representative.

The results are shown in Table 13.4. If, for example, we take married couples aged 65–9, in 1986 they had received total real earnings over the period 1934–83 of 41.6 (taking average earnings in January 1982 as the unit), which includes the wife's earnings; and their basic pension plus other income is 1.8 over the five years (65–9), giving a total 43.4. With the additional pension, this rises to 43.7. In contrast, in 2031, the predicted total earnings over the period 1979–2028 are 72.7, with basic pension plus other income of 2.7, making a total of 75.4. With the additional pension, this rises to 77.1. For this age group, only recently retired, the contribution of the pension is relatively small. If we take married couples aged 80 and over, then the corresponding figures are:

Lifetime income of married couple (aged 80+)

	Earnings	Basic pension + other income	Additional pension	Total
1986	28.8	6.8	0	35.6
2031	66.3	9.9	6.0	82.2

Without the additional pension, income in retirement would have been an equalizing factor, the basic pension (related to current earnings) tending to offset the earnings disadvantage of the earlier cohort. The additional pension means however that the ratio of total lifetime incomes (2.31:1) is almost exactly equal to that for earnings.

The results in Table 13.4 show the total lifetime income to date for

Table 13.4 Estimated lifetime incomes (sum of real earnings plus retirement income)

		1986	2001	2016	2031
		(Unit = 1982 average earnings)			
Age 60–4					
Married couples	– without AP[a]	46.1	59.2	69.3	73.8
	– with AP				
Single men	– without AP	44.3	56.8	66.8	72.4
	– with AP				
Single women	– without AP	36.0	48.8	61.4	71.9
	– with AP	36.3	50.2	63.0	73.7
Age 65–9					
Married couples	– without AP	43.4	57.0	68.7	75.4
	– with AP	43.7	58.4	70.2	77.1
Single men	– without AP	39.0	54.1	65.4	72.6
	– with AP	39.3	55.5	66.9	74.3
Single women	– without AP	33.6	46.3	59.4	71.0
	– with AP	33.7	48.1	62.4	74.3
Age 70–4					
Married couples	– without AP	40.4	54.7	67.5	76.7
	– with AP	40.5	56.4	70.5	80.0
Single men	– without AP	38.7	51.8	64.0	73.4
	– with AP	38.8	53.5	67.0	76.7
Single women	– without AP	31.3	43.9	55.3	72.6
	– with AP	31.3	44.7	59.4	77.4
Age 75–9					
Married couples	– without AP	37.6	52.3	65.8	76.9
	– with AP	37.6	53.2	69.9	81.6
Single men	– without AP	36.0	49.3	64.5	75.7
	– with AP	36.0	50.2	68.6	80.4
Single women	– without AP	29.6	41.3	54.9	68.4
	– with AP	29.6	41.4	60.3	74.3
Age 80 and over					
Married couples	– without AP	35.6	49.3	63.7	76.3
	– with AP	35.6	49.5	69.1	82.2
Single men	– without AP	34.0	46.6	60.2	72.4
	– with AP	34.0	46.8	65.6	78.3
Single women	– without AP	28.6	38.8	52.4	66.4
	– with AP	28.6	38.8	56.7	73.8

[a] AP denotes additional pension.

different age groups in different years. It should be noted that the totals relate to different numbers of years for the different age groups, so that comparisons should be made only within, not between, sections of the table. The first feature is the substantial increase in lifetime income, in real terms, over the next 50 years. This is worth stressing, since studies employing the concept of lifetime income often draw attention to the narrower disparities found *within* a cohort than in the population as a whole. On the other hand, the differences *between* cohorts may be even more marked. For married couples, average lifetime incomes in 2031 are predicted to be 60 per cent (age group 60–4) to 130 per cent (age group 80+) larger than in 1986.

The large inter-cohort difference may simply reflect the assumptions made, and it should be recognized that our projections of real earnings are highly speculative. The assumed growth rate implies that average earnings in 2031 will be £12,530 in terms of January 1982 prices. This increase, slightly over 60 per cent, does not seem particularly large in the light of historical experience. If it were higher, then the differences between generations would be even more marked. A second assumption which would affect the comparison is that the working life remains unchanged. To the extent that younger generations enter the labour force later and retire earlier, the difference in total income (with no allowance for leisure) would be narrowed. Finally, we should note the implications of unemployment. All those aged 65 and over in 1986 are assumed to have entered the labour force before 1935, and their lifetime incomes would be reduced by the effect of the 1930s depression. The unemployment of the 1980s depression reduces the lifetime incomes of all pensioners in 2031.

Against this background, we can assess the effect of the additional pension, since the lifetime incomes are shown in Table 13.4 with and without the additional pension. In general, the new state scheme contributes significantly for widening the already sizeable gap between generations. Taking, for example, the age group 75–9, the additional pension represents in 2031 some five years' earnings (at 1982 levels). To put this in perspective, if unemployment involves a halving of income, then the contribution of the additional pension is equivalent in size (but in reverse direction) to the effect of ten years unemployment.

A second effect of the additional pension is on the position of single women relative to married couples and single men. For the age group 70–4, the additional pension increases the lifetime income of single women by 6.6 per cent in 2031, compared with 4½ per cent for married couples and single men. (It should be noted that single women include widows, and that their lifetime income is heavily influenced by the experience of married couples.) At the same time, the effect of the additional pension is only to reinforce a trend already predicted on the basis of a (partial) move towards equal pay (for the 70–4 age group):

		1986	2031 without AP	2031 with AP
			Percentages	
Lifetime income	Single women / Married couples	77.5	94.7	96.8

The comparison of the lifetime incomes with and without the additional pension allows one to see the effect of Variation 2, at least in the year 2031 when the additional pensions would be effectively halved. Suppose we consider the 'relative advantage' for single women aged 75–9 in 2031 compared with 1986:

with AP   74.3 ÷ 29.6 = 251 per cent
Variation 2   71.4 ÷ 29.6 = 241 per cent

Variation 1 (increasing the basic pension) has the effect of improving the position in 1986:

Variation 1   74.3 ÷ 29.9 = 248 per cent

The 'levelling-up' strategy is therefore rather less effective in reducing the relative advantage. The same applies even more to Variation 3 (100 per cent take-up of SB) which makes virtually no difference to average lifetime incomes. Variation 6 (the tax credit for elderly) also has a limited impact. Finally, Variations 4 and 5 mainly affect the age group 60–4. Since we assume that they induce earlier retirement, lifetime incomes actually fall in these cases, but clearly little significance can be attached to this (our lifetime measure needs to be extended to allow for different working periods).

7 SUMMARY

The main aim of the chapter has been to describe a framework within which some of the key policy issues can be analysed. The framework has been drastically simplified, but it does introduce a number of elements missing from some discussions: for example, the income tax paid on state pensions, the implications for supplementary benefit, and behavioural responses via retirement patterns.

The framework has been used to do some approximate arithmetic with regard to six possible policy variations, and the main conclusions may be summarized as follows:

Variation 1 (Increase in basic pension for those retiring up to 1999)
Gross cost £3 billion in 1986, falling to zero around 2016.
Net cost £2 billion in 1986.
Number dependent on SB halved in 1986.
Reduces inter-cohort differences in lifetime incomes but effect small.

Variation 2 (Scale-down additional pension by half)
Gross saving £1¼ billion in 2001, building up to £5 billion in 2031.
Net saving £3¼ billion in 2031.
Number dependent on SB remains substantial (1–1½ million) in 2031.
Reduces inter-cohort differences in lifetime incomes.

Variation 3 (100 per cent take-up of SB, if feasible)
Cost small.
Number below SB by definition zero.
No noticeable effect on differences in average cohort lifetime incomes.

Variation 4 (Retirement for men at 60)
Gross cost £1¾ billion in 1986, rising to £3 billion in 2031.
Net cost £1 billion in 1981, rising to £1¾ billion in 2031.
Number dependent on SB may increase (with increased retirement).

Variation 5 (Improved benefit for men 60–4)
Gross cost £1½ billion. Net cost £1 billion.
Number dependent on SB may increase (with increased retirement).

Variation 6 (Tax credit for the elderly)
Gross cost £3 billion, net cost slightly smaller.
Number dependent on SB reduced.
Reduces inter-cohort differences in lifetime incomes but effect small.

Finally, the aim of the chapter has been as much to pose questions as to answer them. It is clear for example that we need a more refined basis for estimating the effect of policy changes on the number of pensioners dependent on SB. We need a fuller analysis of the determinants of retirement behaviour. We need to consider more fully the concept of lifetime income and the measurement of the inter-cohort distribution.

14 · SOCIAL SECURITY, TAXATION AND THE WORKING POPULATION OVER THE NEXT TEN YEARS

1 INTRODUCTION

This chapter is concerned with the implications for those in work of likely developments of social security over the next ten years, notably those arising for demographic reasons or because of existing policy commitments, and of different options for policy change over that period. The scope is limited in that it is concerned with the position of those in work, and it should be borne in mind throughout that the changes in policy would have major implications for those not in work, notably the sick, disabled, unemployed, and single-parent families where the parent is not in work.

The determination of long-term policy towards social security is often seen in terms of a trade-off between the generosity of benefits and the 'burden' imposed on the working population in terms of taxes and contributions. The Conservative government has given priority to reducing the tax burden and this – on the trade-off view – implies that a move must be made towards reducing benefits relative to the general level of incomes. An alternative government concerned with raising benefits, or extending their scope, would undoubtedly choose a different policy, but it is often suggested that its room for manoeuvre would be limited by the willingness of taxpayers to finance such improvements.

This kind of trade-off may be illustrated by reference to the Green Paper *The Next Ten Years: Public Expenditure and Taxation into the 1990s* (Cmnd 9189). The Green Paper deals with the totality of public spending, but its analysis may be developed to bring out the significance for social

A revised, and extended, version of a paper prepared for the Conference on Social Policy: Aims and Resources for the 1990s, organized by the Joseph Rowntree Memorial Trust at Leeds Castle, 19–21 September 1984. I am grateful to the participants at the Conference, and to Mervyn King, for their comments.

Reprinted from R. Berthoud (ed.), *Challenges to Social Policy*, Gower, London. [Written in 1984.]

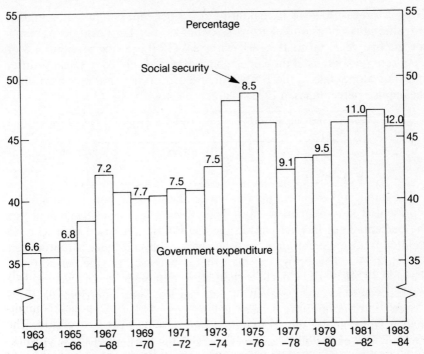

Figure 14.1 General government expenditure and social security spending in relation to GDP (market prices) 1963–64 to 1983–84

Source: General government expenditure from Cmnd 9189, Chart 2; social security spending (figures for calendar years) from *National Income and Expenditure 1983*, Tables 1.1 and 9.4, and comparable tables in earlier years.

security. In Figures 14.1 and 14.2, the information supplied in the Green Paper has been supplemented by that specifically relevant here.

First, there is the ratio of public expenditure to Gross Domestic Product (GDP). As is shown in Figure 14.1, where the ratio is represented by the height of the bars, there has been a general tendency for public spending to rise faster than GDP over the last twenty years. The figures for social security alone are given for alternate years at the top of each of the bars in Figure 14.1. They show that since 1963, social security spending has increased much faster than GDP. In 1983–84, the planning total for social security spending in the UK (*The Government's Expenditure Plans 1984–87*, Cmnd 9143–11, Tables 2.12 and 2.17) was equal in size to some 12 per cent of GDP.

The Green Paper considers the implications of different policies with regard to government spending into the 1990s. These assume that there would be no real increase for five years up to 1988–89, during which period

GDP is forecast to grow in real terms at 2¼ per cent per annum, and then two alternative rates of real growth – either zero or 1 per cent per annum – for the five years up to 1993–94, with real GDP growing at either 1.5 or 2 per cent per annum. If the same assumptions are applied to social security spending alone, taking the 1983–84 figure of 12.0 per cent as a base, then the implied percentages in 1993–94 are:

Assumed spending growth (1988–93) per annum	Assumed GDP growth (1988–93) per annum	
	1½ per cent	2 per cent
zero	10.0	9.7
1 per cent	10.5	10.2

The implications for the tax burden on the working population may be represented in a number of ways. The Green Paper gives prominence to the percentage of income paid in income tax by a married man with no children at average earnings, and the chart published there is reproduced as Figure 14.2. This brings out the general increase over the period up to the mid-1970s, with a decline thereafter, although the decline is less marked when account is taken of national insurance contributions (employee contributions have been added in Figure 14.2 and are shown by the shaded area), and it should be noted that only part of the tax burden is covered, the exclusion of indirect taxes being particularly important in view of the increase in VAT in the 1979 Budget. The Green Paper indicates the effect of the different policies to restrict total government expenditure on the tax burden measured in this way, on the assumption that all of the tax reduction would be concentrated on income tax personal allowances. With 1 per cent growth in total spending in the latter half of the period, and the slower rate of GDP increase, the proportion taken in income tax from the married man on average earnings would fall from 20 per cent in 1983–84 to 17 per cent in 1993–94. With zero growth in public spending and the faster rate of GDP increase, the reduction would be 7 percentage points.

The Green Paper may therefore be interpreted as presenting us with a trade-off between increasing real expenditure on benefits and reducing the tax burden on the working population, and this is the way in which the issue is often viewed. Such a representation serves to bring home the important fact that choices have to be made. It is however a serious over-simplification and potentially highly misleading. First, policy for total social security spending has to be related to that for individual benefits and programmes, an aspect stressed by O'Higgins and Patterson (1985). Zero real growth in total spending may have quite different implications for the level of benefits depending on demographic, behavioural and other changes which affect the number of beneficiaries. In section 2, we examine the spending picture in more detail, working from three different assumptions about the uprating of individual benefits to the implications for

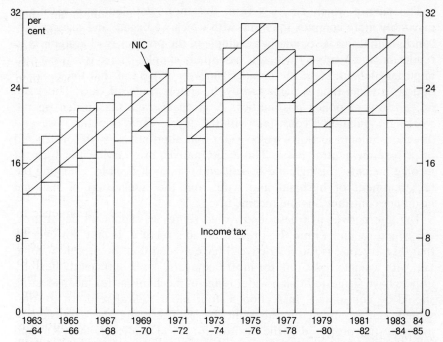

Figure 14.2 Income tax, and employee national insurance contributions as per cent of gross earnings (married man with no children at average earnings)

Source: Income tax from Cmnd 9189, Chart 7. NIC calculated applying rates ruling at 31 October and assuming man not contracted out, based on average earnings of full-time men, all occupations, Great Britain, excluding those whose pay is affected by absence, linked prior to 1970 to the series for average adult male earnings in production industries and some services.

financing. The outcome will depend on economic and social developments, such as changes in the level of unemployment (where we consider a range of assumptions).

The second respect in which the simple trade-off view is misleading is that it only deals with the aggregate cost to the working population, whereas it is the impact on individual families which is of ultimate concern. The married man on average earnings cannot necessarily be assumed to be representative; and we need to take account of the full diversity of family circumstances. In section 3, we present the results of such an analysis based on an extrapolation of the 1980 *Family Expenditure Survey*. This shows the predicted effect of the different spending policies on the *distribution* of net incomes and tax burdens. It considers what can be said about the distribution within the family. The analysis is concerned not only with tax burdens but also shows the implications for marginal tax rates and the incentives faced by individual workers.

The picture which emerges from this more detailed investigation is inevitably more complex than that with which we began, and readers may conclude that this is yet another example of the propensity of academics to render arcane a subject which is essentially simple. There is however an important lesson, since the detailed analysis brings out that the range of options is wider than is suggested by the simple trade-off view. There is a fuller menu of policy possibilities. A given average tax burden on the working population is consistent with the development of policy in several directions, and in section 4 we consider four alternatives, each constructed on a revenue-neutral basis. These alternatives are varying the form of income tax cuts, raising child benefit and making it taxable, changing the tax treatment of husband and wife, and the integration of national insurance contributions and income tax.

The alternatives just described would represent significant departures, but would remain within the present broad structure. It may however be that this structure is too restrictive. I have argued that the present income tax, with a single basic rate for most taxpayers, is not sufficiently flexible. Others have suggested that a wider range of mechanisms for means-testing should be considered. In section 5, four more radical reforms are presented, and analysed on the same basis. These are the extension of means-testing proposed by the Institute for Fiscal Studies (Dilnot, Kay and Morris, 1984), the Basic Income Guarantee proposed by Parker (1984), the negative income tax advocated by Minford (1984), and my own graduated tax/social insurance scheme (Atkinson, 1984).

When one contemplates this wider menu, it becomes clear that more consideration needs to be given to the basic objectives of policy. Why is it that the government wishes to cut taxes? What are the aims of the social security system? We return to these issues in the concluding section 6.

In this chapter, projections are made over the ten-year period to the mid-1990s commencing with 1984–85. Projection even ten years forward involves heroic assumptions about the development of the economy. Here it is assumed throughout that real GDP grows on average by 2 per cent per annum, which lies between the two assumptions described above. It is assumed that real earnings per worker rise at 1.5 per cent per annum, with a range of assumptions about unemployment:

U0   no change in unemployment rate between 1984–85 and 1994–95
U−   3 percentage point fall in unemployment rate
U+   3 percentage point rise in unemployment rate

2 OVERALL PICTURE

The overall picture in terms of total social security spending has been examined by O'Higgins and Patterson (1985), whose forecasts of social

Table 14.1 Social security spending 1984–85 and 1994–95 (projected)

	1984–85 Planning total	1994–95 P1	P2	P3
National insurance	20.7	26.2	24.1	23.2
Child benefit	4.3	5.3	4.8	4.6
Supplementary benefit	6.2	7.0	6.3	6.0
Rent rebates	2.5	2.8	2.0	1.9
Other benefits	1.9	2.2	2.0	1.9
Total[a]	38.4	46.9	42.8	41.1

[a] Includes administration expenses and spending in Northern Ireland not shown above.

security spending for 1993–94 take account of demographic developments affecting the number of pensioners and child benefit recipients and of the changing levels of unemployment induced by different rates of GDP and productivity growth. In general, they assume that there would be no real increases in social security benefits, although they consider variants where there is a real increase in pensions.

These estimates provide a valuable reference point, but they do not go into sufficient detail for the present purpose. Nor do they relate the expenditure to the changes in taxation and contribution rates which are what directly affect the working population. In view of this, we present below a set of estimates built up from the individual programmes, taking as the starting point the planning totals in 1984–85. These planning totals are shown in the first column of Table 14.1, where expenditure in Northern Ireland is treated as a separate category, as in the Public Expenditure White Paper which is the source of the figures.

The analysis in this and the next section is based on three different assumptions about policy towards the uprating of benefits:

P1 all benefit scales, including post-award increases in earnings-related pensions, increased in line with earnings per worker;
P2 all benefit scales, and post-award amounts, constant in real terms for five years and then increased at 1 per cent per annum for the next five years;
P3 all benefit scales, and post-award amounts, constant in real terms.

The first of these assumptions may be seen as maintaining the status quo, as it has generally been interpreted in recent decades. The second and third may be seen as corresponding, in terms of benefit scales, to the Green Paper assumptions about total spending. They would represent a reduction in benefits relative to the general level of earnings.

National insurance

The expenditure on national insurance (NI) benefits, and especially that on pensions, has received considerable attention. The long-term projection of benefits, and the contributions required to finance them, has been the subject of the Government Actuary's *First Quinquennial Review* (House of Commons, 19 July 1982), as well as a number of academic articles, such as Hemming and Kay (1982).

The estimates here are based on those in the Government Actuary's Review. The calculations by the Government Actuary are not directly applicable, since they cover the period 1985–86 to 1995–96 (as well as later years), and assume in the central estimates an unemployment rate of 6 per cent. It is assumed here that the changes over the ten-year period can be applied to that which we are studying (i.e. that they can be displaced by one year) and can be taken as corresponding to the assumption U0 of constant unemployment. This should be sufficient to give at least a broad order of magnitude. The estimates for the increase in NI benefits for our three assumptions P1–P3 may be obtained by the appropriate combination of those made by the Government Actuary (e.g. P2 is based on (b) (i)). These are expressed first in terms of constant earnings levels. On assumption P1, there is an increase of some 9 per cent. This is largely attributable to the rise in earnings-related pensions; the cost of flat-rate pensions being expected to remain more or less unchanged. With assumption P2, there would be essentially no change relative to earnings levels; and with assumption P3 there would be a 3.5 per cent reduction. With our assumed growth of real earnings over the ten years, the overall level of earnings would rise by 16 per cent, so that all three assumptions would imply a rise in real expenditure on NI benefits. This is summarized below:

Assumption	Per cent growth over ten years at constant earnings	in real terms
P1	9.0	26.5
P2	0.4	16.4
P3	−3.5	11.9

The changes in real terms are used to arrive at the estimates in 1984–85 shown in the first line of Table 14.1.

Adopting the same assumptions as the Government Actuary, we may relate the changes in spending to the sources of financing. On assumption P1, the £1.6 billion increase, at the 1981–82 earnings levels used in the Review, is assumed to be financed by an increase of £0.9 billion in contributions, an increase of £0.1 billion in the Treasury Supplement and £0.6 billion via a decrease in the reduction for contracted-out members. As a result, the increase in the percentage contribution rate (Class 1) is 0.3 percentage points. This relatively modest rise, given the increase in total spending relative to earnings, is achieved because of the increased payments by those contracted out and because of the fall in the number of married women benefiting from the option of paying reduced contributions. By the same token, the assumption P2 would allow a reduction of 0.7

percentage points, and assumption P3 a reduction of 1.2 percentage points, in the Class 1 contribution rate. (This rate applies to the total of employee and employer contributions; for the purpose of our analysis we assume that the changes are all in the employee rate.)

The Government Actuary's calculations relate only to the National Insurance fund, but the implications for the government budget do not stop at this point. The Treasury Supplement has to be financed; and the changes in benefit levels will affect income tax receipts. The income tax liability on the state earnings-related pension is likely to be of increasing importance, even when account is taken of the age allowance (see Chapter 13), and we assume here that a third of the increase would be taxable at a rate of 30 per cent. On assumption P1, this more or less counterbalances the increased Treasury Supplement. With P2, the extra tax would permit a reduction in the basic rate of 0.2 percentage points; with P3 the reduction would be 0.3 percentage points.

The Government Actuary provides estimates of the effect of unemployment being higher or lower by 3 percentage points, where this takes account of the change in NI benefits and in contribution revenue. On this basis, we can draw the tentative conclusion that the required Class 1 contribution rate would be 1 percentage point lower on assumption U− and 1 percentage point higher on assumption U+. These calculations may understate the sensitivity to variations in the unemployment rate if receipt of a wider range of benefits is taken into account, including, for example, invalidity benefit.

Other benefits

The prediction of spending on NI benefits involves strong assumptions; this is true to an even greater extent when we turn to the non-contributory benefits. The estimates shown in Table 14.1 for child benefit take account of the expected increase in the number of qualifying children, assumed to be 6.4 per cent on the basis of the increase in the UK population aged under 15 shown in the Green Paper (Table 3). The estimates for supplementary benefit and rent rebates make allowance for the increase in earnings-related pension, which may be expected to reduce the dependence of pensioners on means-tested benefits. These factors tend to cancel. The effect of variations in unemployment is taken into account in calculating expenditure on supplementary benefit. Total predicted spending shows no change in real terms on assumption P3 (with no change in unemployment), whereas on policy P1 the total rises by the same percentage as earnings.

The financing of this expenditure is assumed here to be derived from income tax. If personal allowances and tax brackets increase with earnings levels, then unchanged policy would lead to a rise in revenue at the same rate (this assumes that deductions from the tax base would also rise proportionately). On assumption P1, there would therefore be no adjustment in tax rates. With assumptions P2 and P3, tax could be reduced, and this is assumed to take the form of a reduction in the basic rate of tax of 1.5 percentage points (assumption P2) or 2.0 percentage points (assumption P3). With assumption U−, the reduced cost of supplementary benefit would allow a further 0.5 percentage point reduction; with assumption U+, the tax rate would be 0.5 percentage points higher.

Total

The predictions for total spending under the three policies P1–P3 are brought together in Table 14.1. What do they imply for the overall prospects? If it is the government's intention to hold the total constant in real terms, then it does not appear that this would be achieved even on Policy P3, where there would be a 7 per cent real increase. This would be less if unemployment were to fall, although with assumption U− the increase would still be 4 per cent in real terms. If unemployment were to rise as supposed under assumption U+, then real spending would increase, under P3, by 10 per cent. This latter calculation appears to be broadly in line with those of O'Higgins and Patterson: for example, their scenarios A and B, which involve rising unemployment, show real increases of 10.5 per cent and 8.2 per cent. In order to hold total real spending constant, it appears that it would be necessary to reduce benefit levels in real terms, or to restrict the scope of benefits.

If the aim of the government is to contain the rise in social security spending relative to GDP, then this appears much more easily attained. With policy P1, and constant unemployment, the ratio would exhibit little change, remaining around 12 per cent, but with P2 it would fall to 11 per cent and with P3 to 10.5 per cent. Seen in this way, the continuation of a status-quo policy, maintaining benefits in line with earnings, appears feasible at least into the mid-1990s.

3   IMPACT ON INDIVIDUAL FAMILIES

The implications of the three policies P1–P3 for income tax and national insurance contributions (NIC) are summarized in Table 14.2. For the married taxpayer on average earnings who features in the Green Paper, the impact of these changes is readily calculated. On the assumption that tax allowances and brackets rise in line with earnings, and that the man is not contracted out for NIC, policy P1 would mean a slight increase in the proportion deducted for income tax and NIC, from 29.0 per cent to 29.3 per cent. (In these calculations, 'average' earnings have been taken as

Table 14.2 Predicted tax and national insurance contribution rates, 1994–95

| | Assumptions | | | Variation with | |
	P1	P2	P3	U–	U+
NIC (Class 1)	9.3	8.3	7.8	−1.0	+1.0
Reduction for contracting out	0.9	0.9	0.9	unchanged	
Income tax basic rate	30.0	28.3	27.7	−0.5	+0.5

£182, which generates an income tax burden of 20 per cent as quoted in the Green Paper.) In contrast, the policy P3 would allow a reduction in both NIC and income tax, with the average rate falling from 29.0 per cent to 26.3 per cent. So that the difference between policies P1 and P3, on which we concentrate here, amounts to trading off the lower benefits, relative to earnings, under P3 against a tax cut of 3 percentage points.

It is however clear that the circumstances of individual taxpayers may differ considerably from those assumed in these hypothetical calculations:

1. The man may be contracted out for NIC purposes, in which case the amount paid would rise more or fall less.
2. There may be deductions against taxable income, for items such as mortgage interest, which would reduce the benefit from tax rate deductions.
3. His wife may be in paid employment and also be affected by changes in income tax and NIC.
4. If there are dependent children, then the family may be affected by changes in child benefit.
5. The family may be entitled to means-tested benefits, such as housing benefit.

These different circumstances could be taken into account by extending the range of hypothetical calculations, but this is not sufficient, since we also need to know *how frequently* they are found in real life. We do not want to devote a great deal of attention to combinations of circumstances which are never found in practice. For this reason, any analysis of the impact of the policy changes, and alternatives to them, must be based on evidence from a representative sample of actual families, and this is what is presented below, based on the *Family Expenditure Survey* (FES). The use of data from the *Survey* not only allows us to examine the effect on actual, as opposed to hypothetical, sets of circumstances, but also brings out the diversity of experience which is found in the population. The extent of such diversity is not apparent from aggregate calculations.

The use of evidence from surveys such as the FES is not without difficulty. First, the FES, while a very high-quality survey, suffers from a significant degree of non-response and there are reasons to believe that certain types of income, such as that from self-employment, are understated. In our work, we have attempted to adjust for these shortcomings, in the grossing up to the whole population, and in multiplying up the amounts of income to bring them into line with external evidence. Nevertheless, such adjustments are only approximate. Secondly, we are interested in predicting the effects of changes in policy. This has involved assumptions both about how they would actually work and about the response of families to such changes. In the latter case, we assume for present purposes that there is no alteration in gross incomes, an assumption which may be regarded as equivalent to that made in the official estimates of the effect of direct tax changes.

The third problem with the use of survey data is that it involves substantial computation, and it is not typically easily accessible to the user. Being able to carry out the analysis quickly and flexibly is particularly important when one wishes to consider a number of policy options and where there is room for a range of opinion about the parameters which should be entered (for example, those forecasting demographic changes). The calculations here have for this reason been based on a sub-sample of families in the FES small enough to be analysed on a BBC Micro-Computer. The reduction in the size of the sample, which is 1 in 5 of the families in the relevant FES population, means that the results are surrounded by a greater margin of error; and the program cannot be regarded as a substitute for analysis based on the full sample. Nevertheless, the results seem in general to be quite reliable, and their accuracy should be sufficient for the broad view taken here. (More details of the TAXMOD program in its 1988 version is given in Chapter 18.)

The results here are based on families in the 1980 FES where the head, either male or female, is in full-time paid employment, so that those families are excluded where the head is unemployed, sick, self-employed or retired. The analysis is intended therefore to illuminate the effects on families with a head in employment, referred to for convenience as 'working families'. It should also be stressed that the picture based on the FES is a 'snapshot' and that it does not allow us to follow the changing circumstances of families over time. The heads of families in work at the date of interview may become unemployed; the single-parent families may become two-parent families, and vice versa; wives not in paid work when interviewed may be in employment the next week; and so on. The volatility of circumstances needs to be taken more fully into account, but unfortunately this is not possible with the present source.

In adjusting the figures for our purposes, two steps are necessary. First, we increase the 1980 gross incomes to put them on a 1984–85 basis, adjusting in line with aggregate indicators. It should be emphasized that this does not attempt to 'predict' the 1984–85 situation; for example, no allowance is made for increased unemployment. What the calculation represents is a 'thought experiment' as to the effect of the 1984–85 policy on families in the employment circumstances of 1980. The second stage is the projection forward to 1994–95. This again involves adjustment of gross incomes, which are assumed to rise at the same rate as earnings, and for convenience we express all amounts at 1984–85 earnings levels (so that a policy decision to increase a benefit less than earnings will be shown as a reduction in the benefit). In the case of 1994–95, approximate adjustments are also made for the changing number and composition of families, built up from projections of the number of children, of the number of single-parent families, and of the number of employees in different categories, but they make no allowance for changing unemployment, so that they should be regarded as equivalent to assumption U0.

Our results take account of several important factors missing from the hypothetical calculation for the married man on average earnings. These include working wives, income from sources other than earnings, and deductions from taxable income for mortgage interest. There is contracting out for NIC purposes and some of the wives retain the right to pay reduced contributions. Family net income is calculated allowing for child benefit, family income supplement (FIS), passport benefits and housing rebates. Several of these factors work in the direction of reducing the average tax rate, for example the inclusion of benefits received, although some work in the opposite direction (for example, single people pay more tax than married at any given income). As may be seen from Table 14.3, the average tax rate for the sample of working families is in fact estimated to be 25.4 per cent in 1984–85. It should be noted that the average tax rate calculation, like all those in this chapter, only takes into account income tax and NIC, and the benefits listed, and that it does not include indirect taxes, company taxes, and other forms of benefit.

The projected changes in the average tax rate to 1994–95 depend on two elements. First, there is the changing demographic composition, which may be seen from Table 14.3 to be predicted on unchanged policy to lead to a reduction in the average tax rate (for example, because more children lead to more child benefit) of some 0.2 per cent. The demographic factors appear therefore to be of rather limited significance, although it is possible that our assumptions about the magnitude of demographic change over the next ten years have been too conservative.

The second element in the projections to 1994–95 is the choice of policy option. Under Policy P1, which involves an increase in the NIC rate, the average tax rate is predicted to be higher by 0.9 percentage points than if present policy were maintained. (The same difference is found if Policy P1

Table 14.3 Projected average tax burden, 1984–85 and 1994–95

| | 1984–85 Policy | Policy options 1994–95 | | |
		P1	P2	P3
1984–85 demographic structure	25.4	26.3	24.7	24.0
1994–95 demographic structure	25.2	26.1	24.5	23.9

is introduced with the 1984–85 demographic structure.) This is greater than the apparent rise in the standard NIC rate, and reflects the fall in the reduction for contracting out and the smaller number of married women retaining the right to pay reduced contributions. The same considerations also apply to Policies P2 and P3. Whereas the reduction in the average tax rate calculated at average earnings was 2.7 percentage points under Policy P3, the fall shown in Table 14.3 is 1.3–1.4 percentage points. The difference between policies P1 and P3 is also less: 2.3 percentage points, compared with 3 percentage points in the illustrative calculation. The reduction in the average tax rate is moderated by the existence of deductions against income tax and the reduced value of benefits. If, for example, the married man on average earnings paid £2,000 mortgage interest, then his present average income tax rate would be 13.7 per cent rather than 20 per cent, and he would benefit correspondingly less from the reduced basic rate.

The estimates shown in Table 14.3 assume that unemployment would remain constant (assumption U0), and this is the basis used in the subsequent analysis. The effect of the changes in tax rates and NIC which would be associated with variation in the level of unemployment is illustrated below for Policy P1, where it should be noted that this assumes that the unemployed are drawn randomly from the working population (which is not of course likely to be true in reality):

	Average tax rate P1
Assumption U−	24.9
Assumption U0	26.1
Assumption U+	27.3

A fall in unemployment of 3 percentage points would allow the average tax rate on working families to be reduced by 1.2 percentage points, so that on a status-quo policy the tax burden would fall, rather than rise. This is an addition to the benefit to the unemployed.

As far as the working population is concerned, the choice between Policy P1 and P3 is one between higher child benefit, FIS and housing benefit, on the one hand, and lower rates of income tax and NIC, on the other hand. The latter may be expected to provide more benefit to those with higher incomes; the former is either flat-rate (child benefit) or declining with income. It seems likely therefore that in distributional terms Policy P1 will favour lower-income groups, and this is borne out by the results shown in Table 14.4. For each family, we calculate income per 'equivalent adult', a couple counting for 1.6 single persons, and a child for 0.4. (The choice of such an equivalence scale is open to question; one of the advantages of the micro-computer program is that it allows the scale to be chosen by the user.) The unit of analysis is the tax unit, or man, wife and dependent children, which is, of course, a narrower unit than the house-

Table 14.4 Distributional impact of policy change

	Cumulative shares in total adult equivalent income			
	1984–85	Policy options 1994–95		
	Policy	P1	P2	P3
Bottom:				
10 per cent	4.7	4.7	4.7	4.6
20 per cent	10.8	10.8	10.7	10.6
30 per cent	17.7	17.8	17.6	17.5
40 per cent	25.5	25.6	25.3	25.2
50 per cent	34.1	34.2	34.0	33.9
60 per cent	43.6	43.8	43.6	43.5
70 per cent	54.3	54.5	54.3	54.2
80 per cent	66.5	66.6	66.5	66.5
90 per cent	80.6	80.7	80.6	80.6

Notes:
1. Adult equivalent income calculated counting a couple as 1.6 single persons and children as 0.4 single persons, but with each unit receiving a weight of unity.
2. Distributions calculated with 1994–95 demographic structure.

hold. The figures in the table provide the ingredients for drawing Lorenz curves, showing the cumulative shares in total equivalent income of the bottom 10 per cent, 20 per cent, ... It should be stressed that the distributions relate to the population of working families, not to the entire population, so that they cannot be used to draw conclusions about overall inequality.

Under Policy P1, the shares of the bottom income groups would be slightly increased, since the rise in national insurance contributions, particularly for those contracted out and for married women, would bear less heavily. In contrast, under Policy P3, the shares of the bottom 10 per cent, 20 per cent, up to the bottom 70 per cent would all be lower. The Lorenz curve would lie outside, implying, for examplle, that the Gini coefficient would be higher. The same would be true, to a lesser extent, under Policy P2. How far this could be offset by concentrating the tax reductions on raising thresholds, rather than rate changes, is considered in the next section.

The results in Table 14.4 show the distribution between families with different incomes, and the effects in part reflect the differential treatment of families with different numbers of dependants, of varying composition. Policy P3, by reducing child benefit relative to earnings, will naturally bear more heavily on families containing children. (By the same token, the results will be sensitive to the choice of equivalence scale.) In order to bring this out, we show in Figure 14.3 the differences in average incomes of different family types, cumulating (from the right) from those with the highest number of dependants. (The theoretical rationale for this proce-dure, the analogue of the Lorenz curve when there are differences in family size, is explained in Atkinson and Bourguignon, 1987.) For families with two or more children, the advantage under Policy P3 compared with

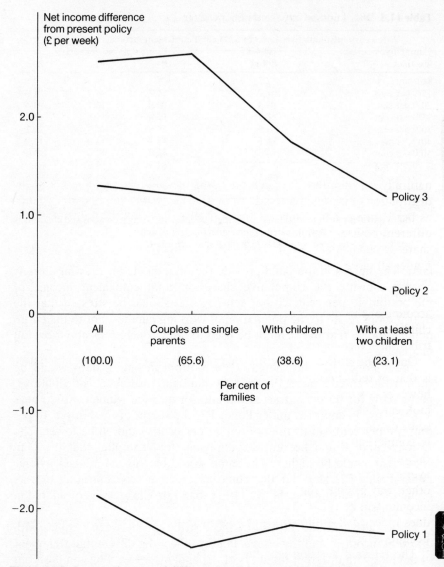

Figure 14.3 Average income of different family types with policies P1–P3

the present policy is an increase in average net income of £1.21, but this is smaller than for families with one or more children, for whom it is £1.81. For all couples (with or without children) and single parents, it is £2.64. There is a distinct gradient. In contrast, under Policy P1, the difference (in this case a loss) is much more similar across family types.

Much less commonly studied than the distribution by families is that *within* families. It is less frequently studied for the obvious reason that our knowledge about the division of resources between husband and wife is

Table 14.5 Wife's net income as per cent of net family income

Cumulative per cent less than	Wife's earnings − tax − NIC + child benefit as percentage of net family income			
	1984–85 Policy	Policy options 1994–95		
		P1	P2	P3
10	32.5	32.1	34.2	35.6
15	39.2	39.2	40.7	41.4
20	45.4	45.4	46.5	47.1
25	52.7	52.7	53.3	54.3
30	64.1	64.4	65.2	65.8
40	80.5	81.4	81.8	81.8
50	94.5	95.3	95.3	95.3

naturally very limited. It is however possible to say something about the distribution of income received. Table 14.5 shows the wife's share, defined as her earnings net of income tax and NIC plus child benefit, under the different policies. For few married couples, only about 1 in 20, does this share exceed 50 per cent, and for more than half it is less than 25 per cent. Under all three policy options there will be a tendency for the share to fall because of the smaller proportion retaining the right to pay reduced contributions. The fall is however more marked with Policies P2 and P3 on account of the decline in child benefit relative to earnings. By reducing child benefit, the government would be influencing the intra-family distribution of income received.

One of the motives for cutting the tax burden on the working population is that of reducing any adverse effect on the incentive to work. This is, however, a more complex matter that at first sight appears, and we need to look carefully at the different types of decision that may be affected. In some cases, it may be the average rate of tax which is relevant. If a person is comparing the net income from working throughout the year with the benefit received if unemployed for the whole year, then a cut in the average rate of tax will raise the attractiveness of working. Turned the other way round, the 'replacement rate', or ratio of benefit to work income, will be reduced. Under Policies P2 and P3, the replacement rate does indeed fall, although most of this is attributable to the reduction in benefits relative to earnings, rather than to the tax changes.

The relevant decision may however be rather different. A person may compare the income from an extra week of work in a year with the benefit received if that week is not worked. In this situation, it may be the *marginal* rather than *average* rate of tax that is applicable. The marginal rate of tax is also likely to be relevant to decisions by those in work: for example, about overtime, intensity of effort or seeking promotion. The impact of the different policies on the marginal rate of tax paid by the family head on an extra £1 of earnings is shown in Table 14.6.

For the person paying basic rate income tax, and below the NIC ceiling, Policy P3 would offer a reduction in the marginal tax rate, compared with Policy P1, of 3.8 percentage points. From the upper part of Table 14.6, it

Table 14.6 Marginal tax rates of family head and wife

(a) *On extra £1 earnings by family head*

Marginal tax rate:	1984–85 Policy	Policy options 1994–95		
		P1	P2	P3
10 per cent or less	1.2	1.2	1.2	1.2
11–20 per cent	—	—	—	—
21–30 per cent	2.4	2.6	5.2	5.2
31–40 per cent	87.5	87.4	86.3	86.7
41–50 per cent	4.8	4.8	3.9	4.0
51–60 per cent	1.0	1.2	1.2	1.0
61 per cent plus	3.1	3.0	2.3	1.9
Average marginal rate	38.7	39.6	36.8	35.6

(b) *On extra £1 earnings by wife (per cent of families where wife in paid work)*
Marginal tax rate:

10 per cent or less	26.3	26.0	26.0	26.6
11–20 per cent	—	0.3	0.3	—
21–30 per cent	0.4	0.4	0.4	0.4
31–40 per cent	66.9	66.9	66.9	66.5
41–50 per cent	3.8	3.8	3.8	3.8
51–60 per cent	2.4	2.4	2.4	2.4
61 per cent plus	0.3	0.3	0.3	0.3
Average marginal rate	29.1	30.6	28.5	27.5

Note: The calculation of the marginal tax rate assumes that means-tested benefits are adjusted immediately.

may be seen that the average reduction for the head of the tax unit is in fact 4 percentage points. For some people, those above the NIC ceiling, the reduction in the marginal rate will be less than 3.8 percentage points, but this is more than offset by the reduction in the number with very high rates arising from the withdrawal of means-tested benefits, commonly referred to as the 'poverty trap'.

In considering the poverty trap, it must be borne in mind that the absolute numbers in the survey are small, and the estimates are subject to considerable sampling error. Our analysis considers therefore as a group all those in the range 60 per cent and higher, rather than the smaller number with rates in the 80s plus. In any case, it seems quite reasonable to treat as 'high' any marginal tax rate in excess of the top income tax rate. Table 14.6 shows about 3 per cent of the heads of working families to be in this position (where the marginal tax rate is calculated assuming that benefits are reassessed), or some 450,000 in total. The majority of these are families paying income tax (30 per cent), NIC (6.85 per cent or 9 per cent), and losing rent and rate rebates (35 per cent). It is clear that a reduction of a few per cent in the income tax rate will make little contribution to reducing the extent of the poverty trap. Policies P2 and P3 do however involve a cut in housing benefit, which narrows the range over which there would be entitlement (partly offset by the reduction in child benefit). From

Table 14.6, Policy P3 would – by cutting benefits – reduce the number in the poverty trap by more than a third, to around 300,000.

Much of the discussion of incentives tends to focus on the head of the family, but the evidence from studies of labour supply (for example, Killingsworth, 1983) suggests that the wife's earning decision may be more sensitive to taxation. In the lower part of Table 14.6 are shown the marginal tax rates faced by working wives. In some quarter of cases the rate is zero, since they are below the tax and NIC thresholds, and these people would not be affected by tax cuts. Nevertheless, Policy P3 offers a reduction in the marginal tax rate of 1.6 percentage points, compared with a rise of 1.5 percentage points under policy P1 (reflecting the rise in NIC rate for married women).

CONCLUSIONS

By adopting Policy P3, rather than P1, the government would be able to reduce the tax rate paid by the working population by an average of 2.3 percentage points. The replacement rate would fall. The marginal tax rates faced by those in work would fall by some 3 to 4 percentage points on average, and the number in the poverty trap would fall by more than a third. This would be achieved at the expense of transferring £3.4 billion less to those not in the working population (under Policy P3 total taxes would be cut by £2.0 billion, compared with a £1.4 billion rise under Policy P1). The distribution of the tax cut would favour middle- and upper-income groups, and coupled with the relative fall in benefits, would reduce the share of lower-income groups. It would favour those without children relative to families with children. The distribution within the family would shift away from the wife towards the husband.

4 VARIATIONS IN POLICY

The policy options open to the government range from relatively limited changes, such as in the structure of income tax, to whole-scale reform. In this section, four changes are considered which may be seen as 'incrementalist' in that they take as their starting point the present structure, rather than seeking to sweep this away so as to start afresh. In each case they are standardized to yield the same revenue, where we have taken Policy P3 as the base (we could equally have taken another base for the comparison). It is important to note that the revenue neutrality is defined for the population of families with a working head, not for the whole population, and that the implications for other groups are not examined.

Alternative A: income tax structure

Under Policy P3, the basic rate of income tax was cut by 2.3 percentage points, but the revenue handed back to the working population could have been used instead to raise the income tax personal allowances, and this is indeed the assumption in the Green Paper. In the alternative policy A, the basic rate is set at 30 per cent, and personal allowances are raised to £2,275 (single) and £3,590 (married), an increase of some 14 per cent. This, together with the other changes under P3, would involve the same net reduction, relative to the present policy, of £2 billion in the net burden on the working population.

The average tax rate is therefore the same as under P3; the difference lies in the distribution of the tax burden and in the implications for marginal tax rates. The policy of raising the tax threshold concentrates most of the gain on lower income ranges. Analysis of the shares of total adult equivalent income received by different groups shows that the bottom half of the distribution do less well than with Policy P1 (although this only shows up in the second decimal place), but they do better than with the present policy, and decidedly better than with Policy P3. The latter comparison is shown in Table 14.7. The share of the bottom 10 per cent, for example, becomes 10.8 per cent rather than 10.6 per cent. Differences of 0.2–0.3 per cent may appear to some readers as of minor importance, but they represent quite sizeable changes, and the overall conclusion must be that the choice of tax structure can make a significant difference to the distributional consequences.

The alternative policy, like Policy P3, involves a reduction in child benefit, and it may be seen from Figure 14.4 that the implications for different family types are very close. This diagram shows the differences in average income for different family groups, again taken cumulatively,

Table 14.7 Comparison of alternative policies

| | Equal revenue basis for families with working head | | | | |
	P3	A	B	C	D
Shares in total adult equivalent income of:					
bottom 20 per cent	10.6	10.8	11.0	10.7	11.0
bottom 40 per cent	25.2	25.5	25.8	25.5	25.8
bottom 60 per cent	43.5	43.8	44.1	43.7	44.2
Percentage with wife's share of income:					
below 15 per cent	41.4	41.4	33.5	40.9	41.1
below 30 per cent	65.8	65.6	59.7	62.5	65.4
Marginal tax rate of head:					
average	35.6	37.4	37.6	36.5	39.7
per cent in excess of 60 per cent	1.9	1.6	1.5	1.9	1.8
Marginal tax rate of wife:					
average	27.5	27.7	33.5	24.9	28.9

See notes to Tables 14.4 and 14.6.

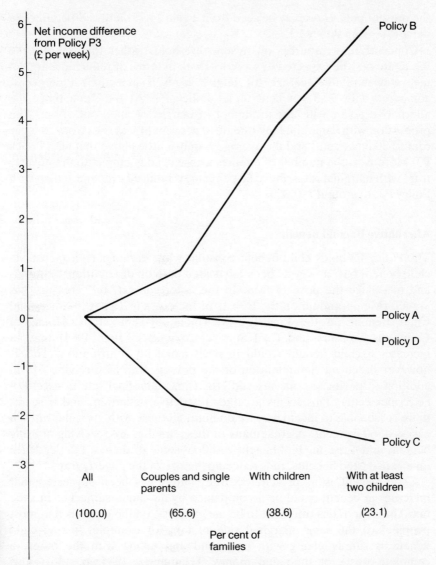

Figure 14.4 Average incomes of different family types

where the differences are those from Policy P3. Differences of less than 10 pence a week are not shown and, since the alternative policy A departs by less than this in all cases, the line is shown simply as horizontal (zero). As far as the within-family distribution is concerned, the policy of raising thresholds provides some additional benefit to working wives, via the increased wife's earned income allowance. But this is still not enough to offset the impact of the reduced child benefit: the proportion with a wife's 'share' of less than 30 per cent is 65.6 per cent, compared with 64.1 under the present policy. As may be seen from Table 14.7, there is little effective departure from Policy P3.

Concentrating resources on raising thresholds rather than cutting the basic rate may be expected to score less well in terms of reducing marginal tax rates, and the average for family heads is indeed 37.4 per cent, compared with 36.5 per cent under Policy P3. At the same time, the alternative policy will take a number of married women out of tax. The proportion with a marginal tax rate of 10 per cent or less rises from 26.3 per cent to 30.3 per cent; and the average is only a little above that with Policy P3. Moreover, the number of families whose head is subject to the poverty trap, with marginal rates above 60 per cent, is reduced even more than with Policy P3, to around 200,000.

Alternative B: child benefit

The Policy P3 holds child benefit constant while earnings rise. *Increasing* child benefit has, however, been advocated both on distributional grounds and to reduce the poverty trap. In the latter context, the Treasury has argued (Memorandum on the Effects of Increases in Tax Allowances and Child Benefit on the Poverty and Unemployment Traps, House of Commons Treasury and Civil Service Committee, June 1984) that an increase in child benefit would in itself make no contribution. This is however based on the definition of the poverty trap as receiving FIS in addition to paying income tax and NIC (i.e. a marginal rate in excess of 86.85 per cent). This seems a rather restrictive definition, and it seems more reasonable to include, as we do here, all those with marginal rates in excess of 60 per cent. A great many of these families are receiving housing benefit, and a rise in child benefit will float some of them off dependence on means-tested benefits, thus reducing the size of the poverty trap.

Child benefit is at present tax-free, but it has been suggested that increases in benefit could be accompanied by making it subject to income tax. This proposal is often felt to be meaningless, on the grounds that most people face the same marginal rate of tax: for example, 'taxing child benefit is simply giving with one hand and taking with the other, a complete waste of time and money' (Hemming, 1984, p. 186). This criticism both ignores the effect on the distribution within the family and fails to address the question as to whose income the benefit would be for tax purposes. If, in the case of married couples, the benefit were treated as the earned income of the wife, then it is not true that the basic rate of tax would be paid in virtually all cases. Some 40 per cent of wives with children are not in paid work, and a sizeable fraction of those who do work are below the tax threshold.

The alternative policy B considers the effect of using the revenue which under policy A financed a higher tax threshold to raise child benefit, while making this taxable as the earned income of the wife. The level of benefit would be £11.00 (and one-parent benefit would become £6.85). For the basic rate taxpayer, the net value would be £7.70, which would represent an increase of 18 per cent relative to present policy; for those not paying tax, the net gain would be 70 per cent (although this may be offset in part by reduced housing benefit).

The distributional impact in terms of adult equivalent income is such that the shares of the bottom groups are significantly higher than under the present system, and a great deal higher than with Policy P3, as may be seen from Table 14.7. For example, the bottom 40 per cent would receive 25.8 per cent, compared with 25.2 per cent under Policy P3. The policy would also have a major effect on the average income of different family types, in a quite predictable way (see Figure 14.4).

The implications for the distribution of resources within the family depends in part on the administrative arrangements for collecting the tax on child benefit. If the tax is levied on the husband, with the benefit being paid in full to the wife, then a sizeable transfer would take place. The calculations in Table 14.7 assume that this would be the mechanism, and the effect is evidently quite dramatic. The proportion of cases where the wife's 'share' is less than 15 per cent would fall to a third, compared with 41 per cent under Policy P3.

The marginal tax rate faced by family heads would be similar to that under Policy A, with an average of 37.6 per cent, compared with 37.4 per cent. Of particular interest, given the Treasury argument quoted earlier, is the estimate that the number taken out of the poverty trap, defined as marginal rates in excess of 60 per cent, would be close to that under the policy of raising tax thresholds. This is an aspect which needs to be examined more fully with a larger sample, preferably pooling the FES data for several years to augment the number of observations, but there appears to be little to choose between the two policies in this respect.

Where the Policy B has an evident disadvantage is that it would raise the marginal tax rate for wives in paid work. This arises because part of the wife's earned income allowance would in effect be absorbed by the child benefit. Indeed, for families with four or more children the wife would become liable for income tax from the first £ of earnings. Table 14.7 shows that the marginal tax rate on the wife's earnings would rise from an average of 27.5 per cent under Policy P3 to 33.5 per cent.

Alternative C: tax treatment of husband and wife

The taxation of the wife's earnings is one aspect of the general issue of the tax treatment of husband and wife. The wife's earned income allowance, and the option of a separate earnings election for wives, mean that there is a substantial degree of independence. The move to fully independent taxation of earnings would require the abolition of the married man's allowance, and it is this that is considered as Policy C, with the revenue being used to raise the tax threshold. (It is assumed for the purpose of the calculations that investment income would be taxed as at present, although this would need consideration.) It seems quite possible that the abolition of the married man's allowance would lead to pressure to make increased provision for those caring for adult dependants, and this aspect would need to be considered.

This policy means that both husband and wife would have a (non-transferable) tax allowance of £2,955, which would represent an increase of some 30 per cent over the single allowance under Policy A. Such a policy would have a distinct tilt against couples (and single-parent families), and this is shown in Figure 14.4. Interestingly, the overall distribution in terms of adult equivalent income is quite close to that with Policy A (see Table 14.7); and the share of family income is shifted slightly in the favour of the wife.

Changes in the tax treatment of the husband and wife are usually discussed in terms of equity, or the financial incentive or penalty to marriage. The effects on marginal tax rates are however quite significant, particularly since separate election will now be advantageous in many more cases. The average tax rate on couples will rise, but for those currently paying higher rates and not choosing separate election (because of the existence of the married man's allowance) the marginal tax rate may fall for both husband and wife. The rate would on average be nearly 1 percentage point lower for family heads, and nearly 3 percentage points lower for wives, than under Policy A. The percentage of wives in paid work with a marginal rate of 10 per cent or less would be 37.4 compared with 30.3 per cent under Policy A.

Alternative D: integration of NIC and income tax

The principle of independent assessment has long been accepted in the case of national insurance contributions (NIC). The increasing convergence of NIC with income tax has however led to proposals that they should be combined. (Here discussion is limited to *employee* contributions.) If they were to be integrated with the present form of income tax, then the consequence would be that contributions would differ according to marital status. This in turn leads to questions about the contribution conditions, which have not always been addressed by those advocating integration. It would presumably not be acceptable to relate benefits to amounts actually paid (which would mean, other things equal, that married men got lower benefits than single men). Under the proposal of integration, it is usually supposed that contribution conditions would be replaced by criteria such as residence, but this would not provide an answer in the case of the state earnings-related pension scheme. These issues are not pursued here, although they are clearly important.

Under Policy D, we consider the effects of integration from the standpoint of contributors, it being assumed that NIC would be replaced by income tax at 39.1 per cent (and the present tax thresholds). The tax would fall on all kinds of income, not just earnings. One of the main arguments for this change is that it would reduce the burden on the lower paid (who at present are liable for 9 per cent on all earnings once they pass the lower threshold) and that it would eliminate the apparently anomalous 'dip' in marginal rates between the NIC upper ceiling and the starting point of higher rates. From Table 14.7, it may be seen that the overall distribution is close to that under Policy B of raising child benefit, although somewhat different groups benefit, as may be seen from Figure 14.4.

The proposal tends to raise marginal rates of tax on two grounds: (i) those in the 'dip' would be paying 39.1 per cent, rather than simply the basic rate of income tax; and (ii) this rate of 39.1 per cent is higher than the combined NIC plus income tax rate (35.5 per cent for those not contracted out) because of the exemption of earnings below the threshold. The average of marginal rates faced by family heads is 4.1 percentage points higher than under Policy 3, although, as may be expected, there is little difference in the poverty trap. For wives, the marginal tax rate is on average higher by 1.3 percentage points.

5   RADICAL DEPARTURES

The changes in policy examined in the previous section would not be minor. The integration of income tax and NIC, for example, would be a significant step. The options would however remain quite close to the structure of the present tax and benefit system. In this section, four more radical departures are considered. In the space available, it is not possible to give an exhaustive analysis, and several aspects of the schemes need further investigation. It should also be noted that, in contrast to section 4, the different policies will not be examined on a revenue neutral basis; the levels of taxation and benefits are those specified by the authors. One of the aims of the analysis is to identify the changes in revenue which would arise as far as the working population is concerned. It should also be noted that the full details of the schemes are not always specified, and that assumptions have had to be made (see the Appendix).

Graduated tax/social insurance

The first of these (Atkinson, 1984) combines raising child benefit (to £17.65) and making it taxable (Policy B), abolishing the married man's allowance (Policy C), and the integration of NIC (Policy D), with the introduction of a graduated income tax structure and a substantial increase in, and extension of, National Insurance benefits. This 'Graduated Tax/ Social Insurance' alternative, referred to for short as GT/SI would involve four ranges of income tax rates, starting at 18 per cent for the first £800 per year and progressing through 33 per cent for the next £2000, and 48 per cent for the next £9200 to 63 per cent. Each adult would have a single, non-transferable, tax allowance of £1,725 per year; and the married man's allowance and wife's earned income allowance would be abolished. Child benefit would be paid to the wife and benefit for the first two children taxed as her income; benefit for third and subsequent children would be tax free. Child benefit and one-parent benefit (£31) would be taken into account (gross) when calculating FIS entitlement. Tax relief for mortgage interest would be reduced to a 15 per cent tax credit.

The effects of the scheme on working families is shown in Table 14.8, which is similar to Table 14.7. One of the main aims of the GT/SI scheme is to improve the benefits paid to those not in the working population, particularly pensioners, those off sick, the unemployed and the disabled. The tax rates have therefore been set to raise additional revenue, and it is estimated that this would be some additional £4.7 billion. The average tax rate for the working population would rise from 25.2 per cent, on unchanged policy, to 28.2 per cent.

The graduated tax structure, and the tapering of benefits by making them taxable, is designed to help those on low incomes, and there would be a substantial rise in the share of the bottom 20 per cent. The Lorenz curve would shift distinctly in the direction of the diagonal. It is also the case that

Table 14.8 Comparison with radical reforms

| | Not equal revenue basis | | | | | |
	P1	P3	GT/SI	BIG	IFS	Minford
Shares in total adult equivalent income of:						
bottom 20 per cent	10.8	10.6	12.2	11.5	11.0	11.0
bottom 40 per cent	25.6	25.2	28.0	27.0	25.3	26.2
bottom 60 per cent	43.8	43.5	46.8	45.7	43.3	44.6
bottom 80 per cent	66.6	66.5	69.4	68.3	66.3	67.4
Marginal tax rate of head:						
average	39.6	37.4	49.9	43.0	40.1	30.2
per cent in excess of						
60 per cent	3.0	1.6	19.7[a]	2.0	11.0	4.2
Marginal tax rate of wife:						
average	30.6	27.7	39.6	40.4	33.1	31.5
Net revenue relative to						
present policy (£ billion)	+£1.44b	−£2.00b	+£4.68b	−£3.15b	+£2.01b	−£12.80b

[a]   2.1 per cent with rates in excess of 63 per cent.
See notes to Tables 14.4 and 14.6.

the wife's share of family income, not shown in
rise: in only 22.3 per cent of couples would it
compared with 41.4 per cent under Policy P3.

The redistribution under the GT/SI scheme is ach.
increased marginal tax rates. The 'average' margin.
heads of tax units would be nearly 50 per cent, compar
under the present policy. Nearly 1 in 5 would face ma.
excess of 60 per cent. These are however predomina.   .n
above-average incomes, and in all but 2.1 per cent of case.   .arginal
rate is the top income tax rate of 63 per cent. The marginal ta.. rate for the
wife would also rise by some 10 percentage points.

Basic income guarantee

The GT/SI scheme would retain the social insurance approach, with
benefits being paid to those in particular circumstances, e.g. retired, sick or
unemployed. The objective of social dividend schemes is to pay benefits
without the need for such conditions. The Basic Income Guarantee, or
BIG, scheme considered here has been designed by Parker (1984) to pay a
basic income to all adults and children regardless of circumstances, with
additions for householders and single parents. All income would be subject
to tax with a single rate replacing the present income tax and NIC, and
higher rates at average earnings and above. The version of the scheme
considered here is the more 'moderate' version 2(c) in Parker (1984),
which has a starting rate of tax of 40 per cent. This version retains tax relief
for pension contributions but not mortgage interest. There would be a
means-tested housing benefit covering rent and rates, and a householder
component, replacing housing rebates. FIS would be abolished.

With the rates of basic income and tax assumed, the BIG scheme would
collect less revenue from the working population than the present policy,
the difference being some £3 billion. If the scheme were to be revenue
neutral for the working population, the tax rate would have to be raised by
some 2 percentage points.

The results in Table 14.8 show that the BIG scheme would provide
considerable benefit to low-income families, and the share of the bottom
20 per cent lies midway between that with assumption P1 and that with the
GT/SI scheme. The BIG scheme is relatively generous to families with
children. Families with two or more children have average net income
which is 150 per cent higher than that of single person tax units, compared
with 129 per cent higher under the present policy (and a similar figure with
the GT/SI scheme).

The BIG scheme means that everyone faces a marginal tax rate of at
least 40 per cent, and it is higher for those paying the higher rates of

, or in receipt of the income-related housing benefit (which ...es a marginal tax rate of 73 per cent). Overall, the marginal tax rate would be some 3 percentage points higher than with present policy. This is a considerably smaller increase than with the GT/SI scheme, although it should be borne in mind that there is a large difference in revenue. For wives, the marginal tax rate would also be at least 40 per cent, reflecting the fact that there is no earned income allowance, and in this case it is higher than for the GT/SI scheme.

IFS scheme

The aim of the GT/SI and BIG schemes is to reduce the extent of means-testing. Moving in the opposite direction is the IFS proposal (Dilnot, Kay and Morris, 1984) to relate child benefit to income, making it a benefit credit, withdrawn at the rate of 50 per cent as income rises. FIS is abolished. The benefit credit is extended to 80 per cent of rent and rates, thus replacing housing rebates, and again this is extinguished at a rate of 50 per cent. NIC is abolished, as is the married man's allowance for income tax, and there would be a basic rate of tax of 34 per cent with a single tax credit against tax liabilities.

Our analysis of the scheme using the FES runs parallel to that carried out by the IFS. Their estimates show an increase in the average net incomes of pensioners, and it might be expected that the overall tax burden on the working population (assuming equal yield at fixed incomes) would increase. Table 14.8 bears this out, showing that there would be a net additional revenue of £2 billion.

Within the working population, there is a redistribution in favour of the lower-income groups, with the share of the bottom 20 per cent being 11.0 per cent, compared with 10.8 per cent under present policy. This assumes that there would be 100 per cent receipt of the benefit credit by those eligible. The overall picture conceals, moreover, substantial differences in the treatment of different families. The average net income of families with two or more children falls from being 129 per cent higher than that of single persons to being 111 per cent higher. The distribution within the family is also likely to be significantly affected, since it is proposed that child benefit credit be paid to the husband through the pay packet.

The average of the marginal tax rates faced by the family head is estimated to be 40.1 per cent, which is below that for the BIG scheme, and well below that for the GT/SI scheme. The fact that it exceeds 34 per cent reflects the substantial number who would be in addition losing 50 per cent in benefit credits. More than 1 in 10 of working families would, according to our estimates, be in the poverty trap; and the proportion would be greater if the taper is extended to recoup overpayments in earlier tax years, which may arise if benefit liability is made cumulative.

Minford scheme

The proposals of Minford (1984) are far-reaching and the analysis here cannot explore all the questions which are raised. Means-testing under his proposals would be extended, not via a child credit or a replacement for housing benefit, but through a negative income tax. Tax thresholds are increased substantially, and all those below the threshold receive a supplement at the rate of 70 per cent. This replaces FIS and housing rebates. Child benefit would be retained. The unit of assessment is taken to be the family, with the separate provisions for wife's earnings being abolished. NIC is abolished, and replaced in our calculations by the 'minimum' provisions for pensions, health, and education.

It is central to Minford's thesis that tax cuts would stimulate output and hence tax revenue. It is not therefore surprising that the revenue calculated assuming fixed gross incomes should be considerably lower than with present policy. Table 14.8 shows that the fall in revenue, on this basis, would be some £13 billion. If, as seems quite possible, stimulating the growth of the economy improves the fiscal stance of the government, then this should evidently be allowed for, but the same consideration applies to the other schemes considered.

The Minford Scheme would, on this basis, make virtually everyone better off, and from Table 14.8 it may be seen that the bottom income groups tend to do rather better, although the extent of redistribution is less than with the BIG and GT/SI schemes. On the assumption that the child benefit continued to be paid to the wife, the intra-family distribution would not be greatly affected, but wives would lose from the abolition of the wife's earned income allowance.

The scheme would reduce the marginal tax rate for most people to 30 per cent, and a quite small proportion would be in the 70 per cent bracket (around 4 per cent). The marginal tax rate faced by wives would however not be reduced.

6   CONCLUDING COMMENTS

In this chapter, we have considered a variety of possible directions in which policy might go in the next ten years. The treatment has necessarily been brief and, particularly in the case of the schemes discussed in section 5, a more extensive comparative analysis is required. The analysis should however be sufficient to indicate some of the choices which have to be made.

In particular, it is clear that the objectives of the government have to be given more careful consideration. We have seen, for example, that the pursuit of Policy P3 would allow the government to reduce the average tax rate, but we need to ask why this goal is pursued – if only because we have identified in section 4 a range of ways in which this could be done, all with the same average tax rate. Does the government want to reduce the basic rate of income tax, as a 'high profile' policy parameter? Does it wish to reduce the tax burden on the average family? Does it wish to reduce the amount taken out of the pay packet? Each of these would have rather different implications. For example, a reduction in the basic rate can be achieved by keeping down the tax threshold: If the thresholds were indexed only in line with prices, not earnings, then the basic rate could be reduced to some 24 per cent by 1994–95. The deductions from the pay packet can be reduced by transferring income from wife to husband, as is brought about by cuts in child benefit.

Cutting taxes may not be an end in itself for the government, but a means to reduce the disincentive effects. This means however that we must examine the source of such disincentives and seek to reduce the tax rates on those people, and on those decisions, which are most sensitive. If the work decisions of family heads are relatively insensitive to taxation, then it may be better to concentrate the reductions in marginal rates on secondary workers. This could, for instance, be achieved by abolishing the married man's income tax allowance and using the revenue to raise the (then common) tax threshold (Policy C). We need also to distinguish between the *distortion* of work decisions and the *reduction* of labour supply. A reduction in tax rates may reduce distortion but cause people to work less.

A policy of restricting benefits relative to earnings would have major distributional consequences. Many of these have not been explored here, since the chapter has focused on the working population, but even within families at work there are important distributional issues. Raising child benefit, under Policy B, has been shown as helping low-income families, but the judgement about such redistribution depends on the view taken about the needs of different family types. Judgements are also necessary about the desirability of redistributing income within the family, an aspect which is not typically incorporated into statistical measures of income distribution.

The concepts of equity and distributional justice need to be further elaborated. We have not considered the role of the individual lifecycle. The distributional impact of the national insurance system as a whole must take into account the lifetime aspects, and the relative treatment of different generations. We must consider ideas of 'fairness' and 'rights'. It may, for example, be that objections to the poverty trap are as much concerned with its 'unfairness' as with any disincentive. The policy towards the treatment of husband and wife for tax and benefit purposes may be significantly influenced by the notion of a 'right' to minimum financial independence which applies as much to individual family members as to the family as a whole.

APPENDIX: SCHEMES ANALYSED IN SECTION 5

BIG scheme

The scheme is based on BIG 2(c) in Parker (1984), where the basic incomes are increased by 15.2 per cent (the increase in supplementary benefit between the November 1981 and November 1983 upratings). The housing benefit householder component and heating allowance are increased by the same percentage. (In the calculation of housing benefit, water rates have not been allowed for.) The higher rates of income tax are assumed to start with 45 per cent at £8,000, with 50 per cent at £16,000, 55 per cent at £24,000, and 60 per cent at £32,000 per year.

IFS scheme

The calculations for this scheme are complicated by the fact that the details in the Appendix to Dilnot, Kay and Morris (1984, pp. 144–51) are not always consistent with those given in the main text of the book. In general, the latter have been taken as authoritative. The levels of the benefit credit are taken directly; the tax credit has been increased in line with the rise in tax allowances in the March 1984 Budget. The benefit credit is applied on a tax unit basis to all those with eligible incomes (assuming 100 per cent receipt). No allowance is made for the extension of the benefit taper to recoup over-payments in an earlier tax year. For the purposes of the higher rate calculations, the tax credit is treated as a tax allowance, and the present higher rate brackets retained.

Minford scheme

The scheme is based on Minford (1984), taking the tax thresholds and health/pension contributions given there. The higher rates of income tax are assumed to be as at present. The wife's earned income allowance, and separate earnings election, are abolished. A negative income tax payment is made where income is below the threshold equal to 70 per cent of the difference (a 100 per cent take-up is assumed). It is not clear whether this would be paid to all those below the threshold or to those who are potentially eligible for FIS or housing rebates. In the calculations, it is assumed that it would be limited to those tax units with children or where the head is a householder. The ceiling for mortgage interest relief of £20,000 is assumed (no figure is given by Minford, but he proposes that it should be gradually reduced). The level of child benefit is taken net of the charges for education and health. FIS and housing rebates would be abolished.

15 · THE ANALYSIS OF PERSONAL TAXATION AND SOCIAL SECURITY

1 INTRODUCTION

Reaction to the Budget is normally focused on the macroeconomic measures announced by the Chancellor. These same measures however have allocational and distributional consequences, at the level of individual families and firms, and about these the Chancellor typically tells us very little.

The March 1983 Budget is a good example. In his Budget Speech, Sir Geoffrey Howe simply told the House of Commons that the proposed increase in personal allowances would benefit a basic rate taxpayer by £2 a week. This figure gave an incomplete and misleading picture of the effects of the Budget. It considered only the increase in tax allowances and took no account of the other changes in income tax, nor in national insurance contributions, indirect taxes and benefits, all of which were announced at the same time. Yet the overall impact of the package of different measures which constitutes the Budget is important and worthy of systematic analysis. How many gainers and losers were there? Who were the main beneficiaries? Who were those for whom the net effect was a loss?

The same applies to proposals for longer-term reform of the tax and benefit system. There has, for example, been interest for some years in the idea of a tax-credit scheme. Yet this has not been subjected to a detailed distributional analysis. The 1972 Green Paper contained only a few illustrative calculations, which took no account of how the scheme was to be financed. There was no attempt to estimate the numbers of families who would gain or lose by significant amounts, nor to characterize who they would be. In the official evidence to the Treasury and Civil Service Sub-Committee in May 1982, the analysis was limited to such statements as 'this would give one-child families a substantial advantage relative to large

With M. A. King and H. Sutherland.

Reprinted from *National Institute Economic Review*, November 1983. [Written in 1983.] The authors would like to acknowledge helpful comments on the first draft of this chapter from the Editorial Board of the *National Institute Economic Review*, B. J. Buckingham of the Department of Employment, R. U. Redpath of the Office of Population Censuses and Surveys, J. Micklewright and N. H. Stern, and to express their thanks to B. Hayes and P. Ramsay for their advice and assistance with the design of computer programs.

families and those without children' (HM Treasury, 1982, p. 233). The extent of such advantage was not documented; nor was any idea given of the numbers of gainers and losers.

These questions are important. The ultimate objective of policy is the welfare of individuals. The impact of policy changes on family resources must therefore be of central concern. The question of who gains, who loses from a change is of more than academic interest. It is for this reason that we have given it priority in the work undertaken by the SSRC Programme on Taxation, Incentives and the Distribution of Income, and in this chapter we describe some of the findings, emphasizing three main features of the research.

First, any analysis must be based on the actual circumstances of a representative sample of families, and not on hypothetical examples. All too often, discussion of policy changes is limited to calculations of the impact on a hypothetical person on average earnings, with two children and whose wife does not work, and who lives in a council house paying average rent and rates. As we show below, such calculations can be highly misleading.

Secondly, we must take into account the responses of families to changes in tax and benefit rates. The figures quoted by the Chancellor are not only incomplete but also reflect only the first-round cash impact of his measures and ignore any responses families may make. Since many policy changes are introduced precisely in order to change behaviour (the 'incentive' effects of taxes) the omission is serious. We illustrate below how behavioural responses may be incorporated into an analysis of the distribution of gains and losses resulting from attempts to increase work incentives.

Thirdly, we attach considerable importance to others being able to reproduce our results and perform calculations of this kind for themselves. For research on taxation to have an impact on policy, it is insufficient that a single group of researchers claims that, for example, 65 per cent of the population would gain from a particular reform. Policy-makers and those engaged in the debate outside government must be able to check the claim for themselves and test other proposed reforms using common methods. Investigating the effects of varying assumptions and policy parameters is part of an educational process which is an essential ingredient in the successful design of a policy package. The computer programs which we have constructed and used to produce the results for this chapter are therefore available to civil servants and other researchers.

2 THE USE OF HYPOTHETICAL FAMILIES IN TAX CALCULATIONS

Most commentators, when considering tax and benefit changes, reach for their pocket calculators and work out the effect of the changes on a series of hypothetical families. At the time of the March 1983 Budget, most of the daily papers published tables showing the changes in income tax at different income levels for single persons, couples where the wife works and couples where the wife does not work (Atkinson, 1983b). These hypothetical families were typically assumed to have no mortgages, and not to belong to an occupational pension scheme. The calculations did not in general allow for national insurance contributions nor child benefit (although these were included by *The Times*) nor for the effects of means-tested benefits. Some newspapers did go further. The *Sunday Times*, drawing on a study by the Institute for Fiscal Studies, took nine households said to 'represent the commonest types', an example being a semi-skilled worker on £129 a week, with one child, whose wife does not work and who lives in a council house. But it is very doubtful whether nine, or even 57, varieties of 'representative' household can provide an adequate picture of the distribution of gains and losses in the population as a whole. The diversity of household circumstances is simply too great.

The potentially misleading nature of hypothetical families is well illustrated by reference to the Tax/Benefit Model tables produced by the DHSS. The results of the model are frequently sought in Parliamentary Questions, and they are exploited for a variety of other purposes, such as the description of the poverty trap given in *Social Trends* (e.g. 1983, chart 5.13). The tables relate to eight different types of family unit (for example, a married couple with two children aged 4 and 6) and are based on a number of other assumptions.[1] Amongst the latter are that the sole source of income is the earnings of the head, that no one else lives with the unit (i.e. that the family unit and the household unit coincide), that the family lives in a council house, pays average rent and rates, and receives no income tax allowances apart from personal allowances.

Because of these assumptions it is clear that there are many ways in which the eight hypothetical families used in the DHSS model fail to capture the circumstances of actual families. If we take a sample of the population, such as the *Family Expenditure Survey* (FES) that we use in our research, then we can see how many are 'covered' by the assumptions made in the DHSS model of hypothetical families. Using data from the 1980 FES for family units headed by a person below the minimum retirement age who was in full-time paid employment, Atkinson and Sutherland (1983a) find that the assumptions about family composition reduce the coverage to 70 per cent (see Table 15.1, line 2), in the sense that 30 per cent of families do not have even approximately the age/size composition of one of the hypothetical types.[2]

The requirement that the head of the unit be a householder reduces the proportion that can be said to be covered to 45 per cent, and excluding units not living in council housing reduces the coverage still further to 13 per cent. If we eliminate from these cases where there are non-dependants

Table 15.1   Families in 1980 *Family Expenditure Survey* 'covered' by
hypothetical family types

	Total family units	Per cent of total FES sample
Total FES sample	5,160	100.0
Covered by hypothetical family types	3,614	70.0
And household head	2,318	44.9
And council tenant	669	13.0
Without non-dependants contributing to rent	497	9.6
No other income in excess of £4 per week	433	8.4
Wife has no income	214	4.1

Source: Atkinson and Sutherland (1983), Table 3.

contributing to the rent, where the wife works, and those with significant unearned income, then the proportion of actual families in the FES accounted for by the hypothetical families in the DHSS model comes down to only 4 per cent (Table 15.1, line 7). Working wives, owner-occupation, and family units who share accommodation are ignored.

The alternative approach is to use a random sample of actual families taken from one of the regular household surveys in this country. This has been our approach, and we are glad to see that it is gaining acceptance (as, for example, in the recent proceedings of the Treasury and Civil Service Committee, 1983).

3   THE USE OF HOUSEHOLD SURVEYS

In seeking data on a sample of actual families to analyse tax and benefit changes, the most appropriate source, because it covers in great detail both incomes and expenditures, is the *Family Expenditure Survey* (FES). Aggregate results of the Survey have been published for many years, but the availability of the data at the level of individual households which has occurred in the last few years – while completely preserving the anonymity of the respondents – has transformed the possibilities for research in this area. Analysis of FES data for individual families has been the main focus of the SSRC research programme.

The FES is carried out on a continuous basis, and normally produces information for some 7,000 households (20,000 people) each year on their income and expenditure. The data can be analysed at the level of the household (all those living together), the family unit (man, wife and dependent children), or the individual. Our concern here is with the family unit, where it should be noted that quite a lot of family units consist of single people. A sizeable number of households contain more than one tax unit, and, conversely, there are a significant proportion of tax units which are not headed by householders (some 25 per cent in the case of the 1980 sample studied below). This fact is often forgotten in calculations which concentrate on householders.

As with all surveys, the FES has a number of shortcomings. First, the sample size, although large in total, is such that the analysis of special groups is often based on a small number of cases. The number of single-parent families in the 1980 FES was 324. If we restrict attention to those where the single parent was in work, then the number falls to under a 100. Caution is therefore necessary in using results for such groups; alternatively, results may be pooled for a number of years.

The second shortcoming of the FES is that there is a substantial degree of non-response. In 1980, the non-response rate was 33 per cent. Even if this were completely random, it would add a further source of sampling variation, and it is one reason why the representation of different groups appears to vary from year to year. (The fluctuating composition of the sample was noted as a problem in the use of the FES in *Economic Trends* (December 1982).) Non-response is not however completely random. Studies by the Office of Population Censuses and Surveys (OPCS) show a systematic tendency for the response rate to fall with the age of the household head and to vary by family type with, for example, households with children having a higher response rate than those without children (see Kemsley, 1975). Building on this work, and that of the Department of Health and Social Security (DHSS), we have attempted to adjust for the differential response by calculating 'grossing-up factors', classified by age and family composition (Atkinson, 1983c). This 'post-sampling stratification' is based on the assumption that, within each family type, non-respondents are similar to respondents, but ensures that the grossed-up totals are in line with the population figures for the numbers in different groups, offsetting both systematic differential non-response and sampling variations.

Non-respondents may be different from respondents not just in family circumstances but also in income, and the third shortcoming of the FES is that it seems to under-represent top-income recipients. A comparison of FES data with those in the *Survey of Personal Incomes* (SPI), based on income tax returns, suggests that the bulk of the distribution is well covered but that there is 'heavy under-representation' of the top 1 per cent (CSO, 1979, p. 11). As an approximate correction for this deficiency, we have increased the grossing-up factor for tax units with incomes at the top (in 1980, above £17,340), based on the SPI.

The fourth problem with the use of the FES is that people may take part in the survey but not fully report their income or expenditure. The understatement of alcohol and tobacco expenditure is well known, although recent research suggests that it may be more a result of differential response to the survey by heavy drinkers and smokers than under-recording by those who do participate (Kemsley, Redpath and Holmes, 1980). In the case of the income data it is often suggested that there is a considerable shortfall in the FES when compared with the national accounts. We have examined this allegation in some depth and have found that much of the discrepancy, notably in the case of occupational pensions, is due to differences in definitions, rather than to under-recording or non-response bias as such. With the exception of self-employment and investment incomes, the FES emerges quite favourably from the comparison (Atkinson and Micklewright, 1983). On the other hand, these two categories do appear to be substantially understated, and in our work on the FES data we have made a proportionate adjustment to the reported income in these categories, taking account of the earlier increase in the representation of the top 1 per cent, with the aim of bringing these more closely into line with the national accounts (Atkinson, 1983c).

These shortcomings of the FES clearly counsel caution in the use of the data. At the same time, their significance should not be exaggerated. The FES compares well with other survey sources. Not only is it carried out by a highly professional survey team, with most exacting standards, but it has been in continuous operation since 1957 and this means that many of the problems of one-off surveys have been overcome.

4 USING THE FES TO ANALYSE TAX AND BENEFIT CHANGES

Statements such as that by *The Times* (16 March 1983) that in the wake of the Budget 'most taxpayers are around £3 to £4 a week better off' can be justified only by examining data for a representative sample of actual families. For this purpose, the FES data described above are the obvious source. Although the *General Household Survey* has a somewhat larger sample, it lacks the expenditure information necessary to treat indirect taxation. There are special studies providing greater detail on particular groups (such as the *Family Finances Survey* of low-income families) but they are not carried out on a continuing basis and are not a random sample of the population as a whole.

Survey data are inevitably out of date. The most recent available to the Chancellor at the time of the 1983 Budget were for 1981. This problem can be handled in one of two ways. One can try to adjust the recorded incomes to allow for changes since the survey date. In some cases this is straightforward. For example, child benefit payments can readily be updated since the statutory amounts are known (although it should be noted that child benefit has consequential effects on the receipt of housing rebates). But for earnings, updating is less easily done, since the appropriate adjustment depends on the timing of pay settlements, to say nothing of variations in overtime hours, bonus payments, etc. Moreover, it is clearly difficult to allow for structural changes, such as the rise in unemployment, where it would be quite inappropriate to simply multiply each observation of an unemployed person by the relevant factor. The alternative is to leave the FES data unadjusted and to convert the policy measures to a 1981 context. This too is unsatisfactory in that it does not allow for subsequent policy changes, a good example being the abolition of the earnings-related supplement to unemployment and sickness benefit.

The choice between these two approaches depends on the purpose of the analysis. If the aim is to examine current policy, such as the Budget, then the first approach must be chosen, with due qualifications being entered about the assumptions necessary in the updating. On the other hand, for the examination of longer-term policy changes the second approach may be preferable, if only because one hopes that the 'medium-term' level of unemployment will be lower than that today. In what follows, our examples are concerned with longer-term changes in taxes and benefits, and we therefore consider their implications *had they been introduced at the time of the survey.* (This differs from the treatment in other chapters.)

The FES contains a great deal of information on incomes and benefits and this is used to calculate the income tax liability and entitlement to means-tested benefits. The calculations allow for income taxation, including the investment income surcharge and the wife's earnings election, national insurance contributions, child benefit, family income supplement (FIS), 'passport' benefits (received when getting FIS), and, in the case of householders, rent and rate rebates. It should be noted that we do not use the information on actual amounts recorded for taxes paid and benefits received. The reason for this is that the analysis of a reform has to be based on calculated payments and receipts, and we wish to place both the present system and the alternatives on a comparable basis. At the same time, we must recognize that a new reform may affect the relationship between calculated and actual benefit. This applies particularly to the question of take-up. In contrast to the DHSS Tax/Benefit Model, which assumes that everyone who is eligible for a benefit does in fact claim it, we allow for non-take-up, assigning a probability that a particular benefit is taken up and randomly allocating units to either the take-up or non-take-up category.

5   AN APPLICATION – A TAX CREDIT SCHEME AND FAMILIES IN WORK

Earlier reference was made to proposals for a tax-credit scheme, and to illustrate the application of the analysis we take a scheme of this type based on the work of Vince (1983) on behalf of the Liberal Party's Taxation and Social Security Panel. We do not follow the scheme in all details, but have taken over nearly all the main features. These include:

1. replacement of national insurance benefits, FIS, passport benefits, child benefit, rent and rate rebates, and supplementary benefit by personal credits, payable to all, with different rates for adults, young people, and children;
2. payment of higher credits for non-earners, including all those over the age of 65, and certain other groups;
3. abolition of all personal allowances for income tax, with all income being taxed from the first £ at a constant basic rate, the higher rate structure being retained, but national insurance contributions being abolished;
4. for householders, a low-income credit, related to family size and income; and
5. a further low-income credit, withdrawn at a rate of 40 per cent as income rises. The details of the credits are shown in Table 15.2.

The tax rate required to finance such a tax credit scheme is not easily estimated. Vince (1983, p. 40) calculates, using the national accounts figures for household income, that a rate of 44 per cent would be necessary for revenue-neutrality. At the same time, he recognizes that this assumes that there is no evasion, that the calculation excludes the cost of the low-income credits, and that no allowance has been made for any administrative savings. To these considerations, we would add the fact that the calculation of the tax revenues to be replaced does not take account of

Table 15.2 Details of tax credit scheme

	£ per week	
	1980 rate	1982/3 rate
Personal credit: everyone aged 18–64	15.10	20.85
Young person's credit: aged 16–17	11.50	15.80
Child credit: aged −15	6.40	10.00
Non-earners' credit: all aged 65 or over, and sick, disabled and unemployed[a]	30.43	45.47
Impaired ability to earn credit: those with disability in work[a]	27.51	30.31–45.47
Higher rate child credit: single parents or disabled parents	11.50	15.80
Widow's credit[a]	16.70	23.00
Householder's low-income credit:		
single	5.425	7.50[b]
married or single parent	9.775	15.00[b]
Low-income credit	15.33–0.4 × income	24.62–0.4 × income

[a] In place of personal credit.
[b] Plus £4.00 (£2.90) 1980 rate per child; reduced if income below £30.00 (£21.70) at rate of 25 per cent single, 30 per cent otherwise, or if income above £61.55 (£38.33) at rate of 40 per cent.

Advanced Corporation Tax; and, more generally, that the relationship between the tax base calculated from the national accounts and that recorded in tax returns needs more careful examination (see Chapter 16). In particular, it seems likely that the feasibility of a tax rate around 44 per cent depends on the widening of the tax base through the elimination of existing deductions. In view of this, we have made the main calculations on the basis of a 44 per cent tax rate but assuming that tax reliefs, apart from that for mortgage interest, and capital allowance/stock relief for the self-employed, would be abolished. We have also shown the implications of raising the basic rate to 46 per cent, as suggested by Vince (p. 41) as necessary to finance the low-income credit.

The introduction of the tax-credit is likely to have substantial distributional consequences. Since one of the aims is to provide more effective income support to those on low incomes, such redistribution is inevitable with a scheme that is revenue-neutral in cash terms. Yet the discussion of the distribution of gains and losses has been limited to hypothetical calculations. No attempt has been made to assess the pattern of gains and losses for an actual sample of the population. This is important, since one of the features of the hypothetical calculations is that they tend to show a majority of gainers from the reform – to a degree that scarcely seems consistent with revenue-neutrality. This aspect has puzzled commentators for a long time. To quote Sir John Hicks' remarks about the earlier Liberal Party scheme of the 1940s: 'It does seem very extraordinary that there are so many pluses in the last column and so few minuses' (Royal Commission on Taxation, 1951, Minutes of Evidence, Third Day, Question 444). In what follows we present the results of our analysis of the distributional effects of the tax-credit scheme described above.[3] For this purpose, we use the FES for 1980, and the parameters of the scheme taken for that year are shown in Table 15.2. In the limited space available in the present chapter, we concentrate on those tax units where the head (whether male or female) was in full-time paid employment. This gives only a partial picture of the effect of the schemes, in that it excludes those families where the head was retired, sick, unemployed or self-employed, but it covers a major part of the population.

The results shown in Tables 15.3–5 are based on calculations for 3,535 tax units in the 1980 FES sample,[4] where we have used the grossing-up factors described earlier. In view of the fact that we are considering only those in work there is no reason to expect that the scheme would be revenue-neutral for the particular sample in question. Table 15.3 shows first the overall distribution of net gains and losses. This brings out the substantial redistribution that would be involved: fewer than 2 million out of 14.7 million families would receive within £1 of their present net weekly income.

One in five would gain £5 or more a week, and a rather larger proportion

Table 15.3 Distribution of gains and losses of net income[a] from tax credit scheme

Numbers in thousands

	Lose:			Lose or gain less than £1	Gain:		
	£15–	£5–£14	£1–£4		£1–£4	£5–£14	£15–
All families							
Number	1,414	3,073	2,816	1,791	2,721	2,622	295
%	*9.6*	*20.9*	*19.1*	*12.2*	*18.5*	*17.8*	*2.0*
Income in relation to SB scale[b]							
Below 160%	9	8	28	7	23	419	235
160–249%	0	53	300	352	875	1,823	49
250–399%	129	1,365	1,519	1,213	1,811	380	11
400% and above	1,276	1,647	970	218	12	0	0
Tenure							
Tenants:							
Number	218	1,168	1,404	941	1,280	1,122	117
%	*3.5*	*18.7*	*22.5*	*15.1*	*20.5*	*17.9*	*1.9*
Owner-occupiers:							
Number	1,196	1,905	1,412	850	1,442	1,500	178
%	*14.1*	*22.5*	*16.6*	*10.0*	*17.0*	*17.7*	*2.1*
Family type							
Single persons without children:							
Number	124	862	1,449	1,137	1,619	358	9
%	*2.2*	*15.5*	*26.1*	*20.5*	*29.1*	*6.4*	*0.2*
Single-parent families:[c]							
Number	4	85	112	19	50	46	12
%	*1.2*	*25.9*	*34.1*	*5.9*	*15.3*	*14.1*	*3.5*
Couples without children:							
Number	812	1,354	627	208	299	482	17
%	*21.4*	*35.7*	*16.5*	*5.5*	*7.9*	*12.7*	*0.4*
Couples with children:							
Number	474	772	628	427	754	1,737	258
%	*9.4*	*15.3*	*12.4*	*8.5*	*14.9*	*34.4*	*5.1*

[a] Net income is defined to include all earnings, self-employment income, investment income, private transfer income, child benefit, FIS, passport benefits, rate and rent rebates, net of income tax and national insurance contributions.
[b] Income in relation to SB scale is defined as net income minus housing costs divided by the short-term SB scale including passport benefits.
[c] In view of the small numbers in this category, the results should be treated with caution.

(30 per cent) would lose £5 or more a week. One in ten families would lose £15 or more a week; and 4 per cent of families would lose £25 or more.

The lower part of Table 15.3 shows the distribution of gains and losses against sub-groups of the population. First, families are classified according to their net income in relation to the SB scale, from which it appears that those with low incomes are predominantly gainers from the scheme and that there are no large gains in the top income group. The second classification is by housing tenure. The tax credit scheme we are examining abolishes rent rebates but leaves the present deductibility of mortgage interest. Other things equal, tenants may, therefore, gain less than owner-occupiers. On the other hand, since tenants tend to have rather lower incomes than owner-occupiers, we would expect them to be disproportionately represented amongst the gainers. In fact it may be seen from Table 15.3 that the percentage gaining £5 or more is identical for the two groups. The main difference is that a smaller proportion of tenants are in the group losing £5 or more: 22.2 per cent against 36.6 per cent for owner-occupiers. Finally, we show the breakdown by family type. This brings out the benefit provided to couples with children: four out of ten gain £5 or more a week. In contrast, more than half couples without children lose £5 or more. It is interesting to note that the changes are less marked for single persons: three-quarters are in the range ± £5. It may also be noted that 61 per cent of single-parent families lose £1 or more a week; the numbers involved are small, but this aspect of the scheme seems to need further investigation.

So far we have been looking at the distribution of gains and losses by household characteristics, but the reverse process may be just as illuminating. In Table 15.4, we classify families by the size of the change in net income and examine their main characteristics. In this way, we are asking directly – who gains and who loses?, which is the kind of question which comes naturally to politicians. Those with losses in excess of £5 under the tax credit scheme have a distinctly higher level of gross earnings for the head of the tax unit, but it is interesting that no pattern is otherwise evident. On the other hand, there is a steady fall in the earnings of the wife (averaged over all married couples), reflecting both the higher taxation of her earnings, with the abolition of the separate earnings allowance, and the association between her participation in paid work and the presence, and number, of children. Both the proportion married, and the proportion of owner-occupiers, exhibit a U-shaped pattern, whereby they are disproportionately represented at both top and bottom of the scale of gains and losses. The analysis can be taken further by examining the individual features of those families who have large gains or losses. This reveals, for instance, the losses where the wife has retained the right to pay reduced rate national insurance contributions – an aspect which is not considered by the architects of the scheme.

Lastly, we show in Table 15.5 the effect of replacing the 44 per cent tax

Table 15.4 Characteristics of gainers and losers from tax credit scheme

	Earnings of head of family £/week	Proportion married %	Average number of children	Proportion of owner-occupiers %	Earnings of wife[a] £/week
All families	114.69	60.1	0.66	57.6	34.39
Net gain or loss:					
lose £15 or more	230.22	90.9	0.57	84.6	75.28
lose £5 to £14	131.93	69.2	0.43	62.0	55.18
lose £1 to £4	103.07	44.6	0.43	50.1	40.28
gain or lose less than £1	89.93	35.4	0.45	47.5	26.91
gain £1 to £4	80.40	38.7	0.53	53.0	14.40
gain £5 to £14	99.92	84.6	1.30	57.2	3.10
gain £15 or more	90.36	93.0	2.48	60.3	1.80

Source: See notes to Table 15.3.
[a] Averaged over all married couples (whether or not the wife is in paid work).

Table 15.5 Effect of varying basic tax rate on distribution of gains and losses from tax credit scheme   Per cent

	Basic tax rate:	
	44	46
Percentage of families:		
lose £15 or more	9.6	14.1
lose £5 to £14	20.9	27.1
lose £1 to £4	19.1	19.3
gain or lose less than £1	12.2	10.6
gain £1 to £4	18.5	14.1
gain £5 to £14	17.8	13.5
gain £15 or more	2.0	1.4
	100.0	100.0

rate used in Tables 15.3 and 15.4 by a rate of 46 per cent. The effect is quite marked. The proportion losing £5 or more rises from 30.5 per cent to 41.2 per cent, and the proportion gaining £5 or more falls from 19.8 per cent to 14.9 per cent. This suggests that the precise determination of the tax rate required to finance the scheme may be crucial to its distributional impact. In current research, we are examining the likely tax base for a tax credit scheme, and extending the distributional analysis to cover the population as a whole.

In this section, we have taken one particular scheme, which has the merit of having been specified in some detail by Vince (1983), in order to illustrate our approach. It should be stressed that we have not attempted any overall assessment of the strengths and weaknesses of the reform as such. In the development of proposals for reform it is likely in fact that there will be a process of iteration, with analysis of the kind described leading to a revision and fuller specification of certain aspects of the proposals, followed in turn by a more elaborate analysis.

6 MARGINAL TAX RATES AND DECISIONS

The analysis of the tax credit scheme given above is based on the assumption that the behaviour of the family is unchanged. In this respect, it is no different from most discussions of tax reform. Yet, clearly, the incorporation of behavioural responses is important and in this and the succeeding section we discuss some of the issues raised and their relation to our research.

As a first step in this direction, we may consider the effect of tax and benefit changes on the incentive to take various decisions. There has for example been extensive discussion of the poverty and unemployment 'traps' and this was one of the topics which concerned the recent Treasury and Civil Service Committee (1983) investigation into 'The Structure of

Personal Income Taxation and Income Support'. The poverty trap refers to the high marginal tax rates which are levied on increased earnings through the combined effect of income tax plus NIC and of the withdrawal of means-tested benefits. The unemployment trap refers to a situation where income in work is little higher than that out of work: i.e. the so-called 'replacement rate' is close to 100 per cent.

The significance of these 'traps' depends on the number of families which are affected, and here the FES provides a valuable source of information. The data have been used by Atkinson and Micklewright (1981) to calculate replacement rates for the unemployed and by the Institute for Fiscal Studies (Morris, 1983) to calculate replacement rates for the employed. Similarly, the FES provides the basis for the official estimates of the number of families affected by the poverty trap. The most recent suggest that 220,000 families face, at least in theory, marginal tax rates in excess of 50 per cent (Evidence to the Treasury and Civil Service Committee Sub-Committee, 1983, p. 254).

In our own research, we have tried to extend the analysis of the poverty trap using FES data. In particular, the standard calculation is based on the additional taxes which result from the head of the tax unit earning an additional £1, whereas this is not necessarily the only nor the most realistic possibility. The family head may be faced with a discrete work decision, such as whether or not to take a second job, for which the increase in earnings is likely to be significantly more than £1. In the case of married couples, the tax on an additional £1 earnings by the wife may be quite different from that on the husband, because of the tax treatment of married women and the earnings disregard under housing benefits. If the wife is not working, then she may consider going out to work, and again the tax rate may be different, as discussed in Chapter 10.

The difference in marginal tax rates is shown in Table 15.6, where we consider three 'margins' at which decisions may be made in addition to the standard £1 extra for the household head. These results are for the same sample of tax units headed by a person in work which we considered in the previous section.

Our calculations differ from those made by the DHSS in several respects. The official figures are based on the recorded receipt of benefit in the FES and show the 'theoretical' effect of a rise in earnings in that they assume that entitlement would be immediately re-assessed. The difficulty with this approach is that quite a number of those currently in receipt would not in fact be eligible on the basis of their current incomes. This is particularly likely to be the case with FIS, where the benefit is paid for a year on the basis of income for a five-week (or two-month) period. Our own calculations are also 'theoretical' in the sense that they are based on calculated entitlement and on an assumption about take-up (each family is given a probability of 0.5 of receiving FIS and 0.75 of receiving housing

Table 15.6 Tax rates at different margins: actual system and tax credit compared

	Head of unit				+£1 earnings by wife[a]		£25 earnings by wife (not working at present)	
	+£1		+£25					
	Actual	Tax credit[b]	Actual	Tax credit[b]	Actual	Tax credit[b]	Actual	Tax credit[b]
	Percentage of relevant tax units							
Marginal tax rate % on								
0	0.2	0.0	0.0	0.0	15.5	0.0	0.0	0.0
1–19	0.3	0.0	0.0	0.0	4.2	0.0	97.2	0.0
20–29	0.2	0.0	0.1	0.0	0.9	0.0	2.5	0.0
30–39	90.6	0.0	93.6	0.0	72.7	0.0	0.1	0.0
40–49	5.2	89.4	4.3	90.8	4.4	99.3	0.1	95.9
50–74	3.3	5.6	1.8	8.6	0.7	0.6	0.1	3.3
75 and more	0.2	5.0	0.2	0.5	1.6	0.1	0.0	0.8
Total	100.0	100.0	100.0	100.0	100.0	100.0	100.0	100.0

[a] For the first four columns, this is all tax units (14.7 million); for the fifth and sixth column this is all units where the wife is in paid work (5.2 million); for the last two columns it is all units where there is a wife who is potentially in labour force but is not at present (3.1 million).
[b] The basic tax rate for the tax credit scheme is 44 per cent.
[c] The percentages may not add to 100.0 because of rounding.

rebates). But they are based on current income and hence exclude those who would not be eligible if reassessed. A further difference is that our figures exclude the receipt of free school meals or welfare foods on the grounds of income but include the passport benefits received together with FIS, which are widely thought to be a major factor in the poverty trap. Finally, we have included the higher rates of income tax.

The results in the first column of Table 15.6 show the standard marginal tax rate on £1 additional earnings by the head of the household. The great majority (91 per cent) of all tax units face a marginal rate in the range 30–9 per cent, made up of the basic rate plus national insurance contributions (81 per cent of all tax units) or basic rate alone (10 per cent of all units). At the same time, there are some who face higher marginal rates of tax: 3½ per cent face rates of 50 per cent or more, representing some ½ million tax units.[5]

It is this last feature which has given rise to concern about the poverty trap. Its significance should not however be exaggerated. We may note from Table 15.6 that at the other margins the numbers with marginal tax rates in excess of 50 per cent are lower: 286,000 where head earns an additional £25; 119,000 where wife earns an additional £1 and 4,000 where the wife starts work and earns £25. The disincentive may therefore be considerably less for decisions such as whether or not the wife works.[6]

In Table 15.6, we also show the effect of the introduction of the tax credit scheme on marginal rates of tax. Attention has typically been focused on the comparison of the basic rate under the tax credit with the combined basic rate plus national insurance contributions under the present system: e.g. Vince (p. 16) compares the rate of 44 per cent with 38.75 per cent (in 1982/3). But this overlooks two aspects. First, the low income/householder credit introduces an additional element of taxation, raising the marginal rate of tax for these families to 84 per cent. From Table 15.6 it may be seen that some 5 per cent of heads of tax units are affected – or more than 700,000 families. Secondly, the abolition of the earned income allowance for the wife, and of the lower threshold for national insurance contributions (these being incorporated in the income tax), means that the marginal tax rate faced by the wife would be raised in a substantial number of cases. This again is an aspect of the proposals which needs further consideration.

7 THE INCENTIVE EFFECTS OF TAXES:
REVENUE AND WELFARE

One of the main arguments underlying the determination of the present government to cut the basic rate of income tax is the belief that this will improve incentives and lead people to work harder. How far this belief is warranted is not a question which we consider here (although as part of the SSRC Programme we are studying the relation between taxation and both hours of work and participation – for example, Stern (1983)). The issue on which we focus concerns the implications of such changes in behaviour, if they take place, for the analysis of revenue and distributional impact.

Suppose that the Chancellor were to consider cutting the basic rate of income tax from 30 per cent to 25 per cent, while reducing the personal allowances to secure revenue neutrality. According to the Treasury 'Ready Reckoner', in 1980/81 the estimated revenue loss from a 1p cut in tax rate would have been £775 billion, requiring a 5.565 per cent reduction in the personal allowances to maintain revenue neutrality (Treasury Background Notes, May 1980).[7] If these figures are extrapolated to the larger change considered here (which is not strictly legitimate), then a 5 per cent cut requires a 27.8 percentage reduction. We can then calculate the implied 'cash gain or loss' for individual families, where this is the change in net income assuming that there is no change in pre-tax income.

Such calculations of cash gains/losses – the sort of number which would be given newspaper coverage – ignore the change in behaviour which the government hopes to bring about. These have implications at two levels: the calculation of what would in fact be a revenue-neutral reform, and the evaluation of the impact on family welfare.

Let us consider first the effect on family welfare, taking the reform specified above. For a single, non-householder, with no children, not contracted out for National Insurance, the budget constraint, in the range above the tax threshold but below that for higher rates, is:

$$N = (1 - 0.09 - t) E + (M + M_t(1 - t) + tA)$$

where N denotes net income, E earnings, M other non-taxable income, M_t taxable income apart from earnings, t the rate of income tax, and A the level of the personal allowance (no other allowances are taken into account). The cut in the basic rate raises the first term, which goes from 61 per cent of E to 66 per cent, but the second term falls unless M_t is more than 2.39 times A. In Fig. 15.1, we show the case where the second term falls, but the cash gain for a person initially at A is positive; it is measured by the distance CG (i.e. assuming gross income unchanged).

The cash gain is misleading as an indicator of the effect on family welfare. First, it takes no account of the fact that the real value of a family's income depends on the prices it faces and that these have in effect changed because of the new marginal tax rate. Leisure has become more expensive. Second, and working in the opposite direction, the family may change its behaviour to move to a preferred position.

One way of allowing for these effects is to calculate the 'welfare gain' (King, 1983, 1988), which is the change in cash income which would be equivalent to the reform at the pre-reform wage level. In a simple

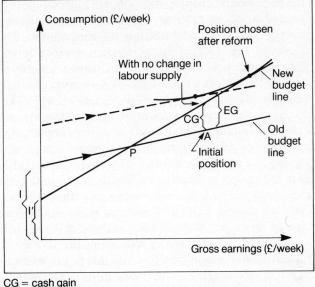

CG = cash gain
EG = equivalent gain

Figure 15.1 Budget constraint and welfare gains for labour supply

model with just labour supply and net income, we can write the family's welfare as a function of the net of tax wage, w, and non-labour income, I (where $I = M + M_t(1 - t) + tA$):

welfare $= v(w,I)$

As tax rates and allowances change, both w and I are affected, and we have a new level of welfare (allowing for any change in behaviour):

$$v(w',I')$$

where the primes denote the new situation. The calculation of the welfare gain, EG, is then defined by:

$$v(w,I + EG) = v(w',I')$$

We are in effect asking how much cash income the family would need at the pre-change net wage in order to be as well off as with the tax change, its 'equivalent income'. (The use of the pre-change wage as the reference point is of course arbitrary, but it seems a quite natural – and easily explained – choice.) This is shown in Fig. 15.1, where EG is the distance between the old budget line and the dashed line which has the same slope but is tangent to the indifference curve passing through the point chosen after the reform.[8]

To this point, we have been considering a specified reform package, but the reform which is possible, under the constraint of revenue-neutrality, depends on the behavioural change. If people are induced to work harder, or if income is redistributed to those with a high propensity to purchase taxed goods, then the required reduction in the allowance would be smaller. In terms of Fig. 15.1, if the point chosen lies below a 45° line through A, then revenue paid by this family in income tax would be higher.

As part of the SSRC Programme, we have constructed (King, 1983, and King and Ramsay, 1983) a computer package, TRAP (Tax Reform Analysis Package), which takes account of both of these aspects – the revenue calculations and the evaluation of the welfare impact. It calculates for a sample of families a tax reform which is revenue-neutral allowing for behavioural change, and the distribution of welfare gains and losses, by decile groups in the sample, ranked according to their initial welfare level, comparing these with the cash gains and losses as defined above. In order to illustrate this, we show in Table 15.7 the results of such a calculation for the sub-sample of single non-householders without children in FES 1980 (chosen since their budget constraint approximates that in Fig. 15.1), with an assumed linear labour supply function, for which the welfare function $v(w,I)$ is readily obtained (Hausman, 1981, p. 41). The wage elasticity (uncompensated) is taken to be 0.3 and the income coefficient (the effect on work of a rise in other income) -0.1.

In the first column of Table 15.7, we show the cash gains for a reform

Table 15.7 Tax changes and welfare for a sample of single non-householders in 1980 FES[a]

Decile groups (ranked in terms of initial welfare)	Gains and losses in £ per week	
	Cash gain[b]	Welfare gain[c]
1 (lowest)	−2.49	−1.57
2	−1.94	−1.01
3	−1.51	−0.58
4	−1.13	−0.20
5	−0.76	0.18
6	−0.36	0.59
7	0.24	1.20
8	0.91	1.88
9	2.02	3.00
10 (highest)	4.96	5.99
Average	0.00	0.95

[a] The sample consists of those family units which are single non-householders without children in the 1980 FES sample described earlier in the article, excluding cases with low earnings or above the starting point for higher rates of tax. The number of such cases is 881, who represent some 4 million in the population as a whole.

[b] The gain calculated assuming behaviour unchanged and taking the revenue-neutral calculation for the sample based on that assumption.

[c] The gain calculated in terms of equivalent income for a reform which is revenue-neutral for the sample allowing for changes in behaviour.

where the revenue-neutral reduction in the allowance is calculated assuming no change in behaviour. For this sub-sample, this calculation gives a 21 per cent reduction in the allowance. In each case the figure gives the average for the decile group, and it may be seen to range from a loss of £2.49 a week at the bottom to a gain of £4.96 for the top decile. The second column shows the effect of taking account of behavioural changes. The necessary reduction in the allowances is calculated allowing for the change in behaviour and now falls to 14 per cent for this sample. The welfare gain is now nearly £1 on average, with the difference between columns 1 and 2 being close to this for all deciles. There is a marked change in the number of gainers and losers: in column 1, with cash gains, the proportion of gainers is 39 per cent, in column 2 it is 60 per cent. The picture in terms of welfare gains is therefore a more rosy one, but it should be noted that the average gain of £1 a week is a balance of large gains at the top with significant losses for those at the bottom. The reform may therefore be unattractive on distributional grounds.

These illustrative calculations are based on an assumed labour supply function which readers may regard as unrealistic (in particular the sizeable positive effect of wages on labour supply). It is however one of the main purposes of the TRAP computer program that the user's own assumptions about labour supply, or other aspects, can readily be incorporated. It is set up as a do-it-yourself package.

8   DIY TAX ANALYSIS

In the analysis of taxation, as with opinion polls, the way in which the questions are posed may be as important as the answers given by the respondents in determining the conclusions drawn. For this reason, it is extremely important that the methods used to investigate tax and benefit changes should be accessible both to policy-makers in government and to those involved in the debate outside government.

The first requirement is that the methods used in making the calculations should be explicit so that other researchers are able to reproduce the results from the underlying data. In the papers which lie behind the research described here, we have tried to give as complete an account as possible of the adjustments made to the FES Base Tapes, with reference to the variables defined there (the data are available on request from the SSRC Data Archive at the University of Essex).

But accessibility means more than explaining the methods used. The policy-maker needs to be able to build in his own assumptions and to consider the particular policy variations which are his current concern. Even if one is sceptical of the need for Budget secrecy, one must accept that there are occasions on which government departments wish to consider policy options without revealing their interest to outsiders. For this reason, one of the aims of the SSRC programme has been to produce tools which can be used by others to analyse policy reforms. In particular, we have developed a range of computer programs. These include TAXEXP, an interactive program for use on micro-computers which allows the user to calculate the gains and losses from a change in policy for a family with characteristics specified by the user. In our view this has considerable advantages over the DHSS Tax/Benefit Model tables, which are at present widely used by MPs and others. The program is much more flexible than the Model tables in that it allows the user to consider a policy change of his or her choice (e.g. to raise child benefit and finance it by an increase in the basic rate), and to specify a range of relevant characteristics of the family, so that, for instance, working wives or investment income (both excluded in the DHSS Model) can be incorporated at will. Moreover, the program calculates marginal tax rates – allowing for different margins – and draws the budget constraint faced by a family.

A second program TAXMOD (see Chapter 18), calculates the distribution of cash gains and losses from a tax change for a representative sample of households drawn from the FES. This program describes the impact of policy changes for actual as opposed to hypothetical families – one of the main points which we have stressed – and allows the user to experiment with different reforms. It again operates on a microcomputer, which means, for instance, that commentators on the Budget can get an immediate analysis of the consequences of the Chancellor's proposals.

The third suite of programs carries out the TRAP calculations described earlier, computing welfare gains and losses, taking into account behavioural responses for each of a sample of households (the number may be varied by the user). The tax reform, and the form of behavioural responses, are specified by the user. The programs may be operated either on a mainframe computer (TRAP) or on an IBM PC micro-computer (MICROTRAP).

These computer programs have been created to exploit the potential of recent developments in computing hardware and software and are likely to reduce the cost of effective policy analysis. The expense of answering a typical Parliamentary Question may be up to £200. For the cost of a few such questions, one could purchase a micro-computer. More importantly, it is our hope that the availability of these programs will permit a wider and better informed discussion of future tax and benefit changes than has occurred in the past.

9   CONCLUSIONS

In this chapter we have described how the analysis of changes in personal taxation and social security can be taken beyond simple statements of the kind 'the basic rate taxpayer would benefit by £2 a week'. The main points may be summarized as follows:

1. The overall distribution of gains and losses resulting from tax and benefit reforms can be assessed adequately only by looking at a representative sample of families, such as that provided regularly by the *Family Expenditure Survey*.
2. In considering the implications for family behaviour, one needs to examine the tax rates at different margins faced by the family. The marginal tax rate on additional earnings by the wife may be substantially different from that on additional earnings by the husband, and it may be quite differently affected by proposed reforms.
3. The behavioural responses of families are important, including the effects on revenue and the evaluation of their welfare consequences.
4. It is essential that the methods used in the analysis should be fully explicit, and the availability of micro-computer programs of the kind produced by the SSRC Programme is intended to encourage better informed debate about these important issues.

NOTES

1. The term 'family unit' is in general applied to a single person or couple, and any dependent children. It is used here synonymously with 'tax unit'.
2. It would be absurd to require that family composition coincide exactly in that the ages of the children be identical to those assumed. All that we have required is that ages fall in any one of the following ranges: 0–4, 5–15, 16–17. (The ranges were chosen on the basis of their entitlement to free welfare milk and free school meals.) In other words, an actual family with children of 2 and 12 would be regarded as 'covered' by the hypothetical case which assumed children of ages 4 and 6.
3. As noted above, we have not followed the scheme in every respect, and in some cases the details (e.g. of the low income credit) are hard to interpret. For a more extensive description see Atkinson and Sutherland (1984b).
4. Those included are tax units where the head is employed, paid in the last pay period, under retirement age, not a married woman, and working sufficient hours to be eligible to receive FIS. Excluded are those interviewed before the start of the 1980/81 tax year (26.7 per cent of the total), so that the same tax parameters apply to all tax units, and those units where the head is in transition between employment states (58 cases).
5. There are a number of reasons why this estimate differs from those in Chapter 10 and Atkinson and Sutherland (1983b), including the fact that the present figures allow for non-take-up of means-tested benefits.
6. It may be noted that there are 1.6 per cent of cases where the marginal tax rate on £1 additional earnings by the wife exceeds 75 per cent. This is in all cases due to the fact that £1 takes them across the lower threshold for national insurance contributions.
7. Full year effect, assuming the same percentage change in age allowance. The comparable figure for 1983/4 derived from Table 5.5 of the *Autumn Statement* (November 1982) is a reduction of 5.73 per cent in allowances.

8. As shown, *EG* is greater than the cash gain, but this is not necessarily the case, as may be seen by varying the shape of the indifference curve in Fig. 15.1. The reason is that the two effects (that associated with the substitution term and the fact that the marginal utility of income changes with the net wage rate) work in opposite directions. If, however, there is a cash loss, as to the left of *P* in Fig. 15.1, then the welfare loss is smaller (the two effects operating in this case in the same direction).

16 · THE COST OF SOCIAL DIVIDEND AND TAX CREDIT SCHEMES

There is renewed interest in social dividend and tax credit schemes as a means of reforming the present income tax and social security systems. Hermione Parker (1982) has proposed a basic income guarantee and Philip Vince (1983) has drawn up plans for a Liberal tax credit scheme (discussed in Chapter 15). Both schemes involve the payment to everyone of a basic income, or credit, the amount being differentiated according to circumstances, and then the taxation of all income. In effect the basic incomes replace both social security benefits and personal tax allowances; and the impact on family incomes depends on the balance between this gain (or loss) and the increased tax, which would be at a single rate over the bulk of incomes.

A crucial issue is, therefore, the rate of tax which would be payable. This depends in turn on the savings on abolished social security benefits, the revenue from the existing income tax and national insurance contributions which would need to be replaced, the cost of the tax reliefs which would be retained and the size of the tax base. Both Parker (1982) and Vince (1983) make estimates of these items, but there are several reasons why a more detailed investigation of the financing of a social dividend scheme seems needed. Most importantly, the estimates of the tax base have been obtained from the national accounts estimates for household income, as published in the Blue Book (*National Income and Expenditure*). These national accounts figures are however rather different from those which enter taxable income as recorded by the Inland Revenue, and one of the main purposes of this chapter is to elucidate the relationship between the two quantities. Other aspects which warrant attention are the treatment of contracting out from the state pension scheme, of tax reliefs, of administrative costs, and of Advance Corporation Tax.

The aim is to examine these aspects of the schemes, taking the benefit

I am grateful to Hermione Parker and Philip Vince for their comments on an earlier version of this paper and for elucidation of the details of their proposals. T. C. Jones of the Central Statistical Office, and M. Haigh and his colleagues at the Inland Revenue, have been most helpful. None of these people is responsible in any way for the conclusions drawn in the chapter. It should be noted that, since this chapter was written, H. Parker has produced revised versions of the Basic Income Guarantee scheme. [Written in 1984.]

side of the equation (the levels of social dividends or credits) as specified by the authors of the proposals. In section 1, the main elements in the calculation are described. Sections 2, 3 and 4 consider the savings on existing benefits, the revenue which would need to be replaced and the cost of tax reliefs retained. Sections 5 and 6 are concerned with the size of the tax base, which is the aspect which raises most questions, and which is therefore discussed in some detail. The final section draws together the different elements and considers the implications for the rate of tax which would be necessary.

1 THE ELEMENTS OF THE CALCULATION

There are five main elements in the calculation of the tax rate necessary to finance the scheme:

  A Cost of social dividends or tax credits.
  B Saving on abolished social security benefits and administrative costs.
  C Revenue raised from income tax and employees' national insurance contributions (NIC) (which are also abolished).
  D Cost of reliefs retained.
  E Tax base.

The calculation of the required basic tax rate is then:

$$t = \frac{A - B + C + D}{E}$$

If the higher rates of income tax, and investment income surcharge, are retained, then the additional revenue should be deducted from the numerator. Conversely, if contracting out for pension purposes is permitted, as with the Vince proposal, then the cost must be added. It should be noted that the calculation is stated in terms which assume that pre-tax incomes and the behaviour of taxpayers would be unaffected by the introduction of the scheme. In the course of the chapter we refer to certain cases where this assumption appears inappropriate and we return to the general point at the end.

In the calculations by Vince for the tax year 1982/3, A = £65.6 billion, and B = £29.7 billion, where the latter allows for the retention of £1 billion worth of existing benefits (1983, p. 54). The revenue raised from income tax and employees' NIC is C = £39.2 billion, where the NIC includes the putative payment if those contracted out had paid in full. Vince then takes the cost of tax allowances retained as D = £5.8 billion, giving a total for $(A - B + C + D)$ of £80.8 billion (rounded), which with a tax base E = £180.9 billion is met by a tax rate of 44 per cent (£79.6 billion) plus £1.2

billion from higher rates and the investment income surcharge. He qualifies the calculation in three respects:

1. A deduction needs to be made from the tax base to allow for evasion ('black economy').
2. No allowance has been made for administrative savings.
3. The cost of the low income credit element of the scheme has not been included.

He suggests (p. 41) that the extra cost could be £3–7 billion.

The Parker calculations are for one tax year earlier (1981/2), and show A = £68.36 billion, B = £31.85 billion,[1] C = £37.42 billion, D = 0, and E = £170.24 billion, so that the required tax rate is:

$$\frac{73.93}{170.24} = 43.43 \text{ per cent}$$

In this calculation, no account has been taken of the revenue from the higher rates of income tax (the investment income surcharge would be abolished), so to this extent the estimate is too high.

In what follows we consider in turn each of the different elements B–E, with the aim of seeing whether a tax rate of 43–4 per cent does indeed seem possible.

2   SAVING ON ABOLISHED SOCIAL SECURITY BENEFITS AND ADMINISTRATIVE COSTS

The estimated savings on social security benefits and administrative costs are made up as follows:

	£ billion	
	Vince 1982/83	Parker 1981/82
Social security (and rent rebates)	30.7	29.48[a]
– Retention of benefits	−1.0	−0.86
Abolition of option mortgage	n/a	0.24
Student awards	n/a	0.65
Free school meals	–	0.10
MSC grants	n/a	1.19
Rate rebates	–	0.35
Costs of administration: income tax	–	0.62
MSC allowances	–	0.08
Total	29.7	31.85

[a] Including costs of administration.
n/a denotes not applicable.

These figures are in large part obtained from the Public Expenditure White Paper. The figure used by Parker for 1981/82, based on the March 1982 White Paper (Cmnd 8494), was the 'estimated out-turn'. According to the

February 1983 White Paper (Cmnd 8789), the actual 1981/82 out-turn was very close. The figure used by Vince for 1982/3 based on the March 1982 White Paper was a planned figure and appears to exclude Northern Ireland; the estimated out-turn according to the February 1983 White Paper was £32.1 billion, including Northern Ireland, making a net saving of £31.1 billion allowing for benefits retained.

In these calculations, there are three aspects which should be discussed. The first two relate to the Parker scheme. First, there is the cost of administration of social security (£1.4 billion in 1981/82)[2] and income tax (£0.6 billion in 1981/82). In taking full credit for this, she is in effect assuming that there would be no remaining administrative costs in the collection of the income tax or in the payment of the social dividend. It seems preferable to take the range with and without this saving, as bracketing the likely actual situation, i.e. £29.85–31.85 billion in 1981/82. Similarly, the Vince figures should be expressed as £31.1–33.3 billion, allowing £2.2 billion for administrative costs.

Secondly, the savings include certain items (student awards, MSC grants, MSC administration) whose abolition does not seem central to the social dividend scheme. Although we follow Parker in including them, their abolition should be seen in the wider context of educational financing.

Thirdly, the Vince calculation makes no allowance for the cost of the state earnings related pension, which would continue. In 1982/83 this is small (£40 million), and we have made no correction, but it would represent a rapidly growing item, of importance in future years.

3 REVENUE FROM INCOME TAX AND NIC

The figures taken by the two authors are:

	£ billion	
	Vince 1982/83	Parker 1981/82
Income tax	30.775	28.21
Advance Corporation Tax (ACT)	not included	2.0
Employees' NIC	8.441	6.81
Self-employed NIC	–	0.38
Voluntary (Class 3) contributions	–	0.02
State scheme premiums	–	not included in calculations

In all cases the figures are estimates: the 1981/82 figures were published in March 1982 and those for 1982/83 in August 1982. More recent figures are £28.7 billion for income tax in 1981/82, £30.5 billion in 1982/83 (*Inland Revenue Statistics 1983*, Table 1.2), and £2.2 billion for ACT in 1982/83 (*Inland Revenue Statistics 1983*, Table 1.1).[3]

There are three issues which need to be resolved. The first concerns

ACT. Since this is in effect income tax deducted at source, it should be included in the costing, as recognized by Parker. It is not, however, included by Vince and this would raise the total by a substantial amount.

The second issue concerns the state earnings-related pension scheme (SERPS) and contracting out of NIC. Under the Parker scheme, SERPS would be abolished, and the treatment of the costs appears correct, with the minor exception that the state scheme premiums should be included (£0.22 billion). At the same time, it should be observed that the abolition would put those at present not contracted out in the same position as those contracted out. The comparison of the effect on net income must therefore take account of the fact that, to finance the equivalent private pension, an additional contribution would be needed. The most straightforward assumption may be that this is equal to the present difference between contracted-in and contracted-out rates.

In the case of the Vince scheme, the state earnings-related pension would be retained (1983, p. 11) and those contracted out would pay a reduced rate (2 per cent lower for employees) on all income (1983, p. 35). In the calculation of NIC, Vince includes the present cost of contracting out (i.e. the putative payments if those contracted out had paid in full). If this equalled the cost of contracting out under his scheme, then the calculation would be correct. Vince himself says that the 2 per cent reduction 'would be equivalent to the 2.5% reduction of the employees' National Insurance contribution at present [1982–83] on the first £220 per week of income' (1983, p. 35). However, it appears that the 2 per cent reduction under the proposed scheme would apply to *all income* received by a person contracted out, earned and unearned. If this is so, then it seems unlikely that the cost would in fact equal that under the present provisions. In what follows, we assume that the size of the deduction would be adjusted to ensure that the cost is no greater. It seems probable that the resulting contracting-out reduction would be less than 2 per cent.

Finally, the Vince calculation refers to the contributions by *employees*, and an addition has to be made for those by the self-employed plus voluntary contributions (although state scheme premiums would presumably continue), which is taken to be £0.4 million.

To sum up, the principle of the Parker calculation is not affected by this analysis, although the revised estimates and the inclusion of state scheme premiums, lead to the rather higher figure of £38.2 billion for 1981/82. On the other hand, to the Vince calculation needs to be added ACT and an allowance for the contribution by the self-employed, which together with the revised estimates gives the figure for 1982/83 of £41.5 billion, rather than £39.2 million.

4   COST OF RELIEFS RETAINED

Under the Parker scheme, all tax reliefs, apart from capital allowances and stock relief, would be abolished, and the only question is whether the government would find it necessary/desirable to compensate any of the losers. Two cases where this seems likely to be the case (for different reasons) are deeds of covenant to charities and the exemption of interest on British government securities where the owner is not ordinarily resident in the UK. In the first case, it is assumed that the government would want to compensate charities for the loss of income. The second case raises the issue of the market reactions to the change in tax status. As noted at the outset, we are assuming that pre-tax incomes are unchanged. The reasonableness of this assumption is discussed at the end of the chapter, but in the case of overseas holders it seems clear that the gross return would have to be adjusted to maintain the attractiveness of British government securities. In order to cover these two items, a sum of £430 million is included (based on *Inland Revenue Statistics 1982*, Table 1.5).

Under the Vince scheme, a number of major reliefs would be retained. These may be divided into two groups. In the first are those reliefs where the total cash cost would be held constant, the relief being provided at source at a rate independent of the income tax rate, as with the present life assurance relief. This is assumed, on the basis of correspondence with Mr Vince, to apply to the relief for pension schemes, self-employment retirement annuities, life assurance premiums, mortgage interest, and the two items noted in the previous paragraph. In the second group are the reliefs which continue to be deductions against taxable income, and which are discussed in the next section. These include foreign earnings and foreign service allowance, interest on National Savings Certificates (and first £70 in NSB), Premium Bond prizes and SAYE, Schedule E work expenses,[4] war widow's pensions, capital allowances and stock relief. The estimated cost of the first group of reliefs under the Vince scheme in 1982/3 is taken from *Inland Revenue Statistics 1983*, Table 1.5:

	£ million
Pension schemes	1,100
Self-employed retirement annuities	390
Life assurance	590
Mortgage interest	2,150
Income of charities, etc.	225
Exemption for non-residents holding British government securities	225
	4,680

5   THE TAX BASE: DIFFERENT CATEGORIES OF INCOME

The estimates by Parker and Vince of the tax base are derived from the *National Income and Expenditure* (Blue Book) table for household income. The elements which made up the total in 1980 and 1981, the years used by Parker and Vince, respectively, are shown in Table 16.1, together with the 1982 figures. Since we are particularly concerned with the relationship between these figures and the present tax base, and since the most recent figures for the latter are for 1978/79, we also show this year (in this case it is the tax year rather than the calendar year).

To arrive at the estimated tax base for 1981/82, Parker increased the 1980 figure by 10½ per cent, giving £174,662 million, and then subtracted £4 billion (+ 10½ per cent) for 'black economy' incomes. To arrive at the tax base for 1982/83, Vince increased the 1981 figure by 7 per cent. These extrapolations of the national accounts figures are, of course, subject to error; and the national accounts figures themselves are typically revised in successive issues of *National Income and Expenditure*. The figure for 1980, for example, in the 1983 edition is some 1.5 per cent below that given in the 1981 edition. It may be noted that the estimate for 1981/82 (taking a ¾:¼ average of the annual figures given in the 1983 edition)[5] is £171.47 billion – or some £3 billion below that predicted by Parker.

Our particular concern is with the relation between the estimated tax base and the income which is actually taxed at present, as recorded in the Inland Revenue *Survey of Personal Incomes* (SPI). The SPI for 1978/79 gives total income of individuals for tax purposes as £106 billion (Table 20). This includes taxable social security benefits, which are excluded from the national accounts given above. If we deduct national insurance pensions,

Table 16.1 Household income from national accounts

	£ million			
	1982	1981	1980	1978/79
Wages and salaries (including HM Forces)	132,971	125,233	118,084	87,754
Income in kind	1,707	1,496	1,496	1,004
Income from self-employment	14,984	13,946	13,860	11,635
Rent, dividends and interest	18,209	15,230	14,123	7,064
Pensions and other benefits from life assurance and superannuation schemes	14,313	13,131	10,502	7,463
Other current transfers	not included	not included	not included	not included
Total	182,184	169,036	158,065	114,920

Sources:
1982: *National Income and Expenditure 1983*, Table 4.4.
1981: *National Income and Expenditure 1982*, Table 4.4.
1980: *National Income and Expenditure 1981*, Table 4.4.
1978/79: *National Income and Expenditure 1981*, p. 117.

which accounted for the great majority of taxable benefits at that time, then the total becomes £101.4 billion, consisting of £96.2 billion earned income and £5.2 billion investment income.[6]

There is therefore a difference of some £13.5 billion between the national accounts estimate and that covered by the SPI. In seeking to explain the difference, it is helpful to consider separately the different categories of income.

Schedule E employment income

National accounts £87,754 million   SPI £84,880 million[7]

+ £1,004 million in kind

The national accounts figure is built up directly from the tax deduction documents returned by employers (a 1 per cent sample of PAYE deduction cards) plus additions for items not covered.[8] There is no reason why it should exactly equal the figure given in the SPI, which is based on a different sample of tax records.[9] There are furthermore the differences in definition, whereby the national accounts figures include employee contributions to pension schemes, an estimate of unrecorded ('black economy') earnings, and untaxed 'income in kind'. Finally, the national accounts exclude work expenses, which would enter the tax base under the Parker scheme.

In order to give an indication of the quantitative significance of these items, we may first note that employee superannuation contributions may be estimated to be some £2,050 million (Blue Book 1981, Table 4.5, taking ¾ of 1978 figure and ¼ of 1979 figure). Second, the national accounts figures include an adjustment for unrecorded earnings. In 1978 it was 1 per cent (Macafee, 1980, p. 85), so that we take £0.89 billion for 1978/9, but it should be noted that the overall 'evasion' adjustment made by the CSO is lower in 1980, 1981 and 1982 than in earlier years (*Economic Trends*, October 1983, p. 78). Adding these two items to the SPI total gives a figure for 1978/9 of £87,820 million (see Table 16.2) which suggests that the large part of income in kind is untaxed (the figure of £940 million is obtained as the difference). Finally, there is the deduction for work expenses. The estimated cost of giving tax relief in 1979/80 was £165 million (*Inland Revenue Statistics*, 1980, Table 1.12), or £510 million if grossed up at 32.4 per cent.[10] A rough estimate of the total work expenses for 1978/9 may therefore be £450 million. This would be added to the tax base in the case of the Parker scheme, but not in the case of that of Vince, where a deduction has also to be made for foreign earnings and foreign service allowance.

In Table 16.2 we also show estimates for the financial years 1981/2 and 1982/3, to which the Parker and Vince calculations relate. These are included in order to fill out the overall picture, but it should be emphasized

Table 16.2 Income from employment in Survey of Personal Incomes (SPI) and Blue Book (£ billion)

	1978/79	1981/2	1982/83
(1) SPI	84.88	121.8	129.6
(2) + employee pension contributions	2.05	3.2	3.4
(3) + allowance for black economy	0.89	2.0	2.1
(4) + non-taxed income in kind	0.94	1.7	1.8
(5) = Blue Book	88.76	128.7	136.9
(6) + work expenses (deducted from the above)	0.45	0.7	0.8

Sources for 1981/82 and 1982/83:
(1) Central Statistical Office (CSO) for 1981/82, extrapolated forward using national accounts.
(2) CSO for 1981/82 and *National Income and Expenditure 1983*, Table 4.5, for 1982/83, where 1982 figure increased to 1982/83 basis.
(3) and (4). CSO for 1981/82, increased proportionately with (5) for 1982/83.
(5) National accounts (*Economic Trends*, October 1983, Table 10).
(6) CSO for 1981/82, based on cost of tax relief for 1982/83 (*Inland Revenue Statistics 1983*, Table 1.5).

that they are based on a number of assumptions and on extrapolation from earlier years.[11] Some items are therefore subject to considerable error.

Self-employment income

National accounts £11,635 million   SPI £7,392 million

Although the Schedule D assessments for income tax are an important element in the construction of the national accounts estimates, they will not necessarily correspond exactly with the SPI,[12] and the Blue Book draws on other sources, notably for farm incomes (based on information supplied by the Ministry of Agriculture, Fisheries and Food), as well as adding in small non-taxable incomes. There are, moreover, important differences between the concept of self-employment income as it appears in the national accounts and that which forms taxable income:

1. Tax liability in general arises on the profits in the accounting year ending in the previous tax year, whereas the national accounts figure refers to currently accruing income. The adjustment for this difference in reference period can be quite substantial: that for 1977/78 is £1,409 million (*National Income and Expenditure, 1980*, p. 113).
2. Capital allowances and stock relief for tax purposes are not the same as capital consumption and stock appreciation used in the national accounts (the treatment of capital allowances is described in Maurice, 1968, p. 385).

The national accounts figures do not, therefore, provide a very satisfactory basis – at least in theory – for the estimation of the tax base. In order to give some idea of the significance in practice of the different elements, we show in the first column of Table 16.3 their estimated magnitude in 1978/79.

Table 16.3 Income from self-employment in SPI and Blue Book (£ billion)

	1978/79	Taxable in 1981/82	1982/83
(1) SPI net income	7.39	10.2	11.0
(2) + small non-taxable income	0.18	0.2	0.3
(3) + capital allowances	1.32	1.9	1.9
(4) + stock relief	0.25	0.4	0.3
(5) + additional farm incomes	0.42	0.5	0.5
(6) + black economy	1.31	2.1	2.2
(7) = Blue Book self-employment income before depreciation and stock appreciation but after deducting interest	10.87	15.3	16.2

Sources for 1981/82 and 1982/83:
(1) and (2). Obtained as residual, divided in same ratio as in 1978/79.
(3) Based on 1980 and 1981 figures in *National Income and Expenditure 1983*, p. 115.
(4) Estimated from cost of tax relief grossed up at a rate of 30 per cent (*Inland Revenue Statistics 1982*, Table 1.5, and *1983*, Table 1.5).
(5) and (6). CSO for 1982/83 and adjusted proportionately with national accounts figure for 1981/82.
(7) CSO for 1982/83 and *National Income and Expenditure 1983*, Tables 4.3 and 4.4 for 1981/82.

First, we add in £183 million of small self-employment income, not at present liable for tax.[13] Second, we add back capital allowances of £1.32 billion (based on *Inland Revenue Statistics 1982*, Table 2.9) and estimated stock relief of £0.25 billion (based on figure for 1978/79 given in *Inland Revenue Statistics 1982*, Table 2.8, netting out the amount recovered). In line (5) is added the difference between the SPI estimate of farm incomes and that calculated by the Ministry of Agriculture, Fisheries and Food, which was estimated at £389 million for 1977/78 (*National Income and Expenditure*, 1980, p. 113), and is taken here to be £420 million for 1978/79. The sum of items (1)–(5) is £9.26 billion. If we assume that the income taxable in 1978/79 corresponds to that arising in 1977, then we can make a comparison with the Blue Book figure for that year.[14] The income from self-employment before providing for depreciation and stock appreciation is £11.51 billion (*National Income and Expenditure 1983*, Table 4.3), for which we have to deduct £0.64 billion interest paid by the self-employed (obtained from Tables 4.3 and 4.4). The difference between £10.87 billion and £9.26 billion is assumed to be unrecorded ('black economy') income, so line (6) is obtained as a residual.

In the second and third columns of Table 16.3, we show the estimates of the different items for 1981/82 and 1982/83. The qualifications made in the case of employment income apply with equal, or greater, force here.

Occupational pensions, etc.

National accounts £7,463 million   SPI £3,410 million
The national accounts figure is built up in the same way as that for employ-

Table 16.4 Occupational pensions and other transfers in SPI and Blue Book
(£ billion)

	1978/79	1981/82	1982/83
(1) SPI	3.41	5.5	6.1
(2) + small non-taxable	0.37	0.6	0.7
(3) + other items	3.68	7.0	7.8
(4) = Blue Book	7.46	13.1	14.6
(5) + other transfers	0.30	0.5	0.6

Sources for 1981/82 and 1982/83:
(1) 1981/82 from CSO, 1982/83 extrapolated in line with Blue Book.
(2) Extrapolated in line with item (1).
(3) Obtained as a residual.
(4) From National Income and Expenditure 1983, Table 4.4, taking 1981/82 as an average (¾:¼) of 1981 and 1982, and 1982/83 as 1982 increased by 2 per cent (to allow approximately for growth in personal incomes 1982^I–1983^I). It should be noted that the 1982 figure used in this calculation differs from that given in Table 16.1, because of revisions to the national accounts.
(5) Extrapolated in line with item (4).

ment income, and the same considerations apply.[15] There is however a much larger proportionate difference to be explained, which is accounted for to only a minor degree by small occupational pensions received by those not covered in the SPI. In line (2) of Table 16.4, we have included £366 million to cover this, based on 40 per cent of the £916 million total referred to earlier. The major part of the difference (line (3) in Table 16.4) arises because the national accounts figure includes a number of items in addition to occupational pensions: lump-sum payments under pension schemes on retirement or death, redundancy payments, the refund of contributions, sums payable on the maturity of life assurance policies, and annuity income. Although certain of these items may, in part, be subject to tax, the amounts are unknown. We have also included (line (5)) estimates of other current transfers which would continue under the social dividend scheme. These include transfers from overseas (e.g. a pension from an overseas government) and from non-profit-making bodies (e.g. trade union pensions or payments by friendly societies). The sum involved is not likely to be large: Jones (1981, Table G) shows current transfers from private non-profit bodies to the household sector of £392 million in 1980. We take a figure of £300 million for 1978/79. It is assumed that the state benefits continuing under the Vince scheme are not taxable.

Again we show estimates for 1981/82 and 1982/83 based on extrapolation.

Rent, dividends and interest

National accounts £7,064 million   SPI £5,210 million
The national accounts estimate is obtained independently, being a residual figure reached after the receipts of other sectors are deducted from total payments. There is therefore no necessary reason why the figures should

Table 16.5 Rent, dividends and interest in SPI and Blue Book (£ billion)

	1978/79	1981/82	1982/83
(1) SPI	5.21	10.9	11.3
(2) + trust income	0.55	1.3	1.5
(3) + untaxed interest	0.25	0.6	0.7
(4) + other differences	1.05	3.2	4.7
(5) = Blue Book	7.06	16.0	18.2

Sources for 1981/82 and 1982/83:
(1) Figure for 1980/81 from Inland Revenue increased by the change in the Blue Book figure for 1979 to 1980 and 1981: i.e. allowing for an average 15-month lag.
(2) and (3). Increased proportionately with Blue Book figure.
(4). Obtained as a residual.
(5) From *National Income and Expenditure 1983*, Table 4.4, 1982 figure extrapolated to 1982/83.

coincide. There is the further factor that certain types of interest are taxed on a previous-year basis.

It is difficult to provide a full reconciliation of the two estimates. The analysis by the CSO of the reasons for the differences beween the national accounts and SPI figures refers to (i) undistributed income of private trusts, (ii) untaxed interest income (co-operative dividends, SAYE, premium bond prizes, the tax-free element of National Savings Bank and other interest, and accrued interest on National Savings Certificates), and (iii) 'other differences' (*National Income and Expenditure, 1980*, p. 113). The last of these includes an allowance for the fact that dividends may not be reported on the tax returns, tax having already been paid at source and there being no loss of revenue in the case of basic rate tax payers, and the reference period adjustment. The amounts in 1977/8 were estimated to be £325 million, £145 million, and £632 million, respectively, making a total of £1,302 million. In Table 16.5, these figures have been extrapolated proportionately to give £550 million, £250 million and £1,054 million for 1978/9.[16]

6 THE TAX BASE IN TOTAL

The present tax base consists in effect of the SPI employment income, the SPI net income (line (1) in Table 16.3), the SPI occupational pensions plus an unknown element of 'other items' (line (3) in Table 16.4), plus SPI rent, dividends and interest, plus an unknown amount of 'other differences' (line (4) in Table 16.5). As we have seen, there are a number of reasons why this differs from the Blue Book concept of household income; and it does not seem that the latter provides a satisfactory basis for estimating the size of the tax base under a social dividend or tax credit scheme. In view of the differences in principle and in practice, it seems preferable to work 'constructively' from the existing tax base, considering the way in which it would be extended.

Table 16.6 Potential tax base (£ billion)

	1978/79	1981/82	1982/83
Present tax base			
(1) SPI employment income (2/1)	84.88	121.8	129.6
(2) + SPI self-employment income (3/1)	7.39	10.2	11.0
(3) + SPI occupational pensions (4/1)	3.41	5.5	6.1
(4) + SPI rent, dividends and interest (5/1)	5.21	10.9	11.3
(5) present tax base: lower bound	100.89	148.4	158.0
(6) + half ('other items' + 'other differences') (4/3 and 5/4)	2.37	5.1	6.3
(7) present tax base: upper bound	103.26	153.5	164.3
Parker tax base line 5			
(8) + work expenses (2/6)	0.45	0.7	0.8
(9) + small non-taxable self-employment income (3/2)	0.18	0.2	0.3
(10) + small non-taxable pensions (4/2)	0.37	0.6	0.7
(11) + other transfers (4/5)	0.30	0.5	0.6
(12) + untaxed interest (5/3)	0.25	0.6	0.7
(13) = Parker tax base: lower bound	102.44	151.0	161.1
(14) + line (6)	2.37	5.1	6.3
(15) + half employee contributions (2/2)	1.03	1.6	1.7
(16) = Parker tax base: upper bound	105.84	157.7	169.1
Vince tax base line 5			
(17) − deduction for foreign earnings/ service allowance	−0.40	−0.5	−0.6
(18) + small non-taxable self-employment income (3/2)	0.18	0.2	0.3
(19) + small non-taxable pensions (4/2)	0.37	0.6	0.7
(20) + other transfers (4/5)	0.30	0.5	0.6
(21) = Vince tax base: lower bound	101.34	149.2	159.0
(22) + line (6)	2.37	5.1	6.3
(23) + half employee contributions (2/2)	1.03	1.6	1.7
(24) = Vince tax base: upper bound	104.74	155.9	167.0

Note: (x/y) alongside entries indicates that they are taken from line y of Table 16.x.

In Table 16.6, we present the main elements of this 'constructive' approach. The top part of the table shows the existing tax base, with two alternative assumptions about the unknown items. The lower bound assumes that none is taxable; the upper bound assumes half of 'other items' and 'other differences' are taxable. A proportion of a half is arbitrary as an upper bound, but there are clearly a number of substantial items (e.g. redundancy payments) which are exempt.

Under the Parker scheme, the tax base would be extended in a number of ways. It is not however clear that all of these would lead to additional revenue on the scale indicated by the present magnitude of the different items. There are certain areas where changes in behaviour seem inevitable.

In particular, the extension of the tax base to include employee pension contributions is likely to lead to a switch to non-contributory schemes. As is argued by Hemming:

> there is no Inland Revenue requirement that employees contribute [to contracted-out schemes] only employers *must* contribute. The most likely outcome is that most schemes would become non-contributory. Employers would make what were previously employees' contributions.
>
> (1983, p. 167)

In view of this, we show a range from zero to half of the amount being included under this heading. The other items are included in full, but this may, for the same reason, overstate their contribution to the tax base. These items are work expenses, which would no longer be allowed, small self-employment incomes and occupational pensions, interest at present tax free, and other transfers (see lines (8)–(12) of Table 16.6).

The tax base under the Vince scheme would differ in that work expenses would continue to be allowed, as would the deduction for foreign earnings/service allowance, and the interest exemptions would remain. The amount for foreign earnings, etc. is estimated from the cost of the tax relief grossed up assuming an average rate of 33⅓ per cent (*Inland Revenue Statistics*, 1982, Table 1.5, 1983, Table 1.5, and 1978/79 based on 1979/80 for 1980, Table 1.12). The treatment of pension contributions is different under the Vince scheme, in that he would retain a subsidy equal in cost to that of the present tax relief. It still however appears that there would be an incentive for all contributions to be paid by employers (since otherwise they would be taxed at 44 per cent or higher). We therefore make the same assumption in line (23) of Table 16.6 as with the Parker scheme (at the same time halving the cost of the relief retained).

How does the resulting tax base compare with that estimated on a national accounts basis? In the case of the Parker scheme, in 1978/79 terms she effectively takes a tax base of £114.92 billion (from Table 16.1) less £2.87 billion for the black economy.[17] It may be noted that the latter is not dissimilar to the £2.2 billion allowed in our calculations (line (3) in Table 16.2 + line (6) in Table 16.3). The resulting figure of £112.05 may be compared with the 'lower bound' of £102.44 billion in Table 16.6 and the 'upper bound' of £105.84 billion. This suggests that her calculations over-state the tax base by between 5.9 and 9.4 per cent. The reasons for the difference in 1978/79 are set out in detail in Table 16.7, the most important elements being employee contributions, the adjustment to self-employment incomes, and the other items paid out by life assurance and pension schemes.

In Table 16.6, the tax base is also calculated for the year used by Parker (1981/2), although the figures need to be reviewed with caution since they are based on less complete information. The resulting tax base lies between

Table 16.7   Reconciliation of 'constructive' and national
accounts-based estimate for 1978/79
(£ billion)

(1) National accounts (Table 16.1)	114.92
(2) − Black economy	−2.87
(3) = National accounts estimate	112.05
(4) + other transfers (4/5)	0.03
(5) + excess of black economy allowance (2.87–2.20)	0.67
(6) − employee pension contributions (2/2)	−2.05
(7) − non-taxed income in kind (2/4)	−0.94
(8) + work expenses (2/6)	0.45
(9) − reference period adjustment/difference in stock relief/capital allowances (from Table 3)	−2.33
(10) − additional farm incomes (3/5)	−0.42
(11) − other items (pension and life assurance) (4/3)	−3.68
(12) − trust income (5/2)	−0.55
(13) − other differences (interest income) (5/4)	−1.05
(14) = 'Constructive' estimate: lower bound	102.45

Note: (x/y) alongside entries denotes that they are taken from line
y of Table 16.x.

£151.0 billion and £157.7 billion, which suggest that Parker's calculations
of £170.24 billion are too high by between 8.0 and 12.7 per cent in that
year.

In the case of the Vince scheme, he suggests (letter to the author) that
the black economy should be taken into account by adding 2 per cent to the
tax rate, which is equivalent with a rate of 44 per cent to reducing the tax
base by 4½ per cent. Applied to the 1978/79 figures, his approach would
yield a tax base of £110 billion. Compared with our estimates of £101.34
billion–104.74 billion, this suggests that he is overstating the tax base by
between 5 and 8½ per cent. Put another way, a tax rate of 44 per cent
would need to be raised to between 48 and 50 per cent, not 46 per cent, if
our constructive calculation for 1978/79 is correct.

7   CONCLUSIONS

The results of our investigation may be summarized in terms of the
elements *B–E*, where we show in each case our estimates (rounded to £0.1
billion), in a number of cases in the form of a range, and in brackets the
original figures, together with a brief explanation of the reasons for the
divergence:

	£ billion	
	Parker 1981/82	Vince 1982/83
B Saving (Section 2)	29.9–31.9 (31.9) With and without admin. costs	31.1–33.3 (29.7) Revised estimates. Northern Ireland. With and without admin. costs
C Revenue to be replaced (Section 3)	38.2 (37.4) Revised estimates and state premiums	41.5 (39.2) Advance Corporation Tax. Revised estimates. Contributions by self-employed
D Cost of reliefs retained (Section 4)	0.4 (0) Compensate charities/ overseas holders	4.7 (5.8) More recent figures (some reliefs under E)
E Tax base (Section 6)	151.0–157.7 (170.2) Payments by life assurance companies, etc. Reference period and other adjustments to self-employment income. Other transfers. Different assumptions about employee contributions	159.0–167.0 (180.9) As Parker *plus* Allowance for continuing tax reliefs

It may be deduced that the necessary tax rate is, in the case of the Parker scheme:

$$\frac{68.4 - \begin{Bmatrix}31.9\\29.9\end{Bmatrix} + 38.2 + 0.4 - 0.9}{\begin{Bmatrix}157.7\\151.0\end{Bmatrix}}$$

$$\underset{(A)\qquad (B)\qquad (C)\qquad (D)}{}$$

$$\underset{(E)}{}$$

where we allow £0.9 billion for the revenue from the higher rates. The range of rates, taking the upper end of each of the two intervals and then the lower end, is 47.1 per cent to 50.5 per cent. In the case of the Vince scheme we have, allowing £1.5 billion from the revenue for higher rates and the investment income surcharge, and £3.0 billion for the cost of the low income credits (the bottom end of the range given by Vince):

$$\frac{65.6 - \begin{Bmatrix}33.3\\31.1\end{Bmatrix} + 41.5 + 4.1 + 1.5}{\begin{Bmatrix}167.0\\159.0\end{Bmatrix}}$$

which gives a range of 47.5 per cent to 51.3 per cent.

The short answer to this question with which we began is therefore that the tax rate required to finance the Parker and Vince schemes is likely to be significantly higher than the 43–4 per cent suggested. The necessary rate is likely to be at least 4 percentage points higher, and may exceed 50 per cent.

The main point that should however be emphasized is that the calculation of the required tax rate is far from a straightforward matter, and that it is surrounded by considerable uncertainty. This applies especially to the magnitude of the tax base, where there are certain items whose taxable status is hard to determine. It should be evident that one cannot simply take the national accounts figures at face value.

This need for caution in drawing firm conclusions is reinforced when account is taken of possible changes in pre-tax incomes. A simple example is provided by the exemption of certain interest income on national savings. The removal of this exemption, as under the Parker scheme, may mean that the gross return has to be raised to retain the present level of holdings, with a cost to the government[18]; conversely, the retention of the relief under the Vince scheme, coupled with the rise in the basic rate of tax, may mean that national savings becomes more attractive, allowing a reduction in gross interest. We have however to go beyond this, to consider the general effect on the level of savings and rates of return. It is moreover possible that wages and earnings will be affected. This is sometimes couched in terms of employers being able to reduce wages, but the assumptions made about the working of the labour market are critical to the conclusions drawn. If, for example, labour supply is reduced, then there may be upward pressure on wages – although total earned income may still fall. Such speculations cannot be further developed within the scope of this chapter, but the general equilibrium consequences of such major changes in taxation and benefits have to be recognized in any attempt to arrive at a definitive answer.

NOTES

1. This allows £0.86 billion for the cost of residual housing and supplementary benefits.
2. This figure is derived from Table 2.12.6 of the 1983 White Paper, with an allowance for costs in Northern Ireland.
3. It should be noted that the 1981/2 figure was affected by industrial action in the Inland Revenue (March 1981–July 1981).
4. Vince states explicitly (1983, p. 31) that employment expenses would be treated as tax-free income.
5. The published quarterly figures do not give the classification by type of income required to construct Table 16.1.
6. Calculated from total earned income and investment income of those covered by SPI (Table 7), less national insurance pensions (Table 21). The net income of those with total income less than £1,000 not covered by the SPI of £916

million (Table 20) is assumed to be 20 per cent self-employment income, 40 per cent national insurance pensions and 40 per cent occupational pensions.

7. Source for this and subsequent SPI figures – *Survey of Personal Incomes 1978–9*, Tables 21 and 27. The figures do not include small non-taxable incomes less than £1,000.

8. The general method is described in Maurice (1968), although there have been certain changes since that date. See also Stark (1978).

9. For example, it is necessary to separate pay from occupational pensions in the PAYE records. It is noted in *Inland Revenue Statistics 1981* that the estimate of pensions differs from that in the SPI for 1978/9 'by more than would be expected as the result of sampling error' (p. 17). The report goes on to say that 'the reasons for the difference are not clear, but may be due partly to the failure to accurately identify occupational pensions in the PAYE returns'.

10. The appropriate tax rate for grossing up is not readily estimated; the figure of 30 per cent is taken as an average of 25 per cent (weight 0.15), 33 per cent (weight 0.8) and 45 per cent (weight 0.05), the weights being based broadly on the SPI 1978/9 (Table 16).

11. The Inland Revenue and Central Statistical Office kindly made available some more recent data.

12. It is understood that for the 1984 Blue Book, the SPI will become the main source, replacing the separate analysis of tax assessments.

13. This is a fifth of the £916 million referred to above.

14. This assumption about the timing is that made by the Inland Revenue: for example, the tables in *Inland Revenue Statistics 1980* relating to 1977 are based on assessments primarily for 1978/9.

15. As pointed out in an earlier footnote, there may be difficulties in distinguishing the two sources of income. This will not affect the total tax base.

16. The schemes do not specify how building society interest would be treated. The SPI grosses up the amount received at the building society composite rate of tax. In our treatment we have assumed that this grossed-up amount would be taxed at the full basic rate.

17. In these calculations we have excluded the £0.3 billion from other transfers and taken the black economy as 2½ per cent (broadly that assumed for 1980).

18. The effects of tax exemption of government bond interest are discussed by Diamond (1965).

17 · ANALYSIS OF A PARTIAL BASIC INCOME SCHEME

1 INTRODUCTION

The idea of a basic income scheme, providing a basic income guarantee in place of all existing social security benefits and levying a tax on all income, has a long history in Britain. The scheme we examine in this chapter can trace its descent (literally) from that put forward in 1942 by Lady Juliet Rhys Williams in *Something to Look Forward to* (1943). Her ideas, together with other proposals for the integration of income taxation and social security, were investigated by the Royal Commission on the Taxation of Profits and Income (1954). The report commented that:

> to the thoughtful observer it has for some time seemed to be a matter for enquiry whether there is not a risk of duplication of effort in a situation in which two State agencies exist side by side, engaging in broadly similar transactions with much the same group of citizens.
>
> (1954, p. 9)

It went on, however, to note:

> The general idea of securing some measure of integration of the income tax and social security systems can readily enough be stated, but to translate that conception into a definite and practicable scheme is a different matter.
>
> (p. 11)

In the decades since then, the idea has been kept alive by a succession of authors, including James Meade (1972), and the son of the original proposer, the late Sir Brandon Rhys Williams, MP, and Hermione Parker, with whom he worked closely.

Examination of the arithmetic of a pure basic income scheme (as in Chapter 16) has shown that the payment of a reasonable level of basic income, sufficient to compensate for the loss of existing benefits, is likely to

With H. Sutherland. The research described in this chapter forms part of the ESRC Programme on Taxation, Incentives and the Distribution of Income, and we are grateful to our colleagues for their help and comments. The partial basic income scheme that we examine is based on the work of Hermione Parker. She has been an active participant in the research but does not necessarily share the views expressed in the chapter. [Written in 1988.]

involve a tax rate significantly in excess of 40 per cent. This has naturally raised questions about the political attractiveness of a pure basic income. In her later book, *Taxation and Incentive*, Lady Rhys Williams herself felt that the rate of income tax 'would be too high' (1953, p. 128), and she put forward a modified proposal, with a lower rate of tax, which did not involve the complete abolition of all existing benefits. Everyone would receive a basic income and benefits would be reduced by this amount (which was a quarter of the national insurance pension for a single person).

Such a *partial basic income scheme* has recently been developed by Hermione Parker (1989), who has suggested that it could provide a way forward that is both feasible and politically acceptable. The consequences of this kind of scheme are however less easily seen than with a pure basic income, since the post-reform situation involves elements of both the current and the basic income systems. This chapter examines the arithmetic of one such partial basic income to see what levels of basic income could be afforded with existing tax rates and who would gain or lose. Would it, indeed, have much redistributive impact?

In our analysis, we have drawn heavily on the BIG Phase I described in Parker (1989), but we have simplified the scheme in certain respects, and the results given here should not be taken as applying to her proposals. It should also be stressed that we are not advocating a partial basic income; our purpose is simply to help others evaluate the potential of this approach.

2   A PARTIAL BASIC INCOME

The scheme that we examine in effect 'cashes out' the personal income tax allowances, abolishing the single allowance, the married man's allowance, the wife's earned income allowance, and the allowance for single parents, but not the age allowance (which would be reduced to £1,040 with an income limit of £8,460). The existing tax rates of 25 per cent (basic rate) and 40 per cent (higher rate) would be retained, but there would be independent taxation of husbands and wives. The basic income scheme envisages that tax expenditures would be phased out and as a step towards this the partial scheme restricts the reliefs for mortgage interest and employee superannuation contributions to the basic rate of tax. Tax would be levied on all income, except that there would be a tranche of earnings (£16.60 a week) for each worker that would be disregarded. This provision in part reflects administrative considerations: the present machinery does not seem capable of taxing all earnings from the first £1. It is also the case that on the benefit side there is typically an earnings disregard for small amounts.

The resulting extra revenue from these changes on the tax side is used to introduce basic incomes. The level of the basic income is taken to be £10 per person aged 16 or over,[1] which is almost exactly the same percentage (24.3 per cent) of the single person's national insurance pension as proposed by Lady Rhys Williams in 1953. This is less than the value of the present single person's allowance to a basic rate taxpayer (£12.52), but there is in addition the tax-free tranche of earnings for all workers which would be sufficient to offset this. The level of the basic income was in fact chosen to be approximately equal in value for a couple to that of the married man's allowance (at present £19.69), so that with the tax-free tranche of earnings one-earner couples gain overall. It would not, on the other hand, be enough to compensate two-earner couples, who would receive less than at present since they would lose the wife's earned income relief. Other losers would be single-parent taxpayers, who would lose the additional personal allowance, and higher rate taxpayers, who would lose since the present allowances are more valuable to them (the single allowance is worth £20 a week).

The partial basic income is intended to replace in part existing social security benefits, so that these benefits are at the same time reduced by £10. They are also brought closer to a basic income in being made tax-free for the basic element (up to £31.15), and with invalidity benefit being brought into line as far as tax treatment is concerned. Further, we assume that the wife's pension is treated as her own income.

Such a partial basic income may be seen either as a compromise solution or as the first stage along the route to a full basic income. The latter takes account of the important consideration that, in terms of practical policy-making, what is relevant is not just the destination of reform but the process of transition by which such a full scheme could be approached.

3   COST OF THE PARTIAL BASIC INCOME

The first question concerns the cost of the partial basic income. The *gross* cost is readily calculated from the number of adults and comes to some £22 billion. The *net* cost however depends on the increased tax revenue that arises from the abolition of the personal allowances and other measures and on the saving on existing benefits. In order to estimate these, we have made use of the tax-benefit model TAXMOD developed at the LSE (see Chapter 18, which describes the qualifications which surround the estimates).

TAXMOD produces estimates of the revenue cost of reform proposals, and we used these to arrive at a scheme revenue neutral in 1988/9 terms.[2] To this end, we iterated on the width of the tax-free tranche of earnings.

(The speed with which TAXMOD operates, performing calculations for 5,824 families in under half an hour, means that one can iterate quickly and it would be quite possible to vary other parameters of the scheme.) The results we obtained are shown below:

	Current	(£ billion in 1988/9) With partial basic income	Difference
Income tax	−43	−58	−15
Basic incomes	0	22	+22
NI benefits	24	18	−6
Income-tested benefits	9	8	−1

The greater part of the finance for the basic incomes comes from increased income tax revenue. Only a small part comes from people being floated off existing income-tested benefits (the basic income would be treated as part of resources for the purpose of assessing Income Support and other means-tested benefits).

4 THE IMPACT ON INDIVIDUAL TAXPAYERS

What is the impact on individual families? Since the scheme is revenue-neutral, there must be losers. Are they all higher rate taxpayers (for whom the loss of the tax allowance is not outweighed by the basic income) or two-earner couples? The main purpose of TAXMOD is to identify the effects of reforms like the partial basic income on a representative sample of the UK population. Table 17.1 shows the estimated distribution of families by range of net income with the tax-benefit system current in 1988/89. (The unit of analysis is the tax unit, referred to as a 'family', and each has a weight of 1 in the table.) The ranges are shown in the first column, and the percentage of families in these ranges is given in the second column. There are for example 11.5 per cent of families with net

Table 17.1 Effect of partial basic income by ranges of net income

Upper end of range £ week	Before change % in range	cumulative %	After change % in range	cumulative %	Average gain £ week
50	11.5	11.5	11.4	11.4	2.32
75	14.2	25.7	14.0	25.4	0.70
100	12.4	38.1	12.6	37.9	0.81
125	10.3	48.4	10.4	48.3	0.40
150	9.2	57.5	9.0	57.3	0.43
175	7.3	64.9	7.6	64.9	0.50
200	7.3	72.2	7.2	72.0	0.75
225	5.8	77.9	5.9	77.9	0.20
250	4.8	82.7	4.9	82.8	0.06
—	17.3	100.0	17.2	100.0	−3.81

Table 17.2 Effect of partial basic income: percentage with gains and losses

Range		Absolute changes of £ a week					
	≤−15	−15/−5	−5/0	No change	0/5	5/15	≥15
1	0.1	2.9	2.6	65.9	6.2	19.4	2.9
2		1.0	8.1	65.4	19.9	5.2	0.4
3		2.1	10.1	40.3	43.9	3.1	0.5
4		5.3	16.8	18.8	57.8	1.3	
5	0.5	8.4	15.5	10.0	63.9	1.6	0.1
6	2.0	9.6	14.5	4.3	68.5	0.9	0.2
7	0.9	8.9	19.6	1.3	66.4	2.9	
8	1.0	7.9	27.5	1.0	59.5	3.1	
9	1.2	2.6	43.0		49.4	3.7	0.3
10	8.6	15.5	49.9	0.6	22.9	2.1	0.4
Overall	1.9	6.7	20.6	25.3	40.4	4.6	0.5

Notes:
1. The range refers to the row in Table 17.1.
2. The blank entries are zero.

incomes of less that £50 a week, who constitute the lowest income group in the table. Table 17.2 makes use of the same ranges (labelled 1–10) and shows the distribution within each range of the magnitude of gain or loss from the proposed reform.

For a sizeable proportion of families, the introduction of the basic income would be exactly offset by the reduction in existing social security benefits. This applies to a quarter of all families (see the bottom entry in the column 'No change' in Table 17.2). For the remainder, there would be a net gain or a net loss, with the overall zero net cost being the result of pluses and minuses cancelling out. This is quite consistent with there being more gainers than losers: there are in fact 45.5 per cent who gain and only 29.2 per cent who lose.

The main part of Table 17.1 shows the distribution by net income before and after the reform. It may be seen that there is a modest reduction in the proportions of families with low incomes. The final column in Table 17.1 gives the average gain or loss by income ranges. This shows a sizeable average loss for the highest income group, reflecting the loss to higher rate taxpayers, but on average a net gain for all other groups, with this being particularly marked for the lowest income group, who gain more than £2 a week on average.

Such averages are however misleading, as is shown by the distribution by range of gain or loss in Table 17.2. Within all groups there are gainers and losers, depending on the precise situation of the different families concerned. In the bottom group there are less than 30 per cent who are actual gainers: about two-thirds are unaffected by the reform (because of the offsetting of the basic income against NI benefits); and about 5 per cent are net losers. Nor do those at the top necessarily lose. In the top group there are a quarter who are net gainers, including some who gain more than £5 a week. It is not even true that most losers are at the top. A fifth of all losers are in the bottom half of the distribution.

This underlines the fact that it may be unhelpful to think about social security reforms in terms of a 'break-even' point below which people gain and above which people lose (or vice versa). Gains and losses depend very much on individual circumstances. We have seen, for example, that one-earner couples tend to gain, and two-earner couples tend to lose, from this partial basic income scheme. It is also the case that single-parent families tend to lose. There are however other factors, such as the extent of investment income, the receipt of particular national insurance benefits, and whether or not families are taking up means-tested benefits.

As Table 17.2 suggests, although there are gainers and losers, the introduction of a partial basic income would not in fact have very large effects on the distribution. Certainly the impact would be much less dramatic than that of a pure basic income. Table 17.3 shows that about 4 per cent lose more than £10 a week and about the same percentage gain more than £10 a week.

These results will doubtless raise questions in the mind of the reader. For example, who are the losers in the bottom group and can this be avoided? How far does the variation in gain or loss by income range reflect the differing numbers of single and married people in the different ranges? What about breadwinner wives? How are gains and losses related to the receipt of current income-tested benefits? One of the attractions of the micro-technology is that the user can choose to explore aspects which look interesting in a particular application. The production of further results can be left at the choice of the user. It is not like a book where there is only a restricted range of options. If the user wants to look at the figures a different way, then providing the programming is sufficiently flexible this can be chosen from the menu (see Chapter 18).

Table 17.3   Effect of partial basic income: distribution of gains and losses

Change in net income (upper end of range) £ week	%	cumulative %
−10	3.7	3.7
−8	1.6	5.2
−6	1.2	6.5
−4	2.7	9.1
−2	14.9	24.0
zero	5.1	29.1
no change	25.3	54.4
2	26.9	81.3
4	2.6	83.9
6	11.3	95.2
8	1.0	96.2
10	0.6	96.7
—	3.3	100.0

5   EFFECT ON MARGINAL TAX RATES

So far, we have looked at the impact on net incomes. The effects on the marginal tax rates are shown in Tables 17.4 and 17.5. Table 17.4 gives the marginal rate on £1 additional earnings by the family head, defined conventionally to be the husband in the case of a couple. Most people are in the 30–40 per cent range, where the marginal rate is 25 per cent basic rate income tax plus NIC; and the average marginal rate is about 33 per cent. The introduction of the partial basic income would not lead to major changes as far as the family head is concerned. A certain number are pushed into the higher rate band by the replacement of personal allow-

Table 17.4   Effect of partial basic income: marginal tax rates for family head

Range of marginal tax rate (upper end) %	Before change		After change	
	%	Cumulative %	%	Cumulative %
10	3.0	3.0	2.1	2.1
20		3.0		2.1
30	17.3	20.3	15.9	17.9
40	72.0	92.3	72.3	90.3
50	5.5	97.9	7.8	98.1
60		97.9		98.1
70		97.9		98.1
—	2.1	100.0	1.9	100.0
Average marginal tax rate		32.7		33.2
Percentage with increased marginal tax rates			5.1	
Percentage with decreased marginal tax rates			2.0	

Notes:
1. The results relate to families where the head is in paid employment.
2. The marginal tax rate is calculated for £1 increase in the earnings of the family head.
3. The blank entries are less than 0.1 per cent.

Table 17.5   Effect of partial basic income: marginal tax rates for wife

Range of marginal tax rate (upper end) %	Before change		After change	
	%	Cumulative %	%	Cumulative %
10	30.9	30.9	6.1	6.1
20	0.4	31.3	0.4	6.5
30	27.4	58.7	53.3	59.8
40	33.8	92.5	36.5	96.3
50	4.3	96.8	0.8	97.1
60	0.3	97.1		97.1
70		97.1		97.2
—	2.9	100.0	2.8	100.0
Average marginal tax rate		27.0		32.2
Percentage with increased marginal tax rates			28.6	
Percentage with decreased marginal tax rates			4.8	

Notes:
1. The results relate to those families where there is a wife in paid employment.
2. The marginal tax rate is calculated for £1 increase in the earnings of the wife.
3. The blank entries are less than 0.1 per cent.

ances by basic incomes and by the mortgage interest and superannuation contribution changes. The number in the poverty trap is slightly reduced, with the number of families receiving family credit reduced only by about one-seventh.

Turning to the marginal tax rate for the wife, we would expect this to go up since the amount of tax-free earnings has been reduced. On the other hand, there is the countervailing factor that independent taxation means that some wives no longer face higher rates of tax on account of their husband's earnings. In order to assess the quantitative significance of these two considerations, we need a model like TAXMOD. From the results, the first of these factors seems to be much stronger, with an increase in the marginal rate for nearly 30 per cent. The average marginal rate for all wives does indeed rise by 5 percentage points.

6   CONCLUDING COMMENTS

We are not attempting here to make a full evaluation of the partial basic income scheme, or to comment on its desirability as a first step towards the integration of taxes and benefits. But there can be little doubt that it represents a 'definite and practicable scheme', as sought by the Royal Commission, and the results from TAXMOD indicate that it could be introduced without having major distributional consequences. There are relatively few families who would experience a large gain or loss, and for a quarter there would be no change.

The partial basic income examined here would not be particularly redistributive, but it provides a platform from which further redistribution could be carried out. The level of the basic incomes (and child benefit) would be the key tools, with increases being financed by increases in the tax rate. If the income tax rate became 40 per cent for all, with national insurance contributions being abolished, the basic income could be almost doubled.

Whether such more far-reaching redistribution would be easier to carry out than via other routes is open to debate. It is indeed possible that making the redistribution explicit in this way is going to make it harder politically to carry out, and this seems to us one of the major question marks that surrounds this kind of reform. In a rational world, the partial basic income may have a lot to recommend it, but political decisions are not made in this way. Less transparent forms of redistribution may be more successful.

NOTES

1. For those aged 16 or 17 in receipt of child benefit, this is made up of £7.25 child benefit plus £2.75 basic income, the distinction being important since child benefit does not enter the calculation of entitlement to family credit.
2. The calculations are made using TAXMOD version 6.3.

18 · TAXMOD

1 OVERALL VIEW

TAXMOD is a tax-benefit model for the United Kingdom which runs on micro-computers and is designed to be accessible to a wide range of users. The model shows the implications of the current personal taxes and benefits for the UK population and allows the user to calculate the impact of policy changes. It is intended as a tool to facilitate assessment of proposed policy changes in terms of their total cost and their effect on individual families. The program is menu-driven and the user is prompted with information about the current tax-benefit system. It may therefore be used to learn about the present system and its complexities.

The program is intended to be as easy to use as possible. No knowledge of computers or programming is assumed. The user types a single command to start the program which then prompts the user for the input it requires. This simplicity for the user is at some cost to the flexibility of the program, but there is a wide range of options and types of output. The program is continually being developed to meet new requirements.

The program has three main stages (see Figure 18.1). In Stage 1, the user has the option of specifying a policy change or of simply examining the present system. If a policy change is requested, the program takes the user through different elements of the tax and benefit system and requests details of the changes. For example, the user may change a single benefit level or tax rate, such as the level of unemployment benefit or the basic rate of income tax. Or the user may make much more complicated changes: for example, the rate structure of the income tax could be changed to give more gradual progression of marginal rates, or national insurance contributions could be integrated into the income tax structure. And quite radical changes, including new benefits such as the introduction of a basic income or social dividend, can be incorporated.

With H. Sutherland. Reprinted from *Tax-Benefit Models*, edited by A. B. Atkinson and H. Sutherland, ST/ICERD Occasional paper No. 10, London School of Economics. Details of TAXMOD are available from Holly Sutherland, ST/ICERD, LSE, 10 Portugal Street, London WC2A 2HD.

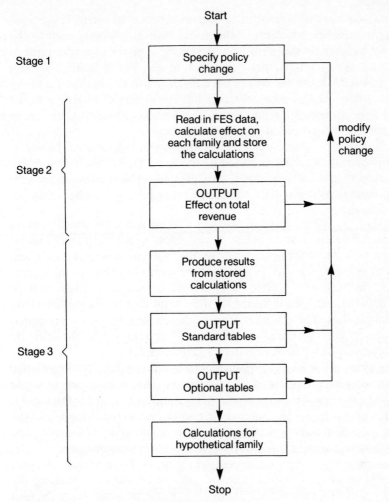

Figure 18.1 Structure of TAXMOD program

Stage 2 calculates the effect of the present system, and of the policy change where one has been specified, for a sample of families drawn from the *Family Expenditure Survey* (FES). The user may specify the sample of families considered, where this may be a sub-group, such as the working population, or the retired. It calculates for each family the net income, and marginal tax rates, before and after the policy change. These variables, together with the family characteristics, are then stored. This takes some time, depending on the type of machine and storage medium being used. As it is proceeding, the user will see the number of families processed to date, and the number of seconds elapsed, on the screen. At the end of this stage, two summary tables appear in turn on the screen. The first of these presents a summary of a number of characteristics of the sample, grossed up to represent their numbers in the population as a whole, such as the number of families on different benefits, or the number of single parents. The second table summarizes the effect of the policy change on the revenue of each tax and the cost of each benefit, also giving the overall net revenue change. At this point, the user has the option of returning to the policy change section, a facility which is particularly useful when one is looking for a revenue-neutral package of measures.

Stage 3 of the program uses the information stored on each family to produce the results that are specified by the user. These results are shown on the screen and, if requested, are printed. This operation is self-contained and does not require the use of other programs. The 'standard' set of results are:

1. Distribution of net incomes or net resources, with and without policy change, and average gain or loss by income ranges.
2. Distribution of gains or losses by income ranges.
3. Distribution of gains/losses in more detail.
4. Distribution of marginal tax rates for heads of families in paid work, with and without policy change.
5. Distribution of marginal tax rates for wives in paid work, with and without policy change.

Thus, for example, the second table can be used to see the distribution of gains and losses for those with net incomes between £100 and £125. In order to produce the set of tables, the program reads the stored data once. Again the user will see the number of families processed to date on the screen as the calculations are being done. The user can then choose from a set of optional tables (there is also the possibility of going straight to them). The options are:

1. Distribution of gains and losses by characteristics.
2. Characteristics: gainers and losers.
3. Distribution of changes in marginal tax rates by characteristics.
4. List cases of large gains or losses.
5. List cases where large changes in marginal tax rates.
6. Lorenz curves.
7. Incomes relative to poverty line.
8. Hypothetical families.

Thus, the first of these shows the distribution of changes in net income for specified sub-groups: for example, those with and those without children, or those who are householders and those who are not. The second approaches the analysis from the opposite direction and shows the features (e.g. proportion who are householders, average number of children) of those in different ranges of gain and loss. This helps identify those who gain and lose from the reform, as does the fourth option which lists the main features of cases where there are gains or losses in excess of a specified figure. The third and fifth options are concerned with the changes in marginal tax rates, allowing the user to identify those families who face increased or decreased marginal tax rates. Each of options 1–7 involves reading the stored data once. The last option allows the user to specify hypothetical families of their own choice. The effect of the policy change on the net income and marginal tax rates for that family is calculated and printed out.

In this chapter, we first describe the different aspects of the model in greater detail, approaching it from the standpoint of the person who wishes to understand what the model can do, rather than from the position of the person sitting at a keyboard actually using it. We therefore begin in section 2 with a description of the output from the model in its present (October 1987) form, so that the potential user can see what results can be obtained. These results show the effects of the present system compared to a policy change, and in section 3 we describe the policy options that can be considered using TAXMOD. Section 4 then outlines the way in which the calculations are made, and the main qualifications that need to be borne in mind in using the results. We then in section 5 take a simple example – that of abolishing the married man's income tax allowance and doubling child benefit/one-parent benefit – to illustrate how the program works and the range of results it offers. (A similar model for France is described by Bourguignon, Chiappori and Sastre-Descals, 1988.)

2 OUTPUT FROM THE MODEL

The simplest output from the model is an estimate of the cost of tax or benefit changes. In some cases, information on the revenue implications is readily available elsewhere and the calculation is simply a check on the accuracy of TAXMOD. Thus the Autumn Statement publishes each year 'ready reckoner' tables showing, for example, the revenue cost of reducing the basic rate of income tax by 1p. Or, the gross cost of £5 increase in the basic national insurance retirement pension may be calculated from the number of pensions in payment. The answers to Parliamentary Questions are another source that is often used.

However, matters are not always that simple. In the case of the pension increase, the net effect on government spending has to take account of reductions in supplementary pensions and housing benefit resulting from the pension increase. The net cost is substantially less than the gross cost. In order to calculate the net cost, the interaction with the other spending programmes has to be taken into account. What is more, the increase in pensions leads to higher income tax revenue, since the pensions are subject to tax, so that the net impact on the government budget has to take the tax side into consideration as well (something which is not typically done in Parliamentary Answers).

The revenue calculations from the model are therefore likely to be of independent interest, since they encompass all aspects of personal direct taxes and benefits. For this reason, we have devoted considerable attention to the problem of grossing-up the calculations for the sample of families in the FES to the United Kingdom population as a whole. The results of the model are intended to apply to the entire UK resident population.

The results at the end of the second stage of the program give estimates of the total cost of each benefit programme and the revenue raised from income tax and national insurance contributions. These may be compared with known administrative totals. The differences that are observed reflect in part shortcomings of TAXMOD, but they also in part reflect differences in coverage. For example, the cost to the Department of Health and Social Security of national insurance pensions includes the cost of pensions paid to those resident abroad or in institutions, who are not covered by our figures. Where a policy change is specified, the total cost of the change is shown at this stage, and the user may wish to return to the beginning to adjust the policy parameters in order to meet some revenue target. Revenue-neutrality, for example, can be achieved by an iterative process involving stages 1 and 2 (see Figure 18.1) – a procedure that was used in constructing the partial basic income scheme described in Chapter 17.

The main use of TAXMOD is to look behind the aggregate revenue figures to the impact on individual families. Stage 3 of the program produces these results. The program performs calculations for individual tax units. A 'tax unit' consists of a single person or a couple, together with dependent children. It does not therefore always coincide with the 'household'. A couple with a 22-year-old son living at home would be one household but two tax units. Here we use 'family' interchangeably with 'tax unit'. The results for individual tax units are weighted, to allow for the differential representation of different types (for example, the under-representation of the unemployed), to give results in terms of distributions.

The first table (labelled Table 1 in the output from the program) shows the distribution of net incomes. Here the user may specify the concept of outcome to be used and the ranges to be shown in the table. The choices of income to be used and the ranges to be shown in the table. The choices of deducts housing costs, and either *total* or *equivalent* income, the latter being total income divided by an equivalence scale. The equivalence scale is specified as 1 for a single person, 1.6 for a couple, plus 0.4 per child, where the last two numbers may be varied by the user. The ranges may be specified in terms of the starting point (for example, below £75) and the width of the interval (for example, £25). After the first five tables are produced, the user has the option of returning to Tables 1 and 2 and giving a new specification. This is useful if the distribution does not turn out as expected (for example, 90 per cent of families are in the bottom range). There is also the option of producing the table (and Table 2) for particular groups: single persons without children, couples without children, and families with children.

Where a policy change has been specified, Table 1 allows the user to compare the percentages in different ranges before and after the policy change. The table also shows the average gain or loss for those in a specified income range in the current situation, so that we could see, for example, that the average gain for the bottom income group is £1.25 a week. The average gain or loss may however be misleading in that there may be great diversity within the group. Information about the *distribution* of changes in income between the present and policy change situations is provided in Table 2. This shows for families with current net incomes in each of the income ranges specified in Table 1 the percentages having gains and losses of different sizes. (The ranges of gain or loss may be specified by the user.) Table 3 shows the distribution of these gains and losses in more detail: by £2 ranges from −£20 to +£20.

The change in net income, or resources, is one of the main variables produced by TAXMOD. The other main output is the *marginal tax rate*, which is calculated for those with positive earnings or self-employment income. There are therefore results both for the head of the tax unit (Table 4), which means single men, single women and married men, and for wives (Table 5). The marginal tax rate shows the amount lost in the form of higher income tax and NIC and lower benefits (FIS or Family Credit, housing benefit, SB or Income Support, passport benefits, NI benefits, and any new benefit) as a result of £1 increases in earnings for the employed or self-employment income for the self-employed. The results show the distribution of marginal tax rates, in 10 per cent ranges with the top range 70 per cent and above, and the average marginal rate. Where a policy change is specified, the percentages with increases and decreases in marginal rate are given.

The tables described above may well lead the user to pose further questions. Who are the families who gain and lose from a policy change? If the change involved an increase in child benefit, then it may not be a surprise to know that the gainers are families with children, but with other policies, or with packages of measures, the beneficiaries may not be so obvious. Options 1 and 3 allow the user to examine the distribution of gains and losses, and the distribution of changes in marginal tax rates, by categories of family: for example, householders compared with non-householders, owner-occupiers compared with tenants, families with compared with families without children, etc. This may show, for example, that large losses are concentrated among tenants.

As is argued in King (1988), we need to consider not only the relation between the characteristics of families and gains/losses but also the reverse relation between gains/losses and the characteristics of families. Which are the families with a gain of £5–£10 a week? How many of them are married? In what percentage of cases is the wife in paid work? Option 2 allows the user to specify ranges of gain or loss and the program then provides information about the characteristics of those in each group. In the case of a user trying to design a reform package, it may be the case that there are too many families with large losses. Use of Option 2 then allows the user to identify their main features. This may then provide guidance as to the changes that need to be made to the package of proposals.

The results from the standard runs may also throw up puzzles. The user may wonder why it is that a cut in taxation may make some families worse off. Help in solving such mysteries is provided by the options which allow the user to print out details of cases where there are large gains/losses (Option 4) or large changes in marginal tax rates (Option 5). The user may specifiy either *increases* or *decreases* in excess of a specified limit. In the case of gains/losses, this may be defined in terms of net income or net resources and may be in total or equivalent terms. In the case of marginal tax rates, it may be the rate faced by either the family head or the wife. So that the user may look at families gaining more than £5 per equivalent adult in net income; or may look at wives whose marginal tax rates are reduced by more than 10 percentage points. The output has the following form (this is a hypothetical example):

> Married couple with four children
> Tenant: housing costs of   £25.78
> Gross income from work of head is   £156.89
> Other income of   £3.24
> Net income before is   £154.01
> After is   £171.08
> Change is   £17.07
> Marginal tax rate before: head 33.85
> After   33.85

(More detail on individual cases can be obtained during the first stage of the program.)

Options 7 and 8 allow further analysis of the distributional results. The first of these provides the figures necessary to draw Lorenz curves for net income or net resources, showing the percentage of total income received by the bottom 10 per cent, bottom 20 per cent, and so on. It is then possible to compare the Lorenz curves with and without the policy change. The curves may be constructed for different sub-groups of the population. The use may specify, for example, that only householders be included, or that the curve be constructed for families with two children. The results record the percentage of the population covered and the mean income. There is also the option of constructing 'generalized' Lorenz curves (Shorrocks, 1983) which show the total *amount* of income received by the bottom 10 per cent, bottom 20 per cent, and so on. Option 8 is related in that it provides the number of families below specified income levels and the amount of their income shortfall from that level. Again there is the possibility of excluding or including different subgroups; and the user may choose an equivalence scale to be applied.

All of the results described relate to actual families contained in the FES sample. The user may however want to show the effect of the present system or of a proposed reform on specified families. The last option allows this possibility. The user has to enter values for all the variables used in the calculations, and this in itself is quite instructive. When thinking of 'typical' families, how many people consider whether there are other adults in the household contributing to the housing costs, or whether the wife has retained the right to pay reduced national insurance contributions? It is such variety of individual circumstances that makes the use of tax-benefit models essential in the analysis of policy reforms.

3   SPECIFICATION OF POLICY CHANGE

At the start of the program (TAXMOD Version 5.1) the user is told that

THE PROGRAM USES THE TAX
AND BENEFIT RATES RULING AT
OCTOBER 1987

and asked

WOULD YOU LIKE TO MAKE A POLICY CHANGE?
IF SO, TYPE Y.   OTHERWISE, TYPE N

If the user enters N, then the program continues to the next stage with no policy change entered. The results then relate to the present system only. If the user elects to make a policy change, the program offers the following:

MENU: You may change
1. Child benefit or FIS/Family Credit
2. National insurance contributions
3. Income tax
4. NI retirement pension and widows benefits
5. Unemployment benefit, YTS and JTS
6. SSP, sickness benefit, maternity and invalidity benefits
7. Housing benefit
8. Supplementary benefit/Income support
9. Introduce new benefit
Type number of item to be changed OR press return to continue

For each item that is chosen, the user is then presented with a screen offering choices concerning the particular tax or benefit. For some of these menus, further sub-screens are available, allowing the user to alter particular aspects of a benefit. Thus, in the case of the income tax, the first screen allows the user to change the personal allowances for single persons, married couples, and single parents, and the basic rate of income tax. It also offers the user the choice of further sub-screens which allow changes in the higher rates, in the tax treatment of husband and wife, of mortgage interest or superannuation contributions, and allow the introduction of an investment income surcharge or an earnings disregard. The menu approach limits the flexibility of the program and it is quite possible that the user may design packages that cannot be fully captured by the policy parameters in the model. When, for example, the Chancellor of the Exchequer introduced reduced rates of NIC, this could not be incorporated without changing the program. At the same time, there is a wide range of choice and it may well be possible to approximate quite closely schemes that are not formally covered by the menus. For instance, at the time of the 1985 Green Paper on social security reforms we found it possible to model many of the proposals without re-writing the program.

In the paragraphs below we describe for each tax or benefit the main policy parameters that can be varied within the program in its present form. The description is not complete, and the user should consult the Manual before using the model.

Child benefit and one-parent benefit

The amount of these benefits may be varied. It is possible to make the benefits taxable and, in the case of a couple, to vary the proportions taxable as the earned income of the husband or the wife. The latter feature is an example of how TAXMOD may alert the user to policy alternatives that otherwise would be ignored. Many people assume that if child benefit were taxable then it would necessarily be taxed as part of the husband's income (see the discussion in Chapter 14).

Family income supplement (now replaced by Family Credit)

The make-up level and the maximum amount of benefit may be varied. These are stated as £X per family plus £Y per child, where there are four age-groups for children. The minimum amount of benefit may be varied. These are the parameters that have in practice been the subject of policy changes, but it is also possible to vary the taper, which has been at 50 per cent since the scheme was introduced. It is possible also to see the effect of complete take-up of FIS, or of calculating FIS on the basis of net rather than gross income.

Family Credit

The amount of the family credit may be varied, stated as £X per family plus £Y per child, where there are four age groups for children. The withdrawal starting point may be varied as may the capital cut-off. The taper may be varied.

National insurance contributions

The contribution rates and thresholds may be varied, the program allowing for two reduced rates with corresponding thresholds. The reduction for contracting out may be varied, as may the reduced rate for certain married women and widows. When the user makes a policy change, the program checks the input for consistency: for example that the reduction for contracting out is not set at such a level as to make the rate paid negative. Self-employed contributions under Classes 2 and 4 may be varied, as may the percentage of class 4 contributions that may be offset against income tax. It is possible to convert contributions to a graduated structure, so that the rate of contribution applies to earnings in excess of the threshold, rather than to all earnings if the threshold is exceeded as at present.

Income tax

The program allows for changes in the single and married personal allowance, the former being also the earned income allowance for the wife. It also allows for separate changes in the allowance for a single parent. The basic rate of tax, and the higher rates and bands (up to 5 bands in all), are policy parameters. In addition there are the following options:

1. The user may vary the tax treatment of husband and wife.
   There are four possibilities:
   (a)   The current tax treatment.
   (b)   Fully independent taxation.
   (c)   Fully transferable allowances.
   (d)   Partially transferable allowances.
   With the choice of fully independent taxation, the user has the further option of exempting married couples over a specified age, and without children, from the policy change, leaving them with a married man's addition if that is to their advantage.
2. The user may introduce an investment income surcharge with a single threshold and rate, and a tax-free band for earned income.
3. The limit on mortgage interest tax relief may be varied, and a further option is to confine relief to a single rate fixed by the user.
4. The amount of superannuation contributions allowed against tax may be limited to a maximum. The rate at which these are deducted may

be confined to the basic rate rather than allowing them against the highest rate paid.

5. The thresholds (single and married) and income limit of age allowance may be altered.

Retirement pensions

The levels of the basic national insurance pension and additions for wives and children and age addition may be altered. The earnings threshold for the earnings rule may be varied, as may that for the wife's addition and for the increase for children. Pensions may be made tax-free. A sub-menu allows pensions to be scaled upwards or downwards.

Widows' benefits

The program allows the alteration of the basic national insurance widows' benefit and the child addition, although account is taken of the fact that some widows receive benefits enhanced by their husbands' graduated or additional pension contributions and some receive less than the basic benefit if their husbands had not fulfilled the contribution conditions. The benefit may be made tax-free.

Unemployment benefit

Unemployment benefit rate may be varied as may the amount of the addition for a dependent spouse. Child additions were abolished in November 1984 (unless the claimant is over pension age) but the program allows these to be reintroduced. It also allows reduced rates of benefit to be reintroduced and for the benefit to be made tax-free again.

Statutory sick pay, sickness and invalidity benefits

The basic rate of sickness benefit may be varied, as may the adult dependant's addition and the child addition. The basic rate of invalidity benefit may be varied, as may the adult dependant's addition and the child addition (and the earnings limit for both of these). The middle and higher rates may be changed, as may the two rates of statutory sick-pay.

Statutory maternity pay and maternity allowance

The maternity allowance may be varied, as may the lower rate of statutory maternity pay.

YTS and JTS

YTS (lower and higher rates) may be varied. The JTS basic rate, dependant's addition, and the earnings threshold for the addition, may be varied.

Housing benefit

Under the 1987 system, the user can vary the housing benefit needs allowances, the earnings disregards, the tapers above and below the needs allowance, for both rent and rate rebates, and the deductions for non-dependent members of the household (either in or out of work) and the minimum payments, again for rent and rates separately. The addition to the needs allowance for pensioners may be altered, as may the special pensioner tapers below the needs allowance. The user may also impose maximum rebates as a per cent of rent and rates (the present maxima are 100 per cent). The 1988 housing benefit introduced under the Social Security Act 1986 applies the same capital cut-off as for Income Support and the housing benefit needs allowances are to be replaced by allowances and premiums which are in most cases identical to those used to assess Income Support. The 1988 housing benefit menu offers options on the tapers and income assessment rules, earnings disregards, and certain premia.

Supplementary benefit/income support

Under the 1987 supplementary benefit, the user may vary the short-term and long-term scale rates, the amounts depending on whether the claimant is single or has a partner, and on whether or not the claimant is a householder. The age of qualification for the long-term rate may be changed. In addition, scale rates can be varied for child dependants, according to their ages. In the case of housing costs, there is a fixed amount for maintenance and insurance if the claimant is liable for these, and a fixed amount towards housing costs for non-householders. If any non-dependants live in the same household then deductions are made from requirements as with housing benefit, and these may be varied. Other policy parameters are the capital limit for eligibility for supplementary benefit, and the minimum payment. Some families, whose SB resources only exceed their requirements by a small amount, and who receive standard housing benefit qualify for housing benefit supplement which is equal to the amount by which their standard housing benefit falls short of their housing costs, less the amount by which their SB resources exceed their requirements. The program does not offer a menu to change housing benefit supplement directly. It is calculated using the policy parameters defined for SB and standard housing benefit and is affected by any change in these. Under the 1988 income support system, the parameters that the user may vary include the weekly amounts (varying by age), the premia for families with children, for a disabled child, for single parents, where one or more spouse is aged over 60, or over 80, or is long-term sick or disabled.

Passport benefits

Certain benefits, including FIS, SB and housing benefit supplement under the 1987 system, act as a 'passport' to a range of health and education benefits. It is assumed that all those claiming these benefits also receive passport benefits worth a standard amount depending on the ages of those in the family. The amount may be varied for each of four types of family member, or passport benefits may be abolished.

New benefit

The last part of the policy change section invites the user to specify a new benefit. This may have four different elements:

1. Basic benefit, in pounds per week, for a single adult, couple, young person aged 16–17, child.
2. Addition, in pounds per week, for having children, for having children under 5, and for single-parent families.
3. Addition for householders which could be lump-sum (pounds per week) or which could be related to housing costs (percentage of rent, percentage of rates, percentage of mortgage interest).
4. Taper with income, expressed as a percentage, with different tapers for single people without children, single-parent families, couples without children, and couples with children.
5. A separate taper for the housing element.

In addition, the user may choose whether or not the new benefit is treated as part of income for the purpose of calculating income-tested benefits.

4   WHAT THE MODEL DOES AND DOES NOT DO

It is important that in considering the results from TAXMOD the user understands how the calculations are carried out, the assumptions on which they are based, and the qualifications that surround them. These are described below under the headings of (a) the use of the Family Expenditure survey data, (b) the calculations for individual families, and (c) the policy measures.

Use of Family Expenditure Survey data

The data used in the present version of TAXMOD are drawn from the 1982 Family Expenditure Survey (FES). The survey is conducted annually by OPCS and is used for many different purposes. It provides a rich source of information for the purpose of constructing a tax-benefit model and is the basis for the IFS and CSO models. At the same time, it has to be remembered that the FES is not designed for this purpose and that considerable care is necessary in its application. Use of the FES for tax-benefit calculations without consideration of the potential problems may lead to misleading results.

The FES sample used in TAXMOD consists of all tax units interviewed in the 1982/3 tax year and before the November benefit up-rating (i.e. between 6 April and 15 November 1982). The resulting sample consists of 5,824 tax units. It should be emphasized that we have excluded no 'difficult' cases on the basis that it is often the large or 'complicated' families who experience unpredictable effects from seemingly simple policy changes. We have therefore made the coverage as extensive as possible given the information contained in the FES. Nevertheless, it should be noted that the FES is a sample of the *household* population and excludes those resident in institutions. This means that the calculations do not cover old people in homes or in hospital, students away at university, people living in army barracks, etc.

The basic unit of analysis is the tax unit. In the majority of cases this coincides with the household. In the, approximately, quarter of cases where there is more than one tax unit in the household, assumptions have to be made about certain elements. We have for example attributed all housing expenditure to the head of the tax unit, with the other tax units in the household being treated as non-dependants contributing to housing costs for benefit purposes. This seems likely to be a reasonable assumption in most cases, but would not be appropriate for 'flat-sharers'. In some cases the correct identification of the tax unit requires careful attention. Examples are provided by cohabiting couples (who are normally treated as married in the FES, but in a few cases this is not done), by absent spouses, and by foster children (coded in the FES as heads of tax units, but who we treat as part of the family).

In order to use the FES data on individual tax units in the model, a number of adjustments have to be made. First, the figures for 1982 are updated to a current tax year basis. For different categories of income, we apply factors derived from aggregate statistics (e.g. the national accounts for self-employment income) or more recent surveys (e.g. the *New Earnings Survey*), but these have to be extrapolated to give current figures. The adjustment factors for each class of income are therefore approximate, and may not reflect the diversity of experience of, for example, pay increases, although we have made a special adjustment to allow for the change in the distribution of earnings indicated by the *New Earnings Survey*. The up-dating of the housing cost variables is based on the rent, mortgage interest and rates components of the Retail Prices Index.

Secondly, there is evidence of understatement of certain types of income by respondents to the FES (Atkinson and Micklewright, 1983); and we have made adjustments to investment incomes and to self-employment income, where in the latter case we assume that the under-stated income is not reported to the Inland Revenue. Thirdly, for certain variables key information is missing for particular families. A prime example is the amount of mortgage interest, where for a sizeable number of cases we have information on the total payment but not on the breakdown between interest and repayment of principal. There are, similarly, problems with missing values for reported rates and water rates payments. Finally, an adjustment is made for the service element paid with rents.

In the FES, there is a substantial degree of non-response, and there is evidence that this varies systematically with household characteristics (Kemsley, Redpath and Holmes, 1980). The OPCS evidence suggests that non-response is related to variables such as the age of the head of the household, the employment status of the head, and the presence of children. Moreover, in using the data from a previous year to model the current situation, it is necessary to adjust for the change in population structure (in this case between 1982 and 1987). We have attempted to allow for these two problems by developing grossing-up factors to be applied to different types of family unit, and the method is described in Atkinson, Gomulka and Sutherland (1988). As is shown there, the choice of grossing-up method may make a noticeable difference to the results.

Calculation for individual families

It should be stressed that the model is purely *arithmetical* in the sense that it makes no attempt to predict changes in behaviour that lead to changes in the gross incomes of families. It assumes that the gross incomes are the same before and after a policy change. The incorporation of behavioural changes is discussed in King (1988), which describes the TRAP model; and the approach has been further developed by Blundell and Walker and colleagues (see, for example, Blundell *et al.*, 1984).

In large part, the program *calculates* taxes and benefits rather than using the reported values from the FES. The reason for this is that we wish to make a comparison with a policy alternative where the amounts must of necessity be calculated. The calculation involves a number of assumptions. Among the most important are that:

1. All income, other than under-stated self employment income, is declared to the authorities.

2. Income is received at the same rate throughout the tax year.
3. Benefit entitlement is related to earnings in the last pay period.
4. Self-employment income is adjusted up to the same date as other sources of income and is treated as current income for tax and benefit purposes.
5. The income of children less than the single person's tax allowance is ignored.

We have however attempted to make use where possible of the data on actual benefit receipt; and this has been a major focus of the research on the ESRC Programme on Taxation, Incentives and the Distribution of Income. For example, the receipt of national insurance unemployment benefit is based on actual receipt, thus allowing for the possibility that people may be excluded from benefit. Similarly, the amount of national insurance retirement pension is based on the observed amount, thus taking account of the additional pension (with an adjustment to project to 1987) increments for deferred retirement, incomplete contribution records, etc. The model allows for the non-take-up of certain means-tested benefits. This is at present allocated at random, with the probability designed to secure the observed proportionate take-up (for example, 50 per cent for FIS), allowing for different take-up rates for pensioners and taking account of the interaction between the take-up of different benefits. (Work is under way to relate the probability of take-up more fully to family characteristics.)

Policy measures

First, it should be stressed that the model does not cover all aspects of government budget. Most importantly, indirect taxes are not covered. This means that any consequences for VAT revenue, for example, are not taken into account in the revenue calculations, and that the model cannot in its present form be used to examine the effects of widening the VAT base.

Secondly, we have not attempted to model all the complexities of the tax and benefit structure. In the case of the income tax, for example, we have not allowed for the allowances for housekeepers, for dependent relatives, for son's and daughter's services, for the blind or for widow's bereavement; and no account is taken of covenants or of the business expansion scheme. In the case of supplementary benefit, we have not modelled the provisions for strikers; the blindness addition is not allowed for; no single payments are covered; and the equal treatment provisions have not been incorporated.

5　ILLUSTRATIVE EXAMPLE

In this section we describe the use of the model (TAXMOD Version 5.1) to examine one frequently discussed reform of the tax-benefit system: the abolition of the married man's additional income tax allowance and the doubling of child benefit and one-parent benefit. The abolition of the additional allowance, reducing the personal allowance for a married man to that for a single person, is a major step towards the independent taxation of husbands and wives. The use of the revenue to increase child benefit is seen as a straightforward way to help families with children.

We take as our starting point the actual October 1987 system, so that the abolition of the married man's allowance results in increased income tax payments for a basic rate taxpayer of 0.27 × £(3,795 − 2,425), or £7.11 a week. Child benefit would be increased from £7.25 to £14.50 and one-parent benefit from £4.70 to £9.40. This may be entered at the policy change stage by using the child benefit menu and the income tax menu. The user may note that one option not considered here, but which could be incorporated, would be to abolish the additional allowance for single parents (which is equal to the married man's addition). This is an example as to how the menus may 'prompt' the user. It is also assumed that the age allowance for a married man would be reduced by an amount equal to the reduction for those below the age of 65, becoming £3,305.

In order to check that the policy change has been correctly entered, the user may request that the calculations for individual cases be printed out during stage 2. An example for a hypothetical family is shown below:

1224

Married couple. Age of husband is 32. Age of wife is 30
with 2 children aged 5–10
Tenant with rent 19.03, rates 8.17, and water rates of 1.73
Does not claim HB

Head is employed with earnings 135.70
and self-employment income 0.00
with work expenses of 0.00
and superannuation contributions of 0.00
and investment income of 0.00
and other taxable income of 0.00
Head pays full Class 1 NIC
Head's normal weekly hours 40

Wife earns 0.00
with self-employment income 0.00
and other taxable income of 0.00

Non-taxable income 0.00
Weight 2643
Total gross income is 135.70

Net income 121.05 <u>WITH POLICY CHANGE</u> 128.44
Difference is 7.39
Marginal tax rate on head 36.00 WITH POLICY CHANGE 36.00

Family pays income tax of 16.93 <u>WITH POLICY CHANGE</u> 24.04
Family head pays NIC of 12.21 WITH POLICY CHANGE 12.21
Family receives child benefit of 14.50 <u>WITH POLICY CHANGE</u> 29.00
Family receives FIS/FC of 0.00 WITH POLICY CHANGE 0.00
Family receives rent rebate of 0.00 WITH POLICY CHANGE 0.00
Family receives rate rebate of 0.00 WITH POLICY CHANGE 0.00

It may be seen that the child benefit is indeed doubled (the changes have been underlined) and that the income tax payment has increased by £7.11, leaving a net gain for this family of £7.39.

The revenue consequences of this reform are relatively straightforward. According to the official figure given in the Public Expenditure White Paper (Cm 56–II, p. 39), the estimated cost of the married man's addition in 1986–7 was £4.45 billion. From the same source, the estimated expenditure on child benefit and one-parent benefit in 1986–7 was £4.66 billion in Great Britain (p. 235) and £0.18 billion in Northern Ireland (p. 312). These figures relate to the previous tax year from that considered in TAXMOD, and one in which the basic rate of income tax was higher, but they suggest a positive cost for the proposed package of several hundred million. However, we have to deduct the saving on income-tested benefits as a result of the increase in child benefit. Estimates of the net cost have been given on occasion in Parliamentary Answers (for example, Hansard, 10 March 1986, col. 385); on other occasions it has been stated that 'estimated savings on other programmes following increases could only be calculated at disproportionate cost' (Hansard, 25 July 1986, col. 667).

It is one of the advantages of TAXMOD that it calculates the net cost of a reform proposal taking account of the interactions between the different elements. So that, although it is less accurate in its treatment of individual elements than, say, the Inland Revenue tax model based on the *Survey of Personal Incomes*, it does provide an integrated picture. The results in the present case, printed out at the end of stage 2, show the following picture:

	£ million
Extra income tax	+4,270
Extra child benefit	−5,053
Saving on housing benefit	+73
Saving on supplementary benefit/housing benefit supplement/passport benefits	+746
Net saving	36

The package would therefore be effectively revenue-neutral.

Turning to the distributional aspects, the user probably has a fairly clear idea what to expect. Married couples without children lose. Those with one child more or less break even, and families with two or more children are net gainers. This all appears straightforward. However, the position is more complicated than may at first appear:

1. Reference has already been made to the saving on income-tested benefits, which means that for some families there is no net gain where the increase is entirely clawed-back (supplementary benefit recipients) or only a reduced gain (housing benefit recipients).
2. For higher rate taxpayers, the value of the married man's addition is greater than the figure quoted above: for the person paying 60 per cent at the margin the loss is £15.81 a week, so that a two-child family would lose.
3. On the other hand, for higher rate taxpayers where the wife has earnings, the wife's earnings election is likely to be attractive, and after the abolition of the married man's addition it would be chosen by nearly all higher rate payers. This reduces the loss and where there is separate election under the present system then the loss would be zero, as illustrated by the hypothetical case below:

1736

Married couple. Age of husband is 51; age of wife is 50
Owner-occupier with mortgage 10.57, rates 8.85 and water rates 2.79

Head is employed with earnings 321.38
and self-employment income 0.00
with work expenses of 0.00
and superannuation contributions of 00.00
and investment income of 3.82
and other taxable income of 0.00
Head is contracted out for Class 1 NIC

Wife earns 229.12
with self-employment income 0.00
and work expenses of 0.00
and superannuation contributions of 13.47
and other taxable income of 0.00
Wife pays reduced rate Class 1 NIC

Non-taxable income 0.00
Weight 4710

Total gross income is 554.31

Net income 392.99 WITH POLICY CHANGE 392.99
Difference is 0.00

Family pays income tax of 117.19 WITH POLICY CHANGE 117.19
Family head pays NIC of 21.05 WITH POLICY CHANGE 21.05
Marginal tax rate on head 27.00 WITH POLICY CHANGE 27.00
Marginal tax rate on wife 30.85 WITH POLICY CHANGE 30.85

The quantitative significance of these different elements can only be assessed by looking at a sample of actual families as in TAXMOD, and we now look at the results which are obtained from the standard set of tables.

Table 18.1 (obtained from Table 1 of the TAXMOD output) shows the distribution of total family net income, before and after the policy change. There are two figures each for the 'before' and 'after' situations: the percentage of all units in that range and the cumulative percentage up to and including that range. In the final column is the average gain for families in that range of income before the policy change. Table 18.2 shows the distribution of gains/losses by the ranges of net income in Table 1. The ranges 0–9 correspond to the ten ranges in Table 18.1. The categories of gain/loss are identified at the head of the table, where the missing category

Table 18.1 Ranges of net income: effect of abolishing MMA/doubling CB

Upper end	Before change %	CUMUL	After change %	CUMUL	Average gain
50.00	12.23	12.23	12.22	12.22	0.24
75.00	15.26	27.49	15.25	27.46	0.22
100.00	13.78	41.27	14.15	41.62	−0.40
125.00	10.84	52.11	10.65	52.27	−0.68
150.00	9.46	61.57	9.09	61.35	−0.12
175.00	7.92	69.48	7.70	69.06	0.41
200.00	6.76	76.24	6.93	75.98	0.49
225.00	5.48	81.72	5.59	81.57	0.37
250.00	4.58	86.30	4.69	86.26	0.79
—	13.70	100.00	13.74	100.00	−0.50

Table 18.2 Gains and losses by range: abolishing MMA/doubling CB

| | The figures show percentage in each row with absolute changes of: | | | | | |
	<−15	−5/−15	0/−5	0/5	5/15	>15
Range						
0	0.00	0.00	0.00	0.00	1.69	0.25
1	0.00	0.13	2.39	0.40	0.92	0.80
2	0.00	7.27	7.66	1.24	2.08	0.34
3	0.00	20.69	4.48	3.51	5.98	1.74
4	0.00	24.62	1.97	7.30	11.40	2.75
5	0.00	29.47	0.18	12.95	17.71	4.03
6	0.00	28.19	0.72	15.27	24.96	1.38
7	0.00	34.29	0.00	15.98	26.17	1.75
8	0.00	35.01	0.00	15.57	31.24	2.09
9	0.70	40.34	3.67	17.12	24.05	2.49
Overall % in each range:						
	0.10	18.84	2.66	7.29	11.31	1.59

The omitted category is 'no change'

is those with no change (so that 100.00 – the sum of row entries = percentage in that income range where there is no change).

The figures for average gain in Table 18.1 show a relatively modest advantage for the bottom income groups, when ranked according to total income, reflecting the predominance in these groups of single persons. Significant numbers of gainers and losers are to be found as we enter the middle ranges, with at first a majority of losers, since there are more couples without children than with children, and then a majority of gainers, although the top group has an average net loss. Overall, gainers and losers are approximately equal in numbers.

It is interesting to see how the results in Tables 18.1 and 18.2 change if we take equivalent income instead of total income, since one would expect families with children to have a lower position in the equivalent income distribution. Table 18.3 shows the effect of taking equivalent income, where the 'standard' equivalence scale of couple = 1.6, child = 0.4 is used. There is now a clear gradient, with the bottom income groups having a substantial positive average gain and the upper income groups, ranked in this way, a sizeable average net loss. Behind these averages are of course a wide spread of individual gains and losses: for example some 10 per cent of the top income group are net gainers.

The differences between Tables 18.1 and 18.3 illustrate the importance of the user being able to choose the format for the results – in this case because of the differential impact by family type. Further evidence about the breakdown between family types may be obtained by choosing the option in TAXMOD that presents its Tables 1 and 2 separately for single persons without children (who are unaffected by the particular measures), for couples without children, and families with children (gaining an estimated £2.2 billion). Further information about gainers and losers may also be obtained by choosing the option to list cases. We may for example look at the cases losing more than £15 a week, and this shows that they are

Table 18.3 Ranges of net equivalent income: effect of abolishing MMA/doubling CB

| Upper end | Before change | | After change | | |
	%	CUMUL	%	CUMUL	Average gain
40.00	9.22	9.22	9.11	9.11	0.83
60.00	17.40	26.61	17.44	26.55	0.80
80.00	19.38	46.00	19.28	45.83	1.00
100.00	14.39	60.39	14.62	60.45	0.85
120.00	10.49	70.88	10.79	71.24	−0.39
140.00	8.49	79.37	8.37	79.61	−0.99
160.00	6.17	85.53	6.25	86.85	−1.79
180.00	4.28	89.82	4.23	90.09	−1.73
200.00	3.13	92.94	3.03	93.12	−2.09
—	7.06	100.00	6.88	100.00	−2.55

couples paying the top rate of income tax or brought into the top band by the abolition of the married man's addition.

The program also summarizes the distributional impact in terms of Lorenz curves, or, more accurately, the information required to draw Lorenz curves. The program interpolates logarithmically the cumulative frequency and cumulative total income to give the Lorenz curve values at 10 per cent intervals. The user has the option of specifying either a 'standard' Lorenz curve or a 'generalized' Lorenz curve, where in the latter case the income totals are expressed in absolute rather than relative amounts (i.e. not divided by total income). In the present case, the total income is essentially the same in the two cases, and the figures in Table 18.4 relate to the standard Lorenz curve. The effects are not large; and follow the pattern that might be expected from the earlier findings. The shares at the bottom increase slightly; those in the middle fall; and the Lorenz curves cross again (just) in the penultimate decile.

Turning to the effect of the reform on marginal tax rates, we may expect that the abolition of the married man's addition would bring some families into the tax net and raise their marginal tax rate. On the other hand, the increase in child benefit may float some families off housing benefit and reduce their marginal rate. And the effect of the wife's earnings election is again important. More wives will be taxed separately and this may reduce the marginal rate for both husband and wife. Again the effect is not as straightforward as may appear at first sight.

Table 18.5 shows the distribution of marginal tax rates on additional £1 earnings or self-employment income (whichever is greater) by head of tax unit. The table only includes heads who have some earned income. The calculation takes account of income tax, NIC, and withdrawal of FIS, SB, passport benefits, housing benefits, and NI benefits where these are withdrawn with earned income. The ranges are 10 percentage points, and those, for example, paying basic rate income tax and standard Class 1 NIC only are in the range with upper end point 40.00 (i.e. from 30 per cent up to but not including 40 per cent). Table 18.6 shows the distribution of

Table 18.4 Lorenz curves

% of families	% of total income	
	Before	After
20.00	5.45	5.47
30.00	10.22	10.24
40.00	16.18	16.17
50.00	23.49	23.42
60.00	33.38	32.29
70.00	43.24	43.17
80.00	56.39	56.37
90.00	72.78	72.79

Table 18.5 Distribution of marginal tax rates for head of tax unit: abolition of MMA/doubling of CB

Upper end of range	Before change %	CUMUL	After change %	CUMUL
10.00	2.82	2.82	2.60	2.60
20.00	0.10	2.92	0.10	2.70
30.00	13.30	16.22	13.64	16.34
40.00	75.36	91.58	75.71	92.05
50.00	3.89	95.47	3.54	95.58
60.00	1.90	97.36	1.92	97.51
70.00	1.12	98.49	1.07	98.57
—	1.51	100.00	1.43	100.00

Average marginal rate: 34.95   35.14
% of units with marginal rate increased 1.81
% of units with marginal rate decreased 1.54

Table 18.6 Distribution of marginal tax rates faced by wife: abolition of MMA/doubling of CB (taking families where she is in paid work)

Upper end	Before change %	CUMUL	After change %	CUMUL
10.00	29.25	29.25	28.57	28.57
20.00	1.35	30.59	1.23	29.80
30.00	5.06	35.66	5.26	35.05
40.00	55.88	91.54	60.59	95.64
50.00	4.33	95.86	1.03	96.67
60.00	1.44	97.30	0.65	97.32
70.00	0.12	97.43	0.00	97.32
—	2.57	100.00	2.68	100.00

Average marginal rate: 29.29   28.89
% of units with marginal rate increased 1.34
% of units with marginal rate decreased 4.50

marginal tax rates on £1 additional work income by the wife, calculated for those families where she is in paid work.

For most families there is little change in the marginal tax rates. But we may note that for family heads the number of cases of a decrease is more or less the same as the number of cases of an increase; and that for wives there are more decreases. Moreover, the size of the change may be quite marked, as is revealed by Table 18.7 produced by selecting the third optional table. This shows the distribution *by changes* in the marginal tax rate for groups with different characteristics.

It may be seen that, where the marginal tax rate falls, the decrease is typically more than 10 percentage points. We have identified two main reasons for this: the exercise of the wife's earnings election, and floating-off housing benefit. Using the option to list cases, taking those where the marginal tax rate of the head falls by 10 percentage points or more, the breakdown between these two may be seen to be approximately equal. The

Table 18.7 Changes in marginal tax rates by characteristics: abolishing MMA/doubling CB

For heads of tax units		
	Children	No children
Fall >10	2.12	0.40
Fall 5–10	0.10	0.02
Fall 2–5	0.14	0.05
No change	94.95	98.96
Rise <2	0.08	0.00
Rise 2–5	0.32	0.00
Rise 5–10	0.78	0.22
Rise >10	1.50	0.36
Average change	0.34	0.04

For wives in paid work		
	Children	No children
Fall >10	4.14	4.52
Fall 5–10	0.00	0.15
Fall 2–5	0.00	0.15
No change	95.16	93.30
Rise 2–5	0.24	0.00
Rise >10	0.45	1.89
Average change	−0.71	−0.12

form of the output shown for each case on the screen is illustrated below for a hypothetical case where the family are floated off housing benefit by the rise in child benefit (the 'change' refers to the change in marginal tax rate of the head):

1575

Married couple

with 2 children

Tenants: housing costs of £19.40

Gross income from work of head is £113.07
Other income of £0.00
Net income before is £115.84
After is £116.80

Change is −33 percentage points

Marginal tax rate before: head 79.85%
After 46.85%

REFERENCES

Abel-Smith, B. and Townsend, P. (1965), *The Poor and the Poorest*, G. Bell and Sons, London.

Akerlof, G. A. (1978), 'The economics of tagging', *American Economic Review*, vol. 68, 8–19.

Allbeson, J. (1980) (ed.), *National Welfare Benefits Handbook*, Child Poverty Action Group, London.

Altmann, R. M. (1981a), 'Take-up of supplementary benefit by male pensioners', SSRC Programme on Taxation, Incentives and the Distribution of Income, Discussion Paper 25.

Altmann, R. M. (1981b), 'The incomes of elderly men in Britain, 1970–1977', PhD thesis, University of London.

Atkinson, A. B. (1969), *Poverty in Britain and the Reform of Social Security*, Cambridge University Press, Cambridge.

Atkinson, A. B. (1970), 'On the measurement of inequality', *Journal of Economic Theory*, vol. 2, 244–63.

Atkinson, A. B. (1983a), *The Economics of Inequality*, 2nd edition, Oxford University Press, Oxford.

Atkinson, A. B. (1983b), 'Newspaper coverage of the Budget – the effect of the March 1983 Budget on family incomes', SSRC Programme on Taxation, Incentives and the Distribution of Income, Research Note 4.

Atkinson, A. B. (1983c), 'Adjustments to the Family Expenditure Survey data', ESRC Programme on Taxation, Incentives and the Distribution of Income, Research Note 7.

Atkinson, A. B. (1984a), 'Review of the UK social security system: evidence to the National Consumer Council', ESRC Progamme on Taxation, Incentives and the Distribution of Income, Discussion Paper 66.

Atkinson, A. B. (1984b), 'Taxation and social security reform: reflections on advising a House of Commons select committee', *Policy and Politics*, 12, 107–18.

Atkinson, A. B. (1985), 'How should we measure poverty?', ESRC Programme on Taxation, Incentives and the Distribution of Income, Discussion Paper 82.

Atkinson, A. B. (1987), 'Income maintenance and social insurance', in A. J. Auerbach and M. S. Feldstein (eds) *Handbook of Public Economics*, vol. 2, North Holland, Amsterdam, 779–908.

Atkinson, A. B. (1988a), 'Measuring poverty and differences in family composition', ESRC Programme on Incentives and the Distribution of Income, Discussion Paper.

Atkinson, A. B. (1988b), 'Income maintenance for the unemployed in Britain and the response to high unemployment', Discussion Paper.

Atkinson, A. B. and Bourguignon, F. (1982), 'The comparison of multi-dimensioned distributions of economic status', *Review of Economic Studies*, vol. 49, 183–201.

Atkinson, A. B. and Bourguignon, F. (1987), 'Income distribution and differences in needs', in G. R. Feiwel (ed.), *Arrow and the Foundations of the Theory of Economic Policy*, Macmillan, London, 350–70.

Atkinson, A. B. and Flemming, J. S. (1978), 'Unemployment, social security and incentives', *Midland Bank Review*, 6–16.

Atkinson, A. B., Gomulka, J., Micklewright, J. and Rau, N. (1981), 'Unemployment duration and incentives: a preliminary analysis of the Family Expenditure Survey data 1972–1977', Unemployment Project Working Note 6, London School of Economics.

Atkinson, A. B., Gomulka, J., Micklewright, J. and Rau, N. (1982), 'Unemployment duration, social security and taxation', Unemployment Project Working Note 11, London School of Economics.

Atkinson, A. B., Gomulka, J., Micklewright, J. and Rau, N. (1983), 'Unemployment duration and incentives: evidence from the Family Expenditure Survey', *Annales de l'INSEE*, vol. 52, 3–20.

Atkinson, A. B., Gomulka, J. and Sutherland, H. (1988), 'Grossing-up FES data for tax-benefit models', in *Tax-Benefit Models*, A. B. Atkinson and H. Sutherland (eds), ST/ICERD Occasional Paper No. 10, London School of Economics, 223–53.

Atkinson, A. B., King, M. A. and Stern, N. H. (1983), Memorandum to the House of Commons Treasury and Civil Service Committee Sub-Committee, House of Commons, 20–11, HMSO, London.

Atkinson, A. B., Maynard, A. K. and Trinder, C. G. (1981), 'National assistance and low incomes in 1950', *Social Policy and Administration*, vol. 15,. 19–31.

Atkinson, A. B., Maynard, A. K. and Trinder, C. G. (1983), *Parents and Children*, Heinemann, London.

Atkinson, A. B. and Micklewright, J. (1981), 'Unemployment and "replacement rates"', Unemployment Project Working Note 8.

Atkinson, A. B. and Micklewright, J. (1983), 'On the reliability of income data in the Family Expenditure Survey 1970–1977', *Journal of the Royal Statistical Society*, vol. 146, 33–61.

Atkinson, A. B. and Micklewright, J. (1986), *Unemployment Benefits and Unemployment Duration*, ST/ICERD Occasional Paper 6, LSE, London.

Atkinson, A. B. and Micklewright, J. (1988), 'Unemployment compensation, employment policy and labour market transitions', OECD, Paris.

Atkinson, A. B., Micklewright, J. and Stern, N. H. (1982), 'A comparison of the Family Expenditure Survey and the New Earnings Survey 1971–1977: Part 11 hours and earnings', SSRC Programme on Taxation, Incentives and the Distribution of Income, Discussion Paper 32.

Atkinson, A. B. and Rahmatulla, A. (1983), 'Family labour supply and benefits in the Family Finances Survey', SSRC Programme on Taxation Incentives and the Distribution of Income, Research Note 3.

Atkinson, A. B. and Rau, N. (1981), 'The specification of income taxation and benefits in models of unemployment duration', Unemployment Project Working Note 9, London School of Economics.

Atkinson, A. B. and Stiglitz, J. E. (1980), *Lectures on Public Economics*, McGraw-Hill, New York.

Atkinson, A. B. and Sutherland, H. (1983a), 'Hypothetical families in the Family Expenditure Survey 1980', SSRC Programme on Taxation, Incentives and the Distribution of Income, Research Note 1.

Atkinson, A. B. and Sutherland, H. (1983b), 'Analysis of reforms of the tax benefit system', Memorandum to the House of Commons Treasury and Civil Service Committee Sub-Committee, House of Commons, 20–11, HMSO, London.

Atkinson, A. B. and Sutherland, H. (1984a), 'TAXMOD: user manual', London School of Economics, London.

Atkinson, A. B. and Sutherland, H. (1984b), 'A tax credit scheme and families in work', ESRC Programme on Taxation, Incentives and the Distribution of Income, Discussion Paper 54.

Atkinson, A. B. and Sutherland, H. (1988), *Tax-Benefit Models*, ST/ICERD Occasional Paper 10, London School of Economics, London.

Banting, K. G. (1979), *Poverty, Politics and Policy*, Macmillan, London.

Barker, D. (1971), 'The family income supplement', in D. Bull (ed.), *Family Poverty*, Duckworth, London, 70–82.

Barr, N. (1987), *The Economics of the Welfare State*, Weidenfeld and Nicolson, London.

Barry, B. (1973), *The Liberal Theory of Justice*, Clarendon Press, Oxford.

Bazen, S. (1984) 'Low pay, minimum wages and family poverty', ESRC Programme on Taxation, Incentives and the Distribution of Income, Discussion Paper 69.

Becker, G. S. (1965) 'The allocation of time', *Economic Journal*, vol. 75, 493–517.

Beckerman, W. and Clark, S. (1982), *Poverty and Social Security in Britain Since 1961*, Oxford University Press, Oxford.

Beveridge, Sir William (Lord) (1942), *Social Insurance and Allied Services*, Cmd 6404, HMSO, London.

Blank, R. M. and Blinder, A. S. (1986), 'Macroeconomics, income distribution and poverty', in S. H. Danziger and D. H. Weinberg (eds), *Fighting Poverty*, Harvard University Press, Cambridge, Mass.

Blundell, R. W., Meghir, C., Symons, E. and Walker, I. (1984), 'On the reform of the taxation of husband and wife: are incentives important?', *Fiscal Studies*, vol. 5, November, 1–22.

Booth, C. (1889–1902), *Life and Labour of the People in London*, Macmillan, London.

Bourguignon, F., Chiappori, P.-A. and Sastre-Descals, J. (1988), 'SYSIFF: a simulation program of the French tax-benefit system', in *Tax-Benefit Models*, A. B. Atkinson and H. Sutherland (eds) ST/ICERD Occasional Paper No. 10, London School of Economics, 97–120.

Bowley, A. H. (1972), *A Memoir of Professor Sir A. Bowley (1969–1957) and his Family*, Chelsea, London.

Bowley, A. L. (1913), 'Working-class households in Reading', *Journal of the Royal Statistical Society*, vol. 76, 672–701.

Bowley, A. L. and Burnett-Hurst, A. R. (1915), *Livelihood and Poverty*, Bell and Sons, London.

Bowley, A. L. and Hogg, M. H. (1925), *Has Poverty Diminished?* P. S. King, London.

Bradshaw, J. (1977), 'A multi-variate analysis of variations in the proportion of households receiving rent rebates', University of York.

Branson, N. and Heinemann, M. (1973), *Britain in the Nineteen Thirties*, Panther, London.

Broad, P. (1977), *Pensioners and their Needs*, OPCS, HMSO, London.

Bullock, A. (1960), *The Life and Times of Ernest Bevin*, vol. 1, Heinemann, London.

Chapman, D. (1951), 'York – laboratory of social welfare', manuscript.

Chesher, A. D. and Lancaster, T. (1981), 'The treatment of unobservables in econometric analyses of labour market transitions', University of Birmingham Discussion Paper A247.

Chilchinisky, G. (1982), 'Basic needs and the North/South debate', World Order Model Project Working Paper 21.

Clark, S. R., Hemming, R. and Ulph, D. (1981), 'On indices for the measurement of poverty', *Economic Journal*, vol. 91, 515–26.

Coates, K. and Silburn, R. (1970), *Poverty: the Forgotten Englishmen*, Penguin, London.

Cole, D. and Utting, J. (1962), *The Economic Circumstances of Old People*, Codicote Press, Welwyn.

Cowell, F. A. (1985), 'Welfare benefits and the economics of take-up', ESRC Programme on Taxation, Incentives and the Distribution of Income, Discussion Paper 89.

Creedy, J. (1980), 'The new government pension scheme: a simulation analysis', *Oxford Bulletin of Economics and Statistics*, vol. 42, 51–64.

Creedy, J. and Disney, R. (1985), *Social Insurance in Transition*, Clarendon Press, Oxford.

Crosland, C. A. R. (1956), *The Future of Socialism*, Cape, London.

CSO (1979), 'Bias in the Family Expenditure Survey: some results', unpublished.

Danziger, S., Haveman, R. and Plotnick, R. (1981), 'How income transfer programs affect work, savings and the income distribution: a critical review', *Journal of Economic Literature*, vol. 19, 975–1028.

Dasgupta, P. S. and Maskin, E. (1986), 'The existence of equilibrium in discontinuous economic games I and II', *Review of Economic Studies*, vol. 53, 1–41.

Deacon, A. and Bradshaw, J. (1962), *Reserved for the Poor*, Basil Blackwell, Oxford.

Deaton, A. S. and Muellbauer, J. (1980), *Economics and Consumer Behaviour*, Cambridge University Press, Cambridge.

Department of Employment (1985), *Employment: the Challenge for the Nation*, Cmnd 9474, HMSO, London.

Department of the Environment (1975), *Poverty and Multiple Deprivation*, Lambeth Inner Area Study.

Department of Health and Social Security (1975), *Two-Parent Families in Receipt of Family Income Supplement, 1972*, DHSS Statistical and Research Report Series, No. 9, HMSO, London.

Department of Health and Social Security (1981), *The Take-up of Family Income Supplement: Note on the Estimate Derived from the Family Finances Survey*, Statistics Branch, HMSO, London.

Department of Health and Social Security (1982), 'Low Income Families – 1979' typescript.

Department of Health and Social Security (1983), *Tables on Families With Low Incomes – 1981*, HMSO, London.

Department of Health and Social Security (1984) *For Richer, for Poorer? DHSS Cohort Study of Unemployed Men*, HMSO, London.

Department of Health and Social Security (1985a) *Reform of Social Security*, vols 1–3, Cmnd 9517, 9518, 9519, HMSO, London.

Department of Health and Social Security (1985b), *Reform of Social Security: Programme for Action*, Cmnd 9691, HMSO, London.

Department of Health and Social Security (1988a), *Low Income Statistics: Report of a Technical Review*, DHSS, London.

Department of Health and Social Security (1988b), *Low Income Families – 1985*, DHSS, London.

Department of Health and Social Security (1988c), *Households Below Average Income: A Statistical Analysis 1981–85*, DHSS, London.

Diamond, P. A. (1965), 'On the cost of tax-exempt bonds', *Journal of Political Economy*, vol. 73, 399–403.

Diamond, P. A. (1977), 'A framework for social security analysis', *Journal of Public Economics*, vol. 8, 275–98.

Diamond, P. A. and Mirrlees, J. A. (1978), 'A model of social insurance with variable retirement', *Journal of Public Economics*, vol. 10, 295–336.

Dilnot, A. W., Kay, J. A. and Morris, C. N. (1984), *The Reform of Social Security*, Oxford University Press, Oxford.

Dilnot, A. and Kell, M. (1987), 'Male unemployment and women's work', *Fiscal Studies*, vol. 8, no. 3, 1–16.

Dilnot, A. and Morris, C. N. (1983), 'Private costs and benefits of unemployment: measuring replacement rates', *Oxford Economic Papers*, vol. 35, no. 4, 321–40.

Dobb, M. H. (1952), 'Review of *Poverty and the Welfare State*', *Economic Journal*, vol. 62, 173–5.

Doeringer, P. B. and Piore, M. J. (1971), *Internal Labor Markets and Manpower Analysis*, Heath, Lexington, Mass.

Domar, E. D. and Musgrave, R. A. (1944), 'Proportional income taxation and risk-taking', *Quarterly Journal of Economics*, vol. 58, 389–422.

Donnison, D. (1982), *The Politics of Poverty*, Martin Robertson, Oxford.

Drèze, J. and Sen, A. (1988), 'Public action for social security', paper presented at ST/ICERD/WIDER Workshop, London School of Economics.

Duncan, G. J. (1984) (ed.), *Years of Poverty, Years of Plenty*, Institute for Social Research, Michigan.

Ellwood, D. T. and Summers, L. H. (1986). 'Poverty in America: is welfare the answer or the problem?', in S. H. Danziger and D. H. Weinberg (eds), *Fighting Poverty*, Harvard University Press, Cambridge, Mass., 78–105.

Elton, D. H. (1974), 'Estimating entitlement to FIS', *Statistical News*, February.

Ermisch, J. (1981), 'Paying the piper: demographic changes and pension contributions', *Policy Studies*.

Feinstein, C. H. (1972), *National Income, Expenditure and Output of the UK 1855–1965*, Cambridge University Press, Cambridge.

Feinstein, C. H. (1976), *Statistical Tables of National Income, Expenditure and Output of the UK 1855–1965*, Cambridge University Press, Cambridge.

Feldstein, M. S. (1976), 'Temporary layoffs in the theory of unemployment', *Journal of Political Economy*, vol. 84, 937–57.

Feldstein, M. S. (1978a), 'The effect of unemployment insurance on temporary layoff unemployment', *American Economic Review*, vol. 68, 834–46.

Feldstein, M. S. (1982), 'Inflation, tax rules and investment: some econometric evidence', *Econometrica*, vol. 50, 825–62.

Fiegehen, G. C. and Lansley, P. S. (1976), 'The measurement of poverty', *Journal of the Royal Statistical Society*, vol. 139, 508–18.

Fiegehen, G. C., Lansley, P. S. and Smith, A. D. (1977), *Poverty and Progress in Britain 1953–73*, Cambridge University Press, Cambridge.

Fishburn, P. C. (1977), 'Mean-risk analysis with risk associated with below-target returns', *American Economic Review*, vol. 67, 116–26.

Fogarty, M. P. (1980), *Retirement Age and Retirement Costs*, Policy Studies Institute, London.

Ford, P. (1934), *Work and Wealth in a Modern Port*, Allen and Unwin, London.

Ford, P. (1939), *Incomes, Means Tests and Personal Responsibility*, P. S. King, London.

Foster, J. E. (1984), 'On economic poverty: a survey of aggregate measures', *Advances in Econometrics*, vol. 3, 215–51.

Foster, J. E., Greer, J. and Thorbecke, E. (1984), 'A class of decomposable poverty measures', *Econometrica*, vol. 52, 761–6.

Foster, J. E. and Shorrocks, A. F. (1984), 'Poverty orderings', University of Essex, manuscript.

Fuchs, V. (1965), 'Toward a theory of poverty', in *Task Force on Economic Growth and Opportunity, The Concept of Poverty*, Chamber of Commerce of the United States, Washington, DC.

George, R. F. (1937), 'A new calculation of the poverty line', *Journal of the Royal Statistical Society*, vol. 100, 74–95.

Goedhart, T., Halberstadt, V., Kapteyn, A. and van Praag, B. (1977), 'The poverty line: concept and measurement', *Journal of Human Resources*, vol. 12, 503–20.

Gourieroux, C. (1980), 'A note on poverty measurement', University of Paris IX, manuscript.

Government Actuary (1975), *Report on the Financial Provisions of the Social Security Pensions Bill 1975*, HMSO, London.

Government Actuary (1981), *Survey of Occupational Pension Schemes in 1979*, HMSO, London.

Gronau, R. (1983), 'Some thoughts on the measurement and welfare implications of equivalence scales', University of Jerusalem, manuscript.

Gueron, J. M. (1986), *Work Initiatives for Welfare Recipients*, Manpower Demonstration Research Corporation, New York.

Hagenbuch, W. (1958), *Social Economics*, Nisbet, London.

Hamermesh, D. S. (1982), 'The interaction between research and policy: the case of unemployment insurance', *American Economic Review*, Papers and Proceedings, vol. 72, 237–41.

Hamill, L. (1978), 'An explanation of the increase in female one-parent families receiving supplementary benefit', Government Economic Service Working Paper 14.

Hardy, G. H., Littlewood, J. E. and Polya, G. (1929), 'Some simple inequalities satisfied by convex functions', *Messenger of Mathematics*, vol. 58, 145–52.

Hartmann, H. (1981), *Sozialhilfebedürftigkeit und 'Dunkelziffer der Armut'*, Kohlhammer, Stuttgart.

Hauser, R., Cremer-Schäfer, H. and Nouverté, E. (1981), *National Report on Poverty in the Federal Republic of Germany*, University of Frankfurt, Frankfurt.

Hausman, J. A. (1981), 'Labor supply', in H. J. Aaron and J. A. Pechman (eds), *How Taxes Affect Economic Behaviour*, Brookings Institution, Washington DC.

Heckman, J. J. and MaCurdy, T. E. (1980), 'A life-cycle model of female labour supply', *Review of Economic Studies*, vol. 47, 47–74.

Heckman, J. J. and Singer, B. (1982), 'The identification problem in econometric models for duration data', in W. Hildenbrand (ed.), *Advances in Econometrics*, Cambridge University Press, Cambridge, 39–77.

Heckman, J. J. and Singer, B. (1984a), 'A method for minimising the impact of distributional assumptions in econometric models for duration data', *Econometrica*, vol. 52, 271–320.

Heckman, J. J. and Singer, B. (1984b), 'Econometric duration analysis', *Journal of Econometrics*, vol. 24, 63–132.

Heckman, J. J. and Singer, B. (1984c), 'The identifiability of the proportional hazard model', *Review of Economic Studies*, vol. 51, 231–41.

Hemming, R. (1983), 'The tax treatment of occupational pension schemes', *The Structure of Personal Income Taxation and Income Support*, Treasury and Civil Service Committee, 20–11, HMSO, London.

Hemming, R. (1984), *Poverty and Incentives*, Oxford University Press, Oxford.

Hemming, R. and Kay, J. A. (1982), 'The costs of the state earnings-related pension scheme', *Economic Journal*, vol. 92, 300–19.

HM Treasury (1982), 'Memorandum submitted by HM Treasury, Department of Health and Social Security and Inland Revenue', in Minutes of Evidence, House of Commons Treasury and Civil Service Committee, *The Structure of Personal*

Income Taxation and Income Support, House of Commons, 20–1, HMSO, London.

Holtermann, S. (1975), 'Areas of urban deprivation in Great Britain: an analysis of 1971 Census data', *Social Trends*, HMSO, London.

House of Commons Social Services Committee (1988), *Fourth Report: Families on Low Income: Low Income Statistics*, HMSO, London.

House of Commons Treasury and Civil Service Committee (1983), *The Structure of Personal Income Taxation and Income Support*, HMSO, London.

Housing Policy Review (1977), *Technical Volume*, HMSO, London.

International Labour Office (1984), *Into the Twenty-First Century: The Development of Social Security*, ILO, Geneva.

Jenkins, S. and Maynard, A. K. (1981), 'The Rowntree Surveys: poverty in York since 1899', in C. H. Feinstein (ed.), *York 1831–1981*, William Sessions Limited.

Jones, D. C. (1934) (ed.), *The Social Survey of Merseyside*, University of Liverpool Press, Liverpool, 3 vols.

Jones, D. C. (1948), *Social Surveys*, Hutchinson, London.

Jones, T. (1981), 'The household sector', *Economic Trends*, September.

Joseph, Sir Keith and Sumption, J. (1979), *Equality*, John Murray, London.

Kaim-Caudle, P. (1953), 'Studies in poverty', University of Durham, manuscript.

Karamata, J. (1932), 'Sur une inégalité relative aux fonctions convexes', *Publications Mathématiques de l'Université de Belgrade*, vol. 1, 145–8.

Kay, J. A., Keen, M. J. and Morris, C. N. (1984), 'Estimating consumption from expenditure data', *Journal of Public Economics*, vol. 23, 169–81.

Kay, J. A., Morris, C. N. and Warren, N. A. (1980), 'Tax, benefits and the incentive to seek work', *Fiscal Studies*, vol. 1, 8–25.

Kemsley, W. F. F. (1975), 'Family Expenditure Survey: a study of differential response based on a comparison of the 1971 sample with the Census', *Statistical News*, November.

Kemsley, W. F. F., Redpath, R. U. and Holmes, M. (1980), *Family Expenditure Survey Handbook*, HMSO, London.

Kesselman, J. R. and Garfinkel, I. (1978), 'Professor Friedman, meet Lady Rhys-Williams: NIT vs CIT', *Journal of Public Economics*, vol. 10, 179–216.

Kiefer, N. M. and Neumann, G. R. (1979a), 'An empirical job-search model, with a test of the constant reservation wage hypothesis', *Journal of Political Economy*, vol. 87, 89–107.

Kiefer, N. M. and Neumann, G. R. (1979b), 'Estimation of wage offer distributions and reservation wages', in S. A. Lippman and J. J. McCall (eds), *Studies in the Economics of Search*, North-Holland, Amsterdam, 171–89.

Kiefer, N. M. and Neumann, G. R. (1981), 'Individual effects in a non-linear model: explicit treatment of heterogeneity in the empirical job search model', *Econometrica*, vol. 49, 965–80.

Killingsworth, M. R. (1983), *Labour Supply*, Cambridge University Press, Cambridge.

King, M. A. (1983), 'Welfare analysis of tax reforms using household data', *Journal of Public Economics*, vol. 21, 183–214.

King, M. A. (1988), 'Tax policy and family welfare', in *Tax-Benefit Models*, A. B. Atkinson and H. Sutherland (eds), ST/ICERD Occasional Paper No. 10, London School of Economics, 10–31.

King, M. A. and Ramsay, P. (1983), 'TRAP – Tax Reform Analysis Package', SSRC Programme on Taxation, Incentives and the Distribution of Income, Discussion Paper 35.

Knight, F. H. (1921), *Risk, Uncertainty and Profit*, Houghton Mifflin, Boston, Mass.

Knight, I. (1981), *Family Finances*, Occasional Paper 26, OPCS, London.

Knight, I. B. and Nixon, J. M. (1975), *Two-Parent Families In Receipt of Family Income Supplement, 1972*, HMSO, London.

Kundu, A. and Smith, T. E. (1983), 'An impossibility theorem on poverty indices', *International Economic Review*, vol. 24, 423–34.

Lancaster, T. (1979), 'Econometric methods for the duration of unemployment', *Econometrica*, vol. 47, 939–56.

Lancaster, T. and Chesher, A. D. (1981), 'Simultaneous equations with endogenous hazards', Hull Economic Research Paper 84.

Lancaster, T. and Chesher, A. D. (1983), 'An econometric model of reservation wages', *Econometrica*, vol. 51, 1661–76.

Lancaster, T. and Nickell, S. J. (1980), 'The analysis of re-employment probabilities for the unemployed', *Journal of the Royal Statistical Society*, vol. 143, 141–65.

Lazear, E. P. and Michael, R. T. (1980), 'Family size and the distribution of real per capita income', *American Economic Review*, vol. 70, 91–107.

Le Breton, M. (1986), 'Essais sur les fondements de l'analyse économique de l'inégalité', Thèse pour le Doctorat d'état, University of Rennes.

Leete, R. (1978), 'One-parent families: numbers and characteristics', *Population Trends*, vol. 13.

Le Grand, J. and Winter, D. (1987), 'The middle classes and the defence of the British welfare state', in R. E. Goodin and J. Le Grand (eds) *Not Only the Poor*, Allen and Unwin, London, 147–68.

Lindbeck, A. (1981), 'Work disincentives in the welfare state', *National Ökonomische Gesellschaft Lectures*, Manz, Vienna.

Lindbeck, A. (1985), 'Redistribution policy and the expansion of the public sector', *Journal of Public Economics*, vol. 28, 309–28.

London and Cambridge Economic Service (1970), *Key Statistics of the British Economy 1900–1970*.

Lydall, H . F. (1959), 'The long-term trend in the size distribution of income', *Journal of the Royal Statistical Society*, vol. 122, 1–37.

Lynes, T. (1962), *National Assistance and National Prosperity*, G. Bell and Sons, London.

MacAfee, K. (1980), 'A glimpse of the hidden economy in the national accounts', *Economic Trends*, no. 136, 81–7.

Macdonald, M. (1977), *Food, Stamps and Income Maintenance*, Academic Press, New York.

Mack, J. and Lansley, S. (1985), *Poor Britain*, Allen and Unwin, London.

Maki, D. and Spindler, Z. A. (1975), 'The effect of unemployment compensation on the rate of unemployment in Great Britain', *Oxford Economic Papers*, vol. 27, 440–54.

Mallender, J. and Ramsden, S. (1984), 'Incomes in and out of work, 1978–82: some results using the DHSS cohort simulation model', Government Economic Service Working Paper No. 69.

Matthewman, J. and Calvert, H. (1987) *Guide to the Social Security Act 1986*, Tolley, London.

Maurice, R. (1968), *National Accounts Statistics: Sources and Methods*, HMSO, London.

Meade, J. E. (1972), 'Poverty in the welfare state', *Oxford Economic Papers*, vol. 24, 289–326.

Metcalf, D. and Nickell, S. (1975), 'Jobs and pay', *Midland Bank Review*, Spring 1985.

Michelman, F. I. (1973), 'In pursuit of constitutional welfare rights: one view of Rawls' theory of justice', *University of Pennsylvania Law Review*, vol. 121, 962–1019.

Micklewright, J. (1984a), 'Male unemployment and the Family Expenditure Survey 1972–1980', *Oxford Bulletin of Economics and Statistics*, vol. 46, 31–53.

Micklewright, J. (1984b), A microeconomic analysis of the receipt of unemployment benefits by males in the UK', PhD dissertation, University of London.

Micklewright, J. (1985), 'On earnings related unemployment benefits and their relation to earnings', *Economic Journal*, vol. 95, 133–145.

Micklewright, J. (1986), 'Unemployment and incentives to work: policy and evidence in the 1980s' in Hart, P. E. (ed.), *Unemployment and Labour Market Policies*, Gower, London.

Micklewright, J. and Rau, N. (1980), 'Analysis of earnings of male full-time workers in the FES 1970–1977', Unemployment Project Working Note 5, London School of Economics.

Millar, J. (1982), *Take-up of Means-Tested Benefits in Work*, Department of Health and Social Security, HMSO, London.

Millar, J. (1983), 'The living standards of low-income one-parent families', University of York Social Policy Research Unit.

Minford, P. (1982), 'The development of monetary strategy', in J. Kay (ed.), *The 1982 Budget*, Basil Blackwell, Oxford.

Minford, P. (1984), 'State expenditure: a study in waste', Supplement to *Economic Affairs*, April–June.

Ministry of Agriculture, Fisheries and Food (1984), *Household Food Consumption and Expenditure: 1982*, HMSO, London.

Ministry of Pensions and National Insurance (1966), *Financial and other Circumstances of Retirement Pensioners*, HMSO, London.

Ministry of Reconstruction (1944), *Social Insurance*, Cmd 6550, HMSO, London.

Moffitt, R. L. (1983), 'An economic model of welfare stigma', *American Economic Review*, vol. 73, 1023–35.

Morris, C. N. (1983), Memorandum to the House of Commons Treasury and Civil Service Committee Sub-Committee, House of Commons, 20–11, HMSO, London.

Moylan, S. and Davies, B. (1981), 'The flexibility of the unemployed', *Department of Employment Gazette*, January.

Narendranathan, W., Nickell, S. J. and Stern, J. (1985), 'Unemployment benefits revisited', *Economic Journal*, vol. 95, 307–29.

National Consumer Council (1976), *Means-Tested Benefits*, National Consumer Council, London.

Nichols, A. L. and Zeckhauser, R. (1982), 'Targeting transfers through restrictions on recipients', *American Economic Review*, Papers and Proceedings, vol. 72, 373–7.

Nichols, D., Smolensky, E. and Tideman, T. N. (1971), 'Discrimination by waiting time in merit goods', *American Economic Review*, vol. 16, 312–23.

Nicholson, J. L. (1949), 'Variations in working-class family expenditure', *Journal of the Royal Statistical Society*, vol. 112, Series A, 359–411.

Nicholson, J. L. (1979), 'The assessment of poverty and the information we need', in *Social Security Research*, Department of Health and Social Security, HMSO, London.

Nickell, S. J. (1979a), 'Estimating the probability of leaving unemployment', *Econometrica*, vol. 47, 1249–66.

Nickell, S. J. (1979b), 'The effect of unemployment and related benefits on the duration of unemployment', *Economic Journal*, vol. 89, 34–49.

Nickell, S. J. (1980), 'A picture of male unemployment in Britain', *Economic Journal*, vol. 89, 34–49.

Nickell, S. J. (1982), 'The determinants of equilibrium unemployment in Britain', *Economic Journal*, vol. 92, 555–75.

Nolan, B. (1987), *Income Distribution and the Macroeconomy*, Cambridge University Press, Cambridge.

Nozick, R. (1974), *Anarchy, State and Utopia*, Basil Blackwell, Oxford.

O'Higgins, M. and Patterson, A. (1985), 'The prospects for public expenditure', in R. Klein and M. O'Higgins (eds), *The Future of Welfare*, Basil Blackwell, Oxford.

Organisation for Economic Co-operation and Development (1984), *Economic Outlook*, December, OECD, Paris.

Orshansky, M. (1965), 'Counting the poor: another look at the poverty profile', *Social Security Bulletin*, vol. 28, 3–29.

Pahl, J. (1983), 'The allocation of money and the structuring of inequality within marriage', *Sociological Review*, vol. 31, 237–62.

Parker, H. (1982), 'Basic income guarantee scheme', Minutes of Evidence, House of Commons Select Committee on the Treasury and the Civil Service, *The Structure of Personal Income Taxation and Income Support*, HMSO, London.

Parker, H. (1983), 'Basic income guarantee scheme: synopsis', Minutes of Evidence, *The Structure of Personal Income Taxation and Income Support*, Treasury and Civil Service Committee, 20–1, HMSO, London.

Parker, H. (1984), *Action on Welfare*, Social Affairs Unit.

Parker, H. (1989), *Instead of the Dole*, Routledge, London.

Parker, S. (1980), *Older Workers and Retirement*, HMSO, London.

Peacock, A. T. and Wiseman, J. (1967), *The Growth of Public Expenditure in the UK*, second edition, Allen and Unwin, London.

Phillips, Sir Thomas (1954), Chairman *Report of the Committee on the Economic and Financial Problems of the Provision for Old Age*, HMSO, Cmd 9333, London.

Piachaud, D. (1981a), 'The dole', Centre for Labour Economics Discussion Paper 89.

Piachaud, D. (1981b), 'Peter Townsend and the Holy Grail', *New Society*, 10 September, 419–21.

Pollak, R. A. and Wales, T. J. (1979), 'Welfare comparisons and equivalence scales', *American Economic Review*, vol. 69, 216–21.

Popay, J., Rimmer, L. and Rossiter, C. (1983), *One Parent Families*, Study Commission on the Family.

Projector, D. S. and Murray, E. G. (1978), Eligibility for Welfare and Participation Rates, US Department of Health, Education and Welfare, Washington DC.

Pyatt, G. (1984), 'Measuring welfare, poverty and inequality', World Bank, manuscript.

Rawls, J. (1971), *A Theory of Justice*, Harvard University Press, Cambridge, Mass.

Reich, C. (1964), 'The new property', *Yale Law Journal*, vol. 73, 733–87.

Rein, M. (1970), 'Problems in the definition and measurement of poverty', in Peter Townsend (ed.), *The Concept of Poverty*, Heinemann, London, 46–63.

Rhys Williams, J. (1943), *Something to Look Forward to*, MacDonald, London.

Rhys Williams, J. (1953), *Taxation and Incentive*, William Hodge, London.

Riley, J. G. (1975), 'Competitive signalling', *Journal of Economic Theory*, vol. 10, 174–86.

Riley, J. G. (1979), 'Informational equilibria', *Econometrica*, vol. 47, 331–59.

Rose, M. E. (1971), *The English Poor Law*, David and Charles, Newton Abbot.

Rothbarth, E. (1943), 'Note on a method of determining equivalent income for families of different composition', in C. Madge (ed.), *Wartime Pattern of Saving and Spending*, Macmillan, London.

Rothschild, M. and Stiglitz, J. E. (1979), 'Equilibrium in competitive insurance markets: an essay on the economics of imperfect information', *Quarterly Journal of Economics*, vol. 90, 629–49.

Rowland, M. (1988), *Rights Guide to Non-Means-Tested Social Security Benefits*, 11th edition, Child Poverty Action Group, London.

Rowntree, B. S. (1901), *Poverty: A Study of Town Life*, Longmans, London.

Rowntree, B. S. (1937), *The Human Needs of Labour*, Longmans, London.

Rowntree, B. S. (1941), *Poverty and Progress*, Longmans, London.

Rowntree, B. S. and Lavers, G. R. (1951), *Poverty and the Welfare State*, Longmans, London.

Roy, A. D. (1952), 'Safety first and the holding of assets', *Econometrica*, vol. 20, 431–49.

Royal Commission on the Distribution of Income and Wealth (1975), *Initial Report on the Standing Reference*, Cmnd 6171, HMSO, London.

Royal Commission on the Distribution of Income and Wealth (1978), *Lower Incomes*, Report No. 6, Cmnd 7175, HMSO, London.

Royal Commission on the Taxation of Profits and Income (1954), *Second Report*, HMSO, London.

Runciman, W. G. (1966), *Relative Deprivation and Social Justice*, Routledge, London.

Rutter, M. and Madge, N. (1976), *Cycles of Disadvantage*, Heinemann, London.

Seers, D. (1956), 'Has the distribution of income become more unequal?' *Bulletin of the Oxford University Institute of Statistics*, vol. 18, 73–86.

Sen, A. K. (1973), *On Economic Inequality*, Clarendon Press, Oxford.

Sen, A. K. (1974), 'Informational bases of alternative welfare approaches', *Journal of Public Economics*, vol. 3, 387–403.

Sen, A. K. (1976a), 'Poverty: an ordinal approach to measurement', *Econometrica*, vol. 44, 219–31.

Sen, A. K. (1976b), 'Real national income', *Review of Economic Studies*, vol. 43, 19–39.

Sen, A. K. (1977), 'On weights and measures', *Econometrica*, vol. 45, 1539–72.

Sen, A. K. (1979), 'Issues in the measurement of poverty', *Scandinavian Journal of Economics*, vol. 81, 285–307.

Sen, A. K. (1981), *Poverty and Famines*, Oxford University Press, Oxford.

Sen, A. K. (1982), *Choice, Welfare and Measurement*, Basil Blackwell, Oxford.

Sen, A. K. (1983), 'Poor, relatively speaking', *Oxford Economic Papers*, vol. 35, 153–69.

Shorrocks, A. F. (1983), 'Ranking income distributions', *Economica*, vol. 50, 3–17.

Smee, C. H. and Stern, J. (1978), 'The unemployed in a period of high unemployment', Government Economic Service Working Paper 11.

Smeeding, T., O'Higgins, M. and Rainwater, L. (eds), (1989), *Poverty, Inequality and the Distribution of Income in an International Context*, Wheatsheaf, London.

Smith, H. L. (1930–35), *The New Survey of London Life and Labour*, P. S. King, London, 9 vols.

Srinivasan, T. N. (1977), 'Development, poverty and basic human needs: some issues', *Food Research Institute Studies*, vol. 16, 11–28.

Stacpoole, J. (1972), 'Running FIS', *New Society*, 13 January 1972.

Stark, T. (1978), 'Personal incomes', *Reviews of UK Statistical Sources*, vol. VI, Pergamon.

Stern, J. (1982), 'Unemployment inflow rates for Autumn 1978', Centre for Labour Economics Discussion Paper 129, London School of Economics.

Stigler, G. J. (1970), 'Director's law of public income redistribution', *Journal of Law and Economics*, vol. 13, 1–10.

Stiglitz, J. E. (1975), 'Information and economic analysis', in J. M. Parkin and A. R. Nobay (eds), *Current Economic Problems*, Cambridge University Press, Cambridge, 27–52.

Stiglitz, J. E. (1977), 'Monopoly, non-linear pricing and imperfect information: the insurance market', *Review of Economic Studies*, vol. 44, 407–30.

Supplementary Benefits Commission (1977), *Annual Report 1976*, Cmnd 6910, HMSO, London.

Supplementary Benefits Commission (1978), *Take-up of Supplementary Benefits*, SBA Paper No. 7, HMSO, London.

Tesfatsion, L. (1976), 'Stochastic dominance and the maximisation of expected utility', *Review of Economic Studies*, vol. 43, 301–15.

Thon, D. (1979), 'On measuring poverty', *Review of Income and Wealth*, vol. 25, 429–40.

Titmuss, R. M. (1962), *Income Distribution and Social Change*, Allen and Unwin, London.

Tobin, J. (1970), 'On limiting the domain of inequality', *Journal of Law and Economics*, vol. 13, 263–77.

Toland, S. (1980), 'Social commentary: changes in living standards since the 1950s', *Social Trends*, HMSO, London.

Tout, H. (1938), *The Standard of Living in Bristol*, Arrowsmith.

Townsend, P. (1952) (Political and Economic Planning), 'Poverty: ten years after Beveridge', *Planning*, vol. 19, 21–40.

Townsend, P. (1962), 'The meaning of poverty', *British Journal of Sociology*, vol. 18, 210–27.

Townsend, P. (ed.), (1970), *The Concept of Poverty*, Heinemann, London.

Townsend, P. (1973), *The Social Minority*, Allen Lane, London.

Townsend, P. (1979), *Poverty in the United Kingdom*, Allen Lane, London.

US Bureau of the Census (1981), *Characteristics of the Population Below the Poverty Level: 1979*, Current Population Report, Series P–60, No. 130, Washington DC.

US Bureau of the Census (1984), *Characteristics of the Population Below the Poverty Level: 1982*, Current Population Report, Series P–60, No. 144, Washington DC.

US Bureau of the Census (1985), *Money Income and Poverty Status of Families and Persons in the United States: 1984*, Series P–60, No. 149, Washington DC.

US Department of Health, Education and Welfare (1976), *The Measure of Poverty*, Washington DC.

van Praag, B. M. S., Goedhart, T. and Kapteyn, A. (1980), 'The poverty line – a pilot survey in Europe', *Review of Economics and Statistics*, vol. 62, 461–5.

van Praag, B. M. S., Hagenaars, A. J. M. and van Weeren, H. (1982a), 'Poverty in Europe', *Review of Income and Wealth*, vol. 28, 345–59.

van Praag, B. M. S., Spit, J. S. and van de Stadt, H. (1982b), 'A comparison between the food ratio poverty line and the Leyden poverty line', *Review of Economics and Statistics*, vol. 64, 691–4.

Vernier, P. (1981), 'Rights to welfare as an issue in income support policy', in P. G. Brown, C. Johnson and P. Vernier (eds), *Income Support*, Rowman, Totawa, 219–32.

Vickrey, C. (1977), 'The time-poor: a new look at poverty', *Journal of Human Resources*, vol. 12, 27–48.

Vince, P. (1983), *Tax Credit – the Liberal Plan for Tax and Social Security*, Women's Liberal Federation, London.

Walsh, A. J. (1972), 'Tax allowances and fiscal policy', in P. Townsend and N. Bosanquet (eds), *Labour and Inequality*, Fabian Society, London, 211–34.

Warlick, J. L. (1981), 'Participation of the aged in SSI', *Journal of Human Resources*, 17, 236–60.

Watts, H. W. (1968), 'An economic definition of poverty', in D. P. Moynihan (ed.), *On Understanding Poverty*, Basic Books, New York, 316–29.

Weale, A. (1983), *Political Theory and Social Policy*, Macmillan, London.

Wedderburn, D. (1962), 'Poverty in Britain today: the evidence', *Sociological Review*, vol. 10, 257–82.

Wedge, P. and Prosser, H. (1973), *Born to Fail?*, Arrow Books.

Weisbrod, B. A. (1969), 'Collective action and the distribution of income: a conceptual approach', in *The Analysis and Evaluation of Public Expenditures*, Joint Economic Committee, US Government Printing Office, Washington DC.

Weisbrod, B. A. (1970), 'On the stigma effect and the demand for welfare programs: a theoretical note', University of Wisconsin Discussion Paper.

Weisbrod, B. A. and Hansen, W. L. (1968), 'An income – net worth approach to measuring economic welfare', *American Economic Review*, vol. 58, 1315–29.

Weitzman, M. L. (1977), 'Is the price system or rationing more effective in getting a commodity to those who need it most?', *Bell Journal of Economics*, vol. 8, 517–24.

White, H. (1981), 'Consequences and detection of misspecified non-linear regression models', *Journal of the American Statistical Association*, vol. 76, 419–33.

Wilson, C. A. (1977), 'A model of insurance markets with incomplete information', *Journal of Economic Theory*, vol. 16, 167–207.

NAME INDEX

Full references to works cited are given in the references.

SUBJECT INDEX